Library of
Davidson College

GERMAN WRITERS
IN FRENCH EXILE
1933–1940

GERMAN WRITERS IN FRENCH EXILE 1933–1940

Martin Mauthner

VALLENTINE MITCHELL
LONDON • PORTLAND, OR

in association with

ejps

THE EUROPEAN JEWISH
PUBLICATION SOCIETY

First published in 2007 in Great Britain by
VALLENTINE MITCHELL
Suite 314, Premier House, 112–114 Station Road,
Edgware, Middlesex HA8 7BJ

and in the United States of America by
VALLENTINE MITCHELL
c/o ISBS, 920 NE 58th Avenue, Suite 300
Portland, OR 97213-3786

www.vmbooks.com

In association with the European Jewish Publication Society,
PO Box 19948, London N3 3ZJ
www.ejps.org.uk

Copyright © 2007 Martin Mauthner

British Library Cataloguing in Publication Data
Mauthner, Martin
  German writers in French exile, 1933–1940
  1. Authors, Exiled – France – Sanary-sur-Mer 2. Authors,
  German – France – Sanary-sur-Mer 3. Political persecution –
  Germany – History – 20th century 4. German literature –
  20th century – History and criticism 5. Sanary-sur-Mer
  (France) – Intellectual life – 20th century
  I. Title
  830.9'9206914'0944'09043

ISBN 978 0 85303 540 4 (cloth)
ISBN 978 0 85303 541 1 (paper)

Library of Congress Cataloging-in-Publication Data
A catalog record has been applied for

The European Jewish Publication Society gives grants to support the publication of books relevant to Jewish literature, history, religion, philosophy, politics and culture.

All rights reserved. No part of this publication may be reproduced, stored in or introduced into a retrieval system or transmitted in any form or by any means, electronic, mechanical, photocopying, recording or otherwise, without the prior written permission of the publisher of this book.

Typeset in 11/13pt Sabon by FiSH Books, Enfield, Middx.
Printed in Great Britain by MPG Books Ltd, Bodmin, Cornwall

Contents

List of Plates	vii
Preface	ix

1.	'Weimar-on-Sea': How Sanary Becomes a Writers' Refuge	1
2.	A 'Slander' on Richard Wagner: The Torment of Thomas Mann	21
3.	A French Envoy Drops a Hint: Heinrich Mann the Francophile	35
4.	Warning in Washington: Lion Feuchtwanger Portrays Life Under the 'Hooked Cross'	42
5.	Émigrés as 'Deserters': Klaus Mann's Literary Feud with Gottfried Benn	51
6.	Cleansing the 'Literary Brothels': German Students Celebrate Their 'Bibliocaust'	61
7.	Rivalry in Ragusa: H. G. Wells Treads the PEN Tightrope	73
8.	'Seppl' and the 'Slimy Frog': A Jewish Publisher Stays on in Berlin	86
9.	'A Reckless Act'? Klaus Mann Launches His Review	99
10.	Watching and Waiting: Thomas Mann Prepares His 'Politicum'	113
11.	'I Have Let My Conscience Speak': Thomas Mann Comes Off the Fence	118
12.	'The Curtain Falls': A Berlin Publisher's Odyssey	129
13.	From Bonds to Blitzkrieg: Leopold Schwarzschild Bares Hitler's War Plans	136

14.	'We Have Just Saved Culture': The Paris Writers' Congress of 1935	148
15.	'I Came, I Saw, I Shall Write': Feuchtwanger's Misguided Mission to Moscow	165
16.	'Canaan-sur-Seine': The Strange End of the *Pariser Tageblatt*	180
17.	'Secret Kaiser' and 'Red Czar': Heinrich Mann, Willi Münzenberg and the *Volksfront*	206
18.	Back from Oblivion: Postwar Germany's Mixed Feelings About Its Exile Writers	228
Bibliography		237
Index		249

List of Plates

1. Sanary shortly after the war
2. A gathering at the Huxleys' home in Sanary: Marta Feuchtwanger, Arnold Zweig, William Seabrook and Lion Feuchtwanger
3. Thomas Mann in Sanary, summer 1933
4. *Die Brennessel* caricatures Heinrich Mann as Marlene Dietrich in *Der Blaue Engel*
5. A portrait of Marta Feuchtwanger by Walter Bondy
6. Lion Feuchtwanger
7. Eva Herrmann
8. Thomas Mann's eldest son, Klaus
9. Gottfried Benn
10. An anti-Nazi cartoon depicts the notorious book-burning that students organised across the country, May 1933
11. H. G. Wells
12. The pacifist writer Ernst Toller in prison
13. Gottfried Bermann-Fischer, Thomas Mann's publisher
14. Thomas Mann's eldest daughter Erika
15. Cover of *Das Neue Tage-Buch*
16. Leopold Schwarzschild
17. Eva Herrmann caricature of Henri Barbusse and André Malraux
18. Lion Feuchtwanger and Bertolt Brecht at the 1935 writers' congress
19. André Gide looks up at E. M. Forster as he addresses the writers' congress in Paris
20. A portrait of Aldous Huxley by Walter Bondy
21. Georg Bernhard
22. The political cartoon was a common Nazi propaganda weapon
23. 'The émigré press ... and its lies factory at work', Nazi cartoon, 1934
24. Heinrich Mann and André Gide
25. 'The pen is mightier ...', cartoon by Walter Trier
26. Thomas Mann in Frankfurt, on his first post-war visit to Germany, 1949

Preface

'A book in *English* about *German* writers in *France*?' The bookbroker was astonished. He looked at me wryly and said, 'You must be joking. No one's going to be interested in that.' Wandering around the London Book Fair, I understood what he meant. It was easy to conclude that, when it comes to popular culture, London is a lot closer to Los Angeles than to Lille or Leipzig.

And yet the fate of the German-language writers who fled Hitler, part of the largest intellectual exodus in history, is a fascinating story. It continues to absorb a great many people, but they are the professionals. They thrive not only on the Continent, especially in Germany and Austria. They also flourish in universities across the English-speaking world: from Beverly Hills through Bloomsbury and Brighton down to Botany Bay you will come across research centres for German and Austrian exile studies, or for German-Jewish studies. You will find the fruits of the experts' research scattered in numerous learned books and journals. Where the academics have had the time or inclination to make their work accessible to the lay reader in English, they have usually chosen to write biographies, or focused on the writers' 'exile in paradise' war years, near Los Angeles. What has been lacking is a book for beginners, a non-specialist narrative about the émigrés' 'locust' years in 1930s France. By taking advantage of the extensive material, mainly in German, produced by these specialists in *Exilliteratur*, I have tried to fill the gap.

Rather than inundate the reader with a plethora of names of writers and their works, many barely remembered, I have selected some of the major events involving émigré writers in the 1930s. I show some of the links in those early years of exile between German writers and their counterparts, especially French and British writers. Above all, I highlight the way political quarrels among the German writers themselves weakened their role in the great ideological battle against the Nazis.

It was while growing up among German and Austrian émigré families in South Africa that I became familiar with the names of famous German-language writers in exile, such as Thomas Mann and Stefan Zweig. Later, while posted to Bonn, I began to read more of their work and to delve into their years as émigrés. As Germany marked the 50th anniversary of the notorious Nazi book-burning in 1933, a flood of books, articles and radio and television programmes streamed forth. Every so often, I came across a reference to an émigré writers' sanctuary, 'Sanary-sur-Mer'.

Although my wife had grown up in Germany, she was as unfamiliar as I was with the writers' French staging post. Our curiosity aroused, we drove down to the Côte d'Azur to find out more. As we turned up, Sanary's church bells were striking six o'clock. Its *pavillon du tourisme* was just closing for the day. I had hardly mentioned 'les écrivains allemands à Sanary' when the friendly official opened a drawer and gave me a set of loose photocopied pages, in French and in German, on precisely that topic. Provocatively titled, 'Qui se souvient encore des émigrants de Sanary-sur-Mer?', its publication date was, appropriately, May 1983.

The leaflet was the work of Barthélémy Rotger, a local historian. He had recorded the writers and painters associated with Sanary and had drawn up a map to indicate where some of them lived. He also reproduced contemporary photographs, including a rare view of the villa inhabited by Thomas Mann – a house subsequently destroyed by German troops. For his labours, the German government honoured Rotger in 1987 with the Federal order of merit, the *Bundesverdienstkreuz*. Thomas Börger, a citizen of Sanary's twin town in Germany, Bad Säckingen, near Freiburg, had prepared the German version of Rotger's text. Later, while strolling around the port, I passed some men playing pétanque and then spotted a plaque that commemorated some of the exiled writers associated with the port.

Revisiting Bonn in 1996, I went to a second-hand bookshop near the university and expressed my interest in *Exilliteratur* and Sanary in particular. The owner told me that Düsseldorf – birthplace of a nineteenth-century German writer who fled to France, Heinrich Heine – had earlier that year hosted an exhibition precisely about Sanary's exiled writers. The exhibition had in fact already opened and closed in Augsburg as well as Düsseldorf, but fortunately was due to end its tour of Germany towards the end of the year in Lübeck – home of Thomas and Heinrich Mann.

In Lübeck I spent a day closely examining the remarkable array of photographs and other exhibits and the richly illustrated catalogue that accompanied it. I came home with a much firmer picture of Sanary's literary significance and decided to ask one of the people primarily responsible for preparing the exhibition, Dr Heinke Wunderlich, if I could call on her at her home in Düsseldorf. Dr Wunderlich, who was teaching German literature at the Bergische University in Wuppertal, proved to be enormously helpful in every way possible, not least in providing me with copies of material from obscure out-of-print journals. If I have been at all able to reciprocate,

Preface

it was by acting as her guide when she joined my wife and me on a trip to New York – her first – to visit an exhibition about Varian Fry, the young American who helped many intellectuals escape from Marseilles after the war broke out.

Through Dr Wunderlich, I became acquainted with Dr Anita Overwien. At her art gallery in Cologne, she was good enough to show me her collection of Eva Herrmann's portraits of the writers the young American artist encountered while living in Sanary. Dr Overwien also provided me with a substantial amount of biographical information about Eva Herrmann.

In London Sybille Bedford, a Sanary resident for many pre-war years, was kind enough to receive me. Over a bottle of white wine at her home in Chelsea, she helped me capture the atmosphere of those faraway years. Sybille Bedford's vivid descriptions in her novels and her biography of Aldous Huxley fired my imagination and reinforced my decision to embark on the journey of literary exploration that turned into this manuscript.

I owe a special word of appreciation to Madame Germaine Poliakov of Massy, near Paris. During an agreeable luncheon in her home, she furnished me with a wealth of information about her Russian father-in-law's extraordinary dispute with the German émigré journalists on the *Pariser Tageblatt*. I am also deeply indebted to Jane Spender, of the International PEN in London, who provided me with many details about the PEN congress of 1933 in Yugoslavia.

I profited from visits to the Royal Library in Brussels, the exile archive of the German national library in Frankfurt, the German literary archive in Marbach and the Monacesia literary archive in Munich. While the British and United States governments halted their cultural activities and disbanded their public libraries in Brussels with the end of the Cold War, the German government decided otherwise, and I was fortunate to find a mine of information in its cultural facility in the Belgian capital, the Goethe Institute. I am obliged to the German radio station *Deutschlandfunk* for providing me with transcripts of relevant broadcast programmes, and to a leading authority on the Mann family, Professor Helmut Koopman of Augsburg University, for giving me information.

Many acquaintances, friends and members of my family showed interest in my work, helped me with their expertise and encouraged me to persevere. The following deserve my special thanks: my wife Heidi, David Burslem, Audri Day, Jana and Moritz Gutmann, Eleanor and Michel Levieux, Professor Norman MacKenzie, Julia MacKenzie, Melanie, Natasha and Hugo Mauthner, Onno Simons,

Adam Steinhouse, Nicola Stephens, and Michael Weiss.

Mark Amory encouraged me by publishing in the *Spectator* an article about Sybille Bedford that I based on my research. For their editorial advice and support, I am indebted to Keith Hart, Philip Hensher, Elizabeth Haylett, Dr Colin Shindler and Professor Edward Timms.

To find suitable illustrations for this book, I was lucky to have the help of Sophie Hartley, who proved to be a highly skilled picture researcher familiar with pre-war cultural and political Europe. For his businesslike way in bringing the manuscript's long gestation to fruition, I wish to express my appreciation to my editor, Mark Anstee.

Finally, I'd like to dedicate this book to Alan Blyth. He recruited me, a raw colonial straight out of school, to work with him in a political bookshop in Westminster some years ago. In that way, he made me familiar with the names of most of the British authors featured in the following pages.

1 'Weimar-on-Sea'
How Sanary Becomes a Writers' Refuge

For seven lean years in the turbulent 1930s, the 'secret capital of German literature' was ... a picturesque fishing village on the Côte d'Azur. Sanary-sur-Mer, a tranquil little port a few miles west of Toulon, acquired its ironic title from the many writers who found a congenial haven there when Hitler forced them to flee Germany.

After the war, the world almost forgot Sanary's role as a bolthole for the German literary diaspora. That ignorance is disappearing, thanks to the extensive literary excavations undertaken by many scholars. More than 40 years after the war ended, the German and Austrian governments acknowledged Sanary's importance, by unveiling a plaque in the port that commemorated 36 of the German and Austrian writers and their families who having fled the Nazis, 'se sont retrouvés à Sanary'.

An impressive roll of writers 'came together' – as residents or as visitors – in 'Weimar-on-Sea'. Lion Feuchtwanger, one of the most widely translated German authors of the era, arrived in Sanary in 1933 and left it only after the war had begun. Thomas Mann spent the summer of 1933 there, visiting it occasionally afterwards from Switzerland, before moving to America. Mann's adult children – his daughter Erika, and his sons Klaus and Golo – were in and out of Sanary in the 1930s. Thomas's elder brother Heinrich found his first refuge there, before moving to Nice.

Berthold Brecht's name is on the plaque. He and Kurt Weill had already been there in the late 1920s, working on the *Dreigroschenoper*. The plaque mentions Bruno Frank, whose works had aroused controversy with their advocacy of Franco-German reconciliation, and Arthur Koestler, the fiery political writer from Budapest who committed suicide in London in 1983.

Other names on the plaque include Stefan Zweig, Joseph Roth, Franz Werfel and Arnold Zweig. Like Heinrich Mann, Roth was an avowed Francophile. He had lived on and off in France before 1933. Franz Werfel and his wife Alma stayed in Sanary after Hitler grabbed Austria. Arnold Zweig, who moved to Palestine, stayed with his friend Lion Feuchtwanger in Sanary. Like many émigrés of that generation, Zweig was a veteran of the First World War. He had achieved fame at the end of the 1920s with *Sergeant Grisha*, a novel based on the true story of a Russian prisoner of war whom the Germans executed.

Egon Erwin Kisch, a Prague-born reporter who rose to become one of Berlin's most famous journalists, visited friends in Sanary. So did Ernst Toller, a familiar figure in left-wing London salons. Robert Musil, the Austrian author of *The Man Without Qualities*, visited a small Austrian colony in nearby Le Lavandou. The plaque mentions none of them.

Today, cultural pilgrims to 'Sanary-les-Allemands' retrace the steps of the refugees. They stroll along the Chemin de la Colline to see exactly where a sombre Thomas Mann sat on his porch and ruminated on Germany's fate. They glance at the mill-tower that a nervous Franz Werfel and his wife Alma rented on their flight from Central Europe to America. They amble down the Boulevard Beausoleil to peer across a luxuriant garden at the Villa Valmer, where a jovial Lion Feuchtwanger dictated a succession of anti-Nazi novels. Visitors have a drink on the terrace of Le Nautique, one of the harbour-front cafés where the refugee writers spent many hours debating how best to fight the fascists. They may overnight in the Hôtel de la Tour where visiting refugee writers stayed, sometimes on their way to or from the Spanish Civil War.

Nowadays the town's tourist office encourages visitors to stray a little further afield towards the Plage de la Gorguette, to see where a famous British writer once lived amidst the refugees and shared in their woes. In a villa above the beach, Aldous Huxley wrote *Brave New World* and *Eyeless in Gaza*. Huxley and his wife Maria – she had come to Britain as a Belgian war refugee – had been living near Paris. They knew the Sanary area, having previously called on D. H. Lawrence there. After paying a last visit to Lawrence on his deathbed in Vence, they decided they wanted to live on the Côte d'Azur. Huxley's novel *Point Counter Point* had sold so well that the couple could afford to buy a house as well as a custom-built Bugatti. The posh stretch of the Riviera between Cannes and Menton they considered too ugly and expensive. They found what they wanted outside Sanary. That was in 1930, before Hitler's ascent to power, and they stayed there until 1937.

Only a comfortable overnight train journey away from Paris, the Sanary region became an idyllic clubhouse for European and American poets and painters in the 1920s. A cheap franc, attractive scenery and sunny skies enticed them to desert the cold grey north.

D. H. Lawrence wintered nearby in 1928, drawn by the presence of Katherine Mansfield; she wrote a poem entitled 'Sanary'. Anthony Powell penned some of his first novel *Afternoon Men* while staying in Toulon. He incorporated his impressions of the port in *What's Become of Waring*, an amusing novel that mentions Sanary. When Evelyn Waugh stayed with Cyril Connolly in Sanary the two of them jaunted around Toulon's red-light quarter. Waugh's reminiscences of 'matelots ... smelling of wine and garlic' found their way into *Put Out More Flags*.

Sanary's Provençal landscape and mild winters appealed to the ailing art critic Julius Meier-Graefe, later hailed by Kenneth Clark for his pioneer work in popularising modern art. He left Germany to settle in the area in 1930. In the same year, growing anti-Semitism drove the writer and translator Wilhelm Herzog to Sanary. René Schickele, another pacifist, joined him there in 1932. A writer of Franco-German parentage, he wasn't a Jew but could no longer bear Germany's harsh political atmosphere. The presence of those three German-language writers in Sanary before the great exodus began helped transform it into 'Weimar-on-Sea'.

Another feature that lured some literati after the First World War was the lax moral climate that prevailed in Paris and along the coast. It was an aspect that especially irked a perhaps hypocritical Edmund Wilson in the United States, and a prudish George Orwell in puritan England.

For Wilson the expatriate aesthetes were cadgers and spongers, or pimps and gigolos, who pretended they'd come over to do some serious writing but had instead slumped into near non-stop boozing and bonking. Orwell mocked the 'drinking, cadging and lechering' that took place in 'those dreadful colonies of expatriates which were dotted all over France during the 1920s', and the way 'so-called artists' spent 'on sodomy what they have gained by sponging'. Orwell was reviewing a book by Cyril Connolly, who followed Huxley to Sanary and lived there for a while. Orwell may have had the port partly in mind, for it undoubtedly had its fair share of droll characters.

One highly visible eccentric in Sanary was Brian Howard, a flamboyant character who served as a model for two memorable if effete Evelyn Waugh characters – Ambrose Silk in *Put Out More Flags* and Anthony Blanche in *Brideshead Revisited*. Though his parents were American, he was born in Britain and had been to Eton and Christ Church, but he went down from Oxford without a degree. Supported by his mother, he was now leading the life of a dilettante troubadour with literary aspirations. In Sanary, he had the chance to entertain the local families by staging his one-act play 'The Secret of Mayerling'. The drama provocatively suggested that the Austrian crown prince Rudolf had committed suicide in Mayerling in 1858, not because of his doomed love for Maria Vetsera who died with him, but because he fancied one of his huntsmen. Howard's German companion Toni Altmann – Christopher Isherwood judged him a 'handsome Bavarian blond' – played the huntsman in question.

A young German woman, pale, blue-eyed and partly of Jewish background, had a role in Howard's play and performed it in exquisite English. Though born in Berlin, where her mother had moved in literary circles, Sybille von Schönebeck's schooling had consisted of private tuition in England, where she later married Walter Bedford. Her mother Lisa Marchesani and her Italian stepfather, an art dealer, had come to Sanary after abandoning Mussolini's fascist Italy. Howard enacted his play in the grounds of 'Bastide Juliette', a house in Sanary's Quartier St Trinide that Sybille shared with Eva Herrmann, an attractive young brown-eyed American artist of German-Jewish origin. As the real drama unfolded in Europe, all three helped bridge the gap between the Anglo-Saxon expatriates and the German émigrés.

Eva Herrmann and Sybille, often seen in trousers, were members of a cosmopolitan crowd of privileged aesthetes, several bisexual or homosexual. They flitted restlessly around the bars, cafés and theatres of Berlin and Munich, Amsterdam and Paris. They haunted Alpine slopes in January and Bavarian lakes or Mediterranean beaches in July. Thomas Mann's eldest daughter and son, Erika and Klaus, observed in their guide to the Riviera, published in 1931, that in summer you could see in Sanary's Café de la Marine habitués in other seasons of Montparnasse's Café du Dôme.

In November 1932, Schickele stopped frequenting the terrace of Sanary's Café de Lyon to avoid the German colony that now occupied his sundowner spot. A month later, he was complaining about the way homosexuals were overcrowding the small resort, one of them boasting 'Gide adore mon livre'. For Schickele, the other side of Sanary's harbour became the 'holy land'.

By May 1934, Schickele was back on the café terrace. It was if drums had announced his presence: 'they all' came along – the father of the painter Balthus, Erich Klossovski; Sybille von Schönebeck; the Huxleys; the literary critic Raymond Mortimer; Feuchtwanger's male and female secretaries; the refugee writer Ludwig Marcuse and others. They 'all' now said France should have marched into Germany in 1933.

'Weimar-on-Sea'

Sanary's expatriate residents would put up visiting friends from the colder north. One of Huxley's regular guests was Edward Sackville-West, a writer and music critic who had been his pupil at Eton. Eddy wrote his novel *Simpson* in Huxley's house, finishing it chez Sybille and Eva. Published as early as 1931, it recounts how a young Nazi machine-guns an English nanny. Sackville-West, who spoke both German and French, dedicated the book to 'Mopsa' – Thea Sternheim, daughter of the German playwright Carl Sternheim.

More significantly, Eddy and Mopsa were part of a crowd of young Europeans who sensed the way the political wind was blowing. Brian Howard was another. He knew Germany well, having visited it partly for medical treatment. While critics judge Howard as an artistic failure, Erika Mann called him 'probably the first Englishman to recognise the full immensity of the Nazi peril and to foresee, with shuddering horror, what was to come'. Eddy Sackville-West and Brian Howard, Eva Herrmann and Sybille von Schönebeck, Erika and Klaus Mann – they were all impassioned anti-Nazis well before 1933.

They were part of an international easy-morals freemasonry that flourished between the wars, and there has probably been nothing quite like it since. Jean Cocteau, André Gide, Julien Green, Christopher Isherwood and W. H. Auden were members of that bohemian clan. Isherwood acted as go-between when Klaus Mann's lesbian sister Erika married a 'delighted' Auden in 1935 so that she could acquire British nationality. Brian Howard told Klaus Mann that 'if she had married me, she would have sometimes SEEN her husband'. A few months later Isherwood reported that Auden was 'very anxious to see his dear wife again', except that she insisted on living in such expensive countries as Switzerland and Holland. It was Isherwood who 'congratulated' Klaus after the Nazis deprived him of his German nationality.

Soon after Auden's marriage to Erika, he wrote a warm letter to Klaus, in a mixture of English and German, saying how much he regretted that his brother-in-law Klaus wasn't at the Mann parental home in Switzerland. Before long, the new Mrs Auden was 'looking out' for someone to marry her friend, Sybille von Schönebeck. Sybille, who occasionally typed Huxley's manuscripts, impressed those who met her as an intelligent and fascinating personality. When the German and English intellectuals met at one of Sanary's harbour cafés, it was Sybille who animated the political discussions.

Sanary had its representative of the American 'lost generation' – a rumbustious, hard-drinking writer. William Seabrook was an adventurer who had already published a couple of best-selling accounts of visits to exotic parts of the world. He was trying to complete a book he had contracted to write about a defrocked European missionary who lived with his concubine in Timbuctoo.

Seabrook and his companion Marjorie Worthington had flown across the Sahara to reach Timbuctoo. There he and the former Père Yakuba drank heavily beneath the desert stars. Seabrook returned in triumph to Paris and invited a group of experts for drinks at his Left Bank apartment so that he could tell them about his 'mission'. Dignified elderly Frenchmen entered to see a Montparnasse harlot hanging by her wrists on the balcony, her toes just touching the floor. She was wearing only a leather skirt, which Seabrook had brought back from Africa. With supreme sang-froid, they said nothing and quickly glanced elsewhere. On another occasion Seabrook appears to have embarrassed his new British publisher George Harrap by entertaining him in a Paris *boîte* where topless waitresses brought the drinks.

To write his book, Seabrook leased from Ford Madox Ford part of an old onion warehouse on Toulon's picturesque Quai Cronstadt, later destroyed in the war. Marjorie Worthington joined him. Seabrook tried to settle down and exploit the diaries, photographs and other biographical material that Yakuba had given him. Instead, he went tuna fishing and boar hunting and resumed his rake's life – gambling, watching pornographic films in the red-light district of Marseilles, hosting caviar-and-champagne buffets, smoking opium with Jean Cocteau and generally drinking himself blind.

Seabrook's literary agent turned up. She threatened to advise his publisher to sue him if he didn't abandon his dissolute way of life and get on with the book. That led him and his long-suffering partner to move to the Villa des Roseaux, on the fashionable neck of land between Sanary and Bandol – and half an hour away from the coastal fleshpots. Their new neighbours were the Huxleys.

Huxley and his wife, who was bisexual, often went over to the Villa des Roseaux in the evening. They had noticed large iron rings hanging from the villa's walls. They had seen Marjorie covered in bruises. Huxley reported that talk of Seabrook's sadistic inclinations had excited Sanary's lesbian baronesses and they were in a flutter of excitement to meet him.

Seabrook's *femme de ménage* was one source of the local gossip that he enjoyed chaining up young women – what Seabrook called his 'twisted sex-driven want'. She had seen 'little Miss' Marjorie Worthington cross herself before letting Seabrook wind rusty chains, two to three metres long, around her dainty hands. No one doubted that sexual games followed and that 'elle doit aimer ça', because Marjorie's shining eyes showed how much she admired her 'wolf'.

Four servants – a cook, a maid, a chauffeur and a gardener – looked after the couple and their eleven cats. Friends from Toulon, Paris, London and New York visited them. Their villa, once a wealthy playboy's property, had a beach that the couple shared with the Huxleys. The racial theories swirling around Europe at the time seem to have influenced the conversation of the two writers. Seabrook and Huxley apparently agreed that a warm climate debilitated blond Nordic types by making their minds torpid and their bodies lazy.

One afternoon Worthington was feeding her cats in the courtyard when Maria Huxley came down the hill. Wearing a linen dress, white gloves and a big straw hat, she addressed Worthington as 'Madame Seabrook' – in fact, she married Seabrook only after they returned to the United States – and invited the couple to dinner the next evening. Both admirers of Huxley's novels, the formally attired American couple nervously approached the Huxley villa. The weak-sighted Huxley rose to greet them, thrusting his head forward to see them better. His 'exquisitely dainty' wife moved about in a white crepe pyjama dress by Molyneux.

Also present was the Huxleys' son Matthew, their niece Sophie and a blonde-haired, red-cheeked German girl wearing a dinner jacket and sporting a monocle. She was introduced as 'La Baronne von Schönebeck'. Conversation inevitably turned to the way the results of Germany's barbarities had already seeped down to Sanary. The Huxleys had noticed the German writers settling in their midst when they returned in June 1933 from a long trip to Mexico and Central America. In Maria's words, 'German Jew authors – and non jewish [*sic*] too – have chosen Bandol and Sanary as a retreat.' Aldous Huxley judged Thomas and Heinrich Mann and 'a rich selection of Jews such as Feuchtwanger and Arnold Zweig' to be 'a dismal crew, already showing the disastrous effects of exile'. Huxley hoped 'we shall not have to scuttle when Tom [Sir Oswald] Mosley gets into power'.

Seabrook suggested that he and Marjorie Worthington host a party for the Germans, and *la baronne* agreed to invite them on their behalf. It was an unusual literary constellation that assembled in the villa's flagstoned courtyard in August 1933. There was Huxley – his recent novel had made Shakespeare's 'brave new world' a household phrase around the world. There was Thomas Mann – winner of the

Nobel Prize for literature four years earlier – and his brother Heinrich, still basking in the fame that *The Blue Angel*, the film version of one of his novels, had brought him and Marlene Dietrich a few years previously. Lion Feuchtwanger was there – the success around the world of his historical novels, especially *Jud Süss*, had made him renowned and wealthy. Arnold Zweig was another guest – his anti-militarist novels had also made him a celebrated author in Germany and beyond.

René Schickele was there. He wondered why Seabrook had arranged such a remarkably alcoholic tea party. While Schickele and Thomas Mann were discussing someone's criticism that Mann's work lacked fantasy, Seabrook interrupted them. Wearing only leather trunks and with a glass of punch in his hand, the hairy-chested American began a drunken oration, half in German, half in French. The gist seemed to be that if German 'senators' – by which Seabrook apparently meant prominent figures in society – had allowed Hitler to shoot them, they would have provoked the world to react, and so changed the course of history.

Thomas Mann noted the al fresco event curtly in his diary: 'After six o'clock to Seabrook, garden party, large group.' Fortunately for posterity, Sybille von Schönebeck, 22 years old at the time, was also present. Years later, under her married name of Sybille Bedford, she left a fuller account in her biography of Aldous Huxley of what she termed an 'incongruous' gathering.

As Sanary's Anglo-Saxon expatriates and German refugees began to mix, relations weren't always smooth. Huxley upset Heinrich Mann when he didn't turn up to hear Mann read from his collection of anti-Nazi essays. Huxley had possibly forgotten that his wife had invited guests for the same evening.

At first Schickele was more flattering about the distinguished British writer in their midst. He found him 'very pleasant' and praised his scintillating intelligence. Over tea in the Huxleys' new kitchen, the two writers talked about Germany. Huxley saw the Nazi movement as a revolt against the spirit. Schickele wondered why Goebbels hadn't used D. H. Lawrence for his cause. Did Lawrence know of Freud, Schickele wondered. He did, but barely and only indirectly, Huxley told him. Later Schickele decided Huxley's intellect was superficial and that cynicism underlay his rationalism.

William Seabrook's party coincided with a cultural turning point in France. America's repeal of Prohibition in 1933, the world economic slump and a dearer French franc made Paris and the Côte d'Azur less alluring adult playgrounds for many of the 'lost generation' of American intellectuals who had flocked to Europe. Seabrook himself returned to the United States in October of that year, to try to cure his alcoholism. He kept in touch with the Huxleys and the Manns.

At the same time, the oppressive new regime in Berlin was beginning to chase into exile a long procession of writers and artists. Hitler's savage new tyranny had disrupted their lives by threatening to throw them into concentration camps, confiscating their homes and other assets, banning and burning their books. Within a few months of Hitler becoming German chancellor at the end of January 1933, and of the burning of the Reichstag that followed a few weeks later, a huge cultural diaspora was under way. France became a favoured refuge.

Most but not all of Seabrook's German guests were among the Jews or left-wing radicals who had fled their *Heimat* earlier that year to avoid arbitrary arrest and imprisonment. They were still adjusting to the shock of being foreign authors in exile. They were wondering how soon the storm would clear so that they could return – and how they would earn a living in the meantime. These political fugitives were replacing the English and American poets and playboys who had been wandering around Europe, but the two groups inevitably overlapped in Paris and on the coast. After mixing with the 'tribe of the emigration', Christopher Isherwood observed that 'when refugees gathered together, there was much wit but no joy'.

How did Germany's endangered writers and journalists decide where to seek refuge? While many of those who were active Communists would flee to Moscow, other refugees tended to choose one of the Reich's neighbours. Zurich, and Vienna until 1938, had the great advantage for writers that they were German-speaking cities. Prague also had a large German-speaking community, while Holland's traditional tolerance drew some to Amsterdam.

What attracted the émigré writers to France? Most of them had a poor knowledge of the French language and were unprepared for the cultural differences that overwhelmed them. On the other hand, Germany's long land border with France made it relatively easy for them to escape illegally. For some it was convenient to cross via the Saar, an autonomous territory administered by France on behalf of the League of Nations until it joined Germany in 1935.

France had a long tradition of offering political asylum. It had absorbed thousands of Russian and Armenian refugees after the end of the First World War. Now Paris quickly became a centre of the political opposition to Hitler. At first, the French authorities were more generous than most other countries in granting entry visas, but they balanced this by issuing few work permits. They preferred to ignore the refugees' often desperate efforts to make a living.

The French capital drew journalists who, like doctors, lawyers, bankers and the business community, believed their best chances of resuming their professional lives lay there. Writers and artists didn't have to live in the metropolis to continue their creative endeavours. Inevitably, some chose to settle in the milder and cheaper South of France. More than 400 refugees settled in the *département* of the Var between 1933 and 1942, most of them choosing Sanary or nearby Bandol and Le Lavandou.

During the early years of exile, before the French government subjected them to its increasingly severe administrative controls, refugees found life in the South of France agreeable, as many memoirs testify. Being beside the cliffs and the sea was like paradise for Marta Feuchtwanger: she found it 'wundervoll'. There was a semblance of the bourgeois domesticity that had surrounded them in Germany: Bruno Frank arranged for the family's German maid and their dogs to join them in Sanary.

The émigrés could subscribe to the words of Charles Trenet's popular chanson of the era, 'Oui, je t'aime, Dans la joie ou la douleur, Douce France'. It wasn't just that the cost of living was low and the climate benign. Travel between Paris and the coastal region around Toulon was convenient: the night train left the Gare de Lyon shortly before half past nine, arriving at Bandol just before eleven the next morning.

At first, many émigré writers naively believed they would soon be able to vacate their 'waiting-room', in Lion Feuchtwanger's phrase, and go home. An atmosphere of optimism prevailed. They assumed they had found shelter from what they expected to be a brief storm, after which Germany would return to normal. Visiting Sanary in the autumn of 1933, Arnold Zweig and Brecht admired the bay, the blue sky and the fishing boats. They spoke of the German people's suffering and of the better future that awaited them after the end of the Third Reich – which they thought was imminent.

Klaus Mann became optimistic after the Nazis had executed Ernst Röhm and other alleged conspirators in June 1934; he was confident that 'it cannot last much longer'. Schickele had heard as early as August 1934 that enthusiasm for the dictators was waning in Italy and Germany. He believed people there had already started to think, and that was the first step; it couldn't be long before Germans began to act.

Many of Hitler's opponents shared the émigrés' wishful thinking, and at first dangerously underestimated the Führer. They consoled themselves with the German adage to the effect that the dish wouldn't be as hot in the eating as in the preparation. The continuing presence in Berlin of Paul von Hindenburg, the venerable and respected president, reassured them. Many took for granted that the Germans would soon regain their senses. After all, 56 per cent of the German electorate hadn't voted for Hitler in March 1933, thus compelling him to bring the ultra-conservatives into his government.

Some Germans expected that the responsibility of being in power would rapidly exhaust the regime, or at least moderate the Nazis' fanaticism. If it didn't, the conservatives' influence might do so. Others thought the armed forces might carry out a coup, or that the government's highly ambitious economic programme would erode its position. And if none of these hopes of collapse from within materialised, then surely France and Britain would put the diplomatically isolated German house in order.

Although a pacifist, Wilhelm Herzog was advocating in 1933 that France launch a preventive war against Germany. His Sanary neighbour René Schickele, also a pacifist, said he agreed – if Herzog would march in the first row. As early as January 1933, Schickele could record ambivalent attitudes among the French. He had seen a peasant spit and curse as a French squadron from Toulon flew past on manoeuvres. The peasant hoped all the pilots would crash and break their necks. Schickele recalled a British paper saying France was armed to the teeth – but peace-longing to the marrow.

Within Germany, many of the country's half-million Jews initially had little sense of the scale of the terror to come. They liked to believe that Hitler's real enemies were the socialists and especially the communists. After the Reichstag fire in February 1933, the Nazis introduced 'emergency' measures that allowed them to place thousands of Communist Party members and other opponents in 'protective custody', usually a concentration camp. The Jews thought they should be patient and avoid panic-mongering. A typically bittersweet joke had two Jews meeting on Berlin's elegant Kurfürstendamm boulevard in the year 2000. 'Well?' asks the first. 'I give the Nazis another three months,' replies the second.

As it dawned on the writers that they wouldn't be going home for a while, they had to give more thought to earning a living in exile. Although most of the displaced authors had immediately lost their main market, they continued to write their novels and biographies, plays and poems. Some turned their energies to forging literary ammunition for the struggle against Hitler. There were reputable German-language publishers outside the Reich, including newly established firms in Prague and Amsterdam, Paris and Zurich, that catered specifically for them. As Berlin didn't necessarily ban all works by proscribed writers, 'harmless' titles might still appear in German bookshops under the imprint of a 'respectable' publisher outside the Reich. Émigrés with a reputation abroad could rely on income from translation rights and foreign royalties. A few had managed to bring money with them. Some could earn modest fees from articles in the newspapers that sprang up in Paris and other exile centres.

As they sat on the verandas of their small Provençal houses and thought of Germany, several writers in Sanary turned to the production of historical works, or biographies of earlier tyrants such as Dionysius of Syracuse. Of course, contemporary concerns led them to draw parallels with their own century. Spending the summer of 1933 in Sanary, Arnold Zweig wrote a major treatise on German Jewry, and the destruction of a creative part of the German population; he used a five-volume Jewish lexicon that Lion Feuchtwanger had brought from Berlin. Bruno Frank, who lived close to Thomas Mann, wrote a fictionalised life of Cervantes that bore the stamp of Frank's investigations into the 'purity' of blood.

Thomas Mann wrote part of his long Biblical novel *Joseph and His Brothers* in Sanary. His daughter Erika finished a children's book. Her brother Klaus worked on essays about Stefan George and Thomas de Quincey, and prepared to launch a literary magazine for the exiles. Their younger brother Golo Mann drafted an essay on Ernst Jünger, which was later published in Klaus's review.

Convalescing in Sanary in 1935, the famous Czech journalist Egon Erwin Kisch – reputed to have introduced to Central Europe the Anglo-American concept of the roving reporter – wrote a book about his abortive trip to Australia. After the authorities had forbidden him, as a member of the Austrian Communist Party, to disembark at Melbourne for a congress against war and fascism, he had jumped onto the pier and broken a leg.

When Brecht visited Sanary, he entertained his fellow exiles by playing the guitar and singing his own songs between Bavarian folk tunes. As a Communist sympathiser, Brecht light-heartedly told his host, the writer Hermann Kesten, that the French revolutionaries would have guillotined him – Kesten – as a bourgeois liberal, along with Beaumarchais, Voltaire and Diderot; later the French communards would have shot him. Kesten replied that Stalin would have expelled Marx, Engels and Lenin from the Communist Party, and banished them and perhaps Brecht as well to Siberia.

Curiously, the refugee writers in Sanary had more contact with one another there than they would have had in Berlin or Munich. They celebrated one another's birthdays; some even fell in love. Together they would sea-bathe, admire the sunrise and stroll beneath the pines or along the beach at sunset. They met in the harbour cafés to dispute whether writers who weren't yet on the Nazi blacklist should avoid a final break with their readers in Germany. As they bemoaned Germany's fate, they planned for their return after the dictator had been toppled.

Above all they witnessed the continent's steady drift to war – Germany's re-occupation of the Rhineland, its bombing of Guernica during the Spanish Civil War, its march into Austria and Czechoslovakia. As the sombre spectre of Hitler gradually overtook Europe, Sanary's agreeable soirées and readings receded into the background. Even the most apolitical of writers realised the imperative need to make a stand. They did what they could, as writers, to oppose the Nazis. They contributed to the anti-Nazi émigré publications that flourished briefly in Paris and elsewhere. As representatives of the 'free' Germany, they sought to force Nazi Germany out of organisations such as the writers' 'parliament', PEN. They attended and addressed anti-Nazi meetings such as the international congress of writers in Paris in 1935. Some joined the international brigades that fought with the Spanish republicans against Franco.

When Arthur Koestler, then a politically active émigré writer in Paris, visited Feuchtwanger's home in 1938, he became embroiled in heated discussions with his fellow refugees about strategies for stopping Hitler. What could they as intellectuals do to arouse democratic Europe's slumbering public and apathetic rulers? The exiles wrangled above all over the wisdom and morality of supporting Hitler's main enemy, the Soviet despot.

At the same time, the approaching war turned a hitherto hospitable France into a more unsympathetic host. When the first German refugees arrived in France in 1933, they could take at face value the words *Liberté, Egalité, Fraternité* that adorned the entrances to official buildings. The populace had fêted them; the authorities had proclaimed it an honour to welcome them to *la douce France*; the press had greeted them warmly and respectfully. By the end of the decade, the French were less welcoming. After fleeing to Paris from Nazi-occupied Austria in 1938, the future London publisher George Weidenfeld found that the 'the prefecture of the police was harsh and hostile'.

By 1938, almost everything German became suspect. Conspiracy theories flourished among the French. Xenophobia and anti-Semitism became more pronounced and an hysterical fear of a treacherous German 'fifth column' spread. That was the background to Eric Ambler's classic espionage thriller *Epitaph for a Spy*, published in 1938. He set it in a fictitious Saint Gatien Hôtel de la Réserve during the late 1930s, close to Toulon. Ambler had stayed in a hotel in the area.

The presence of many Germans among the Hôtel de la Réserve's guests provokes rumours that one could be a spy. Suspicion falls on a German, using an assumed name, who turns out to be the former editor of a left-wing Berlin newspaper. He has managed to reach the south of France but has had to leave his family in Germany. He has a typical émigré background. The Nazis arrest him in 1933, torture him and throw him into a concentration camp near Hanover. They cancel his German nationality and expel him. He flees to Prague, Paris and Switzerland, where he narrowly escapes abduction. Ambler ends the thriller with a piquant twist: the real spy in the hotel turns out to be a Frenchman.

As war approached, and after Stalin's non-aggression pact with Hitler in August 1939, the French saw the émigrés as potential enemies of France, either because they were Germans (even if they had become stateless), or because they sympathised with Stalin. In Sanary, some of the locals who knew little about the Germans around them grew distrustful and even hostile. It became hazardous for the refugees to turn up in certain cafés. As they now had less money to spend, shopkeepers and café-owners seemed less friendly.

The cruellest blow came as war broke out. Hitler's foes in Sanary became 'enemy aliens' for the French. The French war ministry ordered all Germans in France to register, and interned male émigrés. Lion Feuchtwanger found himself detained in Les Milles, a former brick factory south of Aix-en-Provence that the government had requisitioned to serve as the central 'camp de concentration' for the Bouches-du-Rhône *département*. When the people of Sanary saw the German émigrés taken away in a bus, many were apparently unaware that the authorities were going to detain them in camps. Others knew better, yet accepted their internment as a legitimate precaution. After all, those foreigners had been living near the navy's defence installations at Toulon.

Inflammatory articles in some of the regional papers treated all

German émigrés as Nazi sympathisers or agents. One argued that the detention of thousands of 'Saarlanders, Rhinelanders, Israelites and Austrians' was simply an administrative convenience. Another paper complained that the 'concentration camps' weren't full enough because of French complicity and German duplicity. It urged its readers to denounce anyone they suspected: it was better to prosecute the innocent than to overlook just one guilty person.

During the *drôle de guerre*, the French freed bona-fide émigrés. Some Germans joined the French Foreign Legion or volunteered for auxiliary part-military service in the French army. Marta Feuchtwanger secured her husband's release after ten days. She had lobbied French politicians and other personalities, among them Somerset Maugham and Jules Romains, at the time PEN's international president. Maugham told the playwright Jean Giraudoux, then head of the French government's information service, that the French shouldn't antagonise the German refugees because they were likely to influence German opinion when they returned after the war.

Life became ever more difficult in that 'phoney war' phase. The refugees recognised that some French, including officials and those in uniform, were sympathetic and eager to help them. Others seemed increasingly obstreperous. Petty bureaucrats maltreated them in those same official buildings that declaimed *Fraternité*. They blocked the writers' bank accounts, curtailed their freedom of movement and were slow in issuing them with exit permits. The *fonctionnaires* made the foreigners comply with a multitude of formalities covering their identity and their belongings, from their property in France to their cars. Sanary's mayor had to judge the refugees' loyalty and advise his superiors whether to confiscate the possessions of any of them.

Gendarmes subjected émigrés to frequent controls, meticulously searching their homes and checking their documents. On the improbable grounds that Franz Werfel was a communist, police frisked the world-famous novelist and playwright in Sanary's market place. They summoned him to nearby La Seyne for an identity check. They instructed him to darken all 12 windows of his study in the converted tower he and his wife Alma Mahler-Werfel had rented after fleeing from Vienna. One night the police found Werfel using a torch to find a manuscript. They accused him of being a spy who was sending signals to the Germans.

To sort out difficulties with the gendarmes, Alma would employ '*viel Geld*' and offer them a hot drink when the weather was cold. She seems also to have passed generous sums to the *mairie*. Her problems lay elsewhere. It wasn't just Sanary's heat and stinging insects she had to endure. It was also the émigré milieu there. 'At present I'm living in a Jewish-communist clique to which I don't belong', she complained. 'Sometimes I lose my patience ... Thank God, Franz Werfel is now an absolute anti-communist.'

After the Germans launched their western offensive and invaded France in May 1940, the French interned Sanary's refugees again. This time they rounded up women as well, herding them into camps at Hyères and later Gurs, on the edge of the Pyrenees. During his second detention, Feuchtwanger and other refugees persuaded the camp commander to put them on a train headed for the Atlantic coast. From there they hoped to escape from France by boat. Near Bayonne, they learned that a train full of Germans was in the vicinity. Their train turned back as a precaution, taking its passengers to incarceration in St Nicolas camp, near Nîmes. Feuchtwanger escaped from Nîmes to Marseilles. It later transpired that the other train had been full of German refugees, not troops.

After the war, the 'ghost train' episode became the subject of a French novel that was turned into a film, *Les Milles – Le Train de la Liberté*. The screen version suggested the commander at Les Milles was a French 'Schindler' who defied his government's wish to hand over 2,000 refugees to the Germans. A resentful Feuchtwanger, on the other hand, originally called his account of his internment by the French *Unholdes Frankreich* (ungracious, or unkind, France). He softened the title in later editions to *The Devil in France*.

Like Feuchtwanger, Sybille Bedford and Eva Herrmann had been living in Sanary when the war broke out. For a while Sybille Bedford and a close English friend, Allanah Harper, had lived in the former Huxley home. Although the *baronne* had become a British citizen by marrying Walter Bedford, she and Eva now needed permits to travel around the region. After the French began to intern 'enemy aliens', they joined detainees' wives and companions on Sundays in bringing camp inmates their mail as well as food, cigarettes and other comforts. One day the two women alighted from a limousine as the gates of a camp near Toulon were closing. With them was Toni Altmann, Brian Howard's young German companion. Altmann was obeying French orders to present himself at the camp and join the other internees.

As a freelance journalist, Howard had continued to visit Germany after Hitler's rise to power, although some friends frowned on this. He justified these visits to Klaus Mann. To him it was obvious that 'if one is an anti-Nazi journalist' one would want 'to see what one is writing about'. He thought it 'very silly' of anti-Nazis to argue that they 'simply can't go near the place'. Before visiting Germany in 1934, he had asked the German embassy in London whether his anti-Nazi articles in the *New Statesman* might put him at risk. He was alarmed to learn that 'official circles' in Berlin knew about and thoroughly disapproved of 'my few, poor articles'.

For his copy, Howard relied partly on information distributed by Germany's social democrats in exile. He told Klaus Mann he was 'getting a thing called the "Deutschlands-Bericht der Sopade [Social-Democratic *Party Deutschland*]" from Zurich. Why have I never seen it before? It's perfectly wonderful for writing articles out of. Is it reliable?' Using the report Howard had written a piece about the Hitler Youth which the *News Chronicle* had accepted, 'but which they dare not publish, just yet, because it is so astonishing'. The paper also liked his idea for an article 'called something like "Mann against Submen", which would show what one family [Thomas Mann's] was doing against the *Verführer* [seducer]'.

In 1937, during the Spanish Civil War, Howard had urged Klaus Mann to join him, Auden and others in Barcelona. It was full of journalists and inspiring subject-matter, he reported. They might be able to help the Republican government in 'one of the great historical struggles of modern times'. Cyril Connolly had told him that 'for lazy selfish old sissies like ourselves, Barcelona is one of the cheapest and most agreeable towns one could possibly live in'.

As war approached, Howard reflected on what he should do. He was reluctant to kill anyone unless he could be sure of killing only Nazis. Even then, he felt he would be no good at it. His goal was a job in the War Office as a translator or interpreter, so that he could help prisoners of war and refugees. But by the end of 1939, Howard's main concern was to get his German 'secretary' Toni out of Les Milles, the French internment camp near Aix-en-Provence.

Staying in Sanary's Hôtel de la Tour, Howard pulled whatever strings he could to prove to the French that Toni was an anti-Nazi German. Raymond Mortimer had guaranteed that Toni was Howard's collaborator. Donald Maclean, then a young diplomat at the British embassy in Paris, had also vouched for him. Howard had hoped that Feuchtwanger, already released after his first internment, would give him some influential introductions in Paris. He now realised that Feuchtwanger's recent book praising Stalin had discredited the exiled writer.

So Howard went to see if Somerset Maugham, held up at Bandol with his yacht, could help. The 'grinding' encounter with 'Willie' wasn't a success. Howard later complained that Maugham misrepresented their conversation. Without identifying Howard, Maugham recounted how a young Englishman from Sanary called on him for advice. The young man said he wouldn't mind returning to England if he could get something like a job in the Ministry of Information. He then astonished Maugham by allegedly declaring: 'Nothing will induce me to fight. I'm a coward.'

When Howard raised the question of the German internees again a few days later, he learned that Maugham didn't share his vehement indignation at the 'stupidity, high-handedness and brutality' of the French authorities in penning up the German refugees like cattle. Maugham maintained that because Nazi spies were active in the area, the French couldn't let Germans run loose just because they claimed to oppose Hitler. Maugham reflected that 'these men had found safety in France and had enjoyed the nation's hospitality ... now was their opportunity to show their gratitude by accepting with equanimity the mischance that had befallen them.' Howard for his part didn't believe there was a single substantiated case of a 'fifth-column' refugee.

After the French capitulated, Howard tried to get away on a yacht belonging to the ex-Khedive of Egypt, but escape was difficult. With the Germans near Marseilles, the British government hadn't yet sent boats to rescue British citizens living on the coast. Howard ultimately left Marseilles on a cargo boat the day before the Germans entered. Maugham managed to leave from Cannes, where he boarded an empty English coal barge requisitioned by the British vice-consul in Nice.

Brian Howard's account of his last days in France appeared in Cyril Connolly's *Horizon* in 1940. At about the same time, an author who had been one of Connolly's guests in Sanary was writing a satire on Britain's wartime propaganda efforts that maliciously evokes the actively anti-fascist Howard. In *Put Out More Flags* Evelyn Waugh, in the club-land style fashionable between the wars, portrays Ambrose Silk as a 'cosmopolitan, jewish [sic] pansy' who was 'all that the Nazis mean when they talk about "degenerates".' He derisively delineated a 'pale semitic' individual who 'had the flair of his race for comfort and for enviable possessions', and 'the dark nomadic strain in his blood'. *Put Out More Flags* first appeared in 1942.

After the French released Toni Altmann he managed to join the British Army's Pioneer Corps, even though his brother was serving in the German army – they weren't Jews. He moved to the United States, where his marriage to a wealthy American drove Brian Howard to seek solace in alcohol. Howard remained in touch with the Mann family during and after the war. One of his longer book reviews for the *New Statesman* drew attention to the American edition of Klaus and Erika Mann's *Escape to Life*, a series of journalistic portraits of exiled German artists and intellectuals that helped awaken America to their plight.

While undergoing a tuberculosis cure in Zurich in 1954, Howard saw Erika and Thomas again. Mann proved to be 'unexpectedly enthusiastic' about Howard's idea of a last appeal, in the form of a letter to *The Times*, against the re-armament of Germany. Howard went on to buy an old *mas* above Nice. There, he took an overdose in 1958, a few days after a gas leak from the bathroom water heater killed his partner Sam.

Sybille Bedford, who said her name featured on Gestapo lists because of hostile articles she had written for the *New Statesman*, escaped from France via Italy. Aldous Huxley helped her to reach California in July 1940 on an American ship. She later moved to London where *A Legacy*, her highly praised first novel about her family in Berlin, came out in 1956. Her friend Eva Herrmann returned to the United States where she sponsored Thomas Mann's application to become an American citizen. Towards the end of her life, the talented caricaturist turned to the occult. She reported that she had received messages from Winston Churchill and Sigmund Freud, but also from deceased members of the Sanary crowd such as Aldous Huxley, Thomas Mann and Franz Werfel.

As the German Blitzkrieg swept across France, émigré writers were among the thousands who abandoned the capital and headed south. One was Franz Hessel. With Walter Benjamin he had translated Proust's *A la Recherche du Temps Perdu*. In Sanary, Hessel and his family found temporary refuge in Huxley's former house. Another writer was Alfred Kantorowicz, who had helped set up a library of banned books in Paris. He moved into the Feuchtwangers' empty villa and that winter used its bookshelves for firewood. Like many other émigrés, he finally obtained a passage to America from Marseilles.

Kantorowicz was one of Hessel's wet and freezing friends and acquaintances who, in January 1941, waited at the entrance to Sanary's graveyard as Hessel's widow Helen and her two sons approached, accompanying a coffin. Both writers had suffered from the cares and privations of exile, but Hessel never recovered from the dysentery he contracted during internment.

While Hessel and his writings remain virtually unknown outside Germany, the actor Oscar Werner indirectly immortalised him in

François Truffaut's enchanting classic *Jules et Jim*. Freely based on the novel of the same name by Henri-Pierre Roché, the film recounts the triangular Franco-German love affair early in the century between the French writer Jim (Helen's nickname for Roché), Jules, the 'Central European' who comes to Paris, and his wife Kathe (Helen Hessel's second name). In the film, Truffaut turned Kathe from a young German into a young Frenchwoman so that Jeanne Moreau could play the role and sing the haunting waltz *Le Tourbillon*. Hessel's own fictionalised version of his *ménage à trois* appeared posthumously in 1987.

Sanary's role as a 'literary capital' had now ended. After the Allies landed in Vichy-controlled French North Africa in 1942, German troops occupied the small town, but then left the region under Italian administration. The Germans re-entered Sanary following the fall of Mussolini, and requisitioned the Hôtel de la Tour as their headquarters. The Allies began bombing Sanary in 1944, damaging the harbour. As the Germans strengthened the port's defences they systematically destroyed hotels and houses, among them the one where Thomas Mann and his family once stayed. That summer Sanary became part of the war zone, but by August *Résistance* soldiers had appeared and liberated the port. To quote the words De Gaulle proclaimed, on visiting a devastated Toulon in September: Sanary was 'wounded but free'.

2 A 'Slander' on Richard Wagner

The Torment of Thomas Mann

On 'medical grounds', Thomas Mann shouldn't break off his Swiss 'cure': such was Gottfried Bermann Fischer's advice in a letter he sent Mann from Berlin in early March 1933. Bermann Fischer, who was now running his father-in-law's publishing business, the august Samuel Fischer Verlag, urged Mann to wait until there was more certainty about his condition. He feared that a sensitive nature such as Mann's could well be subject to further attacks. Around the same time, Klaus and Erika Mann, telephoning from the family home in Munich, likewise implored their parents to delay their return to Germany. They, however, adduced the 'bad weather'.

Although nearly 58 years old, Mann hadn't been convalescing; nor had the weather in Munich been especially bad. It was Germany's political climate that had changed while Thomas Mann and his wife Katia had been abroad. The couple had planned a fortnight's rest in an Arosa hotel. In the Swiss resort they hoped to recover from a strenuous European tour in February during which Mann had lectured, sympathetically he thought, on 'the sufferings and greatness' of Richard Wagner. From her school in Munich their 15-year-old daughter Elisabeth – 'Medi' – had joined them for a skiing holiday.

Aware that the Nazis might tap their calls, Erika and Klaus Mann expected their parents to understand their cryptic references to the need to linger in Arosa. When Thomas insisted on coming home as planned on 11 March, his children had to warn him more bluntly that it would be unsafe to do so. The Manns agreed to prolong their stay. Thomas Mann never returned to Munich. Since he hadn't consciously abandoned Germany, as so many of his persecuted fellow writers had done, it took him a long time to accept that he, too, had become a political émigré.

It was to mark the 50th anniversary of Wagner's death that Thomas Mann had written down his thoughts about the composer. He completed his essay, which had grown into a 70-page document, the day Hitler came to power in Germany. Munich hosted the lecture's premiere, followed by Amsterdam, Brussels and Paris. In Paris, ominously, Mann met his older brother Heinrich who had just fled there after the Prussian academy of the arts had forced him to resign.

Erika and Klaus Mann had returned to Munich from a skiing holiday in Lenzerheide. Driving them home from the station, the family chauffeur Hans Holzner nervously warned that the local Nazis, who had just taken over the Bavarian government, were looking out for both of them, Erika in particular. Holzner, a strong, young blond man, looked pale and his hands were shaking. He counselled both youngsters to keep off the streets and to tell no one that they were back.

You might have taken Erika and Klaus, 27 and 26 years old respectively, for twins. Both had fresh complexions, dark eyes and strong noses. Erika emphasised her masculine appearance by cropping her dark hair. Klaus was good-looking and liked to affect an aesthete's pose: far-away gaze, handkerchief in the breast pocket of his jacket and cigarette held loosely in his left hand. Both knew they were Nazi targets, even before Erika, at the beginning of 1933, opened an anti-Nazi cabaret, *The Peppermill*, for which Klaus provided some of the political satires. A hostile report in the *Völkische Beobachter* had called for the 'liquidation' of the Mann family. In January 1932, Nazis disrupted a meeting of women pacifists at which Erika was one of the speakers. After she took part in a disarmament meeting in Munich, her enemies called her a 'flat-footed peace hyena'.

Erika and Klaus Mann took the chauffeur's hint. Erika returned to Switzerland that same evening. Her brother looked disconsolately at the family's furniture, their pictures and their books – and invited the chauffeur to share some of his father's best cognac. Next day he caught the train to Paris. Both Erika and Klaus had packed just enough for the few weeks they expected it would take Germany to wake up and return to its senses. Their departure turned out to be permanent exile. Only later would the Manns appreciate the chauffeur's twisted loyalty to the family, when they established that Holzner was a zealous Nazi who had been informing his local party comrades about the Manns' political views and activities.

In Arosa Thomas Mann failed to understand how the political convulsion that had gripped Germany during his absence abroad could endanger him and his wife. It was but two weeks since the Reichstag fire and a week since Hitler's victory in the parliamentary elections of 5 March, which he had called after President von Hindenburg appointed him Chancellor on 30 January. Those were the Weimar Republic's last, semi-free multi-party elections, for the National Socialists, in partnership with the conservative German National People's Party, had obtained an absolute majority in both the Reichstag and the Prussian state assembly.

The new government in Berlin had already imprisoned many of its opponents, and was conniving at widespread acts of political terrorism. A nation-wide exodus of active anti-Nazis had begun. In Munich, one of Hitler's earliest supporters, General Franz von Epp, had taken over the Bavarian government on 9 March, contrary to Thomas Mann's expectations that Bavaria's Catholics would keep the Nazis at bay.

Thomas Mann was hardly a vociferous anti-Nazi. As a young man, he had contributed to the nationalist, anti-Semitic periodical published by his brother Heinrich. As he matured, Thomas Mann's political outlook shifted from the far right to the conservative centre. Leaving Lübeck to join his widowed mother in Munich, he married Katia Pringsheim, member of a wealthy Jewish family. He had entered Munich's upper middle-class society, a culturally liberal yet passionately patriotic community.

Mann had whole-heartedly defended the chauvinistic German social order when the First World War began. He was a 'hurrah patriot' of sorts. Heinrich's disapproval of Thomas's apologetic attitude to Germany's role in that war led to a public squabble, but the brothers were reconciled by 1922. Thomas began to accept the more radical republican views of Heinrich. His third novel, *The Magic Mountain* – the original German version appeared in 1924 – reflected this more liberal outlook. As the Weimar Republic entered its sunset years, Mann wasn't only espousing the struggling and increasingly discredited democracy but also showing more sympathy for socialist ideology. Inevitably, he became the target of right-wing critics.

It was in 1929, the year Thomas Mann received the Nobel Prize for literature, that Samuel Fischer issued a popular edition of *Buddenbrooks*. The family saga had turned out to be one of the first German classics of the 20th century, after Fischer first published it in 1901. The mass sales of the cheap version of *Buddenbrooks* displeased many nationalists. They objected to the novel's frequent use of foreign words, to Mann's portrayal of a wealthy Lübeck family's decline, and to the author's apparent predilection for 'weak' values, such as artistic sensibilities, over 'strong' ones such as commercial rigour. The *Völkischer Beobachter* dubbed Mann a second-rate talent. Extremists threw stones at Mann's Munich home after he protested against Nazi-provoked attacks on left-wing deputies. Ominously, a partly burned copy of *Buddenbrooks* was found near his home.

When the Nazis made important gains in the Reichstag elections in 1930, Thomas Mann called on politicians from the centre and the Social Democrat Party to join forces to counter the rising fascist threat. By the time he set off on his lecture tour, the literary world had acknowledged Mann as an illustrious European figure. But he had also become a thorn, if not a major one, in the side of Germany's extreme right. The Nazi press had been inciting its readers against Mann.

Yet Mann's position differed from that of many other persecuted intellectuals. He hadn't criticised the Nazis in the consistent, uncompromising way his brother had done over the years. Nazis weren't calling for a ban on his novels and stories. Mann wasn't a Jew, a communist or a socialist – and that was precisely why whatever he said carried especial weight.

But what were his political views? As Mann sat it out in Switzerland, his ambivalent conduct corresponded to his unclear status in Germany. Like Hans Castorp, Mann's alter ego in *The Magic Mountain*'s Swiss sanatorium, Mann hesitated uneasily between the proponents of reason and enlightenment and those irrationalists who rejected democracy and freedom.

Mann had to restrain himself. If he returned to Munich, where he had lived since 1898, the new masters might imprison him as a free-spirited intellectual. And if he stayed abroad too long? The Bavarian authorities might classify him as a political fugitive and impound his possessions. Combined with hostile Nazi propaganda, this could lead his German readers to view his conduct as disloyal and to stop buying his books.

Such was the awkward dilemma facing Mann in those early weeks. Acutely conscious of his close ties to German culture and to the German language, Mann hesitated to 'make an open break and shut myself out forever'. Yet the family never returned to the large house he had built close to what became Munich's elegant Thomas-Mann-Allee after the Second World War. In subsequent months constant fits of anxiety, bouts of sleeplessness and stomach upsets assailed Mann as he pondered the disquieting events in Germany and searched for a sensible way out of his predicament.

As his mood swung between hope and resignation, Mann wondered whether he should patiently give the regime a chance. In mid-March, his publisher said Germany was too unsettled for the writer to take any long-term decisions. But Bermann Fischer did advise Mann to pull out of public life, believing he lacked the necessary 'armour'. Mann gave up official responsibilities that 'duty', 'good nature' or 'vanity' had led him to assume over the years. He resigned from the literary section of the Prussian academy of the arts, and from the Munich section of the German writers' guild. The Rotarians took it upon themselves to expel him.

Mann longed to 'free myself with one move from the slings of the world and make a new start'. Yet he didn't want to do anything public that might lead to costly reprisals, however much the new regime distressed him. The news that the Nazis had banned Bruno Walter from conducting in Leipzig and Berlin upset him. He called Richard Strauss and Wilhelm Fürtwängler 'lackeys' for stepping in to take Walter's place. Friends and acquaintances were bringing Mann what seemed like overwhelming evidence of terror and lawlessness in Germany. Their accounts substantiated the disturbing press reports. He had been following the way Hitler's ruthless manoeuvering had secured him parliamentary approval for a ban on communism, and dictatorial powers for himself. The 'revolting', 'sadistic', 'shameless' way in which the Nazis were seeking absolute mastery appalled him.

Mann reflected on the escalating persecution of the Jews, their removal from official legal and medical positions and the nationwide boycott of Jewish shopkeepers, doctors and lawyers that the Nazis planned for 1 April. He registered the increasing violence of attacks on political opponents, including writers. He noted with concern how the Nazis opened the first concentration camp in Dachau for communists and socialists, how they banned liberal periodicals and how they relentlessly imposed cultural uniformity. He was chilled by the photographs glorifying the new regime which filled the pages of Berlin's influential illustrated magazines.

Mann nonetheless considered asking the Bavarian authorities to guarantee his safety so that he could go back to Munich to prepare the family's move to Switzerland. He could then arrange for the transport or storage of the family's household goods, let the house, dispose of their cars and give notice to the servants. He and Katia actually sent their daughter 'Medi' back to school in Munich. She left in tears and would soon be rehearsing the Nazis' favourite marching tune, the 'Horst Wessel' song.

Some sanguine acquaintances tried to reassure Mann that he would not be at risk if he went home. One was convinced that 'they' wouldn't dare lay a hand on him because of the likely reaction from abroad – hadn't the British parliament expressed its concern about reports that Germany was expelling its poets and philosophers? Mann now thought otherwise. Someone sent him an article from a Swiss paper which affirmed that he would be in Dachau by now had he remained in Germany. As an alternative to going himself, he thought perhaps his wife Katia should slip back to Munich to settle their affairs. He then heard that the police were seizing the passports of wives as a way to force their husbands to return. Finally, their son Golo interrupted his studies at Göttingen so that he could temporarily run their Munich home and its staff.

Confident that the Bavarians' national character and their Catholic 'nature' would win through, Thomas Mann estimated that he and Katia would have to stay abroad for a year or so. He considered settling temporarily in Switzerland, Austria or Italy. After friends in the south of France beckoned him, Mann noted in his diary on 4 April, 'Economic conditions point to the south of France.'

Since Erika had brought her father the manuscript of the third volume of his *Joseph and His Brothers*, he set about rewriting a section. It was the first time in weeks that he had busied himself with his huge Old Testament novel. Much as Thomas Mann wanted to 'come to rest' and benefit from a smoothly regulated working routine, he found it difficult to write during those traumatic weeks.

Mann had reason enough to be anxious. The Nazis might use his Jewish parents-in-law as hostages. They had after all confiscated Albert Einstein's house and other possessions. Could he avoid that risk by entrusting his wealth to a Swiss citizen, Mann wondered? According to Bermann Fischer, new German foreign-currency regulations could prevent the Fischer Verlag from sending him his foreign royalties and his monthly remittance of 1,000 Reichsmarks.

Against a background of mounting Nazi pressure to eliminate 'decadent' culture, Mann began to fear that the government might ban his books. How much longer would Berlin let the Jewish firm of Samuel Fischer Verlag – publishers of Kafka, Freud and Trotsky – bring out his works? He knew that the Jewish publishers Ullstein had voluntarily suspended the distribution of an historical novel *Der jüdische Krieg* (The Jewish War) after the Nazis had accused its author Lion Feuchtwanger of spreading 'atrocity propaganda'.

A delay in renewing the Manns' passports, due to expire at the beginning of April, vexed Mann. There was a new ban on travellers leaving Germany if they didn't have a certificate stating that they were politically 'clean'. Could that be another government weapon to harass Mann?

A 'Slander' on Richard Wagner

And then there was that suitcase locked away in his Munich home. It held intimate diaries covering half a century of Mann's life. Mann had sent his son Golo the key and asked him to forward the diaries, at the same time ordering his son not to look at their contents. Golo had naively let the family chauffeur take the consignment to the station. Thomas feared the treacherous Holzner might have handed the case to the Gestapo.

Anti-Semitic comments that Mann noted in his diary in early April reflect his anguished state of mind. A doctor's proposal to sterilise Jews, published in the 'lively government sheet' *Völkischer Beobachter*, prompted Mann to speculate whether something significant was indeed under way in Germany. Jotting down the two words 'The Jews ... ', he affirmed that the 'elimination of [the émigré Jewish theatre critic Alfred] Kerr's arrogant and poisonous *vermauscheln* [jabbering like a vulgar Jew, a meaning that lexicographers have sanitised from modern dictionaries] about Nietzsche is no misfortune; nor in the last resort is the *Entjudung* [removal of Jews] from the judiciary.'

Mann recognised that 'secret, tormented, strained thoughts' filled his mind and that 'undoubtedly something ugly and hostile, something base and un-German in the higher sense', infected him. A few days later, he confided to his diary: 'I would understand the revolt against the Jewish element, if the eradication of the restraining influence of Jewish thinkers on the Germans weren't so dangerous for the Germans, and if they weren't stupid enough to lump my type together with them and expel me too.'

Of course, the Nazis had not yet expelled him, but a return to Munich still seemed unwise. While Golo Mann visited his parents in mid-April – he had obtained a travel affidavit that allowed him to travel freely in and out of Germany – his father told him to instruct their lawyer Dr Valentin Heins to let their Munich house and help to renew their passports. Hoping to get his money out of Germany, he asked Golo to withdraw as much cash as possible from the parents' two Munich banks and bring it to a safe place.

As if he didn't have worries enough, Mann became the centre of a cultural tempest. A group of 45 leading representatives of Munich's administration, commerce and culture had signed a Nazi-inspired public 'protest' against Mann's Wagner lecture. Including some of Mann's former friends, they ranged from the composers Richard Strauss and Hans Pfitzner to the Nazi publisher of the *Völkische Beobachter*, Max Amann. They denounced the 'cosmopolitan-democratic' Mann's 'slander' on the city's own musical genius, the man Hitler had chosen to symbolise German music.

They found especially offensive Mann's suggestions that there was something of the dilettante about the composer, and that Wagner's works provided a rich terrain for Freudian psychoanalysis. Munich's *Neueste Nachrichten* published the protest, and the radio service broadcast extracts. A few days later the newspaper published further names, explaining that it had omitted them because of a 'regrettable error'. For Golo Mann it was a case of naked opportunism by citizens who probably hadn't read his father's lecture but belatedly wanted to join the protest bandwagon. On behalf of the 'Richard Wagner city', Munich's establishment was anxious to show its loyalty to Franz von Epp, the Nazis' new Reich commissioner.

The Bavarian public had originally applauded Mann when he delivered his remarks at Munich university in February. A favourable account of his lecture appeared in the Bavarian *Staats-Zeitung*. After the protests, the paper falsely claimed that Mann hadn't uttered the incriminating passages in Munich. In fact, Mann had conveyed the same sentiments in Germany as he had during his foreign tour. His publishers had reproduced the text in their intellectual review *Neue Rundschau*.

Dismayed by what he considered the burghers' unjustified criticism, Mann replied in the form of an open letter. Newspapers in Berlin, Vienna and Frankfurt – but not Munich's *Neueste Nachrichten* – published his response. Emphasising his devotion to German culture and tradition, Mann pointed out that audiences abroad had applauded his lecture while German diplomats had praised Mann's service to the nation. Yet concern about losing his possessions restrained Mann from expressing publicly the seething emotions that his diary and letters reveal – his outrage at the outcast status conferred on him, and his disgust for the Nazi attitude to the arts. Though he fretted about his expired passport and the unbridled way the new masters were impounding their opponents' wealth, Mann was simply unwilling to do anything that might further provoke German officialdom.

His reticence and the pleading tone of his open letter disappointed Klaus and Golo, his older sons. Golo thought his father should rather have said nothing. Mann's cautious instincts proved to be well grounded. Research carried out after the war indicated that the protest against Mann's Wagner lecture was far from spontaneous. Exploiting the fact that the *Neueste Nachrichten* had fallen under the control of the Bavarian political police, the Nazis had instigated the demonstration to secure grounds for impounding Mann's property, and for placing him in 'protective custody' should he return to the city.

The indignities of the Wagner affair and its aftermath proved to be a turning point for Mann. The abuse poured on him by much of Munich's *Prominenz* convinced him that many of his peers in the Reich wanted to ostracise him. Learning that the Swiss government would be willing to allow him to reside there, he conceived the idea of settling in Basle – a German-speaking city, close to the German border.

But the Manns chose to spend that summer in the south of France, and there were good domestic reasons for doing so. Mann's brother Heinrich had found a temporary French refuge in Bandol, near Sanary. Klaus and Erika, who were familiar with the Côte d'Azur, had also settled nearby, in Le Lavandou. And the two youngest of the Manns' six children, Elisabeth and Michael, were now staying with them.

Mann told his friend René Schickele in Sanary of his intentions. After the First World War the pacifist Schickele had criticised the nationalist Mann in a periodical he edited, but the two had subsequently become friends and both were now part of the Fischer editorial stable. Schickele and his wife Anna offered to help the Manns look for accommodation. Urging them to choose Sanary rather than Bolzano, Schickele claimed the former was 'clean', while the Tyrol was '—-', presumably a reference to polluting pro-Nazis. Schickele advised Mann to stay at first in the Grand Hôtel in Bandol, ten minutes from Sanary and linked by a coach service that ran every 15 minutes.

By now, the Manns had their passports back – but the authorities had not renewed them. The French consulate in Lugano said it would have to consult Paris about permitting the Manns to enter France. Mann decided to use his influence. He sent a telegram to Jean Giraudoux, the French novelist and playwright who had been in the French diplomatic service since 1910 and would later run the French foreign ministry's press section. Meanwhile, as a diversion from their efforts to overcome such bureaucratic hurdles, Thomas and Katia Mann discussed with a friend a German professor's ludicrous suggestion that Mann join the National Socialists to 'ennoble' the movement.

Mann had hoped to motor from Switzerland to France in his Buick. From there he intended to drive to Madrid in May for a meeting of the League of Nations' literary committee, of which he was a member and to which he had appealed for help – fruitlessly as it turned out. Golo Mann had therefore asked 'faithful Hans' to obtain from the local automobile club in Munich – a totally apolitical organisation – the triptyque document needed to drive a car across a national frontier. The chauffeur returned, saying the car couldn't leave Germany as its owner was a 'political fugitive'. Golo suspected that Hans was conniving with the Nazis. When Golo came back from town to the family residence on 26 April, the housemaids confirmed his fears. Brownshirts had searched the house and taken his parents' Buick and Horch into 'safe keeping'.

Golo telephoned the bad news to his father the same evening. Thomas had been floating, with a professor, the idea of a university for émigrés. Mann was so upset that the next day he turned down a request by Brecht, who was in the neighbourhood, to speak with him. But Golo also had good news. The police hadn't found the 60,000 marks – a fortune at the time – that Golo had hidden in the house after managing to withdraw the money in instalments from his father's banks.

Golo, his parents and the family lawyer Dr Heins met for consultations at Rohrschach on the Swiss side of Lake Constance. Over dinner, Golo told his parents about the impounding of their two cars and the search for 'weapons' in their home. He handed over some of his father's possessions that he had brought with him and told him that he could no longer withdraw money from the parental accounts. Until late in the evening and continuing the next morning – perturbed about his missing diaries when he awoke at five o'clock – a nervous Mann struggled with the bleak alternatives facing him: should he return to Germany, or should he prepare for 'war' with the government?

Unable to face either option, Mann settled on a middle way. He would maintain the 'fiction' that he intended to return to Germany soon. He would remove some furniture and he would ask the family lawyer to look after his manuscripts (their fate remains a mystery), as well as pictures and the '*Magic Mountain*' letters Katia Mann had written to her husband while she was convalescing in Davos.

As Thomas and Katia Mann took the train back from Rohrschach, they held hands, and Mann surmised that Katia 'half understood' his worries about 'the secrets of my life' contained in his diaries. Good news greeted him in Basle. The Quai d'Orsay had authorised the pair to travel to France and to reside there. The German police had released the suitcase with the diaries, and it had arrived in Switzerland.

Thomas and Katia Mann continued to question themselves: did they ultimately want to return to Germany, or was it to be 'expatriation'? They concluded that they should go back by the autumn or even earlier, because of the risk of confiscation if they stayed abroad too long. Even as he learned that his wife's brother was among 29 professors who had lost their jobs, Mann still yearned to go back. Germany retained its appeal for him, 'unholy' and 'confused' as it was.

He remained reluctant to antagonise the Nazis. He wouldn't allow the socialist writers' guild in Vienna to publish a letter of sympathy they had sent him, aware that the German regime would condemn even passive opposition on his part. Believing that nothing could dislodge the German government, but that it might change course, he held that he had no right to appeal to the world against it.

Erika and Klaus Mann, as well as Schickele, were house-hunting for the Mann parents when Thomas and Katia prepared to take the train to Toulon. The couple discussed money. It annoyed Thomas that despite his precautions, his loyalty and his reticence, he had probably lost not only his Munich house, furniture and library but also the half of his Nobel Prize money that he had transferred to Germany. Mann believed he had a moral right to keep a present from abroad.

When the Mann parents arrived in Toulon, Erika met them in her Ford and brought them to a hotel in Le Lavandou. While the mosquitoes irritated him, Mann found that the sea acted as an aphrodisiac. As he sat on the veranda surrounded by four of his six children, the hotel's setting on the sea and the sight of a rainbow caused him to break into some strains from Wagner.

Though he and his wife had barely begun to look for a house, Thomas Mann was already wondering whether a hotel wouldn't be more convenient. Was it worth the bother of moving into a house and bringing the maid from Germany if they were going to stay for only three months? With their two youngest children, the parents followed René Schickele's recommendation and moved into the Grand Hôtel in Bandol. It was their tenth station since leaving Munich.

The day they arrived, 10 May, Mann received a customs notice asking for details about a consignment for him that officials had held up on the Swiss–French border. Returning from a walk nine days later, he found the missing case in his room. He burnt its contents, presumably documents revealing his homosexual inclinations as a young man, in 1945.

During his weeks in Bandol, Mann brooded over ways to salvage his assets in Munich. He and his wife arranged for some of their former household goods, their books and Mann's desk to follow a devious route. The Manns could address them to Schickele at his former Black Forest home. From there, Schickele, taking advantage of his French nationality, could have them dispatched as his own possessions across the border to Switzerland.

Meanwhile, Golo had taken along to Berlin the 60,000 marks that had escaped detection in Munich. He had returned to the family home from Switzerland to find that stormtroopers had also requisitioned his car. Realising that he too was now in danger, he left the Bavarian capital and spent much of the following month in Berlin. He took with him his sister Monika, who had been studying music in Florence.

While staying with the Bermann Fischers in their home in the leafy Berlin suburb of Grunewald, Golo met Samuel Fischer himself in the firm's offices, and noted how the old man was blind to the epochal changes taking place around him. He also encountered Samuel Saenger, the managing editor of the Fischer review *Neue Rundschau*, who later that year would hasten to Sanary for crisis talks with Thomas Mann. Through Raymond Aron and other French friends in the capital, Golo arranged for the French ambassador André François-Poncet to send his father's money to Paris via the diplomatic pouch.

His mission accomplished, Golo finally left Germany, accompanied by his sister Monika. They arrived in Bandol on 2 June to the great relief of their mother, who now had her children if not her parents out of danger. A week later Golo went to Paris and fetched the small parcel that the French embassy in Berlin had forwarded to the French foreign ministry.

The news from Germany continued to horrify Mann. Katia's parents visited them and brought not only newspapers, but also first-hand reports of the oppression and anxiety in Munich. Yet Mann still couldn't decide what to do. 'How remarkable,' he told Schickele, 'one leaves one's country and when one wants to go back it has run away.'

Insisting on the risks Mann faced if he stayed abroad, the Fischer Verlag suggested he return to Munich in the autumn. He seemed prepared to do so sooner, if the Bavarian government agreed to guarantee his safety. He thought about approaching none less than Goebbels for help. Hadn't the *Frankfurter Zeitung* called Mann's absence a heavy loss? His adult children tried to sway him against compromising himself in any way.

Mann revealed his unsettled feelings in a letter he wrote to Albert Einstein in mid-May after the savant had praised Mann's conduct. That deserved no praise, Mann said, as what he had done was quite natural for him. What was unnatural was his present situation. The thought of a prolonged absence from his country deeply affected him, a good German. The seemingly unavoidable break with Germany had left him severely depressed and nervous. It wasn't in his nature to seek martyrdom through exile, he told Einstein. That events had forced him into that role showed there was something false and malign about the recent 'German revolution'.

For Mann, that upheaval lacked all the characteristics of true revolutions. Those had won the world's sympathy, however bloody they might have been. This time, Germany wasn't lifting itself up, as the Nazis were proclaiming. The essence of this upheaval was hate, revenge, a mean lust to kill, a petit-bourgeois spiritual shabbiness. He predicted that nothing good could come out of the new regime, 'neither for Germany, nor for the world'.

Meanwhile the Grand Hôtel's management had provided Mann with a table and he started writing again. He sometimes sat in the garden and read. Yet he found the hotel dingy, uncomfortable and beneath the standards to which the family had been accustomed. The noise of traffic disturbed him. Mann yearned for his own house and car – and a smooth routine. He wanted to move, before the high season set in.

During a walk on 27 May, Thomas considered renting a house that his wife had seen in Sanary, where Klaus and Erika had now taken rooms in the Hôtel de la Tour. The next day, a Sunday, he went over by bus and Lisa Marchesani showed him around the property in the Chemin de la Colline. The signora, the German countess von Schönebeck by a previous marriage, knew the owner. The villa was available until that autumn, and Mann liked it. He found it delightfully situated on the cliffs near a pine forest, tastefully furnished and only a short walk from the village. The rent was low and a local house-cleaner who had already worked there might be available. Using a card table as his desk, Mann was already at work when his family moved into the house in June 1933. Thomas and Katia Mann stayed there until moving back to Switzerland at the end of September.

German troops destroyed the villa during the war as part of their preparations against an invasion. Were Mann, today, to inhabit the house built in its stead, he would find a prosperous Sanary that retains much of its old-world charm, compared with many other resorts in the region. He would probably deplore the strip of low-rise 'résidences secondaires' that disfigure the lovely coastline at nearby Six-Fours. He would have to put up with the crowds who holiday in the cheap prefabricated chalets built by a 'fresh-air' association in the forest adjoining his villa. He would have to endure the harsh revving of motorcycles on the roads behind the house, and, in summer, the roar of motorboats accelerating on the sea below. But he would find the property's name unchanged. It is still the *Villa Tranquille*.

3   A French Envoy Drops a Hint

Heinrich Mann the Francophile

Claiming later to have foreseen the Nazi 'outbreak', the Berlin-born Francophile Wilhelm Herzog had settled in Sanary in 1930. From time to time, the German-Jewish writer and translator returned to Berlin to visit friends and give lectures. One such occasion was in February 1933, when Herzog, a fervent pacifist, addressed a human rights gathering in the German capital. It was Heinrich Mann who introduced his long-standing friend to the audience.

During his Berlin visit, Herzog learned that he was being shadowed and resolved to leave Germany straight away. He tried to persuade Mann to accompany him to the South of France. Mann declined the invitation, explaining that he had agreed to deliver the congratulatory speech when the Prussian academy of the arts marked the 60th birthday in March of his fellow-writer, Jacob Wassermann.

Mann's excuse left Herzog unconvinced. He prophesied that Mann would not make the speech. After Mann called him a pessimist who viewed the situation too darkly – a *Schwarzseher* – Herzog replied that he didn't know if he saw black, but he did see 'brown' – a witty reference to the Nazi Brownshirts. That, he told Mann more than half seriously, was why he would be awaiting him in Sanary, where there was a spare bed. He told Mann to telegraph his arrival time.

And that's precisely what Heinrich Mann unexpectedly found himself doing. On 22 February, he sent a telegram from Strasbourg, asking Herzog to fetch him when he arrived at Toulon station. Heinrich Mann had just crossed the frontier and was now seeking refuge in France. He would never return to his homeland. That summer a Nazi law enabled the regime to cancel the citizenship of undesirable Germans and confiscate their possessions. Mann's name was on the first list.

It was an ironical turn of events for a writer who in 1894, the year of the Dreyfus trial, had dedicated his first novel to Paul Bourget, a 'racial psychologist' and co-founder of the extreme right-wing *Action Française* movement. For a while, Mann, influenced by French racists who wrote for German journals, had written anti-Semitic articles in the pseudo-scientific style prevalent at the time. But by the second decade of the 20th century he had evolved into a writer who praised the breadth of the Jewish spirit.

Mann's flight from Berlin drastically changed his life. As a writer, he had enjoyed considerable authority for years, not only among his peers but also in public life. His collected works had already been compiled three times – in 1909, in 1917 and in 1925–32; a fourth version appeared in 1972, after his death, under the auspices of the Communist authorities in East Berlin. Heinrich Mann had held the highest position in the official literary establishment. Some admirers had even urged him to run for the presidency of the Weimar Republic, a suggestion he immediately turned down.

Far less well known today than his younger brother Thomas, Heinrich was more than a successful author of novels, plays and short stories in the early decades of the century. Critics would later complain that his 'lack of economy wore out his readers'. His outpouring of polemical essays and articles on contemporary events had made him a leading publicist, unlike Thomas. Partly under the influence of politically committed French novelists such as Emile Zola, he had come around to supporting radical policies. The reserved and conservative Thomas explained the emotional differences between them by falling back on the duality of their ethnic background. Thomas believed their North European Protestant ancestry dominated his own personality, while the exotic Latin Catholic element in their half-Brazilian mother had shaped Heinrich's more excitable nature.

Born in Lübeck, Heinrich Mann did not complete the school course. He went into the book trade, first in Dresden and then as an apprentice with Samuel Fischer's publishing house in Berlin. From an early age, Heinrich's sickly disposition and his penchant for the Latin European way of life had led him to reside for long periods along the French and Italian stretches of the Mediterranean.

Observing his *Heimat* from a distance, he criticised its ills, whether the materialism and nationalism of the authoritarian Second Reich, the chauvinism and militarism that drove Wilhelm II's empire into war, or the irrational fanaticism that arose during the Weimar Republic. The brothers' opposing attitudes to German society, and especially to Berlin's role in fomenting and prosecuting the Great War, led to an intensely bitter rift between them. It was largely because Thomas warmed, in the early 1920s, to what was by then Heinrich's socialist *Weltanschauung* that the brothers reached a modus vivendi, if not a reconciliation, after they both found themselves in exile. By then Thomas had received the Nobel Prize for literature, and his reputation had begun to overshadow that of his brother.

In his early works, Heinrich Mann criticised and ridiculed both the Prussian obsession with order and authority, and the shady opportunism and *arrivisme* of the flourishing *Gründerzeit* years that followed the completion of German unification in 1871 – the year of Heinrich's birth. That era saw a phenomenal upsurge in economic activity in and around Berlin, and with it the emergence of a generation of nouveaux riches – 'the new rich [*reich* in German] of the new Reich'. Many intellectuals welcomed Mann's corrosive depiction of society, embodied in his satiric turn-of-the-century novel *In the Land of Cockaigne*.

What might strike today's critics, however, are the anti-Semitic strokes with which Mann portrayed some of his characters in that work. Like other novelists of the period, Maupassant in *Bel Ami* for example, Mann liked to target figures from the newspaper and banking worlds. A decadent crowd hovers around the salon of his power-broking financier Türkheimer, who resembles Bismarck's banker, Gerson Bleichröder, himself the victim of anti-Jewish campaigns.

While a liberal economic philosophy had enabled a powerful entrepreneurial middle-class to help turn Germany into a major European power, a paternalist and oppressive political culture kept the working masses in their place. Heinrich Mann's publishers shuddered when they saw the word 'democracy' printed on the publicity leaflet that had been prepared to launch his novel *Die kleine Stadt* (The Small Town) in 1909. They destroyed 20,000 copies and printed a safer version.

His satire on the individual's blind obedience to the Kaiser in *Der Untertan* (roughly, the submissive subject, but translated as *The Man of Straw*) brought him further difficulties. When a first extract appeared in a magazine in 1914, it created an uproar and pre-publication in serial form was suspended at the outbreak of war. After it finally appeared in book form in 1918, however, the work was an immediate literary triumph, some 80,000 copies being sold in a week. In the Weimar years Mann's reputation in Germany as a popular writer rested above all on *Der Untertan*. What finally brought him worldwide recognition was the instant success in 1930 of *The Blue Angel*, the film version starring Marlene Dietrich of his novel *Professor Unrat*.

Although he never joined a political party, Heinrich Mann had constantly swum against the prevailing political currents. He had opposed the conservatism and militarism of Kaiser Wilhelm II's regime, calling for more democracy and humanism. During the 1914–18 War he had refused to let the waves of blind patriotism that swept over the Second Reich engulf him. Mann firmly and controversially advocated Franco-German reconciliation in the 1920s, a decade in which France antagonised the Germans by squeezing out of Germany's struggling economy the reparations imposed on the country by the Versailles Treaty. While Mann didn't hesitate to criticise the Republic's weaknesses, his proposals tended to be imprecise, frequently relying on abstractions such as 'progress', 'justice' and 'democracy'.

Through Félix Bertaux, one of his closest French friends and an expert on German literature, Mann had since 1923 attended the *Entretiens de Pontigny*. He was the first German invited to attend the prestigious, semi-official annual conferences for writers and other intellectuals. There the avowed Francophile met writers such as André Gide as well as other leaders of France's intellectual elite. In 1927, Mann spoke in Paris to mark the centenary of Victor Hugo's birth. Mann was ahead of his times not only in appreciating the need for a genuine Franco-German rapprochement. In 1923 – the year Hitler undertook his abortive putsch in Munich, inflation peaked in Germany and France occupied the Ruhr – Mann was advocating a United States of Europe. In proposing a Europe independent of the 'Anglo-Saxon' and Russian empires, Mann came under the influence of the founder of the 'pan-European' concept, Richard, Count Coudenhove-Kalergi. The link between them was the count's wife, Ida Roland, an actress who had performed in Mann's plays.

By the time Mann left Munich for Berlin in 1927 (at the same time parting from his Czech wife and daughter), he was a widely respected writer despite his left-wing opinions. There was even talk of Mann running as the radical candidate against Hindenburg in the 1932 elections for the presidency of the Weimar Republic. He told Robert Musil of the move to put him forward as *praeceptor Germaniae*: 'an appeal was issued, full of such childish talk about leadership and merit that I said that, eager as I was to oblige, I could not possibly sign in that form.' Heinrich Mann would in effect become a role model during his years of exile in France, while admirers would foist the imposing Roman title on Thomas Mann during his American exile.

Formal recognition of Heinrich Mann's elevated status in the Weimar Republic's literary fraternity came shortly before his 60th birthday. In January 1931, he was chosen to be president of the writers' section of the Prussian academy of the arts. The academy soon turned into an ideological battleground between nationalist and liberal writers.

The celebrations around Mann's birthday, on 27 March 1931, almost had the trappings of a state occasion. One hundred and thirty German and foreign authors signed a message of congratulations. The academy's president, Max Liebermann, as well as the Prussian minister of culture, Adolf Grimme, and Mann's brother Thomas honoured him with speeches at the academy. At a special PEN gathering, Lion Feuchtwanger hailed his achievements. At a banquet of the German writers' guild, Gottfried Benn said that 'in his person I celebrate the most exciting writing of the age ... the most consummate creation in the German language to have been witnessed since the dawn of the century.' A year later Mann endorsed Benn's election to the academy.

It was Mann's conviction that writers should not shy from political responsibilities, a viewpoint that inevitably landed him in trouble once the Nazis took over. In February 1933, while Herzog was in Berlin, Mann's pronounced left-wing stance led him to sign a political manifesto which anti-Nazis were soon plastering over the publicity columns that were a prominent feature of Berlin's streets. This urgently appealed to the communists and social democrats to save the country from sinking into barbarism by forming a united front, ideally in the form of joint lists of candidates for the forthcoming Reichstag elections. Another academy member, the artist Käthe Kollwitz – who had illustrated the cover of one of his novels – as well as Albert Einstein and Arnold Zweig were among those who signed the manifesto.

An outraged Prussian ministry of culture, now Nazi-led, threatened to close the academy if it did not expel Heinrich Mann and Kollwitz. Both stepped down, and only one fellow member resigned in protest. Other members of the literary section thought Mann's action had made his departure inevitable. As they saw it, Heinrich Mann's status was an official one: the social democrats had originally confirmed his election. He was in no position to call for action against the government that succeeded them, even if it was a Nazi-dominated coalition.

By the time the academy came around to regretting Mann's resignation and to thanking him for his achievements, the ex-president was planning to flee. A Nazi periodical in Munich, *Die Brennessel* (Stinging Nettle), had in January 1933 published a grotesque caricature on its cover. The drawing crudely attached Heinrich Mann's head to Marlene Dietrich's body, in her notoriously lascivious *Blue Angel* pose where she flaunts her suspenders. Its caption doctored the words of her famous chanson from the film – 'Ich bin vom Kopf bis Fuß auf Liebe eingestellt' – to read 'From head to toes I'm set on Jews.' The text referred to Mann's inauguration of a Berlin synagogue.

The *Völkische Beobachter* in February described him as 'national vermin' and recommended that someone place a bomb under the 'unpleasant and overweight' writer. The right-wing Hugenberg press had been calling him un-German and Jew-friendly. It was not merely Mann's political views. A history of German literature would point out in 1934 that both the Mann brothers had married Jews. Their mother moreover was of Portuguese origin, and therefore might have had Jewish as well as Negro blood, it noted.

Luckily for Heinrich Mann, the French ambassador in Berlin, André François-Poncet, understood the dangers facing the writer. Greeting Mann at a reception, he hinted: 'If you're crossing the Pariser Platz, you're welcome to use my house.' The skilled diplomat followed that up the next day with a coded warning on the telephone: 'I understand you are going to Paris tonight. Would you be kind enough to visit my mother and give her my best wishes?'

With little more than a suitcase and some notes for his planned historical novel about France's Henri IV, Mann took a train to Frankfurt, changing there to a train that brought him over the border to Strasbourg. He later learned that the Nazis had intended to arrest him, like many other communist sympathisers, after the Reichstag fire at the end of February. His companion Nelly Kroeger, a Berlin bar hostess he had met in 1928, was present when the Gestapo ransacked their Berlin apartment. With a communist friend she would reach Bandol via Denmark that autumn. Mann's ex-wife fled to Prague, where President Thomas Masaryk intervened to prevent the confiscation of Mann's books and manuscripts.

Mann stayed a short time with Herzog in Sanary. There he found his friend Lion Feuchtwanger, whom he knew from Munich days. There was René Schickele, who like him had voiced his misgivings about Prussian militarism and ardently preached European understanding, to no avail. That summer of 1933, Joyce Weiner, later a London literary agent, visited Sanary. Feuchtwanger's secretary Lola Sernau introduced her to the tall, burly Mann. She found the 'bearded giant' taciturn and remote. As they sat in a café, the *patron* played Marlene Dietrich records.

A French Envoy Drops a Hint

When the writer Hermann Kesten called on Thomas Mann in Sanary in September 1933, he found Heinrich Mann there. Conversation inevitably turned to Germany. Thomas declared that the world had never seen so barbaric a regime, never had a people fallen so low. 'My brother is right, don't you agree?' Heinrich asked Kesten. The brothers were dumbfounded: Kesten did not. As a novelist, he believed there was nothing new under the sun. Civilisation had always been a fragile business and it was understandable that exiles would exaggerate their misfortune. Kesten learned later that the Manns thought he was trying to defend the Germans.

Unlike many other refugees, Heinrich Mann had no fears about living in France. Having first visited it as a young man, it was not a strange country. Not only was he well acquainted with France and French culture, he could also speak and write the language. Like his brother and his nephews, Erika and Klaus, Heinrich was familiar with the charms of the Côte d'Azur, which he had discovered well before the First World War.

He and Herzog had travelled extensively in Italy and the South of France, spending more than six months together in Nice before 1914. There Heinrich Mann had worked on his novel *The Small Town*, Herzog on his biography of Heinrich von Kleist. Mann had often stayed in Nice since then. And it was to Nice that Heinrich Mann soon moved from Sanary, preferring to live in a bigger town. He remained in Nice until 1940. During those years of French exile, Mann would return to Sanary from time to time, spending part of the summer with friends in the area. He would also travel frequently to Paris, where he would become one of the most politically active German writers in French exile – and in a sense their 'president'.

4 Warning in Washington
Lion Feuchtwanger Portrays Life Under the 'Hooked Cross'

The host at the dinner in Washington was the German ambassador, Friedrich Wilhelm von Prittwitz und Gaffron. The guest of honour was a small, shy, bespectacled Jew, Lion Feuchtwanger. The day was Monday, 30 January 1933: in Berlin, Germany's newly appointed Chancellor had presided over the first meeting of his cabinet. Next day, the ambassador called his guest and warned him not to return to Germany. Baron Prittwitz would be one of the few senior German diplomats to resign at the time from the diplomatic corps.

Feuchtwanger, a highly accomplished author whose middle-brow historical novels had made him wealthy and famous around the world, was on a lecture tour of the United States lasting from mid-November to the beginning of March. He now astutely predicted that Hitler's arrival at the centre of Germany's political stage was likely to lead to war – or so the story goes. Earlier on in his tour, after a small drop in the Nazi share of the vote, Feuchtwanger supposedly assured the then New York State governor, Franklin Delano Roosevelt, that 'Hitler is over'.

Born in 1884 of orthodox Jewish parents, he had started out as a theatre critic and playwright in Munich in 1908. He based one of his most frequently performed plays on the life of Warren Hastings. Some German theatres rejected it, during the First World War, as too Anglophile. The ravages of that war turned Feuchtwanger towards socialism. In Munich, in the 1920s, he met and discussed politics and literature with Heinrich Mann, 13 years his senior, among others. Brecht, 14 years his junior, would come from Augsburg to borrow money and talk about working together: they successfully collaborated on a play based on Marlowe's *Edward II*.

Almost forgotten today outside the German-speaking world, Feuchtwanger's international eminence rested largely on his historical novels, in particular his first major work *Jud Süß*, one of the best-selling German novels of the 20th century. He based the work on the life of Josef Süß Oppenheimer, a Jewish Don Juan who rose to become financial adviser to the court of an eighteenth-century German duke. Tried for subversion and publicly hanged before he turned 40, the courtier became the classic Jewish scapegoat for some, the stereotypical Jewish wheeler-dealer for others, among them Goebbels.

Feuchtwanger had originally turned the story into a play, before reworking it into a novel that publishers at first rejected. It became a great success after it finally came out in 1925: by July 1931, Germans had bought around 100,000 copies, and there were translations in more than 15 languages. Martin Secker brought it out as *Jew Suess* in London, the Viking Press as *Power* in New York. Arnold Bennett powerfully stimulated sales in Britain with his reference to *Jew Suess* as a novel that enthralled while it instructed. The American critic Clifton Fadiman found *Power* an historical novel of epic dimensions.

By the late 1920s, critics were elevating Feuchtwanger to an honoured place among the foremost writers of Europe. They compared him with Henry Fielding, Alexandre Dumas and Stendhal. His name became a literary by-word in the English-speaking world. *Jew Suess* was turned into a play again, and in time adapted for radio, cinema and television. Years later, when Alistair Cooke turned 90 in 1998, he recalled his 1929 *Manchester Guardian* piece in which he had favourably reviewed Peggy Ashcroft in *Jud Süß*.

Feuchtwanger went to London in 1935 for the première of Gaumont's British film version, starring the émigré Conrad Veidt. In 1940, just as Feuchtwanger was enduring the hardship of French internment, Veit Harlan's German film version of the *Jud Süß* story reached the screen. Before they went into action, SS officers were encouraged to watch a film regarded as one of the most effective examples of Nazi anti-Semitic propaganda.

Feuchtwanger's accomplishments allowed him, after leaving Munich for Berlin in 1925, to build a villa in the fashionable and elegant suburb of Grunewald. He had an extensive library. He employed a secretary, Lola Sernau, to whom he dictated *Erfolg* (Success), a highly popular topical novel that incurred the wrath of the Nazis. Against the background of life in an apparently cosmopolitan Munich and provincial Bavaria in the early 1920s, Feuchtwanger sketched the beginnings of the growing Nazi movement, and especially Hitler's abortive putsch in Munich in 1923.

In the novel Feuchtwanger unmistakably depicts the future Führer in the guise of Rupert Kutzner, founder of the 'True Germans' party; another character is based on Brecht. When Kutzner (with dark moustache and sleek hair plastered over his head) begins to speak, his face becomes curiously mobile with a hysterical vivacity. In a high and sometimes excitable voice, the words flowing effortlessly from his lips, he denounces capitalism and usury and blames the Jews and the Pope for the wretchedness of life in Germany. An international clique of Jewish financiers is supposedly trying to destroy the German people, in the way a tubercle bacillus tries to destroy a healthy lung. To create a robust society, Kutzner wants to eliminate the parasites. Anticipating Feuchtwanger's exile, the work describes how a disillusioned social democrat member of the Reichstag, who has defended a victim of injustice, leaves Germany for a small French fishing village on the Mediterranean.

Feuchtwanger started *Erfolg* in 1927. Published in 1930, the novel became the first volume of what Feuchtwanger called 'The Waiting Room', a trilogy that graphically told the world how the Nazis persecuted their opponents before the war. In his late forties at the time, Feuchtwanger now became the target of anti-Jewish attacks, with Nazi agitators smashing the window-panes of his home. Goebbels called him an un-German Jewish evildoer. The Nazis tried to suppress all mention of *Erfolg* and other works dealing with the Führer's first attempt to attain power.

In those heady Weimar Republic days, in an atmosphere of growing violence and instability, Feuchtwanger worked closely with many other writers and artists who were active in Berlin. Brecht and Arnold Zweig lived nearby. Though he saw Heinrich Mann less often than previously, Feuchtwanger spoke at one of the ceremonies to mark his 60th birthday. Other Berlin acquaintances whom Feuchtwanger would later meet in exile were the writers Carl Zuckmayer, Erich Maria Remarque and Vicki Baum, all highly successful in the English-language world.

Foreign writers such as Sinclair Lewis called on the wealthy and famous Feuchtwanger in Berlin. During the three months he spent travelling each year, he met leading personalities of the era – in 1927 for example, it was Ramsay MacDonald, Bernard Shaw, John Galsworthy and H. G. Wells in London. When his American agent urged Feuchtwanger to tour the United States in 1932, at first he hesitated. He believed he had no talent as a lecturer. Withdrawn all his life, he disliked performing in public; his English was poor; and he was acutely aware of his short stature and timid nature. He believed his voice did not carry, and could not convey the charm and dynamism of his books. He finally agreed to take lessons, and crossed the Atlantic on the *Europa*. It turned out to be a wise decision. Because he enjoyed such a high reputation, Feuchtwanger met Eleanor and Franklin D. Roosevelt during his tour. At the beginning of the following decade, Mrs Roosevelt's influence helped to ensure that Feuchtwanger, trapped in France, managed to reach America.

Feuchtwanger had planned to go back to Berlin on his return to Europe at the beginning of March 1933. As Nazi propaganda had already branded him a traitor to the German people, that course was no longer feasible. Besides his hostile fictional account of Hitler's rabble-rousing activities, Feuchtwanger had demonstrated his support in 1932 for Carl von Ossietzky, the pacifist editor and future Nobel peace prize winner, whom the Nazis charged with treason and sent to a concentration camp.

Instead of going home, Feuchtwanger joined his wife Marta, who was skiing in the Tyrolean resort of St Anton. From there they moved to Switzerland. Feuchtwanger would never again see the country of his birth, the country he had briefly served in the First World War before being invalided out, and the country that had awarded one of his three brothers the Iron Cross.

In Switzerland, where Brecht, Thomas Mann and other exiled writers were temporarily installed, Feuchtwanger learned from his secretary that Nazis stormtroopers had rampaged through his Berlin home and ransacked his library. Nazi students sold and later burned his books. Stormtroopers took his notes and the manuscript of the second volume of the novel he was writing about Flavius Josephus, the Roman-era Jewish historian who propagated a form of world citizenship. The authorities confiscated his house and the considerable cash reserves a highly successful writer such as Feuchtwanger possessed – yet nonetheless ordered him to repay his mortgage out of future earnings.

Feuchtwanger's prospects in Swiss exile were more favourable than were those of most refugee writers. Publishers in many countries translated his books; sales of his historical novels had been especially high in the large English-language market. He nevertheless faced many of the same practical questions as less fortunate émigré authors: where should he live, who would now publish his books in German, could he continue to earn a living without the German market. He decided that he and his wife should leave Switzerland, where he had received menacing letters.

Feuchtwanger tried to rescue what remained of his fortune. He asked both a lawyer and a German friend of Marta's to try to retrieve his funds at the Feuchtwanger Bank in Munich, owned by relatives. Fearing reprisals, the bank resisted. Although a pre-Nazi regulation compelled Feuchtwanger to repatriate foreign royalties, his secretary managed to open foreign accounts for him in the names of her sister, who lived in Switzerland, and of a friend in Scandinavia. Without the lost manuscript and source material about Josephus that he had accumulated at his Berlin home, he could not proceed with the rewriting of the second volume.

A week after Hitler took power, one of Feuchtwanger's German publishers shrewdly removed to Switzerland large stocks of two of his works that it was withdrawing from the German market. As it would be dangerous for the exiled writer to correspond directly with his German publishers, he engaged a Swiss lawyer to carry out the negotiations about the distribution of his books from Switzerland.

Like other émigré writers, Feuchtwanger started to look for a home in the south of France, where life would be cheaper than in Switzerland. The couple took the train to Marseilles and after some inconvenience – their luggage went astray in Lyons and the first hotel was unpleasant – Marta reconnoitred by bus and found temporary accommodation at the 'very attractively situated' Hôtel La Réserve in Bandol. As it was almost empty at that time of the year, she could afford to take extra rooms, including one for her husband's secretary Lola Sernau, who followed them with her typewriter. Lion was soon on the hotel terrace, redrafting the second volume of his *Josephus* trilogy. The Amsterdam publisher Querido, who had set up a branch for the work of German exiles, published it in 1935 as *Die Söhne* (The Sons).

In Sanary, during that summer of 1933, Sybille Bedford helped Marta Feuchtwanger find a house to rent by driving her around in her car, a small Ford that had lost its doors. Marta chose the Villa Lazare, a simple dwelling high above the sea on the Boulevard de la Plage, between Bandol and Sanary. Surrounded by the scent of thyme, rosemary and sage, the Feuchtwangers could descend a rocky path to a small but private beach. Marta persuaded the villa's owner, a lawyer in Toulon, to supply a rudimentary table, some mattresses, a lamp and wobbly chairs. The only heating was the living room fireplace, where Marta would grill food. She later maintained that at first she found her new setting a more than adequate substitute for the home in Grunewald that the Nazis had forced the couple to abandon.

Joyce Weiner, during her visit from London, found the marble-floored villa cool and welcoming. But she did not find Feuchtwanger good-looking. His pebble-thick glasses did not improve his 'visage de singe'. Nor was there anything alluring about his stocky figure as he moved about in brief shorts, exposing his mahogany-tanned torso. Yet Weiner liked Feuchtwanger's genial manner. As he poured scorn on the Nazis, she enjoyed his flow of wit and appreciated what she considered his fluent English.

It was in the Villa Lazare that Feuchtwanger put aside his book about Josephus, and wrote what would be the first anti-Nazi novel written by a German writer in exile, *The Oppermanns*. The British government had commissioned him in April 1933 to write an anti-fascist story as the basis for a film script. The screenwriter Sidney Gilliat travelled from England to the south of France to work with him on the script. Lola Sernau had brought valuable press cuttings about recent events in Germany. Feuchtwanger used these as well as *Mein Kampf* and material from the official German gazette to construct the novel. He based *The Oppermanns* on his own family's misfortunes at the hands of the Nazis, particularly the ruthless way they forced his brother Martin to flee after they had 'Aryanised' his business.

Werner Cahn, who had helped Feuchtwanger with research in Berlin, joined him in Sanary for half a year as his literary assistant, until Feuchtwanger arranged a job for him with Querido in Amsterdam. On a visit to London, Feuchtwanger learned that the British government wanted to abandon the film project; it had decided that it would be unwise to sponsor a piece of propaganda that was bound to offend the new masters in Berlin. As his wife Marta put it, the British prime minister Ramsay MacDonald had resolved to 'swallow' Hitler. Feuchtwanger recalled how earlier that year American politicians he had met in Washington wanted to give Hitler a chance.

Not easily discouraged, Feuchtwanger turned his draft script into a novel. He was determined to exploit his talents to protest at the Nazis' lies and violence. He hoped to warn the public of their cruel and violent persecution of left-wing political opponents as well as the country's Jews, including his brothers. He wanted to use his reputation to tell the world that the Nazis 'were inflexibly determined to transfer the wealth of the Jews to their own pockets, to step into their shoes, to annihilate them.' He hoped to dispel the 'mists of falsehood' and expose for the reading public the true nature of the loutish Nazi 'mercenaries', the surveillance and denunciation of neighbours, the hidden preparations for war. To do all this as rapidly as possible, Feuchtwanger and Sernau worked up to ten hours a day.

Feuchtwanger dictated all that was going through his head. After Sernau had typed a first version, he corrected, re-dictated and re-corrected, using different coloured inks and papers for his various drafts. They completed the manuscript in September 1933 and Querido issued the German version. By November, Martin Secker in London had published James Cleugh's translation. Cleugh turned 'Hakenkreuz' into 'Hooked Cross'. The word 'swastika' was not yet in common use to denote the ancient Sanskrit symbol the Nazis adopted.

Feuchtwanger set his novel in 1932 and 1933. His denunciation revolves around the way the Nazi rabble menaces, humiliates and finally banishes the three respectable, middle-class German-Jewish Oppermann brothers from Berlin – Gustav, a writer; Martin, who runs a furniture business; and Edgar, a prominent surgeon. A fourth brother has fallen in the Great War. None of the three takes seriously the growth of a powerful Nazi movement in the dying days of the Weimar Republic. They can't ignore the unpleasant world of politics, much as they would like to do so.

The regime forces Martin to cede his firm to his main competitor, an 'Aryan'. An anti-Semitic teacher provokes Martin's son to kill himself. A hostile press campaign and the anti-Jewish boycott compel Edgar to abandon his practice and migrate to Paris and Palestine. Gustav flees after the burning of the Reichstag. Realising that he is no longer living in the civilised Germany of Goethe and Kant, he (like Heinrich Mann) has signed a manifesto that condemns the growing barbarity of public life.

After some months in France, Gustav sneaks back into the Reich under a false name, observes the callous acts of the Nazis and tries to join a secret resistance organisation. Arrested, thrown into a concentration camp and released, Gustav returns to the South of France, on the verge of death from the brutal treatment he has endured. An active opponent of the Nazis reassures him: 'The work is going on and we know the truth. They won't get us down.' There lies Feuchtwanger's conviction that it was the writer's job to reveal what lay behind Nazi parades and propaganda.

Feuchtwanger brings in his own experiences in Sanary, though he does not mention the port by name in the book. While in France, Gustav waits at Bandol station for his companion Anna, whom he has not seen for 19 months. Tired after her strenuous work over the past year, she explains that she is looking forward to a lazy time by the sea – walks, bathing and lying in the sun. To cope with her sketchy French she has brought some books and a good dictionary. The couple hire a small car and look for a cheap house in which Anna can spend the few weeks' holiday at her disposal. On the peninsula, they find La Gorguette, a spacious, low-lying and isolated house built on a rocky promontory beside a little cove, and resembling the Feuchtwangers' Villa Lazare, which was located on Sanary's La Gorguette peninsula.

Feuchtwanger uses the Oppermanns to convey the emancipation and integration of German Jews. They are so enlightened and assimilated that Christmas is as important in their household as Chanukkah. Many prosper, and it's this rise to fame and fortune that arouses envy and helps provoke their downfall. He brings out well how minor Nazis – the furniture dealer, the doctor, the teacher – shield uncouth Nazi party thugs and their ideology, and employ threats and violence to uproot their competitors and further their own career and material interests.

Feuchtwanger portrays a stout, elegant Jew who defends the Nazis. Rudolph Weinberg resents the 'whining' of the refugees and wants to give the Nazis a chance: 'One can't sweep without a broom.' He thinks little has changed in Berlin, that the new leaders will improve as soon as they get real power and that 'the whole anti-Semite movement would fizzle out if only Jews abroad would ... stop chattering'.

What might shock today's readers is Feuchtwanger's brand of 'anti-Semitism', common enough at the time. An elderly clerk is 'emphatically Jewish in appearance ... His big nose, overhanging a strong growth of dirty grey moustache'. A doctor, 'born of a poor family in the Berlin ghetto', is 'clumsy', 'insignificant-looking, ugly and inhibited in all directions', 'a grey, ugly dwarf'. He 'reminded one of the caricatures of Jews in the comic papers'.

Feuchtwanger introduces Jaques [sic] Lavendel, an agreeable but ill-mannered 'gentleman from the East' who has married Martin Oppermann's younger sister, to the family's disapproval. A naturalised American, Lavendel is 'an excellent man of business', but has 'no sense of dignity ... of reserve'. Feuchtwanger skillfully turns this crude *Ostjude* into a kind of hero. The Oppermanns have lost their religious roots. At first, they don't want to emigrate because they don't believe the Nazi menace will last. They don't see how the Nazis, on the basis of their foolish race theories, can decide who is a Jew. With millions of copies of Goethe's works in circulation, Germans won't listen to 'the clamour of the barbarians'. Lavendel knows better. Centuries of East European pogroms are in his make-up. It's time to leave to escape the danger, he tries to tell the in-laws.

The novel was still at the printers when Querido had to destroy the first printing. A senior Nazi official in Hanover called 'Oppermann' took offence at Feuchtwanger's use of the name for the fictional

Jewish family. He threatened to have Lion Feuchtwanger's brother Martin, who was still in Germany, sent to a concentration camp. Martin Feuchtwanger persuaded Querido to alter 'Oppermann' to the more Jewish-sounding 'Oppenheim' in the reset German version, which in any case was not going to be available in the Third Reich. The publisher changed the title back to 'Oppermann' again after Martin had emigrated.

The Oppermanns became one of the most widely read fictional accounts of the evolving German tragedy. It provided the outside world with a graphic insight into the grim conditions facing Jews in Hitler's Germany. Richard Grunberger, who as a refugee in Britain was to write a standard social history of the Third Reich, later said he first realised the true nature of the Nazi regime, after reading the novel as a Viennese teenager. The work was soon available in numerous languages and, in translation, sold 257,000 copies within five months. Secker reprinted the English translation in December 1933 and again in the following February; a cheaper edition followed in July 1934. Praise was not unanimous. The satirist Kurt Tucholsky considered the book artistically very bad, flimsy, with cardboard characters; for him Feuchtwanger was absurdly overrated – but good enough for the English.

The Oppermanns became a best-seller in the United States, from where Feuchtwanger's publisher Ben Huebsch reported a storm of press approval. Huebsch sent him the enthusiastic New York reviews – which the émigré press summed up in the audacious prediction that the work would live on long after the world had forgotten Hitler. Feuchtwanger said he had witnessed nothing like it since the publication in Britain of *Jud Suess*.

The novel did more than supplement the income Feuchtwanger had received from the abortive film-script contract. Its success – it was especially well received in English-speaking countries – made Feuchtwanger a prominent spokesman for the opposition to the Third Reich. *The Oppermanns* helped to consolidate Feuchtwanger's position as the leading literary light among the refugee writers in Sanary, and Sanary's reputation as the 'secret capital' of German literary emigration.

Half a century after Feuchtwanger's fruitless negotiations with the British government, the British public at last had a chance to see a screen version of the novel. The British Broadcasting Corporation aired a two-part dramatisation of *The Oppermanns*. It was in German with subtitles, having been produced by and for German television.

5 Émigrés as 'Deserters'
Klaus Mann's Literary Feud with Gottfried Benn

Under a starry sky, the dispossessed and uprooted writers would congregate at the cafés on Sanary's harbour front. One topic that dominated their conversation that first summer was how a renowned writer they once respected now mocked their supposedly carefree life in palatial hotels on the Riviera. The insensitive and sarcastic remarks that Gottfried Benn broadcast over the German radio infuriated writers who had lost their homes and their livelihoods.

Thomas Mann's son Klaus, staying in the Sanary area at the time, was among those offended by Benn's sneer. Until then Klaus Mann had admired Benn as a writer, and considered him a friend. Now, he engaged in a major literary duel with him. The dispute centred on Benn's contention that Germany needed its intellectuals at home to help mould the new society that was taking shape, and that émigré writers had evaded their duty and 'deserted' Germany. (In *Put Out More Flags*, Evelyn Waugh hinted at Auden and Isherwood running away in 1939 to America. Tom Driberg wittily and more openly said 'The dog beneath the skin has had the brains to save itself, Norris-like, by changing trains.')

Few established authors of the era who stayed on in Germany after 1933 enjoyed a high reputation after 1945. Benn was one of them. While 'inner émigrés' tended to brood in silence, others, Benn among them, proclaimed their utmost loyalty to Hitler. They wanted to help rebuild the Reich. They shared the Nazis' hostility towards the 'decadent' culture of the Weimar republic. They approved the way the Nazi government quickly set up state bodies charged with drawing up and enforcing 'health and safety' standards for the arts.

Gleichschaltung was the overall authoritarian concept behind Germany's drive to 'synchronise' the arts. Government agencies used legal and other means to bring cultural organisations into step with Nazi norms. As early as March 1933, a new 'Ministry of Propaganda and Popular Enlightenment', headed by Goebbels, entered the political arena. Goebbels preferred the word 'culture' to 'propaganda', which he thought left an unpleasant after-taste (at that time the word in German suggested advertising publicity), but Hitler turned down his suggestion.

Goebbels, who had tried to become a writer, also presided over the Reich chamber of culture, set up later that year. Its sections were to regulate art, music, letters and the media. All those active in these fields had to join the appropriate section, but were eligible to do so only if they were 'Aryans'. After the Nazis dissolved the German writers' guild (*Schutzverband*), the chamber incorporated its successor, the Reich association of German writers. The law setting up the Reich chamber stipulated that authors who did not register by 15 December 1933 would lose the right to have their books published in Germany.

Among its measures to control the press, the government passed a law in October 1933 that banned Jewish journalists from editorial offices. It set up a centralised bureau to filter foreign and domestic news and 'guide' its presentation. Within the Nazi Party, a new office, headed by Alfred Rosenberg, controlled ideological education. It steered the public actions to outlaw 'decadent' art and music and to burn 'unwholesome' literature. Added to the arrest and detention of writers and journalists after the Reichstag fire, these steps soon intimidated and silenced many of the government's opponents in the arts. The regime rewarded its faithful adherents by appointing them to prestigious positions in the new arts hierarchy. The Nazi campaign mirrored similar moves in the Soviet Union in the early 1930s to control the arts.

Benn sympathised with the aim of 'reawakening' Germany in this fashion and saw no reason to emigrate. Benn's attitude was surprising. He was a churchman's son, he was of French-Swiss origin on his mother's side and he had had a liaison with the German-Jewish poet Else Lasker-Schüler. His support for Hitler upset the émigrés, because of his stature and because he had been in the forefront of avant-garde literature.

Yet even as a young man, there had been a coldness about Benn's nature. A specialist in skin and venereal diseases, Benn served as a doctor with the German army in Brussels during the First World War. He worked in Belgian hospitals that treated prostitutes, and the unemotional poems he wrote on themes such as corpses and flesh shocked his readers. After the Germans judged Edith Cavell guilty of treason in 1915, Benn had to witness the execution of the British nurse and certify her death.

Unlike other authors who had experienced the horrors of the

battlefield, Benn did not turn to pacifism after the war. He nonetheless associated with anti-war writers. In the 1920s Benn's publisher had been the liberal progressive firm of Kiepenheuer, the same that had issued the works of Brecht, Arnold Zweig, Lion Feuchtwanger, Heinrich Mann and other future émigrés.

Benn admired Heinrich Mann's early works and was among the main speakers to congratulate Mann when he turned 60 in 1931. But he angered left-wing writers such as Brecht by praising the literary as opposed to the political Mann. When Benn became a member of the literary section of the Prussian academy of the arts in 1932 – one of the highest honours the state could bestow on a German-language writer – it was partly with the support of Heinrich Mann, president of the literary section.

A year later, however, Mann and the academy itself were in jeopardy. For the Nazis, too many members of that noble fraternity, founded by Frederick the Great, espoused modern cosmopolitan trends in the arts. Mann's call in February 1933 for the political parties of the Left to jointly combat the new barbarism was legal: the Weimar constitution was still in force. It was nonetheless an intolerable affront to the Nazis, and opened the way for the Prussian authorities to compel the academy to demand Mann's instant resignation.

Far from reciprocating Heinrich Mann's earlier support, Benn slipped into Mann's seat in March. He pushed through a proposal that the academy's literary section ask its 27 members if they wished to continue to serve the academy. If they did, they would have to abstain from anti-government activities. They would have to work loyally with the academy in carrying out the national cultural tasks assigned to it in 'the changed historical situation'.

Thomas Mann and Alfred Döblin resigned. Others writers such as Schickele neither signed nor resigned. Franz Werfel was among the 18 members who proclaimed their loyalty, but soon the academy told the Czech Jew that he would have to resign. As the government began to dismiss unsuitable members from all sections of the academy it replaced them with Nazi sympathisers, and the august institution soon lost much of its reputation.

In April, Benn followed up his 'loyalty' initiative with a broadcast from Berlin that justified Nazi opposition to prevailing intellectual currents. His talk was full of heavy abstract concepts and it's difficult to imagine the masses staying tuned to their receivers. Printed in German newspapers, however, the talk had considerable impact. What upset the émigrés was the way a leading German philosopher-poet had condemned the liberalism of the Weimar Republic. The academy's only remaining writer of true distinction had thrown his full weight behind the new regime.

Claiming that intellectual freedom was an anti-heroic ideology and a license to undermine the state, Benn hailed Hitler's Reich as the inauguration of a new historical existence. Even more stingingly, Benn claimed the country's youth despised those Germans who had reacted to the Nazi offensive by crossing the border incognito to look for plots of land in Switzerland. If they had been unhappy with the new regime, he suggested, they should have girded their loins, 'taken the spade' and faced what they thought to be the danger. Benn privately criticised one émigré friend of the Mann family as a traitor who had fled Germany with her money.

That such a highly cultivated man as Benn could adjust so smoothly to Hitler's coarse cultural ideology, and to the crude Nazi attacks on the arts as they flourished during the Weimar Republic, dismayed few more than Heinrich Mann's nephew Klaus. He knew Benn and admired his work. He had based a character on him in a novel published the previous year. Benn's sharp rhetorical blows against the 'traitors' shocked Mann. Mann had previously considered him an intellectual nihilist and was now appalled that Benn should view the new Germany so glowingly.

An outsider, a homosexual (his diaries are explicit, unlike those of his contemporaries, Harold Nicholson and Sir Henry 'Chips' Channon) and a drug addict who later became a cult figure in Germany, Klaus Mann was born in 1906, some 20 years after Benn. While Klaus's father closeted himself in his study, his mother Katia attended to all the needs of her six children, from teaching them to pray and swim to supervising their homework. When Klaus and his clique of schoolmates sought excitement through escapades that verged on the criminal, his parents sent him to what is still a distinguished liberal German boarding school, Odenwald. Klaus left without completing his studies there, and broke off the private tuition he subsequently received at home.

But Mann had benefited from his family background. His mother's wealthy and cultured Jewish family in Munich entertained a cosmopolitan circle of intellectuals as well as society figures. Katia and Thomas Mann introduced their offspring to the magic of theatre and of music, especially the compositions of Wagner. The children met Thomas Mann's Berlin publisher Samuel Fischer, and a Munich neighbour, the conductor Bruno Walter. Leading writers and musicians such as Hugo von Hoffmannsthal or Hans Pfitzner passed through the Mann residence.

Thomas Mann read aloud to his older children from the classics of Russian writers such as Gogol and Tolstoy, and from his own work. Whitman, Rilke, Wilde and Baudelaire influenced Klaus as a youth. Even as a boy Klaus showed interest in writing, although he would later exclaim with a sigh how awful it was that 'in our family just about everything has already been written down'.

Klaus Mann was not yet 18 when, in 1924, he surveyed the bohemian landscape of Munich and left it for Berlin. There his mother's brother found him a job for a short time as a theatre critic. He discovered the capital's theatres, cabarets and other forms of nightlife. His father provided him with the monthly allowance that helped keep Klaus afloat for most of his life and enabled him to travel at will. He lived mainly in hotels and boarding houses or with friends, returning from time to time to his mother for the comforts of an established home.

By 1925, Klaus Mann had published a book of poems, a play with a lesbian setting, and one of the first novels in German to deal openly with male homosexuality – *Der fromme Tanz* (The Pious Dance). He praised as a God-given form of love what was then a crime. For Mann, homosexuals should not deny or resist their inclination. He refused to consider them as degenerate or ill in some way. His father was less tolerant. Thomas Mann found the excesses and extravagances of the younger generation distasteful. In an essay on marriage that appeared in the same year as his son's novel, he cursed 'homoeroticism' as a fruitless and irresponsible form of 'free' love – harsh words from someone who confided to his diary his own repressed longings for other men.

During his Berlin years, Klaus Mann travelled widely, often in the company of his elder sister Erika. His unsettled spirit drove him around Europe's cultural centres, from Budapest, Berlin and Paris to Amsterdam, Sanary and Naples, and to outposts beyond. In his diaries, he noted in dry but meticulous fashion the course of his dissolute days and, being a late riser, more particularly his debauched nights: a procession of hotel rooms, cafés, restaurants, bars and Turkish baths; furtive encounters with male prostitutes; where and when he procured and took the drugs to which he became addicted.

Klaus Mann's profligacy looked like an attempt to rebel against the respectable paterfamilias and his disciplined working routine. Auden later partly blamed Klaus's parents for his unhappy life. By neglecting his education, they had obliged Klaus to enter the literary world in which he could never compete with his father. On the other hand, Auden noted, one of Klaus's younger brothers, Golo, had been well educated and would distinguish himself as an historian.

As Klaus's interest in the major political issues of the moment grew, he came to reject the stereotype, instilled at school, of France as the arch-enemy. Prolonged stays in Paris and on the Côte d'Azur taught him to appreciate contemporary French culture. Gide, Cocteau and Julien Green became his literary models as well as friends. Influenced partly by the views of his father and uncle, he sided with those who criticised much of the pre-war German intelligentsia for supporting the unbridled nationalism that had led to catastrophe. Mann believed the new generation of intellectuals had to encourage Franco-German reconciliation – at that time still a highly controversial concept.

He became enamoured with an even more far-fetched ideal: a united Europe. The founder of the pan-European movement, Richard Count Coudenhove-Kalergi, strongly impressed him at first. Later Mann's enthusiasm for the cause faded as the count, backed by big business, began to view his alliance primarily as a means of opposing the Soviet Union. Klaus Mann nevertheless remained loyal to the general idea of European union.

The economic depression and the results of the Reichstag elections in September 1930, when the Nazis advanced from 12 to 107 seats, brought Klaus Mann closer to everyday politics. He sensed and feared the likelihood of a Hitler dictatorship. He became embroiled in an exchange of letters with Stefan Zweig on the significance of those elections – a dispute that foreshadowed later differences of opinion between them.

Zweig maintained that the Nazis had won so many seats because young Germans had revolted against the slow pace of politics. Mann challenged Zweig's indulgent attitude to the Nazis. He by contrast believed young Germans had voted 'backwards' rather than 'forwards'. In any case, Klaus Mann, who in January 1933 had joined a group of radical left-wing pacifists, knew that the Nazis were likely to harass him.

In his autobiography, first published in English as *The Turning Point* in 1942, Mann considered whether 'we emigrated of our own free will. Not altogether. We couldn't return ... Certain lungs could not breathe the air in the Third Reich ... suffocation threatened in the Heimat.' Mann used the same suffocation metaphor in his novel *The Volcano*. He later amplified his motives for leaving Germany. The Nazis would have beaten him to death or at least imprisoned him, he reasoned. Even had they left him alone, he would have suffocated.

He wanted to fight German fascism from without. He couldn't have become an effective underground fighter, because he and his family were too well known. On the other hand, he didn't consider his family temperamentally suited to belonging to the 'quiet ones'.

The Nazis had never liked him, Klaus said in *Escape to Life*, a book about German culture in exile that he and his sister wrote in the United States in 1939. The aversion was reciprocal, he added. He was not the solid *Blut und Boden* type they favoured. He wrote critical articles about the Nazis and loathed all they stood for. He pointed out that since his 19th year he had – even if with a weak voice and inadequate arguments – publicly condemned reaction, nationalism, imperialism, militarism and exploitation. He believed the Nazis would have killed him had they been able to lay hands on him.

Klaus Mann managed to escape in time. He and Erika were both staying near Le Lavandou when their parents arrived at the coast from Lugano on 6 May. The next day Klaus took the bus alone to Toulon. After an aperitif, a bouillabaisse and wild strawberries at a harbour restaurant, he wandered along to Toulon's red-light district where bar hostesses adorned with roses and sailors' caps sat on his lap and tried to lure him upstairs. Finally, he met a sailor and took him to a hotel. Klaus caught a bus back to Le Lavandou early the next morning. The following day, 9 May, giving Sanary's Hôtel de la Tour as his address, he penned his long polemical letter to Benn. He read out the draft to his parents the same day.

Mann asked Benn to clarify his attitude to 'German events'. He told him he understood his antipathy to the crass materialism of writers such as Brecht. What astonished Mann was not just Benn's support for the new authoritarian state, but also his attack on the émigrés for refusing to dirty their hands and for deserting Germany in its hour of need. He wondered how Benn could remain in the Prussian academy of arts – the only German author 'whom we reckoned to be one of us' who had done so. Mann urged Benn to reconsider his attitude to Nazi Germany.

Klaus Mann couldn't fathom how Benn, who enjoyed such a high reputation among the émigrés, had come around to serving the Nazis. Their baseness was without parallel in European history; the world was outraged by their moral turpitude. Surely Benn's own writings would sound like the purest cultural Bolshevism to the ears of Nazi party hacks.

Mann told Benn he would no longer find his young admirers in Germany. They were living in the small hotels of Paris, Zurich and Prague, while their former idol was consorting with Nazi academicians. Mann sympathised with Benn's hostility to Marxist German literature and the way papers such as the *Frankfurter Zeitung* reviewed literature from a sociological angle. It was nauseating, and no one suffered more from it than Mann himself.

At the same time Klaus Mann had uneasily been observing where Benn's antipathy to those 'bloated fatheads' had led him over the years. There was his ever more vehement irrationality, his gesticulations against 'civilisation'. He had come to favour the cult of force. And, finally, he had turned to supporting Hitler. Mann wanted Benn to know that he counted among the very few whom 'we under no circumstances wanted to lose to the other side'. In a phrase frequently cited afterwards, he warned Benn that 'whoever in this hour adopts an ambiguous stance will never again belong to us'.

Mann had written what he considered a private letter. Benn chose to reply via a second broadcast. Published the next day, this metaphysical 'answer to the literary emigrants' appeared two weeks after the students' book-burning rites across Germany. Taking up Mann's reference to Benn's admirers reduced to the small hotels of Europe, Benn mocked those émigrés in bathing resorts on the Gulf of Lyons who criticised the patriots who had joined in building the new German state. He didn't believe anything would have happened to the exiles had they remained in Germany.

Benn contended that you could profitably discuss recent events in Germany only with those who had lived through them in Germany itself. That view became a key defence of those who remained in the country while withdrawing from public life. For Benn, those who had fled had missed the chance to experience the concept, so alien to them, of *Volk*, rather than think about it in the abstract. There was a genuine national movement afoot in Germany. He didn't mean the theatrical – the torchlight and the music – but an inner process that turned sceptics into supporters.

Klaus Mann, in portraying what was happening in Germany as a threat to civilisation, had often mentioned 'barbarism'. Benn gave the word a positive spin. He linked it to the favourable way late-romantic German authors had reappraised the ancient Germanic pagan cult of nature. How did Mann think 'history' moved, he wondered? Had twelfth-century Europeans discussed and voted on the architectural transition from the Roman to the Gothic style? Benn insisted that 'history's' only method at its turning points was to bring forth a new human type from the inexhaustible loins of the human race. (Gutwetter, a character in Feuchtwanger's *The Oppermanns*, celebrates the advent of the 'New Man'.)

Benn admitted that his view of history was metaphysical, rather than humanist or enlightened. He called on Mann to grasp that events in Germany were not political manoeuvres. A new biological type was emerging, to produce a mutation in history. It had less to do with forms of government than with a new vision of what might be the ultimate great conception of the white race.

Hinting that writers in exile wanted to destroy the German nation, Benn pointed to the millions of victims of Marxist atrocities in the Soviet Union. As a practising doctor, Benn could assure socialist writers in exile that the workers, including former socialists and communists, were better off in Germany than before. Hitler was 'a great individual genius', like Napoleon.

Klaus Mann was in Paris when he heard that Benn's answer had appeared in the press. He found it weak when he read it the next day. But Benn's broadcast unleashed a bitter reaction, and elicited hollow laughter from the refugees. Benn's 'offensive' reply and his mocking suggestion that the writers in exile were having fun in French bathing resorts infuriated Thomas Mann in Sanary. Could Benn really believe that nothing would have happened to the Mann family had they remained in Germany? His daughter Monika had just brought him the news that the Nazis, after blocking his current account, had now confiscated – 'simple robbery' – the 40,000 marks he had deposited in his German savings account.

In Paris Klaus found that exiled writers, like his father, resented Benn's insinuation that they were enjoying themselves at the seaside. Since the Nazis had banned and burned their books, how could they afford Riviera hotels? The Nazis had pulled émigré writers out of bed, tortured and humiliated them, and forced them to flee. Joseph Roth took up Benn's assurance that 'not much' would have happened to Klaus Mann had he stayed in Germany. What did 'Herr Doktor' mean by 'not much': was castration or sterilisation a lot or a little for a writer of Jewish descent, he wondered?

Harry, Count Kessler, the dandified diplomat, writer and philanthropist who left Germany for France in 1933, met a woman in Paris who had just returned from Berlin, where she had spoken with Benn. She reported that he had become a fanatical Nazi who claimed that Hitler's revolution was an historical event of the first order, a total rebirth of the German people and Europe's salvation.

Benn's enthusiasm for Germany's new leaders did not last long. He soon became ashamed at his gullibility. Hitler disgusted Benn by ordering the killing in June 1934 of storm-trooper leader Ernst Röhm and many conservative figures admired by Benn. In 1935, Benn broke with the regime, bitterly retreating into an 'aristocratic inner emigration'. Nazi publications slandered him and castigated his defence of expressionist literature. He was required to prove that the name 'Benn' had no Old Testament roots.

Benn again served as a military doctor until 1936, when the medical association excluded him. Two years later he was forced to resign from the Reich chamber of writers and the regime banned him from publishing further works. The Munich state library placed his books under lock and key. They were accessible only to students of 'degenerate and perverse art' who had permission from the Nazi authorities.

Looking back on the controversy in 1937, Klaus Mann saw it as epitomising the conflict between writers repelled by fascism and those anxious to make their peace with it. For him, Benn was the only significant German writer who had seriously erred into National Socialism. Other writers had perhaps reluctantly accepted the regime's restraints and joined the Reich writers' guild, but they had had done so out of opportunism or fear.

After the war, Benn returned to the medical profession and to writing. Reviewing his life, he said the Nazis had called him a pig, the communists an idiot, the democrats an intellectual prostitute, the émigrés a renegade, and the church a pathological nihilist. He admitted that the 27-year-old Klaus Mann had judged the pre-war political situation more accurately than he, then in his mid-fifties, had done. He acknowledged that he had wrongly lambasted the émigrés for being unable to assess from their Mediterranean resorts what was happening in the Reich.

Benn incorporated Klaus Mann's letter in his autobiography *Doppelleben* (Double Life), published in 1950. But this contrition came too late for Klaus Mann. He had committed suicide in Cannes in May 1949.

6

Cleansing the 'Literary Brothels'

German Students Celebrate Their 'Bibliocaust'

Klaus Mann was drinking an aperitif in Sanary's Hôtel de la Tour a couple of days after he had written his letter to Gottfried Benn. The newspaper he was reading reported that his works were among those German students had burned at carefully orchestrated ceremonies in university towns throughout the country. While considering their action infantile, he nevertheless felt honoured.

Mann was indeed in distinguished company: the students' wrath encompassed authors ranging from Upton Sinclair to Berthold Brecht, from Klaus's uncle Heinrich Mann to Erich Kästner, author of the children's classic *Emil and the Detectives*, and from Marx to Freud. Vandals in Heinrich Heine's home town Düsseldorf destroyed works by the poet, who had found political refuge in France a century earlier.

Supported by Goebbels and his propaganda ministry officials, Nazi students prepared and ignited the pyres on 10 May 1933 – the culmination of a month-long campaign against a wide range of authors and journalists, German and foreign. With their vivid 'purifying' symbolism, the flames served to draw attention to the students' desire to play their part in eliminating the 'rotten' elements in German literature. As a result, many photographers, newsreel camera operators, radio commentators as well as press reporters were present. They ensured that the event received instant publicity in Germany and beyond. Germans could follow the occasion live on the radio. Photographs and newsreels appeared around the globe showing German students throwing tomes on the flames; the illustrations have often appeared since. Reporting the students' boorish behaviour at the time, *Time* magazine called it a 'bibliocaust'.

The students shocked the outside world with what seemed like the revival of a brutish practice linked to less enlightened centuries. They themselves were convinced that they were performing sacred rituals with noble precedents. They began their month-long information campaign by 'nailing', on street advertising pillars and in university precincts, their 'twelve theses' condemning alien writings. That showed the influence of Martin Luther, who had burned papal edicts in 1520.

A later inspiration was the Wartburg festivities of 1817, when radical Jena students had burned books as part of their campaign for political rights and national unity. One of the books had mocked the prevailing anti-Semitic 'Germanomania'. The students' symbolic extermination of the author, a Berlin Jew, inspired Heine's prophecy in his tragedy *Almansor* that 'where one burns books, one will ultimately burn people.' Emigré writers were to recall those words.

More ominously and more recently, students had in 1929 expressed their opposition to the fragile Weimar Republic by burning copies of the Versailles Treaty, the Weimar constitution and international plans drawn up in the 1920s to ease the burden of the post-war reparations imposed on Germany. In the summer of 1932, while vacationing on the Baltic coast, Thomas Mann had received a parcel containing a burned, just-recognisable copy of his popular novel *Buddenbrooks*. He regarded the incident as 'punishment' for having publicly warned the country against the rising Nazi danger.

With Hitler's assumption of power, some right-wing students would inevitably seek to display their support for his cause. They observed the Nazi party bringing about a political and economic 'renewal', and took it upon themselves to perform a similar service in the world of learning. After Goebbels set up his Ministry of Popular Enlightenment and Propaganda in 1933, they established a head office in Berlin for their own press and propaganda service. It was soon instructing local branches how to carry out the planned four-week action. To achieve their goal of 'countering the un-German spirit', the students were to 'cleanse' libraries and bookshops, bring the 'intellectual garbage' to specified locations, and carry out the purification rites on the evening of 10 May.

But which books were they to consign to the flames? Over the preceding years, Nazi publicists had already identified a broad range of tainted writers and themes which they held to be responsible for the country's moral collapse. Helped by the *Kampfbund*, a militant federation to promote German culture, the students drew up blacklists that included supposedly decadent novels, historical works, books on religion, art and philosophy, even children's books.

They would obviously want to condemn political works of a Marxist, Jewish, pacifist or pan-European nature. Freudian-style literature was another category that was ineligible for public protection. Especially undesirable were books with erotic descriptions that sought to arouse readers' baser instincts. As 'normality' was too diffuse a concept when applied to lovemaking, the self-appointed censors adopted 'Germanism' as a more precise criterion. One characteristic of German sexual relations was 'Northern restraint', and consequently moral guardians ruled 'inappropriate' any hint of an 'Oriental' bedroom atmosphere.

Another dangerous sort of reading matter comprised 'unhealthy asphalt literature', written by and especially for those who lived in the big cities. Nazis believed that such works, dealing with unsavoury urban topics such as underworld crime and prostitution, alienated readers intentionally or otherwise from the wholesome values which the right-minded associated with the countryside. They dubbed them 'intellectual nihilism' and established that the authors of these books were generally Jewish *Literaten* – irresponsible and uninspired hacks – as opposed to the more elevated *Schriftsteller* – writers who produced true literature – and above all the *Dichter* – poets and authors whose works were of eternal value. These were subtle distinctions that Lion Feuchtwanger's 'Anglo-Saxon' friends found hard to understand.

Conflicting blacklists emerged and some publishers, among them the celebrated house of Samuel Fischer, urged the authorities in Berlin to approve certain inoffensive titles by otherwise obnoxious authors. For guidance, the students finally followed a semi-official 'index' of about 200 titles by 131 authors, drawn up by the Prussian cultural authorities for their public libraries. Only after the book-burning had taken place did Goebbels's ministry issue official government blacklists for the nation at large.

The students directed their wrath against authors held to be unpatriotic such as Lion Feuchtwanger, Erich Maria Remarque (since he was born 'Remark', Nazis liked to hint that he had reversed his 'real' name, the more Jewish-sounding 'Kramer') and the biographer Emil Ludwig (Nazi publications did not tire of recalling that his name at birth had been 'Cohn').

They also denounced booksellers. In the students' eyes they bore a large share of the blame due to their crucial role in the distribution of the decadent works. Others pointed at what they saw as the machinations of the big Jewish publishing firms, which placed large print orders for their Jewish authors and flooded the market with cheap editions of what the students held to be trash.

There was the harmful role of certain libraries. Students could rely on the public libraries' co-operative staff themselves to remove the offensive works and all reference to them in the catalogues. So they concentrated instead on the 15,000 private lending libraries that had prospered as inflation impoverished Germany's middle class. To meet the upmarket requirements of their readers, the shelves of these 'literary brothels' had displayed books by writers such as Heinrich Mann, Ernst Toller and Kurt Tucholsky. Berlin's lending library in 1932 typically stocked from ten to 100 copies of new books by pernicious authors, among them Thomas Mann, Remarque and Stefan Zweig.

The students produced posters appealing to the public to hand in their Marxist, Jewish and pacifist books. Some booksellers refused to display them in their windows. But Germany's book-trade association swiftly adjusted to the changed climate. Its weekly journal reported without comment the campaign under way. It urged booksellers not to resist the imminent confiscation of undesirable printed matter. It sought to co-operate with the authorities in working out uniform rules on banned books.

On the day after the book-burning, the association published an authoritative list of twelve authors – among them Heinrich Mann and Lion Feuchtwanger – held to be 'damaging to Germany's reputation'. Yet even two days before the auto da fé it was still not clear how binding the published boycott lists would be. Thomas Mann's publisher told him he did not think the move would affect Fischer, as the lists were intended to guide public and private libraries.

As a spectacular debut in Berlin, students from the Institute of Physical Education raided the library of Magnus Hirschfeld's Institute for Sexual Science. A Berlin doctor, Hirschfeld was campaigning for the repeal of paragraph 175 of the Reich's penal code, which outlawed male homosexuality as an act of 'unnatural lewdness' and subjected offenders to imprisonment and loss of civic rights. The law reflected the prevailing attitude in Germany at the time: that homosexuality showed contempt for marriage and would depopulate and seriously weaken the state. Paragraph 175 had its roots in mediaeval theology, which discouraged sexual activity unconnected to reproduction.

Hirschfeld, dubbed the 'Einstein of sex' in Weimar days and later called 'a guru of the gays', had concluded that no clear-cut biological boundary divided the sexes. He argued that homosexuality was neither a sickness nor a crime, but a natural variation of sexual activity. He therefore advocated the abolition of paragraph 175. Although the law had remained in force after the fall of the Hohenzollern empire, Hirschfeld and his followers hoped that society would at least remove the stigma and discrimination associated with gay life, and thereby encourage homosexuals to emerge from their underworld sanctuaries.

Homosexuality did in fact become less of a taboo under the Weimar Republic, and the Prussian government, recognising the Institute's role as a sexual advice centre, administered it as a foundation. 'Deviant' sex became the subject of literary works, films and plays as well as popular reference manuals. Berlin became an erotic eldorado. Its broad-minded attitude to bohemian lifestyles attracted Anglo-Saxon travellers wanting to sample a culture that was less pious and sexually more liberated than at home. A 'Guide to Naughty Berlin' helped them find their way around the underworld of cabarets and brothels. The capital's open promiscuity and its liberation of body and soul allowed an international gay culture to flourish there openly.

Hirschfeld's activities ranged from legal aid and marriage guidance to the treatment of venereal diseases. It was his campaign to decriminalise consensual sex between adult males, however, that made him well known even beyond Germany. Bertrand Russell and Bernard Shaw addressed a congress in London in 1929 of Hirschfeld's world league for sexual reform. Hirschfeld himself conducted André Gide around his premises. W. H. Auden visited the Institute in the late 1920s, after he 'discovered' Berlin. Christopher Isherwood rented digs next door to Hirschfeld's sister's building. What he saw in Hirschfeld's museum embarrassed him, from 'the sexual organs of quasi-hermaphrodites' to a picture by a patient 'of a priapic king who, sprawled on a throne with his own phallus for a sceptre, watched the grotesque matings of his courtiers'.

For Germany's young Savonarolas, however, Hirschfeld, then in his mid-sixties, was a deplorable figure, and it was obvious that as a left-wing Jewish homosexual he would become a prime target for cleansing. Isherwood witnessed the way about 100 students in trucks turned up at the Institute, smashed the doors and rushed inside, all to the accompaniment of a brass band playing in military formation.

On the first floor, they poured ink over carpets and documents before turning their attention to the bookshelves. Photographs show them examining photographs of pin-up girls. They kicked pictures about as though they were footballs, leaving behind a trail of broken glass and frames. At noon, the students' leader made a speech to the crowd that had gathered outside, attracted by the playing of the brass band. The strains of the Horst Wessel song filled the air as the students drove away with their booty. A second attack against Hirschfeld's institute took place that afternoon, when storm-troopers emerged from trucks saying they had to finish the job. With the support of the librarian, himself a Nazi sympathiser, they made a bonfire of the library.

Hirschfeld, at the time on a lecture tour abroad, realised it would be dangerous to go back to Berlin. He began his exile in Paris and then moved to Nice, where he hoped to re-open his institute, but he died in May 1935. Half a century later Charlotte Wolff, a lesbian graphologist who fled from Berlin and briefly stayed in Sanary as a friend of the Huxleys and Sybille Bedford, would publish a biography of this 'pioneer in sexology'.

In Berlin alone, students amassed some 10,000 hundredweight of books and periodicals, the product of raids on the homes of proscribed writers such as Feuchtwanger as well as on bookshops and libraries. Some booksellers had vainly tried to conceal their stocks in cellars, attics, garden sheds or private homes, the police reported. Students sifted through the booty, putting aside scientific and other works that they thought might prove useful to researchers. Authorised scholars could later examine samples of some banned books, locked into special 'poison cupboards' in public libraries. Far from destroying all 'degenerate' books, the Nazis slyly dumped much of the confiscated literature in other countries. That made it even harder for the émigré writers to earn a living from their works.

On the morning of 10 May 1933, newspapers announced and justified the purge that was about to take place that evening. In the carnival atmosphere created by the singing of Nazi songs, members of the Hitler Youth and paramilitary organisations joined the students. Assembled in columns they carried flaming torches to the spot in the various university towns where they were to light their pyres. In Frankfurt, two oxen drew a book-filled wagon normally used to cart manure.

In Berlin, white- or brown-shirted students selected some of the thousands of books and periodicals they had collected and piled them on vans displaying slogans that condemned 'bad' books. With the vehicles in the middle of the procession, the bare-headed students advanced slowly across the city, those in the outside lines carrying torches. They marched through the Brandenburg Gate to the huge empty esplanade, between the university and the Kroll opera house, where they had erected a pyre and a tribune. With storm-troopers and SS squads surrounding the square and bands playing patriotic music, the students paraded a bronze bust of Hirschfeld that they had removed from his institute. It had been presented to him five years earlier to honour his 60th birthday.

Students threw their lighted torches onto the waiting pile of faggots which was soon ablaze. A chain of students passed the books and periodicals from the vans to a companion standing on a platform alongside the pyre. His role was to throw one book after another into the flames, uttering a denunciatory *Feuerspruch* for the author concerned: Marx was an enemy of social cohesion; Heinrich Mann an enemy of morality; pacifist authors were enemies of patriotism; Freud had advocated excessive subservience to instinct.

The throng heard a condemnation of Erich Maria Remarque for his 'literary betrayal of the World War soldiers' and a call to the population to take up arms. Franz Werfel's works turned to ashes although, just days before, the Czechoslovakian Jewish novelist had vainly offered his loyalty to the new regime.

A woman squeezed her way through the crowd, carrying a shopping bag with books and shrieking 'Here, please, these too.' Goebbels drove up and made a speech that many couldn't hear, despite the loudspeakers. He of course proclaimed that a new spirit would rise, phoenix-like, from that evening's ashes. 'Sami' Fischer's daughter Brigitte, witness to what she considered a witches' Sabbath, recalled how the flames made the dwarf-like Goebbels look like a ghost. She observed some of the silent crowd trying to salvage works from the fire.

One of the most memorable literary reactions to the book-burning was that of Oskar Maria Graf, a Bavarian writer who had been confined to an asylum for two years during the Great War for failing to obey orders. He was absent from his home in Munich when the police came to arrest him in 1933. They nonetheless confiscated most of his manuscripts, his laboriously assembled source materials and many of his books. He then learned that the Nazis deemed his books inoffensive, apart from his main work, *We are Prisoners*. He was aghast that the Nazis had chosen him to represent the new German spirit.

Protesting that he did not deserve such dishonour, he publicly appealed to the authorities to burn his other works also. Graf condemned the way a twisted spirit of nationalism motivated the Third Reich. It had rejected most representative modern German literature, had driven the best German writers into exile and suppressed their works, and had persecuted, imprisoned, tortured, murdered or driven to suicide the friends of freedom. 'Now it claims me as a representative of that spirit,' he declared in disgust.

Graf's 'protest' found its way into the *New York Times*, under the heading 'Wants His Books Burned'. His widely published gesture inspired a poem by Berthold Brecht. Probably no other text by a German writer in exile became so closely associated with the book bonfires and was reprinted so often. Nazi students in Munich were eager enough to fulfil Graf's wishes. In the presence of their professors, they burned his books on the campus. Graf ended up in the United States, where he was a founder of the publishing firm Aurora.

After the students had destroyed blacklisted books, they encouraged booksellers to fill their shelves with *Mein Kampf* and related volumes, and with *Heimat* literature, which exalted true German virtues and values. They did not interfere with authors who wrote 'traditional' works.

Did the students significantly 'cleanse' the German mind? Many blacklisted books probably survived – in second-hand bookshops or concealed in attics and cellars. As Germans could travel abroad until the outbreak of war, those curious enough could read what the banned authors were writing in exile. Still, the students' action did help the government carry out its broader programme to bring the arts into step and purge the influence of harmful intellectuals. In that way they had fulfilled one condition for victory, Hitler told the Nazi's ideological leader Alfred Rosenberg at the end of 1933. The students' campaign reinforced the government's other steps to 'synchronise' the written word: harnessing the press, forcing 'decadent' writers to leave the country, depriving publishers of their freedom to choose what to publish, dissolving the writers' associations and reorganising the academy of the arts. In future, no publisher could issue in Germany books that disparaged the new state.

Many of the prominent authors who did stay in Germany began to practise a form of passive resistance: they stopped writing. Nationalist writers such as Hanns Johst now rose to prominence. They generally did so more because of their public support for the Nazis than for the literary quality of their writing. Austria re-enacted the book-burning rite after Hitler annexed his homeland in 1938.

As a carefully staged media event, the students' book-burning revelries proved highly successful in drawing the world's attention to the barbarous nature of the new government. In London, British communists responded by opening a Karl Marx memorial library in Clerkenwell that same year – the 50th anniversary of the political theorist's death.

In Paris, the guild of German writers in exile turned an artist's studio on the Boulevard Arago into a 'Freedom Library' of burned and banned books. They were resolved to preserve the works of the despised writers. Inaugurating the Library on the first anniversary of the bonfires, Heinrich Mann declared that if one silenced a people, their books would speak. Egon Kisch told two representatives from the German Embassy at the ceremony that he approved of their presence: they would be able to register that the battle against Hitler and his savages would continue relentlessly.

André Gide and Romain Rolland, a winner of the Nobel Prize for literature, joined Lion Feuchtwanger as the Library's honorary presidents and Heinrich Mann presided over its committee. The French publisher Gaston Gallimard lent his prestige. André Malraux planned but failed to bring out a French-language anthology of *écrivains brûlés*. Émigrés who had managed to bring their libraries with them donated books when they had to flee overseas, or when they found they had too little space for them in their hotel rooms and could not afford storage dues. The journalist Georg Bernhard lent the Library the books he brought from Berlin: he reckoned there were 8,000 volumes. The Freedom Library acquired books at auctions. Apart from the many thousands of books it housed, the Library went on to amass leaflets, illegal newspapers, camouflaged and coded communications and relevant photos. The Library lent nothing, but became a valuable documentation, exhibition and propaganda centre.

In November 1936, Goebbels and the Nazi writers' association organised a book exhibition in the Boulevard St Germain that tactfully excluded Nazi books about persecution, rearmament and racial theories. The German Freedom Library filled the gap by organising a counter-action in the same Latin Quarter artery. Its ten-day exhibition attracted publishers from Europe and beyond. The exiled writers reminded Parisians that the Nazis had burnt books by many non-German writers, among them Balzac, Barbusse, Flaubert, Gide, Maupassant, Molière, Rolland, Voltaire and Zola.

The refugees displayed the worst examples of Nazi propaganda: Julius Streicher's *Der Stürmer*, the SS paper *Schwarzes Korps* and a poster for that year's Olympic Games in Berlin, showing marching soldiers on either side of an athlete.

Surprisingly, the exiled writers revealed some of their 'Trojan horses', the illegal leaflets and booklets smuggled into Germany to try to stiffen anti-Nazi resistance. They camouflaged their material by copying the cover and first pages of authentic material circulating freely in Germany. What looked like an index of Berlin street names reproduced the gazeteer's original introduction, before giving the text of a speech to communist youth. A prize-winning 'German Mythology' turned out to be a German anthology of left-wing writers in exile.

Soviet agit-prop techniques to win over workers inspired an exhibition in Paris to mark five years of Nazi rule. A didactic series of panels vividly covered the gamut of Nazi misdeeds, from the camps to the bombing of Spanish civilians. The German ambassador intervened via the Quai d'Orsay and the police swiftly removed some exhibits, among them a brochure prepared for the exhibition. The organisers then put it on sale at a nearby store, informing vistors that the ambassador was to blame for the ban. At the ambassador's behest, the police ordered them to remove the reference to his role. They also cancelled some lectures by exiled authors.

In Britain, a society of the 'friends' of the burned books became active. To help secure the Library's finances, Lion Feuchtwanger arranged for its secretary, Alfred Kantorowicz, at that time a communist writer, to call on Lionel de Rothschild in London. He hoped that a friendly nod from the second Baron – who in May that year with the Marquess of Reading had set up a British fund to help German Jews – would have a domino effect on the great and the good in the city.

An impoverished Kantorowicz later ruefully acknowledged that he was not up to the occasion. Lord Rothschild had invited along a multi-millionaire to hear about the Library. As the guest spoke German without an accent, an uneasy Kantorowicz tactlessly mistook him for the German correspondent of a socialist newspaper and the discussions went awry. The shabbily dressed Kantorowicz departed from the aristocratic residence feeling his host had almost expelled him.

Later visits to London from Paris were more fruitful. In the spring of 1934, Ernst Toller arranged for Kantorowicz to meet the Countess of Oxford and Asquith, a gifted writer and leader of society, and widow of the former prime minister. She invited Kantorowicz and his wife to lunch and learned from him about the exiles' library, the role of its French supporters and the émigrés' hopes for similar assistance from her side of the Channel. Margot Asquith was convinced and immediately telephoned H. G. Wells and Wickham Steed, former editor of *The Times* and an authority on Central Europe.

She arranged for Kantorowicz to see Steed that same afternoon, and Wells the following day. Kantorowicz thought Steed so well informed and enthusiastic about the initiative that he assumed Lady Oxford had discussed it with him beforehand. Steed agreed to serve on a British committee. Encouraged by the outcome, Kantorowicz found it easy to persuade Wells to become its president.

It was simple to convince other leading liberal and left-wing establishment figures of the day to join the bandwagon. They included Bertrand Russell; the *New Statesman*'s editor Kingsley Martin; the London School of Economics' political guru Harold Laski; Vera Brittain; the Marxist scientist J. B. S. Haldane, his wife Charlotte and his sister Naomi Mitchison, both campaigning writers; and Hubertus Friedrich Prinz zu Löwenstein-Wertheim-Freudenberg, a left-wing Catholic aristocrat writer who had fled to Britain.

The next stage was the organisation of a fund-raising event in London on 10 May 1934, the first anniversary of the book fires. Kantorowicz was to explain succinctly the Library's genesis and objectives at a press conference planned for April in Lady Oxford's London residence. Before he left Paris, Kantorowicz prepared his text and arranged for a translation. It turned into a 40-page lecture that he reckoned was going to take him at least 90 minutes to read aloud in his faltering English.

Kantorowicz and his wife were on the Calais-Dover ferry, the day before the press conference, when he discovered that he had absent-mindedly left his notes in the Paris taxi that had taken them to the station. (The taxi-driver brought the draft of the original speech back to his Paris hotel and Kantorowicz later turned the text into an English brochure. It was still in use when the tenth anniversary of the book-burning was commemorated in the United States in 1943.)

In London, Kantorowicz fathomed that it was too late to try to reconstruct the text. His wife suggested that in its place he dictate the key points in German. A refugee friend translated the new version, now condensed to fill only four pages. It was ready 15 minutes before the press conference began. Kantorowicz stuttered as he delivered his plea for financial support in his own poor English. His oration lasted almost a quarter of an hour. Lady Oxford congratulated him. She had found it all very impressive, except that his speech had been a little too long.

Nonetheless, the press covered the conference well. At the same time, the British committee appealed to thousands of intellectuals across the country for an annual contribution of five shillings. By now, the wide support the British public was showing for the refugee writers was disconcerting the German embassy in London. With the backing of ultra-conservative figures it organised a reception to counter the one the committee was going to hold on 10 May 1934. Kantorowicz thought that the embassy's action served merely to generate more publicity for his cause.

As Lady Asquith's home was too small, the Countess of Rosebery and Hubertus Prinz zu Löwenstein were 'at home' at 16 Bruton

Street in Mayfair. There a liveried servant announced each of the weighty and wealthy guests – including the Rothschilds – as they mounted the stairs to greet their hosts, the Countess of Oxford, the Viscountess Rhondda (her weekly *Time and Tide* was a 'Salvation Army shelter for destitute ideologues,' according to Malcolm Muggeridge) and members of the committee. Margot Asquith insisted on having a nervous Frau Kantorowicz at her side, reassuring her there was nothing to fear. 'Just shake hands and smile,' she instructed her.

In brief speeches, Wickham Steed and others appealed to the guests to donate generously. Over tea, debutantes collected pound notes and cheques on silver trays. It was a glittering and successful occasion, and raised enough money to keep the Library in Paris going for at least two years.

Over the rest of the decade, the Library's fortunes mirrored those of the refugees themselves. The Spanish Civil War and the Moscow political trials divided the library's friends into those who rejected the communists' methods, and those who continued to support or at least sympathise with them. In the winter of 1937, Walter Ulbicht's apparatchiks took over the Library. The headed paper changed: André Gide was no longer president because he had written a critical book on the Soviet Union. With the outbreak of war, and once the French government began to intern 'enemy aliens', the French police closed the Library and confiscated its contents. When the Germans occupied Paris in 1940, some 20,000 volumes and the valuable records of the anti-Nazi centre fell into Nazi hands. What happened to them is unknown.

After the events of May 1933, who would have expected German students to burn books again as a form of political agitation? Yet in 1967, rebellious students disrupted a meeting of Günter Grass and other German writers and burned – not the works of the writers, but right-wing publications such as the mass daily *Bild Zeitung*. The students were protesting because Grass and company had not taken a sufficiently left-wing stand against the reactionary material.

7
Rivalry in Ragusa
H. G. Wells Treads the PEN Tightrope

A few weeks after the Nazi book-burning revels, a mixed bag of writers journeyed by rail to Trieste. There they boarded the MS *Krajl Aleksander*, a steamer bound for Ragusa, today better known as the Dalmatian resort of Dubrovnik. They were sailing down the Adriatic to attend the eleventh congress of the writers' 'League of Nations', scheduled to take place in Ragusa's municipal theatre.

Even in an era when international junkets were less common than they were to become, cynics would dismiss as a talking-shop the body that described itself as a world association of poets, playwrights, editors, essayists and novelists – PEN. Like several other international organisations set up to better man's lot, this literary parliament traced its origins to England. In 1921 Catharine Amy Dawson Scott, a novelist of the period, founded the English PEN club in London. Rapidly spawning other national centres, it assumed the task of repairing the amicable links among writers of diverse nationalities which the 1914–18 War had damaged.

The 'fraternity of authors' began to hold international gatherings in 1922. At its congress in Brussels five years later, John Galsworthy declared there would be no politics in PEN. It would not interfere in a country's political affairs, and it did not want to become the tool of governments or parties. Galsworthy was PEN's first international president – his *Forsyte Saga* had made him famous across the Continent.

Now, six years later, Ragusa was expected to test PEN's credo severely. Whether and how PEN should react to the Nazi persecution of writers seemed likely to override other topics. Some feared that if members infringed the Galsworthy doctrine, they would splinter PEN and drastically shrink its influence. Others held that Ragusa would be the right moment to condemn Berlin's cultural outrages, and to help the many exiled writers who had lost their livelihood. With that in mind, Felix Salten, author of the children's classic *Bambi*, asked Stefan Zweig to join him as an Austrian participant.

Zweig said he did not want PEN to present him as a hero and martyr, 'which I am not'. Zweig thought Jews should keep away from anti-German demonstrations. He went off to Switzerland so he would not have to take a clear stand. When the official invitation came, his wife Friederike telegraphed that her husband was absent and would not be taking part in the congress.

The waves of Nazi repression had scathed the German PEN club itself. Its chairman, the drama critic Alfred Kerr, had fled to France from Berlin on 15 February, the day the Prussian academy expelled Heinrich Mann. In March, the club's executive resigned. While the rump PEN hoped to replace it through democratic procedures which included Jews, the government and Nazi cultural officials had other ideas. They exerted pressure on the organisation. The result was that the administrators who took over in April represented the propaganda ministry, a combative association to promote German culture called the *Kampfbund*, and the Nazi *Völkischer Beobachter*. They promised to work harmoniously with Germany's 'national reawakening'. A leading Nazi playwright, Hanns Johst, succeeded Kerr. He also became president of the Reich's chamber of writers.

The German PEN announced that the men who had chosen the new board were veterans in the battle for German freedom; bringing recognition to the German spirit in art was their vocation. It affirmed that at Ragusa Berlin's three representatives would present the new Germany: a nation where character and honour determined every action.

The German club reported the changes to PEN's London headquarters a month before the congress. Hermon Ould was in charge of PEN's relations with its branches abroad. Born in 1886, Ould had spent two years in prison as a conscientious objector during the World War. The 'cockney internationalist' was hostile to the loud bellicose voices from Germany. A militant in literary matters, Ould believed writers had a duty to defend freedom on the intellectual battlefield. As a minor British playwright, he was familiar with the German literary scene and contributed to German theatre publications. He knew and admired Ernst Toller, a leading German pacifist playwright, and had translated some of his works. Photographs show him as an earnest, bow-tied intellectual who could have fitted in with the Auden-Isherwood crowd.

Ould warned the Berlin branch of the literary fraternity's unease. Writers were bound to raise questions at Ragusa. Did the German delegation still accept PEN principles? Did it oppose political curbs on books? Would the German PEN recruit members because of their literary distinction, rather than their race or creed? Why had prominent writers such as Heinrich and Thomas Mann become ineligible for membership? Why did Alfred Kerr have to resign? Ould also wondered why the new executive members had no previous ties to the organisation.

Even in Germany, some questioned the literary credentials of the three men chosen to represent the Reich at Ragusa. Would they have enough authority among their peers to overcome the hostility they were likely to face there? Hanns Martin Elster, who had served as treasurer during Kerr's presidency, worked as a journalist on Nazi publications. Edgar von Schmidt-Pauli was a 'throne-room reporter' who had published flattering books about the men in Hitler's inner circle and Hitler's struggle to achieve power. Fritz Otto Busch specialised in articles about naval warfare.

Shortly before the congress opened, the German PEN in Berlin told its delegation to quash all malicious criticism of Germany, especially any agitation over the book-burning. It should counter moves by the 'Hebrew' delegation to incite the international PEN to defy Hitler's Germany, and denounce foreign support for Lion Feuchtwanger and the biographer Emil Ludwig.

The Berlin centre denied that it had expelled Heinrich Mann, Thomas Mann or Alfred Döblin. It argued that Kerr had resigned on his own initiative, because he had chosen to live outside Germany. Anticipating that some persecuted German writers might turn up in Ragusa and cause mischief, the German PEN asked the Yugoslav hosts whether any German members had registered directly, instead of through the Berlin body.

As the steamer approached Ragusa, the writers informally discussed whether they should react to Nazi persecution of writers. They understood that they might be sailing into a political storm, however distressing that would have been for Galsworthy. He had been PEN's international president for eleven years when he died on 31 January 1933, a day after Hitler became Germany's political leader. Over the next three years, H. G. Wells was to preside over what he called an 'international net of literary societies'. By that time PEN had branches in more than 30 countries, including Palestine.

Nobody could be sure that the congress would place the three German delegates in the dock. Though few participants were true Nazi sympathisers, others were expected to join these in preventing the congress from challenging Berlin. Many regarded themselves as poets, not politicians. They feared the German group's reaction if

PEN interfered in the Reich's political affairs, and turned the congress into a tribunal to condemn Germany.

As delegates prepared their positions on board ship, the Germans found a number of Swiss, Italian and Dutch writers to support them. Confidential talks with English and French participants showed that 'all are against us'. The two countries would not oppose motions to criticise the book bonfires and persecution of the Jews. The Germans feared they might have to withdraw from the congress before it started – a humiliating step to envisage. They embarked on prolonged and conciliatory conversations with individual members in a bid to 'clarify the situation'.

They identified their main opponents as Shalom Asch, representing writers in Yiddish, and the dark-haired, bearded Benjamin Crémieux, an influential and erudite French Jewish writer and translator who advised the publisher Gaston Gallimard. They believed Crémieux, the secretary-general of PEN's French section, wanted to manoeuvre them into walking out even before the congress opened. They suspected he was undermining their discussions with H. G. Wells. Determined to take part in the sessions, they prepared themselves for the hurdles that lay ahead.

To their relief, President Wells did not want a showdown. A passenger on the Adriatic crossing, he had been living in the South of France with the writer Odette Keun, an exotic character of Dutch and Italian parentage, but the relationship had soured. Wells had left their *mas* near Grasse to catch the train from Cannes to Trieste, and would never return. He had earlier abandoned Rebecca West for Odette Keun. Now Wells was reviving his romantic friendship with Maxim Gorky's former mistress and muse, Moura Budberg, whom he had first met in 1914. He planned to spend an early summer holiday with her after the PEN conference, in the 'fresh green loveliness of Austria'.

Despite Wells's efforts to find a middle way between French 'obstruction' and Berlin's orders, the talks on the boat were inconclusive. Delegates scheduled a further confidential pre-congress meeting in Ragusa's Hotel Imperial. The Germans used the intervening period to build alliances and ward off future attacks.

At the hotel, the French continued to assail the Germans. Then a more accommodating atmosphere developed. Wells let Henry Seidel Canby, the bald, bespectacled president of the American PEN and a co-founder and editor of the *Saturday Review of Literature*, propose an anodyne motion that ignored German misdeeds. It spoke about the general need to prevent political misuse of PEN clubs.

Rivalry in Ragusa

As Canby had done little more than reaffirm PEN's admirable goals, the Germans accepted the phrasing – conditionally. They agreed that Schmidt-Pauli, who spoke English well, knew many delegates and showed diplomatic tact, should approach the president. He was to ask Wells to assure them that no delegates would introduce any other motion attacking Germany.

Although victory seemed in sight for the Germans, they were not altogether sanguine. But they did not put all the blame for their misfortunes on their fellow delegates. They deplored above all the intemperate way émigré writers had inflamed the congress against them. They considered reports in the foreign press to be totally distorted. As they awaited Wells's reply, the Germans believed they had weakened French influence and persuaded other participants that Germans were not the barbarians portrayed in the atrocity tales of the agitators. Schmidt-Pauli meanwhile was delighted to learn that Wells did not envisage another motion for the first working session on Friday, 26 May. Especially gratifying was the news that participants would not discuss the Palestine group's hostile motion, as it had not turned up. It had cabled starkly that while the Germans were in Ragusa, they had nothing to do there.

Wells did warn Schmidt-Pauli that it would be hard for him to prevent someone from unexpectedly introducing a motion. He advised the Germans to squeeze out time for other discussions by dragging out the debate on the insipid American motion. The Germans appreciated Wells's 'loyal' attitude towards them. It seemed as if consensus had triumphed over confrontation. Delegates could now settle down and enjoy Yugoslav hospitality. They could look forward to a local troupe in colourful national costumes performing a Balkan classic, Gundulic's *Dubravka*, with the arcades of the ducal palace as a romantic backdrop. They could relax in their exotic surroundings. Crémieux was delighted to 'breathe the gentle seas of southern Europe'. Asch called Ragusa 'Salzburg-on-sea'. Wearing a beret, a portly Wells strolled in the spring sunshine.

But suddenly the atmosphere turned tense. At a meeting on the afternoon of Thursday, 25 May, PEN's executive committee learned that Ernst Toller had appeared on the scene. One of the émigré writers most hated by the Nazis had temporarily left his Swiss exile to attend the congress. The *New York Times* reported his arrival. Toller's presence electrified other members; his reputation was such that he could throw the meeting into total disarray.

Toller's combat experiences in the War had turned him from an impassioned patriot into a pacifist. Although he played a leading part in Bavaria's short-lived Soviet republic, Toller's belief in non-violence led him to tear up arrest warrants and annul death sentences. In powerful speeches, he sought to convert the masses to his ideal of a 'revolution of love'.

After the crushing of the communist uprising in Munich, a court had sentenced Toller to five years' detention for treason. In prison, he wrote expressionist plays that established his reputation in Germany and beyond. Critics hailed him as the German proletariats' playwright. He later abandoned party politics, but remained a radical intellectual. He moved to Berlin, where he worked as a journalist.

An occasional visitor to Sanary, where Lisa Marchesani would invite him to dinner, Toller was a powerful orator. He undertook several lecture tours, among them visits in the 1920s to the Soviet Union and to the USA. He was a long-standing PEN member and had attended previous PEN congresses. Any public utterance by such an outspoken opponent of the Nazis as Toller could force the organisation to ignore the lofty Galsworthy doctrine of non-interference – and break with Germany.

But it was not Toller who challenged Canby's pusillanimous compromise at the opening session. Wells had barely invited participants to state their views on Canby's insipid wording, when the French unexpectedly announced another motion. Its content was unknown even to Wells. The Germans, however, had heard that it was explicitly unfriendly to them. A wrangle over procedure followed. The French and their allies wanted delegates to hear the French draft before the debate began. Wells said they would have to wait until they had debated the American one.

Delegates unanimously adopted Canby's text. An agitated auditorium now heard the Germans threaten to walk out if Wells broke PEN rules and allowed discussion of the French draft. Wells saved the situation by calling for an adjournment, ostensibly so that the French could make copies of their motion. They arranged for further talks in the Hotel Imperial that afternoon. Behind the French text were Crémieux and Jules Romains, a prolific author who had recently embarked on his 27-volume novel *Men of Good Will*, and who ranked at the time with Bernard Shaw and Pirandello as a popular playwright.

This time the German victory seemed decisive. The French retreated and agreed to turn their motion into a *déclaration*. They would delete all unfriendly references to Germany. Their wording would mention the recent destruction of books and the forced resignation of professors – but would not cite any country. Delegates would vote, without discussion. That would stop Toller and Asch from speaking up, contrary to earlier announcements. A relieved German delegation could abstain.

Combined with their threat to walk out, the Germans' backstage manoeuvres had succeeded. Thoroughly prepared by their political masters in Berlin, they had skilfully exploited the rules of procedure and courted participants who were unfamiliar with their negotiating style, based on secret agreements, manipulation and pressure.

When the afternoon session opened, an hour late, the Germans assumed Wells would welcome the revised French draft, read it out and call on delegates to vote on it straightaway. Wells stunned delegates as he announced that he would, after all, allow discussion if anyone wished to speak.

What had gone wrong? Perhaps delegates misjudged Wells. In his mid-sixties at the time, the prolific writer remained rich, famous and influential, even though his major works – such as his novel *Kipps* or his popularised *Outline of History* – were well behind him. Political questions had always interested him. He had joined the Labour Party in the early 1920s and tried to become a member of parliament. Even his early science fiction had exhibited a concern for social problems. The horrors of the First World War had led him to campaign for a world state.

Wells objected to Jews for the same reason he despised Scotsmen: they 'clustered close' in families, gangs, clans and nations. Yet he was unlikely to sympathise with ultra-nationalist writers in Europe. He wrote one of the earliest novels in English to warn the public to take seriously the fascist menace – *Meanwhile*, which appeared in 1927. *The Autocracy of Mr Parma*, published in 1930, was also likely to displease the new German Ministry of Enlightenment. It dealt with the disasters that ensue when an Oxford don, who has become leader of a fascist movement of national regeneration, rallies European reactionary forces for a crusade against Bolshevism.

The Germans suspected the coup de théâtre in Ragusa had its origins in London. They thought Ould and Toller had played a key role in stiffening the president's resolve to deal firmly with the Germans. Delegates as a whole deplored Wells's decision, after all their efforts to emasculate the French draft. Jules Romains praised the Germans' courtesy and amenable conduct. He predicted disaster if the assembly could not agree amicably and unanimously. Schmidt-Pauli conferred with Toller and was astonished to find a 'loyal' Toller willing to postpone his intervention. Toller insisted only that Wells let him question the German delegation the next day.

An adamant Wells maintained his decision, recalling that a vital PEN function was to promote untrammelled discussion. Observing that some writers had come to Dalmatia to express their concern about their German colleagues, Wells called on Toller to take the floor. Delegates stood up and shouted as Toller prepared to speak. The Germans objected on a point of order and threatened to walk out.

Ould now intervened. Instructed by London headquarters to ascertain the German branch's reaction to Hitler, Ould wanted to know if the Berlin PEN had condemned the ill-treatment of German intellectuals and the book bonfires. Had the German club expelled members because they were communists or held communist views? If so, it had itself meddled in politics. Schmidt-Pauli sprang up and protested. He offered to answer Ould's questions if he repeated them the next day in line with the rules of procedure.

Wells was unmoved and called on Toller to speak. The Germans threatened to withdraw their support for the French text that the writers had so laboriously drawn up. Wells refused to bargain, declaring that Ould's questions were legitimate and that anybody could speak on what the German PEN had done.

Toller was about to begin his long-awaited speech when Schmidt-Pauli picked up his file, gave the Hitler salute and warned Wells, in English, that it would be his fault if the German group withdrew from the congress completely. He and his colleagues left the theatre and uproar broke out. Amidst the hostile cheering, the Germans thought they detected sympathetic applause from their 'allies', including some of the French. Austrian, Swiss and Dutch delegates supported the Germans by withdrawing temporarily, but returned to their seats before the tumult had died down.

Toller postponed his speech. On the next day, 27 May, after Shalom Asch had spoken, Schmidt-Pauli entered the auditorium with a note. It said that the Germans were departing in protest against the discussion of Germany's internal affairs. The Germans apologised to the city authorities for their absence from the reception they were hosting that evening.

Toller at last took the floor. He regretted that the Germans were no longer there to answer his charges. He wondered how they reconciled their support the previous day for literary freedom with events in Germany, particularly the German PEN's exclusion of ten members. Rhetorically he asked what it had done to protest the book-burning, or the persecution of musicians such as Bruno Walter and artists such as Paul Klee.

The hall filled with applause. Toller's speech was the high point of the congress and most persecuted writers abroad would welcome it as such. Most but not all: Stefan Zweig resented Toller's appearance at the congress. He maintained that it had distracted attention from the shameful fact that none of the 'Aryan' German writers left alone by the Nazis had sided publicly with those oppressed writers who had been their colleagues for so long. Zweig found their silence more disgraceful than the attitude of the Nazi government, which was merely fulfilling its party programme. Zweig compared the petty silence of the novelist Gerhart Hauptmann and others with what he saw as Furtwängler's admirable public stand on behalf of his fellow conductor Bruno Walter.

In its revised, emasculated version, the French *déclaration* was carried by 10 votes, with two against and 14 abstentions. It seemed Toller's speech had achieved nothing. He had provoked the Germans to leave the proceedings, but they had not resigned from PEN. Delegates even voted to maintain a German representative on PEN's executive committee.

The German delegation thought it had made a triumphal exit. It claimed that Wells's clumsy behaviour had enabled it to achieve a range of successes which its enemies had not intended. The congress did not condemn the Reich's persecution of its writers. It did not oblige the Berlin delegation to answer awkward questions. It avoided taking a decision on a proposal to provide the persecuted writers with material help and legal aid.

For the *Neue Zürcher Zeitung*'s correspondent, the three-day event severely damaged PEN's significance as an independent writers' movement. It blamed Wells for his high-handed disregard of the rules of procedure. He had let an irresponsible minority upset efforts to draft a statement in line with PEN principles. The Swiss paper linked Wells's behaviour to the fact that the Nazis had publicly burned one of his works.

For Wells, Ragusa was 'stormy but entertaining': the violent Nazi persecution of writers had forced the 'weak but widespread organisation' to forego 'amiable exchanges' and champion freedom of expression. For him, PEN's effectiveness lay in its ability to generate wide publicity for its activities.

The British press was inclined to agree that Ragusa had been a victory of sorts for the anti-Nazi camp. *The Times* interpreted the French *déclaration* as a slap in the face for Berlin even if it did not mention Germany. The *Manchester Guardian* called Wells 'a lion in the PEN'. It sympathised with Wells as he faced 'the almost impossible task of keeping politics out of the discussion, of pacifying the more excitable delegates who were burning to attack the Hitler regime, and of seeing that the German delegates had fair play'.

The Observer claimed to have saved Wells's opening address for posterity after a young man from Oxford had taken it down in longhand, but failed 'to fill it in later on'. As Wells had his notes and the paper's special correspondent knew shorthand, they agreed on a 'bargain'. Wells would dictate his address, the journalist would deliver a transcript and Wells would 'submit' to a ten-minute interview. The weekly praised Wells for the 'serious exchange of views' achieved at Ragusa, 'instead of the usual junketing, excursioning and exchange of harmless compliments'.

Stormy sessions and earnest debates looked woefully inadequate to the exile community in Paris. Hitler was trampling European culture to the ground, putting writers behind bars or forcing them to flee, and burning their books – and yet PEN had failed to throw out the German group. It had not even managed to agree on steps to help penniless writers. A leading exile weekly, the *Neue Tage-Buch*, told its readers not to get agitated about the affair. The PEN crowd, it suggested, were a cynical lot who swarmed to PEN banquets but did not really take the organisation seriously.

Yet the congress turned out to be a short-lived victory for the Nazis. That November, Edgar Schmidt-Pauli travelled to London for a meeting of PEN's international committee at the Mayfair Hotel in Piccadilly. He had studied at Cambridge University and spoke good English. As no one else was anxious to put him up, Marjorie Watts offered him her husband's dressing room in their small Georgian house at 1 Holly Place in Hampstead. The daughter of PEN's founder, she found Schmidt-Pauli a charming guest. He 'brought clothes for every conceivable occasion – a dinner jacket and tails, dark suit, tweed suit, and even morning coat'. Matching overcoats and a hatbox accompanied him.

Dressing for the PEN dinner held on the eve of the meeting, Schmidt-Pauli asked his hostess whether he should wear his Iron Cross. Watts replied that she thought not, on the whole. Crémieux and Toller were among the dinner guests. Schmidt-Pauli was upset that no one invited him to speak, whereas Crémieux was allowed to expound for a quarter of an hour on PEN's ideals. Despite an uneasy tension, the guests restrained themselves.

The following day, however, the committee questioned Schmidt-Pauli about the German PEN's actions. It resolved that the way it had excluded its communist members was incompatible with the PEN constitution. Wells proposed that the German PEN renounce its affiliation until it were again prepared to take members irrespective of race or political creed. Schmidt-Pauli, the sole dissenting voice, drew the obvious conclusion: German writers would have to work for world peace in their own way.

The German branch formally withdrew from PEN in November 1933, a few weeks after Germany had left the League of Nations. Presided over by Hanns Johst, and with Gottfried Benn as vice-president, a Union of National Writers replaced the Nazified German PEN Klub. Hanns Martin Elster went over to Britain in 1935 to try to heal the wounds. Over breakfast in the Savoy Hotel, the Marquess of Lothian, a prominent figure in fostering good Anglo-German relations and later ambassador in Washington, advised Elster not to judge Britain by its press. On his return, Elster told Johst that the German books on display in London bookshops were mainly by émigrés; the position was even worse in Oxford and Cambridge.

With the Nazi PEN branch out of the way, persecuted writers in Paris and elsewhere began to woo its international secretariat. Ernst Toller, who had lost his German citizenship in August 1933, joined Lion Feuchtwanger, Klaus Mann and Heinrich Mann among others in lobbying PEN's head office in London to recognise a new group representing the German writers in exile. The twelfth international congress, held in Edinburgh in June 1934, unanimously agreed to do so after Wells had praised Schmidt-Pauli as a 'good fellow and obstinate fighter' who 'had had to be sacrificed on the altar of his instructions from Berlin'.

Official international recognition by PEN helped émigré writers break out of their isolation. At a PEN gathering in Paris in 1937, Feuchtwanger mingled with James Joyce, J. B. Priestley, Franz Werfel, André Maurois and Karel Capek. An international PEN membership card became a valuable form of identification for stateless refugees. They could resettle in other countries with less trouble. They could more easily approach writers in host countries and take part in official events. PEN offered persecuted German writers a respected forum not bound to any political group. It helped them publicise the Third Reich's philistine measures against its intellectual opponents. Refugee writers now found it easier to tell the world of the 'other' Germany and the 'free' German literature in exile.

At first, the Galsworthy rule of non-interference remained intact. But gradually PEN acknowledged that it would have to be more political if it wished to defend its enlightened principles more effectively. By 1939, PEN had become bolder: its members made speeches at an international congress of writers it sponsored during the New York world fair that a few years earlier, they would have judged as ultra-radical.

Based in Paris, the German PEN group in exile contributed to the change. The outspoken Heinrich Mann served as its president from 1933 until he fled France in October 1940. The German PEN in exile resurfaced in Britain; its new president was the sharp-tongued Alfred Kerr. (His daughter Judith Kerr wrote a children's classic about her youth in Paris, *When Hitler Stole Pink Rabbit.* In 2001, his grandson Matthew Kneale won the Whitbread Prize for his novel *English Passengers*). Its secretary was Rudolf Olden, a former political journalist in Berlin, who now reported on the British political scene for the émigré daily in Paris. A lawyer by training, he lectured at Balliol College, Oxford, and helped secure the release of émigré writers interned by the French. The British interned Olden after the war began.

H. G. Wells became honorary president of the British committee of the Library of the Burned Books. He was in Russia the next year, urging Soviet writers to establish a PEN branch. Jules Romains succeeded him as president of the international PEN in 1936, fleeing to America after German troops invaded France. Canby became professor of English and American Literature at Yale University. A disillusioned Toller, 46 years old, committed suicide in New York in May 1939, shortly after addressing the PEN congress in New York. In the *New Statesman*, Kingsley Martin said Toller was 'in his prime as a writer'.

After the war broke out, Ould and the English PEN's president, Storm Jameson, helped persecuted exiled writers overcome the bureaucratic barriers to refuge in Britain. Ould worked to secure the release of Alfred Kerr from British internment. Ould died in 1961. Benjamin Crémieux, whose family had lived in Languedoc since the 14th century, was caught hiding in southern France and deported to Buchenwald, where he died in 1944. Ironically, he had written theatre reviews during the 1930s for what became a notorious anti-Semitic publication, *Je Suis Partout*.

The British allowed Olden to emigrate and, in September 1940, he embarked at Liverpool on the 11,000-ton *City of Benares*. Among other refugees on board were Thomas Mann's daughter Monika and her husband. The vessel, the pride of the peacetime run from Britain to the jewel in its crown, was part of a convoy to North America taking 406 passengers, mainly children evacuees. On the night of 17 September, a torpedo from a German U-boat tore through the ship. Among the 256 who drowned were 77 children. So too were Rudolf

Olden and his wife and, in front of her eyes, Monika Mann's husband.

Writers re-established a 'normal' German PEN club in 1949 but, by 1951, Cold War politics had driven members into an East German and a West German PEN. As late as 2002, there was still a PEN club for German writers abroad. Moves that year to dissolve it were inconclusive: delegates to the PEN congress in Macedonia failed to agree.

8 'Seppl' and the 'Slimy Frog'
A Jewish Publisher Stays on in Berlin

Though the pretty Villa Tranquille lacked hot running water, Thomas Mann felt more comfortable there than he had during his four preceding months of hotel life. At his new home in Sanary Mann spent evenings on the terrace in front of his study, smoking cigars, observing the stars and reflecting on life's strange ways. He went for walks with his wife Katia. Gradually he recovered the serenity he needed to resume the disciplined working days he had imposed on himself over the years. The view over the Mediterranean soothed his troubled spirits. He enjoyed his early-morning sea-bathe – 'definitely the best time for me' – and local strawberries for breakfast. Soon the Manns were mobile again: their purchase of a Peugeot cabriolet constituted a high point of their stay in Sanary.

They had the family around them. Their elder children Klaus and Erika, as well as Thomas's brother Heinrich, called on them. From his quarters chez Seabrook, Golo Mann would come over to his parents around noon, after a morning during which he sea-bathed, made himself a continental breakfast, read, and transcribed in his diary his reflections on the Third Reich and its philosophy. He would join the family for another swim and stay for lunch and dinner. In the afternoon, he would tell his younger siblings Elisabeth and Michael, then 15 and 14 years old respectively, about the dramas of Schiller and the historical works of Sallust.

Sometimes Thomas Mann would join acquaintances over an aperitif at one of the harbour cafés. Shortly after their arrival in France, Thomas and Katia Mann had met Lion Feuchtwanger and his 'Egyptian-looking wife' at a local hotel. Feuchtwanger's United States publisher Ben Huebsch, founder and head of the Viking Press, met Mann during his visit to Sanary. The Manns entertained and were entertained. In the Villa Tranquille's garden, close friends as well as the family celebrated Katia Mann's 50th birthday, on 24 July 1933, with peach champagne.

Sybille Bedford and her mother frequently dropped in on the Manns, who were familiar with the local gossip about Signora

Marchesani's drug-taking habit – that 'elle se pique'. The Manns invited the Huxleys, whom they had met at the Meier-Graefes. When Mann went to the Huxleys for tea on one occasion, he found Paul Valéry there, and the hours of conversation in French left him fatigued. The publisher in exile Kurt Wolff, who was to establish the Pantheon Press in New York in 1941, came over from Nice to visit the Manns. Mann went to see an Italian exile, Count Carlo Sforza; he was a former ambassador in Paris who had resigned from the diplomatic service in protest against Mussolini's regime. Two other Italians in exile were present, both distinguished historians, Gaetano Salvemini, who later that year took up a chair at Harvard, and Guglielmo Ferrero.

A typical Sanary day for Thomas Mann, as he recorded for 27 July 1933, comprised a sea-bathe, drafting and correcting texts, writing letters, going for a stroll with his wife and hosting with her a gathering in the garden of the Villa Tranquille that evening. Among the guests were the Seabrooks, the Feuchtwangers, the Arnold Zweigs and his secretary, and Wilhelm Herzog. Mann told his guests that they would later look back fondly on their stay in Sanary, and that such would certainly be his own sentiment.

Thomas Mann's serenity during those summer months was far from complete, however congenial his stay in Sanary might be. While walking together one summer morning along Sanary's harbour front, Thomas Mann asked Herzog whether he had heard that the Nazis had revoked Heinrich Mann's German citizenship. Herzog said he had. Mann asked him whether he, Mann, should ask German president Paul von Hindenburg for the same treatment as his brother. That would be more than a gesture, it would be a deed, Herzog assured him. Mann said he would give further thought to the idea, and Herzog assumed he would not act on it. When Thomas Mann finally lost his German nationality, it was not at his own request.

At the time, Mann was more worried about renewing than relinquishing his passport. Did he really want to do it, he asked himself. Wouldn't that imply an endorsement of the detestable new regime? Other conflicting thoughts plagued him. What about his blocked savings and the family's Munich house and other possessions? Weren't the Nazis less likely to confiscate them if he returned to Germany? And if he didn't, where should the family settle? The Manns had rented the Villa Tranquille until the middle of September, and it was not yet clear if Signora Marchesani's German friends would want the house after that.

A house in Nice was available; the rent was reasonable and it would be pleasant to winter there. And it might be sensible, Mann thought, to keep his distance from Germany. But did he simply want to extend the provisional solution he and Katia had found in Sanary? No, Mann yearned to settle more permanently. He was inclined to keep to his original plan and return to Zurich or Basle – to 'German cultural terrain'.

Mann's health remained delicate and he often took sleeping pills. He noticed how his hair had turned much greyer. One underlying issue tormented him as a writer. Where did he stand in relation to the grim news from Germany? Was he to remain a silent witness, or should he side with the persecuted? Because Mann couldn't answer this primordial question, émigré publications criticised his ambivalent posture, even if they didn't name him. His indecision provoked a tug-of-war for his conscience. Erika and Klaus wanted to pull him into their camp, centred on Paris. His Jewish publishers in Berlin wanted Thomas Mann to keep his ties to Germany.

Born in what was the Hungarian part of the Habsburg empire and is now Slovakia, Samuel Fischer started as a bookseller in Vienna, before moving to Berlin. The Fischer house he established there in 1886 did much to mould cultural life in the German-speaking world during the first two decades of the twentieth century. 'Sami' discovered Gerhart Hauptmann and other avant-garde naturalists. Schnitzler, Freud and Kafka were in his net. So were Ibsen, Shaw and Wilde, as well as Tolstoy and Dostoyevsky. With its enviable list of renowned authors, the firm featured among the most illustrious of German publishers in the Weimar Republic. Since its heyday, however, the Fischer Verlag had failed to keep up with the new generation of young writers who were coming to the forefront. Critics noticed that Fischer was losing its edge, however high its reputation remained among the public.

As Fischer's only son had died young in 1913, the publisher decided to groom his son-in-law, a volunteer in the Great War, to become his deputy. Gottfried Bermann had wed Samuel Fischer's elder daughter Brigitte in 1926, and now styled himself 'Bermann Fischer'. 'Sami' persuaded him to give up his position as a distinguished surgeon in a Berlin hospital. Handsome, charming and a gifted musician, Gottfried showed unusual business acumen. By the time he took over the day-to-day running of the Fischer business in 1932, he had made a smooth transition from maladies to manuscripts.

Samuel Fischer taught Gottfried Bermann Fischer the secrets of publishing and showed him how to handle difficult writers such as

Thomas Mann. Bermann Fischer and his young wife were soon welcoming to their Berlin home not only celebrated German-language writers – Carl Zuckmayer, Joseph Roth and Ernst Toller – but also foreign literary personalities such as Jean Giraudoux and Raymond Aron.

In 1929 Bermann Fischer had overcome the stubborn resistance of his father-in-law and taken the firm down-market by introducing cheaper 'department-store' editions of selected Fischer bestsellers. Bermann Fischer chose Thomas Mann's *Buddenbrooks* as the first in the series. Some 600,000 copies were sold in the first two months, and sales soon exceeded one million. Even today, you sometimes see that popular edition on the shelves of German middle-class homes. By 1933 Fischer had sold more than 130,000 copies of *The Magic Mountain*, first published in 1924. Mann was the firm's most prestigious and valuable author, especially after he received the Nobel Prize for literature in 1929.

As the senile Fischer found it ever harder to deal with house authors, he tended to bother less about business or technical questions such as royalties. 'Sami' nevertheless insisted on coming to the office for a few hours every morning and continued to handle personally the firm's correspondence with his close friends, among them Schnitzler and Mann. He did so in that first summer of Hitler's rule as if little of great consequence had occurred. Bermann Fischer on the other hand sensed the dangers ahead: other Jewish publishers were leaving, now that many of the works on their lists were by 'undesirable' authors and no longer on sale in Germany.

Yet sound business considerations lay behind Fischer's decision to remain in Berlin. The firm's catalogue list comprised many writers of world renown whose works were still freely available in Germany: the likes of Joseph Conrad, Hermann Hesse, Eugene O'Neill, Bernard Shaw – and Thomas Mann. As Bermann Fischer himself put it, the new rulers might not love some of those hallowed names but they hadn't banned any of them. Could a firm so deeply rooted in German soil as Fischer thrive elsewhere, Bermann Fischer asked himself? If the Fischer Verlag moved out of Germany, wouldn't many of its authors in Germany do the same? And if they did, wouldn't they provoke the Nazis to ban their works?

Bermann Fischer had a further justification for staying in Berlin: he believed he was ensuring that books from the liberal, independent publishing firm he managed would continue to influence the German public. You couldn't say the same of the publishers in exile and the lists they were feverishly preparing, he would point out. Fischer's decision to stay put was a noble act as far as Bermann Fischer was concerned. After all, Hitler might turn out to be no more than a passing cloud.

Perhaps the main reason why the Fischer Verlag didn't transfer its activities beyond the Reich had less to do with business or politics than with the founder's mental decline. 'Sami' Fischer hadn't fully grasped what was happening on his doorstep – he was far from alone – and he wanted to stay put. His death in October 1934 would have removed that impediment had not his widow, who kept an interest in the firm, proved equally reluctant to leave the capital. Only in 1939 did she finally agree to emigrate from Germany. In those early years of Hitler's ascendancy, therefore, Bermann Fischer didn't really have much choice; circumstances compelled him to practise a cautious and conciliatory policy of business as usual. It was a strategy that provided him with some unusual publishing experiences.

On one occasion, a police official called on Bermann Fischer to inform him that, according to complaints received by the police, the firm was displaying too many photographs of Jewish writers in its reception room in Berlin. When the official proposed their removal Bermann Fischer refused, saying he would rather take down all the portraits of Fischer authors. That would be a regrettable step, thought the police officer. Bermann Fischer therefore asked him to indicate the offensive faces. The officer pointed out various writers whose beards presumably summoned up rabbinical associations; among them were Henrik Ibsen, Bernard Shaw and Lytton Strachey.

More awkward was the sequence of events after Bermann Fischer decided, in 1932, to commission a book on the new recreation of flying. He had asked Heinrich Hauser, a writer who was good at describing technical topics for lay readers, to learn to fly and write a book about it. Hauser delivered his manuscript in January 1933. While ostensibly about flying as a pastime, the author's real aim was to promote the mass training of combat pilots. His book carried illustrations of aircraft bearing swastikas and enthusiastically described a storm-troopers' air-rally near Berlin.

Fischer was preparing to publish the book in May that year. In April, while Bermann Fischer was visiting his father-in-law who was taking the waters in Rapallo, his Berlin office telephoned to inform him that Hauser wanted to dedicate the book to Germany's first minister of aviation, a flying enthusiast who also happened to be prime minister of Prussia – Hermann Göring.

If Fischer refused Hauser's request, the Nazis would surely close down the firm. If it assented, that act of servility would as surely bring Bermann Fischer eternal condemnation from the 'emigration' in Paris, with which, after all, he felt a close association. Bermann Fischer played the ball back into Hauser's court. As a Jewish publisher couldn't ask Göring to authorise such a dedication, he told Hauser that he himself would have to approach his idol if the matter was so important to him. Bermann Fischer reasoned that Göring would turn down the request, but he was mistaken. Within a few days, Göring had replied positively, sending his letter directly to the publisher.

For Bermann Fischer there was no escape. He had to publish a book dedicated to an arch-enemy and persecutor of Jews, and accept the consequences of Hauser's 'treachery'. The 'emigration' ridiculed him. After receiving a copy of the work, artist George Grosz, who had been friendly with Hauser, wrote a satirical letter of appreciation. Heinrich Mann mockingly hoped that 'poor' Bermann Fischer's action would not upset the Jews' god too much. Bermann Fischer shunted Hauser and his works on to another publisher.

Bermann Fischer's travails were far from over. A novel he published in 1934 contained a footnote about the small band of Germans who remained grateful to the Jews for their contribution to German culture. Bermann Fischer found it courageous for an author to write that, and 'not cowardly' of the Fischer Verlag to print such sentiments at that time. Both author and publisher, however, soon faced threats that increased in violence until Fischer removed the offending footnote from the third printing.

Its disappearance did not escape the observant eyes of the exiled writers in Paris. Taking his cue from the book's title, 'The Swing', Leopold Schwarzschild, editor of the Paris émigré weekly *Das Neue Tage-Buch*, wryly commented that perhaps the incident would inspire a Fischer author to write a new 'Swing' novel, this time with Bermann Fischer as the protagonist. After all, he had swung backwards and forwards a long time before he decided to continue running his father-in-law's firm under the control of the Reich chamber of culture. That Bermann Fischer had not become giddy showed what strong nerves he had, Schwarzschild concluded.

For a while, the firm published more or less normally under the Nazis. Bermann Fischer even joined an official committee charged with curbing *Schmutz und Schund*, 'smut and trash' in literature. The Nazis hadn't seriously harassed the firm, and they hadn't searched its editorial premises let alone closed it down, he could note at the beginning of April 1933. To keep out of trouble during the Nazi boycott of Jewish businesses, Bermann Fischer visited his in-laws in

Rapallo. On a trip to Paris, he boasted that the Nazis hadn't forced him to allow a Nazi party cell to operate within his firm.

In 1935, the Gestapo came around in large trucks to Fischer's Berlin depot to remove stocks of works by banned authors. Although they found only ten to 20 copies of each title, they didn't investigate further. Otherwise they would have looked around in Leipzig, Germany's chief book-production centre, where Fischer stored many thousands of books in its main warehouse.

Despite Bermann Fischer's sang-froid and his willingness to compromise, his mood fluctuated. He became less sanguine when he learned that the conservative German People's Party, which many hoped would restrain the Nazis, had left the coalition with Hitler and dissolved itself. At times, he appeared to be a troubled man who feared the Nazis would expropriate the Jews. He would argue both for and against emigration. He thought about negotiating a fallback arrangement whereby he could contract a publisher outside Germany, to handle the works of Fischer authors who might become blacklisted in Germany.

In the spring of 1933, however, Bermann Fischer's prime concern was to safeguard the firm's position in Berlin. If the business was to carry on as usual, it had to make sure it didn't give the Nazis an excuse to ban any books by its distinguished authors. Conscious that the slightest slip-up could bring the curtain down on Fischer and Thomas Mann, the firm's star property, Bermann Fischer was especially nervous about the way Mann was hesitating in the wings.

He repeatedly assured Mann that his position was special, for he had not fled Germany but chosen to reside abroad temporarily, after completing a lecture tour in neighbouring European countries. If Mann were now to prolong his absence abroad, Bermann Fischer feared, he might well provoke the Nazis to take official action against him. Such a move could ruin Mann – and the Fischer Verlag. Bermann Fischer suggested what seemed like a fair quid pro quo. Since you want the Nazis to release your assets, he told Mann, why don't you placate them and return home? In early May, he provided a persuasive list of reasons why Mann shouldn't stay abroad indefinitely. He pointed out that Fischer needed permission to transfer royalties abroad to a German who was still administratively a resident of the Reich. Mann's opponents were likely to criticise what they viewed as his rejection of Germany, and such a hostile campaign could intimidate his readers in the country.

Bermann Fischer didn't see how moving back to Basle would guarantee Mann's security, especially as extreme right-wing movements were flourishing in Switzerland itself. There were the uncertainties surrounding the continued distribution of Mann's books in Germany. Foreign markets would provide only a limited compensation for the loss of the German market.

Mann's contract with Fischer forbade him from ceding the German-language rights for the book he was writing at the time to a foreign publisher. The German authorities might even compel Fischer to assert its rights, because such a cession would divert earnings from Germany and so infringe its foreign-exchange regulations. As if those were not reasons enough, Bermann Fischer rubbed more salt in the wound: Mann's expired passport could give the government the legal justification, after a certain time had elapsed, to confiscate 'all your possessions'.

What solution did Bermann Fischer have in mind? Nothing less than to ask the new propaganda minister, Dr Goebbels, to guarantee Mann's safety in Berlin and an official solution for his passport and other problems. Such a request would reassure Mann that he had tried everything, and at the same time keep the door open to an orderly legal move from Germany.

Bermann Fischer believed this major gamble could succeed, because of positive developments in Germany. He detected clear efforts in the Reich to reinstate the rule of law. Mann's name had not appeared on any of the boycott lists, and a Berlin newspaper had published some distinctly friendly remarks about him. Bermann Fischer believed the Bavarian government was acting independently of Berlin in punishing Mann. He therefore suggested that Mann leave Munich and settle instead in one of Berlin's pleasant villa suburbs. There, among reasonable and like-minded people, he could continue his literary activities undisturbed.

Even if Mann were unwilling to come home, Bermann Fischer had to ensure he didn't jump overboard and join a publishing house outside Germany. That would lead his readers to conclude that Fischer had lost its semblance of independence, even if there were nominally no change in its ownership. And the government would show less restraint towards a Fischer without Mann. The question was whether Mann was prepared to remain so closely associated with a publisher who was behaving so obsequiously. Malicious gossip had it that Bermann Fischer was collaborating with Goebbels in trying to get his star author back to Nazi Germany.

The follow-up to Mann's Wagner lecture showed how reluctant Fischer was to risk anything that might upset the regime's supporters. Hans Pfitzner had justified the protest he had ignited. He defended the Munich burghers who had disapproved of the lecture. It wasn't merely the content of Mann's speech but the fact that Mann, considered abroad as a weighty German voice in matters of the mind, had delivered it beyond Germany's frontiers in front of the whole world. The foreigners might have misunderstood the speech, the composer feared. Mann drafted a reply for Fischer's intellectual review. In it, he attacked the 'chauvinist mob' in Germany for deliberately misinterpreting the nuances of his speech.

Bermann Fischer's deputy Peter Suhrkamp claimed that Mann's text had missed the deadline. It did not appear in Germany, or elsewhere, until 1974. As a protesting Erika Mann suspected, the true explanation lay elsewhere. Suhrkamp sensed that publication of her father's article could harm the firm. Through his act of voluntary self-censorship, he hoped to preserve such freedom as Fischer retained. Mann could have used the incident as an excuse to take his work to an unshackled publisher beyond the Reich. He was, however, morally bound to Fischer and understood that the firm was safeguarding his own interests, particularly prospects in Germany for the forthcoming *Joseph and His Brothers*.

Mann had been writing this Old Testament novel with frequent interruptions since 1925. What he first envisaged as a short story now looked like becoming a huge opus. Mann jealously guarded his manuscripts. To gain some idea of the contents, his publisher relied on extracts that appeared in intellectual periodicals, including the firm's review. Only when Mann had finished writing the second volume in June 1932 did he send Fischer the manuscripts of the first two volumes, *Tales of Jacob* and *The Young Joseph*.

By the summer of 1933, Mann was well advanced with the third volume. Fischer and the author originally planned to bring out *Joseph* as a whole, but the expected trilogy had turned into a tetralogy. For economic reasons Alfred A. Knopf, Mann's American publisher since 1916, wanted to publish the volumes consecutively. He was awaiting Helen Lowe-Porter's translation of *Tales of Jacob* so that he could bring out the first volume that autumn, even though Fischer had not set a publication date for the German version.

That caused Bermann Fischer to warn Mann of the disturbing political consequences 'for all of us' if the United States edition were allowed to appear before the German one. Such a step would furnish Mann's German readers, who honoured him and were patiently awaiting the work, with an excuse to boycott his novel. Knopf in effect forced Fischer to schedule a first printing of 10,000 copies of *Tales of Jacob* for publication at the beginning of October 1933, earlier than planned.

The second and third volumes were to follow in the spring and autumn of 1934. Fischer would be issuing the volumes singly for the same reason as Knopf: it would be easier to sell the lengthy novel. Though Knopf subsequently had to delay the first volume's appearance in the United States, because the translator needed more time to complete her work, Bermann Fischer ignored that delay.

Other hurdles faced Bermann Fischer that summer. For Erika and Klaus Mann it was unthinkable that the 'magician,' as they called their father, should heed Bermann Fischer's advice and go back to the Nazi dictatorship. Even though Fischer had published their travel book in 1929, the indignant Mann siblings were striving to pull their father away from the firm. Their father's close ties to the Berlin publisher, and the way Bermann Fischer was trying to appease the Nazis, deeply disturbed them. Bermann Fischer annoyed them by alleging that Klaus was spreading disparaging rumours about him. Erika called Bermann Fischer a 'slimy frog' and appealed to her father to reject his impertinence. She told her brother that the 'Berswine' (*Bersau*) wanted all émigrés to shut up so that the Nazis would leave him, the 'Berdirt' (*Berdreck*), in peace. Klaus thought Bermann Fischer was 'a harmless blockhead who was turning into a big danger'.

Klaus Mann had been spending much time in Amsterdam, where the Dutch publisher Emanuel Querido had agreed to help him launch a literary review intended to serve as an unfettered substitute for Fischer's journal. Querido, a social democrat of Portuguese Sephardic origin, had set up a German-language branch of his firm and was preparing to bring out works by banned writers, among them Heinrich Mann, Joseph Roth, Alfred Döblin and Lion Feuchtwanger. The Dutch concern was to become the most renowned publisher of German-language writers in exile.

Klaus Mann had told his father about Querido's plans and Thomas Mann knew Bermann Fischer was thinking about letting the Dutch firm handle Fischer books that Germany might suddenly ban. For Thomas Mann, the question now was whether he remain loyal to Fischer or follow other anti-Nazi German writers in changing to one of the publishers springing up in cities outside the Reich. Mann still had the choice, unlike most of them.

Convinced that the Nazis had already brought the 'compliant' house of Fischer to heel, Erika and Klaus urged their father to let Querido publish his works in Amsterdam. If he did so, they said, he would be making a political statement with worldwide repercussions. Erika warned her father that he had nothing further to seek in

Germany. A Querido representative was ready to take the next train to Sanary if he 'smelled' the smallest chance of getting at 'Seppl' – *Joseph and His Brothers*.

Klaus Mann assured his father that, even if the Querido imprint brought only a limited readership, it would avoid a repetition of the hostile reception which official Germany had given his Wagner lecture. In addition, Querido would be free to transfer Mann's royalties. Klaus confirmed that Querido was interested in publishing his father's work and said he would pay a very large amount of money for the rights.

Soon Bermann Fischer was expressing concern over reports that Mann might allow a firm outside Germany to publish *Joseph*. While Bermann Fischer had opened talks with Querido about his contingency plan to share 'undesirable' writers with other publishers, he in no way considered the negotiations relevant to Mann's forthcoming novel. He resented Querido's attempt, as he saw it, to poach Fischer's celebrated author, even if he welcomed the way Querido offered exiled writers a fresh opportunity to publish their works outside the Reich. Bermann Fischer impressed upon Thomas Mann that his case was different. He was not a banned writer, his books could still appear in Germany and he should therefore let a German firm handle his forthcoming novel. Bermann Fischer warned Mann that if he chose an exile publisher for *Joseph*, the German government would probably ban his other books.

By July 1933, Bermann Fischer could be reasonably sure that his arguments had prevailed and that Fischer would retain the prize. At Mann's request, he had come down to Sanary towards the end of June. Mann had found his visit 'not unpleasant'. Bermann Fischer's good relations with Querido pleased him. As a sop, Mann considered giving Querido a planned book of his essays.

Mann was now reading the *Joseph* proofs and considering embellishments. He fancied decorations with Hebrew script but feared they would make it look like a kosher restaurant. In mid-August, he told Bermann Fischer that he thought he had moved his audience – about 20 guests gathered in the Villa Tranquille's garden – when he read aloud the chapter from *Joseph* about Jacob's marriage.

Mann's second son Golo suspected that Bermann Fischer had tried, during his visit to Sanary, to persuade his father to come back to Germany. In fact, Bermann Fischer did so in writing after he returned to Berlin. He told Mann about a new law: 'it provides that Germans who have left the Reich and who do not return when ordered, lose their rights as citizens. Their wealth is confiscated. It is to be feared that you will receive such a summons. If you think you will return one day, it would seem necessary to act now. Negotiations later will certainly be futile.'

As Berlin had not so far moved against Mann, Bermann Fischer said, it was Mann who was putting the government in the right by staying away. He was giving the government 'leverage for measures against you, as your continued absence will lead them to infer that you have made a final decision against Germany'. Warning Mann that he could not judge the situation 'correctly in that refugee atmosphere', Bermann Fischer said 'we shall be glad to meet you at the border'. He urged Mann not to hesitate too long. In Germany, one could assess the situation more calmly than abroad.

Mann's public attitude remained confused, even if he privately approved a 'revolt' against Hitler's dictatorship. He declined to sign an oath of loyalty that would have allowed him to join the Nazi-controlled writers' guild, but told its president that he wanted to remain part of the German literary scene. At the same time he recognised that he could not 'shilly-shally' much longer. He wondered whether he could work in Germany's stultifying intellectual atmosphere.

The question of his return now became academic. His lawyer had learned that if Mann did return to Munich, the Bavarian political police would arrest him because of his anti-'national', pro-Jewish and pro-socialist outlook. Reinhard Heydrich, a recent recruit to the SS, had signed the arrest warrant. Eight years later, he would draft Hitler's plan for the 'final solution'.

When news came that the police had confiscated the family home, where Mann had lived for 18 years, Mann concluded it would be senseless to publish *Joseph* in Germany. Bermann Fischer should leave the book to Querido, Mann now pleaded. He disingenuously suggested that such a cession was a temporary, minor matter. The novel would be given away only in the sense that it would bear the Querido rather than the Fischer imprint.

Great excitement prevailed at the Querido offices in Amsterdam when Klaus told them they might get *Joseph* after all. There was talk of telephoning Bermann Fischer and sending someone to Sanary to talk to Mann. But they had underestimated Bermann Fischer's resolve. For him there could be no question of leaving it to Querido. With one stroke, Germany would ban all of Mann's work, he told the author. To bring home the potential loss, Bermann Fischer emphasised how well his books had been selling in recent weeks. With publicity preparations for *Joseph* well under way, a decision to publish outside Germany would create a commotion. Think of your German readers, he entreated Mann.

Furthermore, Bermann Fischer announced, Mann's lawyer had negotiated a favourable settlement for him. Mann could declare that he had left the country, and pay the punitive tax levied on those who 'fled' the Reich – 25 per cent of the value of their belongings. He would become a non-resident German elegible for the return of his assets, which the authorities were holding in lieu of the tax. He could leave in Switzerland the possessions he had already sent from Munich. And nothing prevented any longer his receiving substantial royalties from Germany, Bermann Fischer assured Mann.

It seemed a satisfactory outcome in the circumstances, and Bermann Fischer's arguments prevailed. After all his prevarication, Mann decided to remain true to his German readers and to one of the last major liberal publishers left in Germany. Fischer would publish Mann's novel in Berlin as planned, and that would show whether the Nazis would allow the firm to continue to operate in Germany.

By the end of August, Mann was telling his publisher that he would create no further difficulties. He was not altogether sanguine about his decision, for it was at this time that the Nazis revoked his brother's citizenship. How much longer could he hold back from demonstrating publicly against the 'rogues' regime', he pondered. 'Whatever one does is wrong,' was his exasperated conclusion.

After much soul-searching, Mann had agreed to let matters take their course. A few days later, however, he found himself in the midst of a fresh crisis. Bermann Fischer had destroyed his correspondence with Querido and co-operation between the two publishing concerns was no longer on the agenda. More seriously, the continued publication of Mann's work in Germany was in jeopardy. Both the Fischer Verlag's fate and Mann's access to his German readers hung in the balance. The cause was none other than Mann's own son Klaus.

9 'A Reckless Act'?
Klaus Mann Launches His Review

Klaus Mann had been wondering what life held in store now that he and his sister Erika had fled Munich and cut their ties with Germany. What he really wanted to do was emigrate to the United States, but only if Erika accompanied him and if they had enough dollars to live on. He thought he should concentrate in the meantime on Paris, where he had provisionally settled and where he believed he had a fair chance of earning a living.

Klaus pestered his friends to help him find a job in publishing or journalism. Christopher Isherwood advised Mann to see if Jonathan Cape was interested in publishing an English edition of his novel about exiles in Paris and underground resistance in Germany. Brian Howard offered to arrange for Thomas Mann's translator, H. T. Lowe-Porter, to translate an article by Klaus. 'Her real name is Mrs E. A. Lowe and she lives in Oxford,' Howard told Mann. He thought she would do it for nothing and, in that case, Howard would send the money to Querido in Amsterdam. Warning Mann that the *New Statesman* would pay only four or five pounds, Howard thought they should rather approach the *News Chronicle*. But Howard found it hard to place Mann's material, even though he liked it. Noting that in Britain 'people seem to want facts more than general information', he tactfully explained that Mann's work was a little abstract for that part of the English literary market that paid well.

Starting a review for the émigré writers now engrossed Klaus Mann. The wealthy industrialist father of a Swiss friend refused to fund his project, predicting that the cleansing new forces at work would wash away what he presumed would be a colourless, internationalist magazine. Instead, Klaus Mann approached a fellow émigré who had set up Querido's German-language branch in Amsterdam. Querido agreed to cover the printing and distribution expenses of a monthly periodical. As a result, Mann now spent some five months a year in Holland. During the rest of the time he criss-crossed Europe, often prowling around louche establishments in search of drugs and sexual satisfaction. Sometimes his escapades brought him close to danger.

In Toulon, he had a 'horrible adventure' when two young men beat him up and robbed him. Blood streaming down his face, Mann reported the incident to the police, who took him to the hospital. The attack found its way into the local newspaper, but its garbled version referred to a 'Thomas Klau' who worked at Sanary's Hôtel de la Tour. Otherwise, Klaus Mann reflected, the Nazi press would have had a field day reprinting the story.

Aldous Huxley, André Gide and Klaus's uncle Heinrich agreed to serve as patrons of Mann's magazine, which he called *Die Sammlung* because he aspired to 'collect' the voices that Hitler had tried to silence. Huxley offered him an article – 'deux ou trois de ces petits essais concentrés' – about his recent travels in Central America and arranged a German translation of his English text.

Mann solicited articles from the many other famous writers he knew. He emphasised that the journal's approach would naturally be one of basic opposition to the Nazi regime, but avoiding day-to-day politics. Hermann Hesse, a German writer who had been living in Switzerland since 1914 and who had become a Swiss citizen in 1923, proved a hard fish to catch. Mann flattered him: his work would give the periodical a certain nuance. He tried to snare him: the first issue would carry pieces by Stefan Zweig, Aldous Huxley and Joseph Roth. But Hesse resisted. He wanted to see the publication first. In any case he had nothing ready, and did not see himself being able to write an article in the near future. A wary Hesse instructed Mann to exclude his name from the flyer's list of forthcoming contributors.

Klaus Mann tried the same approach to entice Stefan Zweig to submit anything he wished. He told Zweig he could expect to be in the company of André Gide, Hermann Hesse and Heinrich Mann. Zweig, then in his early fifties, was living in Salzburg and had become an internationally famous writer of verse, plays, short stories and biographies – and a passionate pacifist. German students had burned some of his works that May. Yet he thought little of writers who entered the political fray. He simply did not believe they had any chance of changing the views of convinced Nazis.

Zweig nevertheless seemed to be more forthcoming than Hesse. He was ready to support Mann's periodical provided it did not have an overtly aggressive character. He could offer an extract from the book he was writing about Erasmus of Rotterdam. (The book would show Zweig's indirect way of entering the political arena. He expected readers to associate the way Martin Luther had defeated the great Dutch humanist with the way Hitler was crushing humane Germans.)

Yet Zweig also procrastinated. There were too many exile journals and publishers about, and too many editors were asking him for contributions. In 1918, he pointed out, enthusiasts in various countries had established some 800 ineffective peace unions and 200 peace journals, instead of one powerful organisation. He embroiled Klaus Mann in correspondence about the urgent need for leading émigré writers to unite. Meanwhile, the deadline for the first issue of the review passed. Zweig cabled that he needed another week. Then he explained he was not satisfied with what he had been writing and needed a rest. Mann sensed that Zweig wanted to have nothing to do with his venture.

Sybille Bedford was among the friends who offered to help Mann in his quest for worthy contributors to his review. Roy Campbell – Bedford explained that he was the 'English poet-bullfighter near Marseilles' – agreed to contribute a poem. When Bedford drove over, Campbell showed her the 'promising beginning' and swore he would complete it straightaway, but there is no trace of it in the magazine. (On moving to Spain, Campbell found the coast full of German refugees who were, he claimed, using Comintern money to set up sex-clinics and communist cells. Near Benidorm, Campbell came across some Germans disturbing a church service. He boasted that he caught the largest one, a Dr Meyerstein, broke his glasses and his watch and then throttled out his false teeth and broke them as well.)

Sybille Bedford had more success with Raymond Mortimer. When Mann published the 'notes' about English novelists by the 'famous London avant-garde critic', he found it necessary to append a footnote: Mortimer had handed down disrespectful judgments about some of his great fellow writers (Galsworthy, for example, was 'as humdrum and dreary as dishwater') that Mann as editor would not have presumed to make.

Brian Howard was sure that with Huxley's help he could arrange an English-language edition of *Die Sammlung* that would circulate on both sides of the Atlantic. He saw a place in England for a socialist, anti-fascist monthly magazine with the 'best writers in it'. 'Good young' writers and 'the older men like Bertrand Russell, Havelock Ellis and Leonard Woolf' would contribute.

In Berlin, meanwhile, Thomas Mann's publishers had heard of Klaus's review. It made them distinctly uneasy. Unlike his father, the young Mann was an outspoken critic of the Nazis. Bermann Fischer tried to intimidate Klaus. He hinted that the German authorities might well interpret offensive remarks about Germany in the review as 'his master's voice'. Irritated but undeterred, Klaus Mann in

August 1933 proudly issued a prospectus that heralded an impressive roster of future contributors.

Among the literary notables were Jean Cocteau, Alfred Döblin, Sinclair Lewis, H. L. Mencken, Robert Musil, Romain Rolland, Joseph Roth, René Schickele, Stefan Zweig and, most significantly, Thomas Mann. Hesitating about approaching his father directly, Klaus had asked Erika to sound him out. Thomas Mann cabled that he didn't object to his name appearing in the prospectus. He proposed to write about Karl Barth; the anti-Nazi Swiss theologian was teaching in Germany, but would have to resign the following year.

The first number of *Die Sammlung* appeared in early September 1933. Despite Klaus Mann's earlier reassurances, émigrés and enemy alike judged the publication to be political as well as literary in nature. An unmistakable tone of opposition to the Nazi regime filtered through its pages, especially in Heinrich Mann's aggressive opening article. In it, he called for effective joint opposition to the Nazis, averring that 'never has such an avalanche of lies descended on a nation'. An article by Klaus himself criticised Gottfried Benn – at the time still an open Nazi sympathiser – for defending 'those who degraded the spirit'. Alfred Döblin and Alfred Kerr, two politically vocal German Jews who had found refuge in France, contributed articles and so did the Austrian-Jewish novelist Joseph Roth.

Thomas Mann, who received his copy of *Die Sammlung* on 2 September, thought his son had played a trick 'on us' in carrying Heinrich Mann's polemical piece in the first issue. By the time *Die Sammlung* was available, Klaus Mann sensed that he might have jeopardised his father's position. He told his father he had become 'a little restless' after including his father's name in the prospectus and after he saw what a stir the first number, particularly Uncle Heinrich's article, had caused. He realised that nervous cramps might have afflicted Bermann Fischer. In that case, Klaus would admit he had erred.

Thomas Mann, Alfred Döblin, Stefan Zweig and René Schickele, as well as their German publishers, were now in a most awkward position. They were writers who had publicly associated themselves with the review and hence, indirectly at least, with its attacks on the Nazis. Yet their works were still on sale in the Third Reich. The thought of punitive action by the Nazis alarmed their German publishers, who resolved to persuade their writers to withdraw their support for Klaus Mann's enterprise.

Bermann Fischer arranged for his colleague, the elderly Professor Samuel Saenger, to enter the fray. Saenger telephoned Mann from

'A Reckless Act'?

Paris on 5 September 1933 to say he was coming to Sanary on the overnight train for urgent talks with Mann and Schickele. Mann sensed what was in store for him. That July he had allowed Bermann Fischer to deny claims by an anti-Nazi exile publication in Amsterdam that he was one of their regular contributors. This time another Amsterdam-based publication was involved, but it was his own son's, and he had unambiguously agreed to write for it.

A vulnerable Thomas Mann was in an almost biblical situation. He had to decide whether to stand by his son – or to shield Fischer, a reputable firm that had served him well over many years and that was about to bring out the first volume of what Mann deemed one of his greatest achievements. Mann plagued himself with the likely consequences if he refused to sacrifice Klaus. The Nazis might ban his books, beginning with *Tales of Jacob*. If they did not sever his ties to his many German readers, they might confiscate his royalties. In addition, Mann's lawyer might fail to negotiate the return of his confiscated assets.

Heinrich Mann strongly encouraged his brother and Schickele to repudiate Klaus's review. He saw himself as the cause of their problems. Thomas Mann fretted at the thought of rousing a horde of agitated émigrés in Paris into mocking him. The rest of the world would surely criticise his hopelessly equivocal attitude toward the Third Reich. Mann would pay a heavy price if he disassociated himself from the review, but it would be a moral rather than a material one. Was he prepared to do that?

Saenger – during his two days in Sanary – underlined the precarious position in which Fischer 'firm and family' found themselves. Although Nazi louts had threatened 'Sami' Fischer, Saenger said that the old man would let himself be clubbed to death rather than leave Germany. Finally, Thomas Mann and Schickele submitted, as Döblin had done earlier while Saenger was in Paris. Schickele claimed Saenger's pitiful appearance, rather than what the professor said, caused him to concede.

In a telegram to the Fischer Verlag, Mann said he reserved the right to work occasionally with a literary journal of a European nature that counted world-leading names among its contributors. But, he added, his collaboration did not mean he identified himself with any particular article. That thin disclaimer was 'all' that Saenger had achieved, Mann told his son – yet it still left a sour taste in Thomas Mann's mouth.

It was too thin for Fischer. Back in Berlin Saenger cabled Mann on 12 September that the firm needed a stronger disavowal, in which

Mann confirmed that his son had misled him about *Die Sammlung*'s literary character. The Mann parents drove over to Schickele's to discuss the matter. Although Mann had already drafted a reply saying he could not honourably go beyond his first statement, he changed his mind and sent Fischer a second telegram – 'probably an unsatisfactory compromise but unpleasant enough', he told Klaus.

A grateful Bermann Fischer assured Mann that 'our situation, into which the irresponsible attitude of the publisher of *Die Sammlung* brought us, was no less unpleasant than yours.' He recognised that his firm might have created the awful impression 'outside' that it had switched to the Nazi side. While no one knew how much longer the firm could survive in Berlin, the main point was that Fischer could for the present go on serving Mann effectively.

Bermann Fischer argued that, while those outside Germany might be better able to judge the general situation inside the country, 'we' could better appreciate the harmful effects of Klaus Mann's review. Bermann Fischer was not opposed to what he called public polemics. His attitude was that open debate would fail to influence the enemy if the opposition included émigrés, and above all Jews. They had to stay on the sidelines. By taking part, they merely provoked agitators and their inflammatory publications to throw dirt 'at us'. In Bermann Fischer's view, it had been extremely shortsighted of 'K.' to undertake a task for which he had neither competence nor vocation. The Gestapo had informed the propaganda and interior ministries, and Bermann Fischer was sure they would act against the journal's collaborators.

Apologising for the difficulties his request had caused Mann, Bermann Fischer explained that too much had been at stake: 'I had to have something to prevent the worst. So far, I have not used the material and I shall not do so unless circumstances compel me. You can rely on me not to make any unnecessary use. I fully appreciate how unpleasant a careless step can be for you, but also for our reputation abroad.'

Meanwhile, the prevaricating Stefan Zweig finally said he would not contribute an article. He explained that he had irritated other editors by refusing them an article after Klaus Mann had announced Zweig's collaboration with *Die Sammlung*. Zweig said he would not write for any editor until all had worked out a common approach. He therefore asked Mann to remove his name from the list of future contributors.

Zweig's withdrawal bitterly disappointed Klaus Mann. He told Zweig he was aware of the 'senseless denials' Fischer was extracting from his father and the others. It was a sad and ludicrous affair. Virtually none of the great names, whose word in that hour of destiny would have had some influence, was willing to be identified with those who were fighting. As Klaus Mann saw it, those intellectuals outside Germany who still had something to lose were avoiding any action against Germany that might harm them.

Klaus wondered what purpose was served if émigré publications in Paris attacked the Nazis, while Zweig, Mann's father, Döblin, Hesse and Schickele kept silent. He reproached Zweig for holding back even non-political articles from publications that criticised the German government: 'You want to avoid offending Goebbels.' A discouraged Klaus Mann wondered upon whom 'we can rely when all those we had most trusted leave us in the lurch because of their concern for the "German market".'

He did not convince Zweig, who criticised Mann for announcing a literary review and then producing an aggressive political periodical. Zweig said that like Klaus Mann's father, he had not published in any journal within or without Germany for the past seven or so months, because he did not want to give the enemy any excuse to say he had provoked them. He begged Mann to understand how 'we feel obliged to act responsibly towards those friends who had remained in Germany. For a Jew especially, that feeling must be even more intense'.

Fischer brought out the German edition of Thomas Mann's *Tales of Jacob* on 10 October 1933. By that time, the author had left Sanary to settle in Switzerland. As Bermann Fischer feared, Klaus Mann's *Die Sammlung* unleashed intense hostility in Germany and soon the nation's new literary mentors reacted. They declared that writers who agreed to write for *Die Sammlung* no longer placed any value on German readers. Hanns Johst, unaware that Thomas Mann no longer resided in Germany, suggested to 'My dear Himmler' that he, Munich's police commissioner at the time, bring the son to heel by sending the father to the nearby Dachau concentration camp.

Far more danger lurked in an official warning carried in the *Börsenblatt*, Germany's book-trade journal, the day *Jacob* was published. In it, the Reich office in charge of promoting German writers announced bluntly that Germans would be committing treason if they bought the works of those authors whose articles were 'besmirching the country's name from abroad in the most ignominious fashion'. Directed by Alfred Rosenberg, the leading Nazi ideologue, the Reich organisation called for a boycott of the authors and controls on the distribution of *Die Sammlung* and other exile literary periodicals. It pointed out that some German publishers had announced forthcoming works by writers who were among Klaus Mann's contributors, present and future.

Bermann Fischer knew he had to neutralise the lethal statement, and he therefore played his trump card. He sent the authors' telegrams to the publishers' weekly and their contents became public on 14 October. In his second cable to Fischer from Sanary, Thomas Mann confirmed that the nature of the first number of *Die Sammlung* didn't correspond to the original programme.

Schickele's disclaimer was stronger. He made the statement precisely as requested by Fischer. He said *Die Sammlung*'s political character had painfully surprised him. As Klaus Mann had solicited him solely for occasional contributions to a purely literary periodical, he disassociated himself utterly from the Querido publishing business. Alfred Döblin in Paris also disavowed all literary and political connections with *Die Sammlung*.

Stefan Zweig had been travelling for weeks, and was in London when he heard in November of press attacks on his statement to the *Börsenblatt*. He claimed to know of no such statement. He then learned that his Berlin publishers, Insel, had released without his approval a 'private' letter he had sent them at their request, and in which he too distanced himself from *Die Sammlung*. In a stream of letters, Zweig now tried to clarify his position. He asserted that his publishers had arbitrarily fabricated the statement without consulting or informing him. Romain Rolland was among those who thought Zweig had merely created more confusion, rather than prove his innocence.

An embarrassed Zweig assured Klaus Mann that he would never have publicly disavowed him. Because Insel had published the disclaimer without his knowledge, Zweig said he wouldn't let the firm publish his book about Erasmus. That was a public indication of how little he cared about safeguarding his sales in Germany. Zweig went further: he left the firm that had published his books for 28 years.

But Zweig also scolded the young editor, telling Klaus Mann that the whole affair had made him sick. The way Klaus Mann had politicised his magazine was exasperating. For a politically neutral periodical was vital to prevent German literature from collapsing (as had happened in Russia after 1917) into émigré literature on the one hand and state-controlled literature on the other. Zweig told Mann he had wasted a great opportunity; there were already enough combative publications.

The authors' disavowals infuriated the German émigré community in Paris and elsewhere. Their journals published pages on the controversy and debated whether Thomas Mann and the others were justified in appeasing their publishers. Thomas Mann's capitulation disenchanted many, even if they found parts of *Die Sammlung* too polemical.

Schickele told Thomas Mann that the waves of disappointment provoked by their group – the 'four swine' – hadn't overspilt beyond the émigré 'family paddling pool'. Not altogether accurately, he maintained that the French and the rest of the world were ignoring the whole affair, the French presumably because the émigrés were getting on their nerves.

Klaus Mann refrained from responding publicly to the unfortunate consequences of his editorial decisions. He did, however, publish in *Die Sammlung* a devastating letter from Romain Rolland, in which he remarked that Victor Hugo wouldn't have kept out of politics while exiled on Guernsey. In private, Klaus Mann made his views clear. He warned Bermann Fischer that historians would record the way he had engineered the retractions: 'When we no longer have any other function, we shall ensure that all this is not forgotten.'

Few reacted more violently than did Joseph Roth. The Galician-born author had been working for the *Frankfurter Zeitung* and went into French exile early in 1933. The first issue of *Die Sammlung* carried an extract from a forthcoming novel of his that Querido would publish later. Bermann Fischer had already upset Roth that summer, when he appeared in Paris amidst reports that he hoped to persuade some exiled writers to sever their links with foreign publishers and come into the Fischer fold. Roth publicly lambasted Bermann Fischer both for remaining in Germany and for the disclaimers in the *Börsenblatt*. He said he would no longer allow his work to be published in the 'Third Reich, formerly known as Germany'. Thomas Mann, in his diary, dismissed Roth's 'dubious' open letter as 'tasteless', adding a snide reference to Roth's fondness for the bottle.

As Roth prepared to assault Döblin, Schickele and Thomas Mann – 'he writes better than he thinks' – he was dismayed to learn – 'like a blow to the ears' – that his friend and countryman Stefan Zweig had also disavowed Klaus Mann. Even if *Die Sammlung* were to be wrong a thousand times, Roth told Zweig, it would still be right 'compared with Goebbels, murderers, those who despoil Germany and its language – those stinking Luther-farts'.

Zweig should have fought with all his might against the regime, Roth told him. If unable to do that, he should at least have remained quiet. Zweig surely knew that a state official owned the Insel publishing concern, so that Zweig's retraction couldn't have remained private. Every ordinary German citizen, including the publishers at Insel and Fischer, was an arse-licking state employee, and Roth wished the concentration camp upon the lot of them. Roth warned Zweig that he would have to choose between him and the representatives of the Third Reich. The next day Roth wrote to say he had reread his letter and wanted to assure Zweig that he wasn't drunk when he wrote it. He again appealed to his colleague not to betray the 'emigration'.

Zweig tried to reason with Roth. Unlike younger authors, he and Thomas Mann had ties to publishers that couldn't be broken overnight. Fischer was demanding 200,000 marks to surrender its rights to publish the works of Jacob Wassermann. Yet money wasn't the issue, for him. He appealed to Roth to believe him rather than cry 'traitor' straight away. He defended Thomas Mann as an honourable Aryan who had no need to partake of the Jewish soup. However much one might protest, Zweig maintained, one couldn't ignore 70 million potential readers in Germany.

The *Sammlung* affair dealt the anti-Nazi struggle a cruel blow. The exiles believed that Thomas Mann above all, because of his exalted status as a Nobel Prize-winner, had played into the hands of Berlin. The Nazis could contend that they had cleansed the country of pernicious Communist and Jewish writings, while continuing to honour great writers such as Thomas Mann. Reluctant to accept that he had behaved opportunistically, Thomas Mann went on the offensive. He told his critics that he wasn't prepared to sacrifice his work, or disappoint and bid farewell to those many Germans who had listened to him and had waited for years for his new work, just to see his name on the masthead of a magazine.

Mann was far from ready to lend his considerable authority to the anti-Nazi opposition. 'My behaviour and views are in no way formed or influenced by the émigré front,' he wrote in early 1934; 'I stand on my own two feet and am not in touch in any way with the German émigrés who have been dispersed around the world.'

He nevertheless had to convince Klaus, whom he termed a proud anti-opportunist, as well as Erika, that his action was justified. His daughter had implored him to clarify his political position in exile and to express his firm opposition to Bermann Fischer as well as to the Nazis. Thomas Mann explained that people inside Germany assessed publishing prospects in the Reich quite differently from those outside. From outside, he did not reckon a highbrow publisher or journal could function normally in Germany. He had therefore tried to persuade Bermann Fischer to let Querido issue his *Joseph*.

Bermann Fischer had refused precisely because he believed that *Joseph* was one of the works that would salvage the firm's position in Germany as a liberal publisher. As the publisher was determined to carry out the experiment, Mann felt obliged to help ensure its success. In recent weeks, he pointed out, sales in Germany of his other books had been better than for a long time – orders for his latest work were in the thousands. It therefore wasn't senseless or dishonourable of him to accommodate Fischer's concerns.

What, Thomas Mann rhetorically asked his son, if Fischer's gamble now paid off, and the Nazis didn't dare impede the publication of Mann's new book – the work of an outcast, a work whose Old Testament contents could be regarded as offensive to the regime? What if *Tales from Jacob* sold well? That would be far better and far more galling for the authorities than a whole truckload of émigré polemics.

Father reprimanded son for knowing full well that 'the character of the first number of *Die Sammlung* didn't correspond to the original programme', as Thomas Mann had admitted to his distraught publisher. He remonstrated with Klaus for printing Heinrich Mann's fiery article in the first issue. That decision had determined the journal's anti-Nazi essence more irrevocably than if the article had appeared in the third or fourth issue. Klaus had acted recklessly towards other writers who had agreed to help him, in his father's view.

Schickele also tried to justify what he had done, though he later regretted his telegram and the way he had compromised Klaus Mann. He told Joseph Roth he shouldn't have condemned him, Schickele – the most painful experience the affair had brought him – without first hearing his side. Roth's howling with the wolves surprised him. Schickele explained that he had, after all, left Germany voluntarily, before receiving any threats from the Nazis. He had resigned from the academy of the arts, unlike other writers who had signed the oath of loyalty, and had nevertheless been expelled.

Schickele thought writers should let their work be published in Germany for as long as possible, if they could do so with decency, because a 'free' word there was more important than all the execrations and curses of émigrés, which no soul in Germany would ever hear. He personally wouldn't seek the political limelight because he would land in the Communist or the French nationalist camp, and would feel uncomfortable at either political extreme.

A far less-established author than Mann and virtually unknown in the English-speaking world, the ailing Schickele admitted he relied entirely on Fischer for a living. He didn't want to do anything that would endanger the publication in Germany of his forthcoming novel, and its newspaper serialisation, for which he had signed a contract for 4,000 Reichsmarks. At stake, he estimated, was an amount that would cover his living expenses for one year.

Joseph Roth later told Döblin that he wouldn't sit at a table with him until Döblin had justified his telegram to Fischer. Döblin explained that his two oldest sons were in Germany at the time, and Saenger had intimidated him by mentioning concentration camps.

Obsessed by the unpleasant affair, Klaus Mann inclined to blame himself. He conceded that it had been tactless to mention Schickele's pacifist background in the congratulations he had published in *Die Sammlung* on Schickele's 50th birthday. Klaus Mann had thought that as the Nazis were harping on that point, why shouldn't his friends also do so? He didn't mention again those authors whom he had expected to write for him, though it was too late to remove their names from the covers of the first two books that Querido published.

Klaus Mann never said that his review would be non-political, only that it would not concern itself with everyday politics – too fine a distinction perhaps. Inevitably, a strong anti-Nazi flavour permeated such articles in the review as those dealing with the churches' resistance to Hitler, compulsory military service, and the possible re-incorporation of the Saar into Germany. Many articles on foreign affairs were political in nature: the Palestine problem, France's Stavisky financial scandal, Austria's political ties to the Reich, or moves among exiles to build a Popular Front.

It is hard to see how a review dealing with the humanities could have ignored such far-reaching contemporary topics, especially as most of them impinged on the intellectuals' everyday life. Klaus Mann did concentrate, however, on broadly cultural themes, allowing his contributors to present a wide range of views and making no effort to find a common denominator. Apart from Austria's banning *Die Sammlung* in 1934, there is little evidence that the periodical's contents influenced any government, friendly or hostile.

On average, about two thirds of the 3,000 copies of each issue printed were sold. It is unlikely that *Die Sammlung* ever made a profit, and increasing financial difficulties forced Querido to halt its publication in August 1935. Klaus Mann told Huxley the sad news and thanked him for his support. Huxley had earlier apologised to Klaus, in French, for neglecting his review. Besides his poor German, he said, weak eyesight rather than 'une mauvaise volonté' had forced him to ration his reading.

Over its two years of existence, *Die Sammlung*, its editor and its publisher earned widespread admiration among the émigré community. Brian Howard – his German companion Toni helped him understand the articles – thought it a 'magnificent production' and regarded it 'as the literary headquarters against fascism'. Literary historians later praised the way the review exalted militant humanism and rebutted Nazi ideals and values. Perhaps the greatest tribute paid to Klaus Mann's enterprise is the fact that the complete set of *Die Sammlung* was reprinted twice after the war.

The review brought under one literary roof work by distinguished German and foreign authors as diverse as Brecht, Cocteau, Einstein, Gide, Hemingway, Huxley, Kafka, Pasternak, Roth and Trotsky. Sybille Bedford discussed Huxley's *Beyond the Mexique Bay*. At Mann's request, Walter Benjamin submitted a critique of Brecht's *Threepenny Opera* in its novel version. Mann returned the article after they disagreed about the fee. One famous author is conspicuously absent from *Die Sammlung*'s pages – Thomas Mann.

On the other hand, Thomas Mann's consolation was that his telegram to Fischer produced the desired result. Rosenberg's office withdrew its accusations after Bermann Fischer published his authors' disclaimers. The government did not interfere with the sale of Mann's novel. German newspapers reviewed the book. Bermann Fischer's deputy Peter Suhrkamp secured a further victory for Mann: the Nazi cultural authorities would consider him a non-resident and therefore not require him to sign the 'loyalty' declaration. And Mann's lawyer negotiated the payment of the emigration tax and the re-opening of his account so that Fischer could pay Mann his royalties.

Bermann Fischer's political poker had paid off, and he could claim a great success for the Fischer Verlag. His robust nerves had safeguarded the German market for Fischer's authors, even if by the summer of 1933 the Nazis had abolished basic human rights and the parliamentary system, removed Jewish professionals from government service (which included schools and universities) and launched a boycott of Jewish businesses.

Fischer could publish the first four volumes of the collected works of Franz Kafka. In 1934, a Fischer catalogue announced books by other Jewish authors – Alfred Döblin, Jakob Wassermann, who had recently died, and the Austrian Arthur Schnitzler. *The Young Joseph*, the second volume of Thomas Mann's *Joseph and His Brothers*, also featured. A first run of 10,000 copies appeared in April 1934.

Bermann Fischer was vindicated, even if his manoeuvres – what the émigrés considered his intrigues against Klaus Mann and his determination to conciliate the Nazi political and cultural overlords – were to tarnish his reputation. Bermann Fischer nevertheless had little illusion that his luck could hold indefinitely. He still pondered how to transfer Fischer to another country while retaining the firm's valuable rights to the extensive German market.

Of the journals that succeeded *Die Sammlung*, Klaus Mann thought that *Maß und Wert*, based in Zurich, best carried on in its tradition. He worked for it, as did Döblin and Schickele. Thomas Mann was one of its publishers. Towards the end of the decade, a famous English-language novelist in Paris agreed to contribute to *Maß und Wert*. But when he recalled that Thomas Mann had criticised Germany in the 'politically oriented' periodical, he changed his mind. James Joyce did not want Germany to ban *Finnegan's Wake* because of his supposed political bias. Thomas Mann would have understood.

10 Watching and Waiting
Thomas Mann Prepares His 'Politicum'

As he moved into the Villa La Tranquille in Sanary, that summer of 1933, Thomas Mann was brooding sullenly upon his own silence. He had taken his time in the 1920s before supporting the Weimar Republic, and later espousing the era's socialist ideals. Now his role in the *Sammlung* affair made it especially awkward for him to declare openly his opposition to Hitler's dictatorship, however much he might privately approve a 'revolt' against the new rulers in Berlin. He recognised that many of his admirers, including that vociferous and irascible émigré crowd in Paris, impatiently awaited a signal from him. He could not remain politically mute indefinitely.

Or could he justify his remaining on the fence? After all, there were still those in Germany and abroad who remained unsure how to judge the drastic measures that came thick and fast, following the collapse of the Weimar Republic. Many still admired Germany's contributions to civilisation, and sympathised with the hardship it had endured since 1918. Perhaps, they reasoned, the harsh steps ordered by the Führer were necessary to restore the country's fortunes. With anti-Semitism common among the ruling classes in other European nations, there was a tendency to give Nazi propaganda the benefit of the doubt, and consider the wailing of the Jewish émigrés as probably exaggerated. Above all, numerous influential voices welcomed Germany's position as a bulwark against communism.

Thomas Mann attempted to steer a middle course. In the spring of 1933, the president of the Prussian arts academy had asked Mann to sign the declaration of loyalty to the new regime drawn up by Gottfried Benn 'in view of the changed historical situation'. Instead, Mann resigned, as he had from other official positions. Aware that his gesture would appear as an affront, he explained that he wished to concentrate on his personal projects. Mann assured the president that he in no way intended to work against the government, and that he wished to continue to serve German culture.

That *Tales of Jacob* sold well in Germany was a 'wonder' for Mann. It compensated him for the 'painful confusion' his *Sammlung* 'rescue act' had aroused 'in many hearts I respect'. His brother Heinrich reassured him. Even though the Nazis had sentenced Heinrich in absentia to 18 months' imprisonment and had put him on the first list of Germans to lose their nationality, Heinrich told Thomas he had been right to let Fischer publish the novel in Germany. Heinrich encouraged Thomas to keep his access to readers in Germany: 'If I had been able to do it myself, I would have done exactly the same – namely, continue the struggle against Germany's rulers from inside.'

Heinrich had received encouraging letters from Germans who had been reading his earlier works, or his topical articles which anti-Nazis had smuggled into the country. 'How I should like to be able to publish in Germany,' he exclaimed. When a group of left-wing writers in exile asked him to criticise his brother, he refused. Klaus Mann was also reluctant to condemn his father, even in private. But Mann's wife Katia regretted that her husband didn't break with 'this cursed gang' of his own free will, as so many other writers had done.

So did the intellectuals who had emigrated to Paris, Prague and beyond. They looked to Thomas Mann to denounce the Nazi regime unambiguously. If a distinguished non-Jewish German of international stature such as Mann were to sound the alarm, the world might take notice. Yet as late as November 1933, Mann was still contemplating a return to Germany. Mann thought that he, unlike Gerhart Hauptmann or Richard Strauss, could maintain an attitude of solemn isolation and refuse to make himself conspicuous. In the end, however, Mann didn't seek permission to go back.

Reports that the government in Berlin opposed moves by the Munich authorities to revoke his citizenship raised his hopes of regaining his confiscated assets. In the spring of 1934, he wrote a long abject letter to the Reich ministry of the interior in Berlin, asking it to renew his passport and to urge the Munich regional government to return his house and possessions. He told the ministry that he opposed National Socialism, but that since 'History' had spoken he had remained silent and withdrawn from public life. He believed that this 'separation from his fatherland was a temporary episode dictated by destiny'. Mann never received a reply.

Outward success, the continuing sales of his work in Germany, brought no inner peace to Thomas Mann. His diaries record how, despite his many hesitations, he realised he would eventually have to break openly with the regime. He collected newspaper articles about events in Germany and busied himself with drawing up what he called his 'politicum' – the political affirmation for which his fellow émigré writers were waiting – only to put the drafts aside.

How, he asked himself, could he abandon his German public, adjust to living indefinitely beyond his German-speaking *Heimat*, learn a new language? He hoped the dictatorship would not last that long. His friend René Schickele saw the restless Thomas Mann as someone who clung with every fibre to Germany: he wondered how Mann would survive if those links were severed. That was not such a far-fetched apprehension, considering how many émigré writers did commit suicide.

Mann's daughter Erika was, meanwhile, still adroitly canvassing on behalf of Querido in Amsterdam. Her father could not have a better, a more commited publisher, she assured him. The firm would be making him an 'offer' for his collection of essays, the third volume of *Joseph* and whatever else was ready beforehand. Erika pointed out that Querido had published books by Alfred Döblin, Joseph Roth and Jacob Wassermann that had sold well in Germany and elsewhere. Querido could not understand why Mann did not liberate himself from Fischer and join what was the biggest and best German publisher abroad.

Erika hinted that 'If you were lost to Querido, all could turn out badly' for her brother Klaus. His review was doing moderately well, but his position at Querido was insecure. Erika was displeased to learn that her father had encouraged a Zurich publisher rather than Querido to acquire Fischer's rights to publish his forthcoming collection of essays. That would be unfriendly and harmful to the Amsterdam publisher now that Klaus and Querido were so closely linked, Erika told her father.

Querido offered 10,000 Swiss francs for Mann's essays. But Fischer, unwilling to cede the rights, published the essays as *Sufferings and Greatness of the Masters* in 1935. It was the last work by Thomas Mann to come out in Germany until after the war. As Schickele discovered when he tried to take his work to Querido, it was not a simple matter for an expatriate writer to seek a publisher outside the Reich: the Fischer Verlag threatened him with legal action.

By the summer of 1934, Mann's sentiments seemed to be swinging towards making the break with Berlin. He judged the time right for issuing the statement he had in mind; he feared he might regret having delayed too long. He reprimanded Bermann Fischer for his blindness to the horrors the Nazis were perpetrating in Germany. Mann hoped the publisher would reflect on his views and not dismiss them as 'émigré mania'. Mann warned Bermann Fischer that he might 'jump off the Fischer vessel'. Stefan Zweig encouraged Mann to make a decisive statement.

As late as 1935, Bermann Fischer was still preventing Mann from doing so. Mann had agreed to address a League of Nations gathering in Nice. He prepared a speech championing a militant humanism and criticising the way certain governments were turning the masses into fanatics. Bermann Fischer persuaded Mann to call off the journey on the supposed grounds of ill health. Someone read a watered-down version of Mann's lecture on his behalf.

Within Germany, there was mounting evidence that the Nazis were unlikely to welcome Mann back into the *Heimat*. He knew the government was considering whether to deprive him of his German nationality. On his 60th birthday, on 6 June 1935, there were no official congratulations from Berlin although the literary academy had made such a proposal to the government. After earlier hints that he might get his Munich property back if he kept his mouth shut, he was infuriated to hear that the Bavarian political police had let his house to unsatisfactory American tenants. Later, the SS would requisition the residence and turn it into a *Lebensborn* – a 'burn' or 'spring of life' where, as part of Heinrich Himmler's 'master race' programme, SS officers sired superior 'Aryan' stock with selected females.

Abroad, the whole world seemed to be watching and waiting. In the summer of 1935, during Mann's visit to the United States to receive an honorary degree from Harvard, more than 30 prominent United States writers and critics implored him to use his influence to improve the lot of the persecuted artists and Jews. A gesture from him would encourage the oppressed in their struggle, and help those Americans trying to curb the rise of fascism in their own country. Ella Winter, Malcolm Cowley, Lincoln Steffens, John Dos Passos, Langston Hughes and Clifton Fadiman were among those who signed the letter. They never received a reply.

Yet the worsening political situation in Europe was edging Mann away from the ambiguous position he had upheld for the past three years, as his letters and diaries indicate. He recognised that neither Germany's neighbours nor the German people themselves would halt the advance of the Third Reich. Germany had left the League of Nations in October 1933. Hitler had ordered the Röhm massacres in 1934. A month later he liquidated Engelbert Dollfuss, the conservative Austrian chancellor, after Dollfuss (nicknamed 'Millimetternich' because of his short stature) had outlawed the Austrian Nationalist Socialist Party. A huge majority of the German electorate supported

Hitler when he usurped the presidential office after Hindenburg's death, and combined it with the post he already filled as chancellor. In 1935, a large majority of the Saar's voters said they wanted the territory to be part of Germany again. Hitler re-introduced military conscription. He decreed the infamous anti-Semitic laws in Nuremberg.

Yet it wasn't Hitler's tyrannical measures that finally caused Mann to launch his 'politicum'. It was a long-distance telephone call – from Gottfried Bermann Fischer in London. Mann had publicly rescued the besieged Fischer Verlag once before, at the heavy price of distancing himself from his own son. Now, his publisher again begged Mann to intervene, and help clear the illustrious firm's name.

11 'I Have Let My Conscience Speak'

Thomas Mann Comes Off the Fence

Reports had reached the émigrés in Paris that Gottfried Bermann Fischer was trying to move the publishing firm out of the Reich. They made malicious remarks about his exertions. He in turn retorted that, unlike Fischer, competing German-language publishers in Paris, Prague, Zurich or Amsterdam had no responsibilities in Germany and nothing to lose there. He insisted that by carrying on in Berlin till 1936, he had enabled Thomas Mann and Hermann Hesse among others to flourish financially.

At the same time, Bermann Fischer had to admit the Nazis were making Fischer's situation untenable. By the end of 1933 Fischer held huge stocks – some 780,000 volumes – that it could no longer put on the German market. A nightmare scenario obsessed Bermann Fischer. What if the Nazis wrested control of Fischer from its owners, just as they were 'Aryanising' the illustrious *Frankfurter Zeitung*? No doubt they would retain the shells of the two Jewish concerns, respected around the intellectual world, while changing their contents. (In *The Oppermanns*, Feuchtwanger describes step-by-step how the Nazis took over Jewish businesses.)

As sole inheritor, 'Sami' Fischer's widow Hedwig could veto plans to sell the firm. But Bermann Fischer, as business manager, had authority to divide the firm into a German and a non-German section. He saw this as the only solution, as he contemplated ways of setting up the Fischer concern in exile. To this end he opened negotiations with the German government. He would need permission to take with him stocks of books by authors he would be publishing abroad. He would have to settle the question of the firm's financial reserves. And he would have to ensure the 'foreign' Fischer's access to the crucial German market.

It was in an anxious frame of mind that Bermann Fischer visited the propaganda ministry. A warm reception awaited him. The official responsible for dealings with publishers had a nephew who knew Bermann Fischer's deputy, Peter Suhrkamp. (It was Suhrkamp's new wife who told Bermann Fischer that Germany's Jews, having enjoyed so many fat years, should now have to endure some lean ones.) To Bermann Fischer's relief, he could let Suhrkamp negotiate with the ministry. After almost a year, his deputy concluded the talks in December 1935.

One section of the house of Fischer, about 45 per cent of the business, would become a new company to be established outside the Reich. It would retain the right to issue works not only by Thomas Mann but also by Hugo von Hofmannsthal, André Maurois, Arthur Schnitzler, Bernard Shaw and Carl Zuckmayer among others. Bermann Fischer could take existing stocks of their works away with him. The other part of the firm would stay in Berlin under Suhrkamp's direction. The banker Hermann Abs helped Suhrkamp raise 200,000 Reichsmarks to buy out Hedwig Fischer for the rights to such 'approved' authors as Hermann Hesse and Gerhart Hauptmann.

When reports of Bermann Fischer's dealings appeared in the émigré press in Paris, exiles inevitably construed them as collaboration. In London in January 1936, the publisher phoned Thomas Mann to complain about an 'outrageous' article on precisely such lines. He feared it would upset his moves to start a partnership with Heinemann, the leading British publishing business run by Charles Evans. There was a long-standing bond between the two celebrated firms – William Heinemann, the firm's founder, had known Samuel Fischer.

The 'outrageous' article had appeared as part of the review of the week in the issue dated 11 January of *Das Neue Tage-Buch*, the Paris émigré weekly edited by Leopold Schwarzschild. Untitled and unsigned, it observed that the Nazis ensured with the utmost severity that no 'non-Aryans' exercised any authority in the field of German culture. Nowhere else did they apply their 'cleansing measures' more strictly. Even suburban cinemas had to be under 'Aryan' control. Yet the regime had left the firm of Fischer – an important purveyor of German culture – in the skilled business hands of Samuel Fischer's son-in-law. For the *NTB* it seemed to be the only instance where Goebbels and the Nazi arts hierarchy had accorded a distinguished Jew such exceptional treatment.

Recalling the privileged legal status enjoyed by a Jewish elite at some European courts in earlier centuries, often in return for financial services, the article described Bermann Fischer as a *Schutzjude* – a 'protected' Jew – in the Nazi publishing world. While the Nazi press showered dirt on some of Bermann Fischer's authors, and the police manhandled others, no Goebbels organ had ever uttered a single angry word about Bermann Fischer or his firm, the

NTB pointed out. Not even Julius Streicher's notoriously anti-Semitic *Der Stürmer* had questioned the fact that in 1936 a Jew still headed one of the country's biggest publishers. How had Bermann Fischer attained this favoured position? Was it because his books included obsequious dedications to Göring, or did he pay a higher price, the *Tage-Buch* wondered.

The journal surmised that Bermann Fischer had failed to relocate in Switzerland because the firm's close ties to the Nazi cultural establishment had harmed its image in the confederation. The open way Bermann Fischer had been preparing the move, the *Tage-Buch* reasoned, suggested that the German authorities favoured Bermann Fischer. How else could he have obtained permission to transfer funds abroad, but by offering some worthwhile concession in return?

For the *Tage-Buch*, the propaganda ministry had an interest in seeing Fischer re-emerge as a 'camouflaged publisher in exile'. The Nazis could expect Bermann Fischer to publish only books that did not offend Berlin. In addition, his competition would make life harder for genuine German publishers in exile, who did not have to respect the views of Berlin.

That mischievous *NTB* article prompted an indignant Bermann Fischer to call Thomas Mann. Would Mann and two other well-known Fischer authors, Annette Kolb and Hermann Hesse, protest publicly at Schwarzschild's unjustified attack? He insisted that he had operated in Germany in the same way as other firms. He had not bypassed foreign exchange controls. He thought it shameful that some Jewish émigrés should undermine the efforts of other Jews to get out of Germany.

Even before Bermann Fischer's phone call, Mann had planned to protest to the exile weekly – but privately, as was his wont. The Zurich city authorities, who were intervening on Bermann Fischer's behalf to get him a work permit, had telephoned Mann to check the truth of the *NTB* article. They indicated it would embarrass them if Bermann Fischer were some kind of Nazi agent anxious to settle in Switzerland.

Now, sensing that his publisher was 'understandably' very distressed, Mann concluded that he had to make a public gesture in defence of Fischer. He informed Schwarzschild of his intentions. He sent Annette Kolb a draft press statement that already had Hesse's approval. He explained that its purpose was not only to help Bermann Fischer transplant the firm, but also to reject 'certain Nazi methods of the émigré press'.

Mann told Annette Kolb that Bermann Fischer had been trying to publish in Germany in the old spirit – something 'we' knew from the beginning was a hopeless endeavour. Now Bermann Fischer had also recognised that fact, and was therefore trying to move the firm to another German-speaking country. 'Everyone' had regretted and criticised Bermann Fischer's delay in joining the emigration, Mann wrote. But it was spiteful and unjustified to presume that Goebbels had commissioned Bermann Fischer to move abroad, and that the publisher was acting as the propaganda minister's emissary. Mann believed Schwarzschild's aim was to scupper Bermann Fischer's efforts.

Mann's family disapproved of Bermann Fischer's attempt to dispatch the renowned writer once more into the fray on his behalf. Katia told her husband that she opposed Bermann Fischer's request, though she appreciated the need to protect him from the otherwise catastrophic consequences of the *Tage-Buch* article. Erika sympathised with her father's desire to ensure that Germans could continue to read his books. But she wanted to ask him a fundamental question: which publisher was to represent her father, the most distinguished living figure of German letters; with whom, and against whom? She did not see how her father could hover above the mêlée indefinitely. He had to belong to 'them' or to 'us'. She admitted her side was nothing special, but it would certainly be more effective if he joined it.

While Thomas Mann regretted that Bermann Fischer had not left Germany earlier, he sympathised with his publisher's predicament. He saw the embarrassing dedication to Göring as an isolated mishap, the result of the firm's commitment to a house author who had since gone elsewhere. What impressed Mann was that Fischer had, despite ever-harsher laws, continued to publish books by Jewish writers. Mann resolved to try to rescue Bermann Fischer. On 18 January, the *Neue Zürcher Zeitung* carried a 'declaration' by Mann, Hermann Hesse and Annette Kolb.

The three writers praised the way Bermann Fischer had, over the preceding three years and 'under the most difficult circumstances', managed the firm in the spirit of its founder. Proclaiming their continuing loyalty to their publisher, the writers called the *Tage-Buch*'s reproaches and innuendoes unfounded, and seriously damaging to Bermann Fischer.

Erika told her father his action had saddened her. In his first public utterance since the Nazi take-over, and that in a Swiss paper unsympathetic to the émigré cause, Mann had backed 'a faceless business Jew' clever enough to exploit her father's attachment to Sami Fischer. At the same time, Mann had criticised an outspoken opponent of the Nazi regime, Leopold Schwarzschild. She complained that Bermann Fischer, having earlier swayed Mann to detach himself from her brother and his review, had now prodded her father into striking a blow against the emigrants as a whole. Bermann Fischer was thwarting the émigrés' efforts to oppose the Nazis.

Erika accepted that Schwarzschild had been unfair in 'denouncing' so sharply a Jew who wanted to emigrate. On the other hand, she told her father, Bermann Fischer must have had good relations with Goebbels – how else could he have carried on publishing for so long in Germany? She assumed that Bermann Fischer, in negotiating part of the firm's transfer abroad, must have assured the propaganda minister that the Fischer Verlag would not help émigré writers. That, she thought, surely justified Schwarzschild's warning to those not in the know about the 'false émigré', Bermann Fischer.

What particularly upset Erika was that her father had chosen to support Bermann Fischer publicly. Simply allowing the Berlin firm to bring out his books had, in her view, sufficed to show that Mann considered him a worthy person. On the other hand, by leaving Germany her father had demonstrated his rejection of the Nazis, even if he had not expressly articulated it.

Erika wondered why her father's first public support for a victim of injustice should concern Bermann Fischer, when he had defended other personalities through private letters. When Mann in 1935 proposed the award of the Nobel peace prize to the writer and pacifist Carl von Ossietzky, whom the Nazis had sent to a concentration camp in 1933, his letter to the Nobel Prize committee was not for publication. When Knut Hamsun, the Norwegian writer and Nazi sympathiser, opposed Mann's recommendation, Heinrich Mann reacted publicly, but Thomas remained silent. And it was in the form of a private letter that Thomas defended Heinrich after a hostile review in the *Neue Zürcher Zeitung* of his historical novel about Henri IV.

Even though Erika's mother Katia would have preferred her husband to maintain his reserve, she urged Erika to see the issue through Thomas Mann's eyes. His declaration was not disreputable, unlike Schwarzschild's perfidious charge that Goebbels was using Bermann Fischer to harm exile publishers. It was 'unfair' – Frau Mann used the English word – to go on about the unfortunate dedication to Göring. Far from conferring favours on the Fischer Verlag, the Nazis had forbidden the firm from publishing further works by René Schickele and by Harry, Count Kessler (who would die in exile in southern France the following year). Katia Mann pointed out that it was still business more or less as usual for some other Jewish publishers, such as Bruno Cassirer and the musical publisher Peters. (Some 27 Jewish editorial businesses still functioned in Germany as late as 1937. All had to close instantly in December 1938, following *Kristallnacht*.)

Schwarzschild's 'vulgar, Nazi-like methods' had angered Mann. He assured his daughter that it was nonsense to argue that Goebbels wished to transfer Bermann Fischer abroad as a Nazi agent. Bermann Fischer had nobly continued to bring out books by Jews. Suggestions that Berlin was treating him favourably, despite increasingly severe laws, were hateful fantasies. He told Erika confidentially that Bermann Fischer wanted to conclude his negotiations with Heinemann, leave Germany and then surprise the German authorities with his fait accompli.

Mann explained that Bermann Fischer's goal was to head the German section of a new firm, Fischer-Heinemann, based in London as well as Zurich or Vienna. Backed by British, American and Swiss capital, the undertaking would be strong enough to ward off political pressures. If Fischer-Heinemann could sell Mann's books in Germany, despite all he had done to provoke the government, so much the better; if not that was par for the course.

Mann told Erika about an internal report prepared for the Swiss publishers' association: this claimed that if the Swiss authorities let Bermann Fischer set up in the confederation, it would provoke an 'outburst of anti-Semitism' similar to the one produced by 'Jewish cultural domination' in Germany. If Schwarzschild had known of it, Mann assured his daughter, he might have grasped how his article was helping Bermann Fischer's opponents.

A week after Mann, Hesse and Kolb had publicly defended Bermann Fischer, Schwarzschild published his 'reply to Thomas Mann'. What astonished him, he said, was how swiftly Mann had come to Fischer's rescue; after all, Mann had taken years to clarify his thoughts on other matters. He found this 'error' far more serious than Mann's earlier capitulation in 1933 to Bermann Fischer's 'blackmail' over Klaus Mann's literary review.

Schwarzschild argued that virtually the whole of German literature had been 'transferred' abroad since the Nazis came to power and it was now 'hibernating'. Never before had a country's whole literature had to flee the clutches of a regime determined to destroy or deform it. Exiled writers and their publishers in Holland and Switzerland faced a small and declining number of readers.

Now Gottfried Bermann Fischer had appeared on the scene,

seeking to establish another publishing firm outside Germany. In Schwarzschild's opinion, his record since the coming of the Third Reich revealed his poor understanding of literature, deficient mind and lack of character. Schwarzschild recalled Bermann Fischer proudly telling him in Paris about the gracious way the Nazis were treating him, and how they had honoured him by inviting him to a meeting of the official body that dealt with *Schmutz und Schund* – 'smut and trash' literature. Bermann Fischer had expected that the Nazis would exceptionally allow him to stay in business. Surely, Schwarzschild reasoned, Bermann Fischer should have appreciated he was dealing with intellectual goods, not with leather or textiles, and that he would have to conform to the regime's restrictions.

Schwarzschild wondered what type of publishing firm Bermann Fischer would open abroad. It would be either a truly emigrant concern free from Nazi pressures, or one that would respond to directives from Berlin. If the first, Bermann Fischer might exploit Fischer's hefty reputation and financial reserves to bring out new authors, if there were any. That would merely dilute the already meagre purchasing power of an inelastic market, so that all publishers and authors in exile would be worse off.

Bermann Fischer might, on the other hand, try to bait some of the established writers with more attractive conditions. They would initially be better off, but such a policy would weaken other publishers and in the end sap the emigrant literary community as a whole. Had a Nobel laureate [Thomas Mann] ever before used his authority for such a mercantilist venture since the Nazis' rise to power? Schwarzschild unkindly remarked.

The *Tage-Buch* editor did not believe that Bermann Fischer had renounced his efforts to continue publishing in Germany; instead the Reich had renounced its claim on his services. The Nazis had struck his name off the official book-trade register. Schwarzschild thought Mann had missed an opportunity to tell Bermann Fischer that being a rich young man, in all 'fairness' he should return to the medical profession or open a braces factory. Mann could have done so in confidence, even though all Europe would have heard about his message. In that way, Mann would have shown that there was still a certain nobility among Germans, at least beyond the Reich's borders.

Schwarzschild argued that a Fischer based outside Germany might look like an émigré publishing business, but its fortunes would depend on whether Berlin allowed it to sell its books by Mann, Hesse and others on the German market. In that situation Bermann Fischer would not dare to publish anything remotely unfriendly to Berlin, even by a tolerated author such as Mann. Schwarzschild pleaded with Mann to end his association with a 'pseudo' publisher in exile. In continuing to let Fischer handle his work, Mann would be enabling the enemy to boast that it permitted the sale of his books, even though Mann opposed the regime.

It was not Schwarzschild's arguments that caused Mann to climb off the fence, but the sarcastic reply to them that Eduard Korrodi, the *Neue Zürcher Zeitung*'s influential arts editor from 1914 to 1950, published in his paper on 26 January 1936. Known to be unsympathetic to the literary exiles, Korrodi challenged Schwarzschild's 'mercantilist' affirmation that the emigrants had transferred Germany's literary 'wealth' abroad just in time. For him it was 'ghetto madness' to identify German literature with those writers, primarily Jewish, who had fled the country. German literature had not emigrated: Korrodi named a dozen national writers who had not budged, among them some names that are still respected such as Gerhart Hauptmann, Hans Carossa, Ernst Jünger and Ricardo Huch.

Korrodi wondered exactly what had left Germany. He could not think of one true *Dichter*, one genuine poet, who had emigrated. It was primarily the 'novel industry' and a handful of experts in that field who had gone abroad. They could hardly represent the whole of Germany's literary treasure. Korrodi understood why some respected German writers abroad did not care to identify with that émigré clique – an obvious reference to Thomas Mann.

Korrodi's polemic provoked Klaus Mann to send his father a telegram, urgently appealing to him to reply to the Swiss journalist's 'disastrous' article. Erika Mann went further. No other family member rebuked Thomas Mann so severely for his hesitant attitude. She now begged her father to cease obstructing the refugee writers' resistance, and face the fact that he was part of the literary emigration.

The moment had finally come: Mann was at last ready to release his 'politicum' to the world. Helped by her mother and her younger sister Elisabeth, Erika drafted the reply for him. Thomas Mann's response took the form of an open letter to Korrodi, and the *Neue Zürcher Zeitung* published it on 3 February 1936. Mann, who was acquainted with Korrodi, agreed with him that Leopold Schwarzschild might be a brilliant polemicist on political issues but that literature was not his speciality. Schwarzschild had certainly exaggerated in claiming that most of Germany's contemporary literature had abandoned the country. Of course, Mann concurred, there were still notable pens in Germany – but perhaps some of them had 'emigrated' in spirit while forced for various reasons to remain physically in the Reich. Mann also agreed with Korrodi that German literature incorporated works in that language by Swiss, Austrian or Czech authors, such as Hermann Hesse and Franz Werfel, who were not émigrés.

But Korrodi had erred in confusing émigré literature with Jewish literature. He and his brother Heinrich were not the only distinguished non-Jewish writers who had left Germany. Mann cited as other examples Annette Kolb, Leonhard Frank and Oskar Maria Graf. Korrodi had similarly strayed in suggesting that no German poets lived in exile; Mann mentioned Brecht, Johannes Becher and someone Korrodi himself admired, the poet Else Lasker-Schüler.

Mann pointed out that the novel, rather than 'archaic' drama and poetry, had become the dominant and most representative literary art form. It was novelists who analysed and criticised modern society's problems and who could employ science, music and myth, irony and inquiry in crafting their prose. He cited a recent review by Korrodi in which the critic acknowledged the role of Jewish writers in giving the typical German novel a broader European and international character. Thomas noted that he and his brother Heinrich were non-Jews who had helped to bring about that change. In a remark that revealed how racial theories of the era continued to influence Thomas Mann, he attributed his and Heinrich's broader vision to the Latin and Swiss blood in their veins – their mother was partly Brazilian, while their father had Swiss antecedents.

What made the Jews international in outlook, for Mann, was their European-Mediterranean component, a quality that was also an intrinsic part of being German. Without it, the Germans would be a useless primitive people instead of a leading cultural nation. From that observation Mann went on to infer that the Nazis' hatred of the Jews was equally a rejection of European and Christian civilisation, and that it threatened to alienate the land of Goethe from the rest of the world.

Mann declared his 'profound conviction that no good can come from the present German regime, neither for Germany nor for the world'. That conviction had caused him to stay out of Germany although he had deeper intellectual roots there than did the German authorities who had been dithering for three years over whether to deprive him of his nationality. He was certain that both his contemporaries and posterity would judge that he had acted rightly in siding now with those who had been compelled to renounce their fatherland.

'I Have Let My Conscience Speak'

Mann had at last publicly rejected Nazi Germany. For the first time, he explicitly declared his solidarity with the exiles. He wrote in his diary, 'I am aware of the implications of the step I took today. After three years of hesitation, I have let my conscience and firm conviction speak.' Mann's avowal was immediately recognised as a literary landmark in the opposition to Hitler. Stefan Zweig told Mann his letter had historical significance; he hoped 'the gentlemen in Paris' would now cease to blow hot and cold toward him and simply honour him. In Sanary, Ludwig Marcuse observed that a stream of visitors could talk about nothing but the 'Thomas Mann affair'. He told Klaus Mann – an *enfant terrible* if ever there was one – that he had baptised his father the *'père terrible'*.

Klaus congratulated his father, while warning that his act would provoke the Nazis to retaliate. The government waited until December 1936 before doing so, possibly to avoid unfavourable publicity while Berlin was preparing to host that year's Olympic Games. It then revoked Mann's German nationality, as well as that of his wife and their four younger children. Unlike many other less famous émigrés who had become stateless, Mann could still travel freely: the previous November the government in Prague had granted him Czechoslovak citizenship.

Mann's political declarations now became more frequent. Among the most notable was his response to the university of Bonn, which informed Mann in December 1936 that because he had lost his German citizenship the university would withdraw the honorary doctorate it had awarded him. It was a step the university later regretted and annulled.

Mann, who by that time had received an honorary doctorate from Harvard, told the university of Bonn he no longer derived any pleasure from its award, as German universities bore such a grave responsibility for the misfortune that had befallen them. The published version of Mann's reply, in which he accused Hitler's regime of ruthlessly ruining Germany spiritually and physically in its determination to prepare the German people for war, appeared in several languages around the world. After illegal copies began to circulate in the Reich, Goebbels ordered German editors to treat Mann as a non-person.

Was Mann wrong to hesitate so long before making his definitive break with the regime? The émigrés in Paris thought he should have used his authority and prestige far earlier. They deeply upset Mann by saying his stubborn defence of Bermann Fischer had been tantamount to supporting the Nazis, and by calling his years of vacillation a 'stab in the back'. As he saw it, the world knew the Nazis had affronted him and his family, and that they had confiscated their possessions. Mann maintained he had always protested radically, in his reserved way, against the new despotism.

Mann thought his delay in doing so openly was justified. For otherwise, refugee polemics would have drowned his voice and dissipated his moral sway. Instead, he claimed, he had built up a reserve that could one day prove to be more useful. In any case, he believed in a division of labour: why should he compete with a brother who was so excellent as a political writer?

What was important now was that Mann had removed a major cause of discord in the exile community. In the high noon of the Third Reich and during the forthcoming years of war, he rose to probably the greatest international prominence ever achieved by a German writer. In the eyes of the civilised world, he became the counter-figure to Hitler, embodying the 'other', the 'free' Germany. In the cafés of Left Bank Paris, the refugees conferred on him the witty sobriquet, 'His Emigrance'.

12 'The Curtain Falls'
A Berlin Publisher's Odyssey

Somewhat naively, Thomas Mann hoped his 'excommunication' in December 1936 would not 'seriously' harm his publisher. Gottfried Bermann Fischer, however, knew 'the curtain had definitely fallen'. What he had long dreaded came suddenly upon him, like a powerful shock.

Had Bermann Fischer been altruistic or had he been opportunistic? Had he kowtowed to the Nazis when, for example, he asked his writers to sign a loyalty declaration? Had he, however unintentionally, let the Nazis exploit him? The debate smouldered for decades, and not only in Germany. A leading London publisher, in 1996, dismissed damaging insinuations that Bermann Fischer in some way helped Hitler. Tom Rosenthal, linked to two pillars of postwar Anglo-Jewish publishing – André Deutsch, and Secker and Warburg – noted that Fischer was one of many Jewish cultural undertakings that tried to keep afloat in those early years of Nazi rule. He argued that their 'continuance might have helped to ameliorate and even criticise the intellectual horrors of Nazism'.

But now, Bermann Fischer would have to start anew. He couldn't turn back; he had to undertake the painful process of severing his ties with the land of his birth, with his childhood, with his student years – with the land for which he had fought in a world war. He would have to follow the stony path into exile taken by other German publishers before him. Frustration and failure, humiliation and imprisonment, were to accompany his efforts to transplant his part of Fischer beyond the grasp of Germany's 'new order'. The great publishing firm would traverse a decade of near attrition before it could ultimately blossom again, in postwar West Germany.

With Thomas Mann's support, Bermann Fischer was trying to relaunch the 'exile' Fischer in Zurich, where Mann now lived. Until then the name of Samuel Fischer had been enough to open virtually all doors. It was therefore a severe blow when the Swiss government rejected his application. It wasn't that Berne disapproved of Fischer's concessions to the Nazis. What worried the Swiss police was that a Swiss-based Fischer publishing business might now lean too far to the left, and that could cause problems with the big neighbour to the north.

Bermann Fischer detected machinations elsewhere. In his view, Eduard Korrodi had intrigued behind the scenes. He believed the arch-conservative, anti-Semitic literary critic of the *Neue Zürcher Zeitung* had mobilised an apprehensive Swiss publishers' association to lobby the authorities against the potentially powerful competitor. An appalled Hermann Hesse thought the Swiss should have rejoiced at the prospect of welcoming a publisher who had the rights to Thomas Mann's works, instead of excluding Bermann Fischer because he was a Jew.

Unlike other publishers who went into exile, Bermann Fischer was obsessed with the idea that he could flourish professionally only in a German-speaking country. After the Swiss setback, he prepared to try his luck in Vienna. Hitler's savage campaign to undermine the Austrian government and incorporate his native country in the Reich heightened political tension between Berlin and Vienna. That led to bureaucratic impediments, such as Berlin's imposition of a 1,000 Reichsmark levy on Germans who wished to travel to Austria. Bermann Fischer and his wife were in Zurich at the time, and decided not to risk returning to Germany to seek the necessary stamp in their passports. Instead, the couple boarded a train to Vienna and managed to enter Austria illegally by concealing themselves in the carriage toilets during the passport controls at the frontier.

On their arrival, disappointing news from London tempered their good luck. The original plan was to associate Heinemann with a Swiss-based Fischer. Now, in view of the deepening political instability in Austria, Charles Evans thought a partnership with a Vienna-based Fischer was too risky. Bermann Fischer was nonetheless able to open his firm in Vienna in April 1936. From there he could distribute in Germany the works of some of his authors. The authorities also allowed him to bring out of Germany more than 700,000 'undesirable' books and store them at a local bookbinder's premises.

In Vienna, Bermann Fischer and his wife took a small house that, they conjectured, had accommodated stable employees from the nearby Schönbrunn palace in imperial days. They found the Viennese unexpectedly and wildly confident about their country's political prospects. Benito Mussolini and Neville Chamberlain would not hesitate, the locals believed, to halt Hitler's annexation manoeuvres and back the Austrian government's resolve to stay independent. Surrounded by his Berlin furniture and pictures, and by his library of first editions and dedicated copies, Bermann Fischer all too easily found a new serenity. He would later look back without regret on his decision to move to Austria.

Professionally, Bermann Fischer was pleasantly surprised to discover how many readers of German books there were in other European countries as well as in the Americas. He realised that in the past, the firm had neglected its overseas markets. He was soon issuing works by a respectable list of authors, ranging from Paul Claudel and Paul Valéry to Hugo von Hofmannsthal and Annette Kolb. Eve Curie's biography of her mother Marie turned into a bestseller. As the Nazis had banned Robert Musil's *The Man Without Qualities*, Bermann Fischer was able to acquire the rights from Musil's German publisher.

Vienna offered the Bermann Fischers a rich social life. There were visits to the Salzburg festival and to opera performances conducted by Bruno Walter and Arturo Toscanini. The couple enjoyed winter vacations in the nearby mountains and summer breaks on the Austrian lakes. They mixed with leading intellectuals and politicians. They congregated in the home of Franz and Alma Werfel, Sigmund Freud received them and Robert Musil visited them. Werfel's publisher lived close by in a small baroque *Schloss*.

But it was a deceptive Austrian idyll. That autumn of 1936, the new firm published *Joseph in Egypt*. It was the third and now penultimate volume of Thomas Mann's magnum opus. Mann gave a public reading from the novel in Vienna, while he and his wife were visiting the Bermann Fischers. The two couples then went to the opera to hear Bruno Walter conduct the third act of Mann's favourite opera, *Tristan and Isolde*. They entered to the unpleasant odour of stink-bombs that Nazis had thrown into the auditorium. At the end, Walter and the orchestra were performing to a half-empty house. His wife was crying in her box. (Around the same time, British students threw stink-bombs from the gallery into the Oxford Union's debating chamber. They were protesting at the presence of Randolph Churchill, who had come along to get the Union to expunge its notorious resolution declining to fight for king and country.)

When the Manns again visited the Bermann Fischers in January 1937, the hosts were among the first to hear Mann publicly read his reply to Bonn university's decision to rescind the honorary doctorate it had awarded him. A particularly embarrassing incident for Bermann Fischer involved the famous German writer Gerhart Hauptmann. The playwright, then in his mid-seventies, was to visit Vienna for a production in the Burg theatre of his early work, *The*

Rats. He asked Bermann Fischer, who had been his publisher in the Berlin days, to arrange a reception at his home. Earlier in the century, Hauptmann's naturalist novels and plays, expressing sympathy for the oppressed from a social democrat position, had provoked bans and scandals. Later they had earned him the Nobel Prize, as well as honours from a host of distinguished institutions, including Oxford and Columbia universities. The Nazis, however, tolerated rather than revered Hauptmann.

Bermann Fischer invited about 80 of Vienna's most prominent actors and artists. Three days before, Hauptmann asked him to cancel the event: Hauptmann feared that his presence in the émigré publisher's home on such a public occasion would cause him difficulties in Germany. When Hauptmann attended a performance of his play, a caustic Bermann Fischer noted that he was in the imperial box in the company of the German ambassador. With 'profuse apologies and lame excuses', Hauptmann and his wife came to the Bermann Fischers for dinner the following evening – 'secretly and incognito so to speak', the publisher recorded.

Despite the political turmoil surrounding him, Bermann Fischer had not contemplated another move, but his new-found tranquillity came to an abrupt end after less than two years. At the beginning of March 1938 Pierre Bertaux, a former Berlin neighbour who had become a French authority on German literature, telephoned from Paris to urge the family to prepare to leave the country. It was too late: on 11 March, a telephone call rudely awoke Bermann Fischer, who was enjoying an afternoon nap. A friend told him Nazi troops were preparing to occupy the country. The Austrians had thought they were going to decide in a referendum a few days later whether they wanted to join Germany. But Hitler had acted pre-emptively, correctly assuming – as the cheering street crowds would prove – that the great majority wanted the *Anschluss*.

With their three daughters, the Bermann Fischers prepared to take the train to Bermann Fischer's mother-in-law in Rapallo. At the station in Vienna, where controls had immediately been set up, a porter asked them what passports they were carrying. 'German', said Bermann Fischer. 'That's good. You wouldn't get out any longer with an Austrian passport,' the porter replied.

In Rapallo, the family were walking to their hotel room when they bumped into a beaming Gerhart Hauptmann. He raised his arms and exclaimed enthusiastically, 'It's the fulfilment of Heinrich Heine's dream. Vienna is going to be the capital of Europe.' A puzzled Bermann Fischer wondered how this elderly poet's patriotism caused him to imagine that the Jewish Heine could have approved of Hitler's coup.

Bermann Fischer had left behind in Vienna all the firm's records and correspondence. Two days later, the Gestapo occupied the family's home and confiscated their possessions. The Nazis subsequently disposed of them in the state auction-house. A Nazi engineer took over the publishing business, but it was later closed down. Bermann Fischer's thoughts turned to the ultimate refuge – America. Who else to approach but Thomas Mann? He was on a lecture tour of the United States and about to take up an academic position at Princeton University that autumn.

Mann cruelly advised Bermann Fischer to go back to being a surgeon rather than stay in the world of books. Writing from the Beverly Hills Hotel in April 1938, he warned Bermann Fischer, now in Zurich, against setting up in the United States. Mann told him that his 'policy all these years, your ties with Germany, which you maintained until they were broken for you, and even the character of your Viennese enterprise, which remained geared to the German market, have made the terrain here most unfavourable for you. Unlike all European countries, this is the only land where a really deep antipathy to the character of present-day Germany prevails.'

American intellectuals had so decisively rejected Nazi Germany, according to Mann, that they were unlikely to welcome a publisher who had failed to take an unequivocal stand at the outset, and who appeared to have cooperated with the new dictatorship. Mann recalled that Bermann Fischer had never wanted to run an émigré publishing firm. Even in Vienna he had rejected the idea. Mann said he could not contradict those who claimed that Bermann Fischer, now in an impasse, had forfeited the moral right to set up a German émigré publishing house.

Mann rebuked him for lacking the will and vision to make sacrifices and do what Querido had done: publish books and a review outside Germany. Bermann Fischer had remained firmly attached to Germany, leaving only when there was no longer any future for Jewish publishers. What opportunities the Fischer Verlag would have enjoyed, had it gone to Switzerland promptly in 1933 or 1934, Mann unkindly remarked. Instead, the Swiss turned down his belated initiative. Fischer's project for a worldwide firm with Heinemann of London had come to nothing. The limited business in Vienna had held out scant prospect, and had now reached its predetermined end.

Bermann Fischer's American plans, like his Vienna undertaking, needed Mann's reputation and help. Knowing that many would disapprove of such support from him, Mann was disinclined to provide it. He coldly told Bermann Fischer, 'Don't say that that is hard and horrible of me, bearing in mind our long-standing relationship. I have been true to you longer perhaps than I should have been. It seems to me the situation now requires a separation of the personal from the professional.'

Although Mann had approved of and benefited from Bermann Fischer's publishing activities between 1933 and 1938 in Berlin and Vienna, he now tried to sever his ties with his publisher. It was a harsh attitude that echoed the way he had earlier distanced himself from his son. As critics would later judge, such an unforgiving attitude did not show 'His Emigrance' at his best.

Mann's remarks devastated Bermann Fischer. He told Mann that he was not going back to the operating theatre. After 13 passionate years in publishing, he would not give up a task that was now more important than ever. While he had expected 'certain circles' to discredit him at that difficult time, he never imagined Mann would join them and leave him in the lurch. Bermann Fischer thought he had acted faithfully towards Mann. They had agreed on the timing of the firm's move from Germany, yet now Mann was joining those who criticised the firm for remaining in Berlin until 1936. Bermann Fischer emphasised that in 1933 and 1934 the Nazis would not have allowed Fischer to publish a single book outside Germany, or transfer any book rights abroad.

Bermann Fischer maintained that the Nazis had closed his Vienna office, and confiscated his personal and commercial assets, because of his effective anti-Nazi activity in the Reich. Émigré publishers, on the other hand, had been unable to do anything inside Germany. He complained that a small but loud section of the exiles had scorned him for rejecting their form of political struggle, because he believed other methods to be more useful. They wanted to exercise a form of intellectual totalitarianism similar to that employed by the Third Reich, he said.

Bermann Fischer and his family settled in Stockholm after the Swedish government authorised him to restart his business there. They felt increasingly uncomfortable and threatened as German propaganda blossomed in Sweden. Bermann Fischer and his wife noticed that the government and the royal family were promoting a pro-Nazi atmosphere in the country. Bermann Fischer spent more than two months in a Swedish jail. The American author Hendrik Willem van Loon, best known for his popular history *The Story of*

Mankind, helped the Bermann Fischers obtain American visas. They reached the United States in 1940, via the Soviet Union and Japan.

With Fritz Landshoff, his former competitor at Querido in Amsterdam, Bermann Fischer founded the L[andshoff] B[ermann] Fischer publishing corporation in New York. (After the Germans occupied the Low Countries in 1940, they confiscated Querido's stocks in Amsterdam. Emanuel Querido, although in great danger as a Jewish left-wing Dutch publisher, refused to hide. In July 1943 the Nazis deported him and his wife to Poland, where they perished.)

The Fischer warehouse in Vienna was destroyed during the war. Bermann Fischer's former deputy Peter Suhrkamp administered his half of the Fischer firm in Germany, until the Nazis arrested him in 1944 and sent him to a concentration camp. After the war the British let Suhrkamp continue to run Fischer, as 'Suhrkamp, formerly S. Fischer'. When Bermann Fischer returned to Germany, each publisher set up a separate firm and their authors could opt for one or the other. Today, Fischer flourishes in Frankfurt, in no small part because it continues to bring out the works of Thomas Mann.

13 From Bonds to Blitzkrieg

Leopold Schwarzschild Bares Hitler's War Plans

In September 1936, René Schickele told a friend about a 'monster tea' party that the 'world famous *Dichter* Lion F[euchtwanger] and his Queen of Sheba-like wife' had hosted in Sanary. Among the guests were popular Sanary residents – Sybille Bedford, Eva Herrmann, Maria Huxley – but also a visiting couple, 'Schwarzschild und Frau'.

While most stars of Weimar journalism failed to sparkle as brightly in exile as they had in Germany, Leopold Schwarzschild was a notable exception. Born in Frankfurt in 1891, Schwarzschild had co-founded *Das Tage-Buch* in Berlin in 1927, serving as editor and publisher of what would become a leading liberal left-of-centre weekly. Then, as later, his success lay in the fact that although he edited a political review, he had no ties to any political party and gave more space to economic topics than did his competitors.

After first fleeing to Austria, where his wife's family lived, Schwarzschild emigrated to Paris. As luck would have it, he came across an Amsterdam barrister who, alerted by an English friend, offered to help Schwarzschild finance a weekly in exile. Lion Feuchtwanger lent what he called a large sum to Schwarzschild and later realised that the editor would probably be unable to repay it. Schwarzschild's re-born <u>Neue</u> *Tage-Buch* appeared from July 1933 until May 1940, longer than other exile periodicals. It has come to be regarded as the most important German exile journal, and the one that had the most influence beyond what Schwarzschild called the 'sullen émigré clique' around him.

His wife Valerie, who came of a wealthy Viennese clothing-manufacturing family, visited rather than lived with her husband in Paris. In exile, she continued to lead a life of pleasure and extravagance, with little respect for conventional norms of matrimony. Although Schwarzschild received a generous salary, he tried, he told her, to lead a life that was modest to 'frightfully frugal, even without an egg in the morning'. He felt, however, that his free-spending spouse thwarted and neglected him. 'I am not a plant that flourishes in the desert,' he complained. Their mutual reproaches offer an insight into how the strains of exile aggravated personal relations.

Schwarzschild told Valerie that he missed the normal domestic comforts of the middle class, and did not want to spend so much time in cafés and restaurants. To reduce his outgoings he moved from his hotel to an apartment. As it was just off the Place Vendôme, the move did not produce enormous savings. He tended to shun self-catering and usually ate at his local café, though occasionally he enjoyed lunch and dinner in some style at restaurants. Klaus Mann had lunch with him in a good Hungarian restaurant. Schwarzschild enjoyed a night on the town in a group that included Alma Mahler-Werfel. The company went to a Left Bank restaurant, where they consumed grilled truffles and drank water-glass quantities of superior cognac drawn out of a barrel. They then crossed the Seine to Fouquets on the Champs-Elysées, and finally proceeded to a dance hall.

During a marital dispute in the spring of 1934, Valerie tore strips off her husband and said she had been advised to look for another man. She then 'vanished' to Switzerland, telling him she would come back only when there was more money. Schwarzschild lamented that he saw no incentive in having and working for a wife who, like a migratory bird, came in the financial spring and flew away in the financial autumn.

In September 1934, Schwarzschild sharply reprimanded Valerie. When he first arrived in Paris, he reminded her, she had offered him conjugal support and she was pleasant. 'But you did not lift a finger,' he wrote to her, 'you created scenes when asked to sew on a button or discuss our joint finances, you thought of nothing other than how to continue the life to which you had been accustomed – car, travel here, travel there.'

Schwarzschild was on the verge of 'jumping sideways' – as the Germans phrase an extra-marital relationship. An acrimonious Leopold confessed to Valerie that 'You have told me often enough that you do not love me and there can be no denying that the unavoidable result is that we stand on an equal footing in that respect ... there is a woman who claims to love me very much, that is, a woman who would give what you did not.' He enjoined Valerie either to come back to him and settle down to a true marriage, or to agree to a proper separation.

Valerie did neither. She kept on paying brief visits to her husband, but did not change her way of life. She travelled by air or in expensive wagons-lits, stayed in the most elegant hotels, remained an exceptionally well-dressed woman and drove her own car. She would spend summer in Ascona or on the Riviera, and go skiing in winter. She was a member of the Racing Club de France, and as late as 1937 could afford a new Lancia sports car. She continued to have affairs, some stormy, with a series of lovers. As Schwarzschild could not change her ways he joined her, spending the occasional brief holiday with her in luxury hotels on the Côte d'Azur – a practice that led to bitter gossip among his less fortunate colleagues.

Despite their turbulent relationship, the couple remained married. Later a widowed Valerie went to some trouble to consolidate Leopold's niche in history by bringing out two selections of his articles in book form. Asked how high the circulation of her husband's illustrious periodical had been, Schwarzschild's widow vaguely but optimistically recollected that sales never exceeded 50,000 copies. Researchers subsequently estimated that its widely fluctuating circulation could rarely have gone beyond 15,000 copies. Perhaps Valerie Schwarzschild said or meant 'fünfzehn' rather than 'fünfzig' thousand.

In the *Neue Tage-Buch*'s 24 pages Schwarzschild balanced editorials with reports on political, economic and military themes. In the first issue, published in Paris in July 1933, he explained that the new review's coverage of Germany would emphasise facts more than its predecessor had done. In Berlin, background analysis and comment had been the priorities because hard news was available from many other sources. As Germany's new dictatorship was intent on obscuring facts, Schwarzschild's goal in exile was to expose what lay behind German officialdom's version of events – or behind its silence.

Despite the difficulties involved in transplanting a periodical from Berlin to Paris, Schwarzschild's journalistic talent ensured that the *NTB*'s standards remained high, consistently distinguished by its accurate analyses of events. Few other refugee journals penetrated as effectively the deliberate obfuscation surrounding the Nazi re-armament drive. More than most other journalists in exile, Schwarzschild and his contributors delved deeply into Germany's budget and economic policy. They closely examined official documents as well as the German press for clues about what was really going on.

Underlying Leopold Schwarzschild's researches into the statistics issued by banks and economic institutes lay a conviction that Germany was preparing for wars of conquest. His concern was to lay irrefutably bare, to sceptics on both sides of the Channel, the devious ways in which the German government, contrary to its international obligations, was re-arming the country.

That Hitler had rapidly embarked on extensive public-works projects had soon become obvious to the outside world. Such visible signs as the construction of the autobahn network, a scheme planned in the mid-1920s, convinced many observers of Hitler's determination to create jobs. Penetrating analyses in Schwarzschild's *Das Neue Tage-Buch* revealed what lay behind the state's outgoings. The periodical showed how the Nazis' creative book-keeping concealed a build-up of the country's military might – and a parallel substantial rise in the public debt. Gleaning data from documents on Germany's imports of raw materials and outlays for aircraft, tanks, barracks and other military purposes, the *NTB* staff scrutinised and interpreted the data – and generally arrived at accurate conclusions.

Such was the case in 1933, for example, when the Reichsbank announced a change in its statutes. It said it would henceforth be authorised to purchase – and not only give short-term credit on – fixed-interest bonds issued by the central and regional governments and other public authorities. Dr Hjalmar Schacht, brought back that year to preside over the bank, assured the business community that the amendment was a technical one without further significance. Schacht, who had been a member of the Social Democrat Party after World War I, had already served as Reichsbank president from 1923 to 1929. He had turned to the National Socialists because he opposed the Versailles treaty and the severe reparations it imposed on a defeated Germany. His influence enabled him, as the regime's financial architect, to draw leading industrialists and financiers into the Nazi orbit.

From their editorial offices in the rue du Faubourg St Honoré, opposite the British embassy, Schwarzschild and his colleagues on the Paris weekly reacted sceptically to Schacht's bland assurances. Even before Keynes had published his *General Theory*, they grasped that Hitler was driving the country into a deficit-spending spree as he sought to expand employment, revive the economy and above all build up the Reich's military strength. The Führer's ambitious economic programmes required vast monetary disbursements that conventional sources of revenue, primarily taxes, alone could not have covered.

Georg Bernhard, an occasional contributor to *Das Neue Tage-Buch* until he became editor of the exile daily *Pariser Tageblatt*, doubted that the Reichsbank's measure was as harmless as proclaimed by Dr Schacht. After all, German governments had until then severely circumscribed the central bank's power to lend money to official bodies. With a public still traumatised by the hyperinflation of the 1920s, the country's financial watchdog had been scrupulously restraining access to its resources by government agencies.

For *Das Neue Tage-Buch*, therefore, Schacht's step was more than financial fine-tuning; it had considerable political significance. The revised rules allowed the bank to inflate the money supply in a disguised fashion. In purchasing such official bonds once offered to the public, the Reichsbank would be injecting fresh money into the economy. Its book-keepers could enter the bonds as assets covering the issue of bank notes, so that for accounting purposes there would be no expansion in the supply of money.

Schwarzschild's weekly explained how in theory the Reichsbank could now better serve the state's financial needs, not least for military purposes. Was it doing so in practice? The government assured the public that its debts had barely risen, despite its raft of programmes to reduce unemployment. A wary *NTB* continued to scrutinise Schacht's ruses. In the spring of 1934 it showed that the government had concealed a substantial rise in the public debt.

How high exactly was the debt? As the authorities perfected ways to disguise their manipulations, it became harder for the Paris journal to go beyond estimates. In 1935 its journalists noticed a sudden increase in Germany's liquidity, after years of tight money. They suspected that the German war machine was covering its growing cash requirements in some occult way. 'From where does Hitler get his money?' was the headline of one *NTB* article. Like a detective investigating a crime, Schwarzschild had uncovered what had happened, even if at first he could not quantify the money-laundering operation.

The government's explanation for the increased amount of cash in circulation was that resources spent on 'job creation' – an umbrella term that included military expenditure – had streamed into the money market. That might be true, wrote Schwarzschild, but only partly so. It was just as accurate to say that the government had sucked money from the economy to pump into job creation. To do so it had borrowed billions from the reserves of private companies and individuals, and further billions from commercial banks and savings institutions.

In return for the money it siphoned out of the economy, the government increased its debt by providing bills of exchange. Whereas the public would normally consider these a short-term capital investment, the government had persuaded businesses and banks that they were as good as bank notes, because they could convert the bills into cash at any time. Skimming and recycling money in this fashion would not in itself cause an increase in liquidity, Schwarzschild noted. But as the savings in the private sector dried up, the Reichsbank must have turned to printing money – and that would explain the observed growth in liquidity.

The *NTB* still had to quantify the growing public debt. It now uncovered a major financial instrument that Schacht had devised to help Hitler disguise his enormous rearmament effort and the accompanying inflationary pressures. It was the 'Mefo-Wechsel' system, and Schacht, who became economics minister in 1934, developed it, backed by Krupp, Siemens, Gutehoffnungshütte and Rheinmetall – four industrial heavyweights that were also leading defence contractors. With the modest sum of 1,000,000 Reichsmarks as capital, the companies set up the 'Metallurgische Forschungsanstalt mbH', an institute with limited responsibility that ostensibly would carry out metallurgical research. When the Wehrmacht negotiated arms-procurement contracts with industrial concerns, it paid them with promissory notes known as 'Mefo-Wechsel' – Mefo bills of exchange.

The Mefo procedure brought the government political and economic advantages. For book-keeping purposes, the government treated Mefos as commercial instruments, and so didn't have to include them in its statistics of military orders. In that way Berlin could veil the true extent of the German rearmament effort operated through the Mefo institute. Economically, Schacht's genius was to exploit the Mefo as a device to finance prodigious outlays on building up the fighting forces, without the Reichsbank having to print more money.

The central bank could do this without infringing the country's banking legislation and without mentioning the Mefos in its published accounts. The authorities distinguished 'Wechsel' from 'credit', which would have revived fears of inflation. Germany's internal liabilities could remain unbalanced, without weakening the country's credit rating and thus provoking a flight from the Reichsmark.

Mefos were an indirect credit granted to the government by the Reichsbank, which guaranteed this financial paper. A business could exchange 'Mefos' for cash at commercial banks. The banks in turn would hold what for them was equivalent to money as part of their normal cash reserves, confident that they ran no risk. If a bank did present a Mefo to the Reichsbank, the central bank issued a new Mefo, so that it never called in its loan to the government.

Schacht had expected that the German economy would flourish and so allow the Reichsbank to buy back the Wechsel it had issued. Hitler, however, used the increased revenue to reinforce the country's war capacities, rather than repay the debts. That led Schacht to resign in 1939, both as economics minister and as Reichsbank president. Some 12 billion marks' worth of Mefos were issued during the lead-up to war.

The *Neue Tage-Buch* not only uncovered the Mefo mechanism, but also ingeniously analysed Mefo statistics to work out the extent of the national debt. When the German authorities claimed that the country had a public debt of 4.3 billion marks at the end of May 1935, the *NTB* promptly challenged the figure. Schwarzschild's weekly showed that since Hitler's assumption of power in January 1933, the government had additionally run up through the Mefo mechanism a concealed 'black' debt of some 18.3 billion marks.

To reach this conclusion, Schwarzschild and his colleagues correlated three sets of official figures. The Reich statistical office published the proceeds of the tax levied on bills of exchange such as the Mefos. Every month, an institute for economic research provided details of new bills of exchange. Every quarter, the same institute announced the value of the bills in circulation. Using these variables, the exile journal showed that the government had falsified the extent of its debt. A week after Schwarzschild detailed the scope of Berlin's shrouded stratagems, the government indirectly confirmed his conclusions by prohibiting further publication of data on the Wechsel tax. Revelations about the extent of Germany's internal financial liabilities were no longer possible.

Yet Schwarzschild's paper continued to beaver away on unearthing what lay behind official pronouncements. Staff compared a range of statistical yearbooks and government reports for the Weimar era with those issued after 1933. If the government suspended publication of certain data, the journalists suspected it was to conceal information linked to war preparations. After looking at figures of imports for raw materials used in military production, they observed that the government paid those bills promptly, although it was claiming at the same time that it lacked the foreign exchange to pay for other imports.

Schwarzschild opened his pages to Berthold Jacob, an exiled journalist with military expertise, whom the Nazis had abducted from Switzerland and then released under diplomatic pressure from the Swiss. Though Jacob greatly overestimated the number of aircraft at the Luftwaffe's disposal, his analysis of official defence documents, especially the armed services lists, led him to conclude correctly that the German government was shaping the air force into an offensive arm.

Well before the French general staff, Jacob's articles noted the important role that Germany's tanks were acquiring, identifying General Heinz Guderian as the army's chief tank expert. In 1934, Hitler, aware of the benefits of armoured units operating independently of the mass of infantry, authorised the new Wehrmacht's first tank battalion. As early as 1934, Schwarzschild's paper was forecasting that a Blitzkrieg would be the most likely form of German attack, as proved the case when Guderian's Panzers invaded Poland and France.

When Germany's cement industry boomed after Hitler's occupation of the Rhineland in 1936, Schwarzschild signalled its significance to his readers: Germany had embarked on the construction of the defensive Siegfried Line on the Franco-German border. He drew attention to the tenfold rise in the capital of the Junkers aircraft-manufacturing firm and to the automobile industry's announcement of full employment in its sector.

Schwarzschild spotted the big increase in investments by IG Farben, at the time one of the world's leading chemical undertakings. As a producer of synthetic substitutes for crucial raw materials such as oil and rubber, IG Farben was to become one of Germany's vital industrial assets during the war. It was to manufacture the Zyklon-B poison gas used in the death camps, among them its own at Auschwitz. After the war, the Allies broke it up into Hoechst, Bayer and BASF – modern Germany's three largest chemical companies.

Das Neue Tage-Buch sometimes got its interpretations wrong. It erred in asserting (in a typical example of émigrés' wishful thinking) that autarchy would lead to hunger among the German population. Overall, however, Schwarzschild and his colleagues uncovered a stream of facts that led them to reach strikingly accurate and significant conclusions. Even if some pieces did not fit properly, their articles constituted a mosaic that offered readers a reasonably exact picture of Hitler's war preparations.

Precisely because of his effective sleuthing, Schwarzschild became one of the few exiled journalists whose Cassandra-like writings carried some weight among French and British opinion-makers. His circle of readers extended well beyond the Central European emigrants who languished in the cafés of Paris and Prague. His hard fact-finding approach made the paper the object of attacks by the German press. But the *NTB* also became one of the most frequently cited exile journals: papers such as *Le Figaro*, the *Daily Mail* and the *Manchester Guardian* quoted from its reports. Schwarzschild proudly told his wife that after the French press picked up an *NTB* article about Germany's rising imports, an American embassy messenger had collected 12 copies of the issue and embassy staff had cabled the article to Washington.

Schwarzschild hoped to broaden his journal's influence by starting an English-language version. Ernst Toller arranged for him to have talks with the *New Statesman* in London, but they proved fruitless. Instead, the *NTB* used journalists from mid-stream French papers, such as *L'Echo de Paris* and *Le Figaro*, which had good links to the French armed services and French heavy industry. It regularly published articles by French and British politicians and writers. In its first issue, Sir Austen Chamberlain, a former foreign secretary, called the 'new German spirit' the 'worst Prussian imperialism, strengthened by barbarianism and race hatred'. In August 1933, Winston Churchill pleaded for arms control instead of disarmament. Pierre Mendès-France analysed German dumping practices. Wickham Steed denied a German newspaper's claim that, in 1922, Lloyd George had engineered his resignation as editor of *The Times*. Another journalist contributor was Robert Dell, the *Manchester Guardian*'s Geneva correspondent.

Bertrand Russell set out to answer the question, 'Can the World be Saved?'. Aldous Huxley looked at the prospects for fascism. When the weekly reviewed the English edition of his *Beyond the Mexique Bay*, it highlighted his suggestion for a psychological world conference to reduce race hatred. Asked by the *NTB* for his views on Nazi race theory, Bernard Shaw replied, 'Don't waste your time on this pseudo-Nietzschean Northern Races Theory. There is no such thing, and soon there will be nothing called Race in the world – except for the race of greyhounds that chase electric hares.' In 1933, André Maurois reviewed H. G. Wells's *The Shape of Things to Come*, in which Wells predicted that a major European war in the 1940s would begin on the Polish border.

Besides the foreign press, a host of foreign politicians, diplomats, bankers and the upper echelons of the armed forces closely followed the *NTB*'s efforts to unravel details of Berlin's military preparations. They were more interested in such information than they were in accounts of the fratricidal ideological disputes that filled other émigré papers. During his wilderness years, Winston Churchill used information from the *NTB* when preparing his speeches. The paradoxical result was that while German 'reactionaries' detested

Schwarzschild, British and French right-wing nationalists and conservatives admired him. Colonel Blimp was not Schwarzschild's friend, but the enemy of his enemies.

Although Schwarzschild opposed the West's appeasement of Hitler, he did not advocate a preventive war against Germany. He believed its neighbours should strengthen their military capacities and form an alliance to isolate the Reich and dissuade it from pursuing its aggressive aims. At first, he urged the democracies to join forces with the Russian and Italian dictatorships, and with Austria's 'clerical fascists'.

In the campaign launched in Paris to form the German Popular Front, the moderate left-wing Schwarzschild worked alongside the well-disciplined communist refugees. His sympathy for the far left dissolved in 1936, however, when Stalin's political trials turned him into a foe – an hysterical one, in the view of some fellow journalists – of what he called the 'red fascists'. For Schwarzschild 'Bolshevistery' was the original disease, the '*Ur-Syphilis*' without which the fascist or Nazi scourges would never have existed.

While French and British conservative 'diehards' admired the man who called strongly for collective resistance to Hitler, many of his anti-fascist companions in exile began to detest him. Some German communists absurdly accused Schwarzschild of working for Goebbels, but they hoisted themselves with their own petard. His weekly had suggested in February 1937 that Stalin's agents could have used hypnosis to extract confessions from the accused in the Moscow political trials. That same month it ran a letter supporting the article's hypothesis, from a Dr Marcel Strauss who claimed he had formerly been in charge of the university hospital in Strasbourg.

A few days later, a communist German-language paper in Prague published an article headlined 'Press Scandal – Revelations in Moscow Trial – A Crass Case of Trotskyist-Fascist Conformism – Goebbels in *Neue Tage-Buch* – Working for Hitler.' Its communist author claimed he had unmasked Schwarzschild's journal as a Nazi organ. The 'proof' he advanced was that the Strauss letter was similar to one that had appeared a few weeks earlier in a Nazi newspaper in Berlin. That showed how the *NTB*'s editorial staff resembled the Goebbels lackeys, the communist journalist claimed. He said that when it came to slandering Soviet justice, both used the same sources and collaborators. The *Pariser Tageszeitung* published similar allegations against the *NTB*.

The journalist stumbled, however, by mockingly informing his readers that the Strasbourg doctor did not live at the address 'indicated' in the letter, and that there was in fact no such Doctor Strauss. Schwarzschild pounced triumphantly: how could the journalist have checked the authenticity of the address? Although the actual letter sent to the *Neue Tage-Buch* gave an address, Schwarzschild had not reproduced it in his publication. Beyond his editorial staff – and they had not disclosed it – only those involved in drafting and sending off the bogus 'Strauss letter' to the *NTB* could have known the Strasbourg address. The communist journalist had unmasked himself.

Schwarzschild's censure of Thomas Mann's German publisher, Bermann Fischer, his unbridled attacks on the German communists, and his criticism of his fellow émigré journalists on the Paris exile daily in their drawn-out dispute with their proprietor showed a rare independence of spirit. But his non-conformist attitude added to the strife the refugee intellectuals created among themselves as they tried to build a united resistance to Hitler. They seemed to be more concerned with fighting one another than with resisting the common enemy.

Schwarzschild's violent anti-communism led him to set up a 'free' writers' association as an alternative to the fellow-travelling guild of German writers in exile. Many émigrés shared his opinion that it had become a communist front organisation. After the Nazi-Soviet non-aggression pact, however, Schwarzschild appeared to have lost his capacity for reasonable judgment. He denounced Lion Feuchtwanger as the laureate among 'Soviet agents'. Coming from a fellow émigré, such allegations harmed Feuchtwanger, who at the time was enduring French internment and hoping the United States would grant him asylum.

A week later Schwarzschild condemned Klaus Mann in the same terms, although Mann had greatly admired Schwarzschild's journalistic achievements and had contributed nearly 30 articles to his journal from 1933. Schwarzschild's accusation of treachery was similarly unhelpful to Mann, who was living in the United States with only a visitor's visa. What had infuriated Schwarzschild was that Mann had not answered directly a question from the German-American Writers' Association, 'Do you approve of the Hitler-Stalin Pact – Yes or No?'

Schwarzschild ceased to review books by communists or fellow-travellers, an exception being Feuchtwanger's account of his visit to Moscow. He began to lose the services of communist sympathisers such as Feuchtwanger, as well as independent left-wing writers, who were offended by his virulent hostility to Stalin. In that era of appeasement, they considered that the Soviet tyrant, who had provided military support to the Spanish Republicans, remained the only major opponent of Hitler whose deeds matched his words.

The *NTB* appeared for the last time on 11 May 1940. The French interned Schwarzschild in various camps from 14 May, then let him join a special foreigners' unit in the French army. He was demobilised in July and managed to flee, via Marseilles, Spain and Portugal, to New York, where he disembarked in September. Klaus Mann, among others, helped him reach America: Mann had proposed Schwarzschild's name to the Emergency Rescue Committee, the influential body set up in New York with Roosevelt's backing that saved hundreds of intellectuals trapped in France. Klaus Mann had resolved never again to shake the hand of someone he regarded as a slanderer who had stabbed him in the back, but he did not wish Schwarzschild to fall into Nazi hands.

In New York, besides a flow of anti-communist and other articles on current affairs, Schwarzschild wrote a well-received *World in Trance*, published in London in 1943. One of the best-known communist apostates, Arthur Koestler, praised the work for containing 'the most concise summary of the Seven Years' Blindness' of the Europeans and Americans to the rise of Hitler during the 1930s. Émigré polemics continued even after the war. Fellow émigrés smeared him as a 'German McCarthy', after he published a critical book about Karl Marx.

In September 1949, Schwarzschild attempted to gas himself in his New York apartment. He died in Italy the following September, while on a prolonged visit to Europe. Schwarzschild would have turned 60 that December. Officially, a heart attack caused his death, but drugs may have induced it.

14 'We Have Just Saved Culture'

The Paris Writers' Congress of 1935

'I have been blackmailed into promising to attend an international writers' congress in favour of free speech in Paris on the 21st of this month,' an unenthusiastic Aldous Huxley wrote to his brother Julian from Sanary, early in June 1935. He didn't indicate the 'blackmailer's' identity. During his Sanary years, as bellicose voices roared ever more loudly, Huxley reflected constantly on the role of 'literature for peace'. Influenced by Freud's writings and by esoteric gurus, he concluded, perhaps optimistically, that peace propaganda had to be a set of instructions in the art of modifying character. That was how he put it in *Eyeless in Gaza*.

Huxley frequently used his authority to promote 'the peace business'. He had served with Heinrich Mann and André Gide as a patron of Klaus Mann's literary review. He asked his brother Julian to see if any major scientific body in Britain was prepared to send an official representative to a peace conference. He wrote political pamphlets and attended international gatherings, well aware of the prestige his reputation contributed to such events.

Huxley feared that the gathering in Paris would be an 'intolerable bore', but at the same time believed it was his duty to be present. Some of his émigré neighbours also accepted an invitation to Paris, while sharing Huxley's apathetic attitude. How, they wondered, could poets and artists, armed with pens and brushes, halt fighter planes? Like Huxley, Lion Feuchtwanger portrayed himself as the victim of subtle intellectual blackmail. He claimed he had agreed to go to the congress, after submitting to the 'joint efforts of the French and Russians', specifically André Malraux and Mikhail Koltsov, *Pravda*'s correspondent in Paris, and representative in France of the Soviet writers' union. Heinrich Mann went up from Nice, assured that he would figure prominently in the proceedings. Gide, Malraux, the pacifist Henri Barbusse and Romain Rolland jointly signed telegrams to Klaus Mann and others, 'strongly insisting' they take part and reply urgently.

Held during four sweltering June days, the congress was probably

'We Have Just Saved Culture'

the most impressive gathering of writers to take place in the ideologically fragmented 1930s. The Mutualité, a new *palais* just off Place Maubert in the Latin Quarter, belonged to the French Socialist movement's welfare insurance organisation. Its main auditorium, in the basement, could seat more than 2,000, while a smaller hall on the first floor could accommodate 900.

Each day, audiences running into many hundreds thronged the building to hear the writers – around 230 from nearly 40 countries. They ranged from major figures such as E. M. Forster, Berthold Brecht, Boris Pasternak and Robert Musil, to minor ones such as Paul Nizan, a schoolmate of Sartre's and a temporary convert to communism, and two Americans, Waldo Frank and Michael Gold. Trotskyist and conservative writers were simply unwelcome. Others were surprisingly and conspicuously absent, among them Thomas Mann, Stefan Zweig, Upton Sinclair, H. G. Wells and Bernard Shaw.

Officially, the point of the congress was to rally writers to the 'defence of culture', congress-speak for the persecution of intellectuals and the growing threat of war in Europe. Behind the nebulous phrase lay the intention to attract writers who normally steered clear of day-to-day politics, or who did not want to be too closely associated with communist demonstrations. That so many writers should have come at all to Paris was in itself a remarkable achievement. It reflected not only the writers' wish to demonstrate their support for the congress's goals but also its efficient organisation.

Although the congress was ostensibly a non-party occasion, several participants realised or at least assumed, even in the preparatory stage, that the Soviet Union was its chief sponsor. To most, it was clear that the prime impetus for the event came from Russian, German and French writers who, if they were not at that time Communist Party members, were at least active fellow travellers. Gide and Malraux, who dominated the congress proceedings, were prime examples.

International conferences at which writers and other intellectuals called on governments to avert war, defend culture and resist the fascist menace had been taking place in European capitals even before the Führer's ascendancy in 1933. There had been such a gathering in Berlin in 1929, while in 1932 Amsterdam was the venue of a significant anti-war assembly of pacifists, including Heinrich Mann and Albert Einstein.

In the 1920s, writers joined 'proletarian' or 'revolutionary' literary bodies set up to arouse 'progressive forces' to defend the Soviet

Union against those perceived campaigns to undermine it by the 'reactionary' forces of 'imperialist monopoly capitalism'. Prominent among these left-wing movements was the revolutionary writers' association, a kind of literary Communist International, based in the Soviet capital and often known by its Russian acronym, *Morp*. It provided the impetus behind the organisation of the Paris congress.

One of *Morp*'s chief co-ordinators in Paris and other émigré centres in Western Europe was the poet Johannes Becher, a German communist who found refuge in Paris and Moscow. With Gottfried Benn and Brecht, he was regarded as a legendary figure of the early Expressionist era, though their ideological paths then diverged. Many years later, Becher would write the words of East Germany's national anthem and become its first minister of culture.

The son of a judge, Becher was still at school when he bungled a suicide pact with his older lover. He shot her dead, while the three bullets he fired at himself left him gravely wounded. Thanks to his father's influence, a Munich court acquitted Becher, ruling that he had been mentally unstable at the time. He took to morphine and carried out a second unsuccessful suicide attempt. After studying philology, philosophy and medicine, Becher began to write Expressionist poetry with a strong left-wing bent. His verse became more distinctly proletarian in tone after he joined the German Communist Party in 1919. He paid his first visit to the Soviet Union in 1927, and in 1928 co-founded the association, or *Bund*, of German proletarian revolutionary writers. He was convinced that the Russian revolution heralded a Socialist utopia.

The doctrinaire tone of some of Becher's work bewildered even Klaus Mann, who had joined the association. Mann told the poet that he preferred his lyric verse to his enthusiastic 'hymns' to the Soviet Union. Betraying the doubts that filled his own mind, Mann said he envied Becher's conviction that the communists had almost achieved a paradise on earth. A book of Becher's verse published in 1925 contained such extreme language – it included a blasphemous Marxist 'Lord's Prayer' – that he was arrested on charges of treason. Although he was released after three days, following vehement protests by Feuchtwanger, Hesse, Thomas and Heinrich Mann, Maxim Gorky and Barbusse, his trial dragged on for nearly three years before he was amnestied.

Becher fled to Leipzig after the Reichstag fire, tipped off that storm-troopers would probably arrest him at his home in Berlin. Friends provided him with a false passport that allowed him to travel to Prague as a representative of the Leipzig fair. After reaching

'We Have Just Saved Culture'

Moscow in April 1933, Becher went on to become an official of the third Communist International, a member of the central committee of the German Communist Party, and the editor of a Marxist review. It was, however, in his capacity as a *Morp* representative that he mobilised German exile writers in France, as well as those French writers and artists who had set up their own revolutionary association.

Becher travelled to émigré centres in the west, primarily to herd 'progressive' German writers into active anti-fascist groups. The problem was that many had not fraternised in such a way in Weimar days. During the 1920s, Germany's bourgeois intellectuals and politicians proved unreceptive to communist calls for violent revolution and dictatorship of the proletariat. German Marxists had violently criticised liberals and social democrats for supporting the conservatives in vigorously repressing the communists.

After 1933, both sides recognised that years of bitter rivalry on the left had merely served to ease the National Socialists' advance to power. The Soviet authorities in Moscow also changed course: they prepared to exhort Europe's communists to emerge from their isolation and embrace the social democrats – whom they had previously denounced as 'social fascists' – as their *compagnons de route* in the struggle against the common enemy in Berlin.

Becher's two Moscow-inspired journeys to the west reflected the ideological about-turn in the Soviet Union. His first voyage, in the summer of 1933, took him to Prague, Vienna, Zurich and Paris. Shortly before he left, Brecht told him that left-wing writers were becoming discouraged and confused. Brecht had recently returned to his exile in Denmark after touring émigré centres. He found that it was getting harder for writers to continue their 'revolutionary production', now that they were widely dispersed and deprived of their former contact with the proletariat. As they had to spend more time on earning a living, they were compromising in all directions. They were turning to writing innocuous children's books, pseudonymous novels and 'kitschy' film-scripts with bourgeois concerns, Brecht complained.

Brecht urged Becher to organise a conference to work out ways in which 'colleagues' could fight back. 'Authoritative friends' such as leading communist journalists Karl Radek and Koltsov should attend – to give a lead and to help counter the émigré writers' diminishing sympathy for the Soviet Union. Brecht wanted such a meeting to set specific goals; one would be the publication of a new encyclopaedia that could serve as a reference work for criticising fascism.

In Vienna, Becher found three feuding groups of writers – Nazis, 'patriots' who supported the country's leader Engelbert Dollfuss, and a loose collection of left-wing radicals – but he nonetheless managed to set up an anti-fascist group. In Salzburg on the other hand, he was unable to call on Stefan Zweig and Carl Zuckmayer.

Further frustration awaited him in Paris, where he wasted many hours between appointments. Some German writers were on summer vacation and others were too busy, particularly those who were helping the leading German communist publicist Willi Münzenberg prepare his documentary *Brown Book on the Hitler Terror*.

Becher was shocked to find that about 30 German writers in exile knew little of the literary theory required of proletarian revolutionary writers. He diagnosed that some had sublimated their feelings of persecution and panic by absorbing Trotskyist ideas. One German émigré had become so deranged that he was muttering about the need for a second political party in Russia. To help these comrades 'catch up', Becher wanted to form a group to educate them, especially about the perils of Trotskyism in literature. As a form of education from below, he foresaw 'control' evenings at which participants would critically discuss writers' works. Some comrades told him the Communist Party should help writers improve their theoretical knowledge by inviting them to pay extended visits to the Soviet Union.

Looking at ways of expanding publishing prospects for the exiled German writers, Becher considered a suggestion that they draft booklets to be smuggled into the Reich, where many Germans apparently had a poor opinion of those who had fled the country. Some émigré publications alarmed him. Communist writers said they had stopped writing for one review, because it represented French imperialist interests. Another publication was suspect because a convicted fraudster edited it and because of hints that the French government financed it. Moreover, Becher learned, its bewildering mixture of articles included some by Zionist apologists and by writers hostile to the Communist Party.

Becher adduced an article about France as an example of the inadequate theoretical background of some émigré writers in Paris. The author referred to France as a 'free and happy' land, and proposed that French families invite German émigrés to their homes so that the two cultures could mingle with one another. The 'theoretical confusion' in the cultural section of Münzenberg's *Brown Book* on the Reichstag fire, which dealt indiscriminately with all banned and burnt books, further dismayed Becher.

'We Have Just Saved Culture'

From his meetings in Paris and elsewhere, Becher realised that not all refugee writers wanted to play a prominent part in the political resistance. Some worried that such a step could endanger relatives they had left behind in Germany. Others thought it could lead their host government to expel them. Even those bourgeois writers who felt that they ought to join in the struggle keenly debated the form their participation should take. Were writers whose work had hitherto ignored contemporary politics now supposed to move into the political arena? Could writers in exile simply carry on as if nothing had happened? Should their writing reflect their persecuted status? Or should true artists resist attempts to turn them into political agitators, following the example of Thomas Mann and Stefan Zweig? (Auden and Isherwood soon became disgusted with 'the united front, the party line, the anti-fascist struggle'. They resolved to 'be artists again', not 'amateur socialist agitators'.)

Fortunately for Becher, there was already a forum in Paris that served to indoctrinate politically receptive writers – the German writers' guild (*Schutzverband Deutscher Schriftsteller*). In Weimar Germany, its primary function had been to look after its members' commercial and legal interests. After Goebbels dissolved the guild, exiled members of the Berlin branch re-established the association in Paris in the summer of 1933. Militant Marxists soon brought the *Schutzverband* under communist influence and changed its raison d'être: the guild now expected its roughly 150 members to concentrate on the common struggle against Nazi Germany. Publicising the fate of politically persecuted writers, especially those languishing in German jails and camps, became one of its cardinal concerns. In May 1934, in a symbolic act of defiance, Heinrich Mann and Lion Feuchtwanger went to Paris to open the guild's 'freedom library' of works banned and burnt by the Nazis.

Guild activities included invitations to the public to hear exiled authors lecture or read from their works, or to discuss the writers' current output. The guild found for example that those of Feuchtwanger's novels dealing with the Nazi phenomenon were firmly against Hitler in theory, but remarkably unclear about how to destroy fascism in practice. A few weeks before the Paris congress, in a bid to refute contentions that there was no such thing as an 'exile literature', the guild published an anthology of work by authors considered to represent the new genre. Thomas Mann was not among them – nor were anti-communists living in France such as Joseph Roth and Leopold Schwarzschild. Most of the contributions were by 'socialist' writers.

It was also Becher's task while in Paris to rally left-leaning French writers. Inspired by the example of the international association of revolutionary writers in Moscow, André Gide, Henri Barbusse and Romain Rolland had in 1932 set up their *Association des Écrivains et Artistes Révolutionnaires*. Dedicated to the proposition that revolutionary writers and artists could not be neutral in purveying culture, the association expected its members to commit themselves – *s'engager* – to resisting the fascist danger and to developing a proletarian culture.

French intellectuals sensed an added urgency when in February 1934, a year after Hitler came to power, French right-wing groups provoked serious anti-Semitic riots in Paris. France's communists and socialists joined forces in an effort to extinguish the flames of fascism. Becher tried to build bridges between these left-wing French and German writers in Paris, but found that relations between the *Morp* in Moscow and the *Association* in Paris were poor. He saw a key *Association* figure, Louis Aragon, only twice, and then briefly and after much trouble; the French communist writer claimed he was too busy.

Becher returned to Moscow convinced that a west European base was necessary to prepare the literary assault on fascism. First major steps to that goal would be a well-organised international conference of anti-fascist writers, and a permanent secretariat. A publication was needed to refute Trotskyist arguments and to allow émigré intellectuals generally – doctors, teachers, scientists, architects – to express their views. Becher recommended that Moscow invite more writers to pay longer working visits to the Soviet Union. One of his goals here was to counter Trotskyist and social democrat critics who complained that Moscow was not doing enough to help the émigrés.

Becher made a special effort to enlist the support of well-known writers who had not taken a clear stand. He urged Eva Herrmann, who had been his lover in the 1920s and was now living in Sanary, to put pressure on Feuchtwanger, her current lover. He asked her to approach Heinrich Mann, who had not replied to letters from Moscow, as well as his brother Thomas. He tried to get Stefan Zweig to end his silence and write for Moscow-sponsored émigré publications.

He was able to work on some of the well-known *engagé* German and French writers, including Klaus Mann, Barbusse, Malraux and Aragon, when they attended the first Soviet writers' congress, held in Moscow in August 1934. The meeting has gone down in literary history as the occasion when the communists instituted 'socialist realism' for the arts.

'We Have Just Saved Culture'

Although some regarded the new cultural canon as a corset for left-wing writers, others saw it as a liberal step away from the communists' previous insistence that all literary endeavours take the form of 'agit-prop'. It reflected the radical change in Comintern policy as European communist leaders, shaken by the spreading fascist threat, prepared to hug their more moderate colleagues on the left.

Marxist writers could henceforth evoke conflict so long as it were finally resolved. They had to portray 'positive' heroes and a shining socialist future on the horizon. 'Zhdanovism' – after Andrei Zhdanov, the speaker who expounded the doctrine in Moscow – enjoined writers to reject 'bourgeois objectivity' with its emphasis on the shadowy side of life. Klaus Mann hoped the doctrine would disappear when the Soviet Union no longer felt itself so threatened.

The move to form a literary alliance was part of a broader campaign covering the arts – Hanns Eisler composed a stirring Popular-Front song – that was intended to prepare the way for a political anti-Hitler coalition. As Marxist literary theory changed, so did its vocabulary: instead of 'proletarian,' 'revolutionary' and the defamatory 'fellow-traveller', the communists adopted the blanket 'anti-fascist' to describe all those writers they wished to keep in, or entice into, their camp.

Stalin himself, even as he prepared to liquidate his opponents, indirectly helped Becher by making communism more respectable: the Soviet Union established diplomatic relations with the United States and joined the League of Nations in 1934. If the communists were now willing to moderate their previous dogmatic position, some social democrats were more than ready to meet them halfway, as Becher discovered on a second mission to the bourgeois world in October–November 1934. The Communist International had sent him to form an international organisation that would attract a broader spectrum of writers than the *Morp* had been doing; it would 'defend culture', rather than promote a proletarian revolution.

In the west, Becher learned that the Moscow writers' congress had encouraged foreign writers to join the anti-fascist cause, however indifferent or even hostile they might have been to Marxist doctrines. The idea of an international writers' congress was gaining ground, even if a few points remained unclear. Some émigré writers posed a question about Trotsky that Becher could not answer on the spot: had not the fascist upsurge in Germany, Austria and Spain confirmed predictions by the ostracised old Bolshevik, at the time in French exile, that Europe would pass through a reactionary period? If so, how could the communists continue to assert that their revolution was advancing, they wondered. Becher asked his superiors in Moscow to prepare an authoritative explanation.

As he conversed with the exiled writers in Paris, Becher came up against a peculiarly literary hurdle – the *Erbfrage*. In essence, the question was, who had 'inherited' Goethe and the other great German poets and playwrights of the past. Nazi cultural leaders had debated the issue. In 1934, a Berlin professor suggested to the annual meeting of the Goethe society in Weimar that Goethe and the other classical masters were the 'first National Socialists' – a bold assertion that sought to introduce a new layer of ideological legitimacy to the regime.

For a leading Nazi 'philosophical' authority such as Alfred Rosenberg, on the other hand, there was no room in the Nazi pantheon for someone who could never have accepted the 'dictatorship of a concept'. Later, Goebbels came to Goethe's defence by banning a book alleging the poet had murdered Schiller as part of a freemasons' conspiracy. So too did Baldur von Schirach, the half-American Nazi youth leader, who asserted that Goethe would have approved of pupils going to school in military uniform.

Nazi pretensions led émigré writers to dispute claims that Goethe would have been a Nazi had he been living a century or so later. Goethe's *Egmont*, for example, showed he would have been on their side, they insisted. So would Schiller; émigrés pointed to his *Don Carlos*, with its ringing plea for the removal of Spain's feudalistic and oppressive yoke from Flanders.

Unfortunately, some Marxist literary theorists preferred to 'disinherit' the German-language classics. They maintained that 'true' art and literature dated from the Bolshevik victory in Russia's civil war in 1921. Others held that genuine literature had to be distinctly anti-fascist. Even Heinrich Mann, a non-Marxist socialist, at one stage considered the earlier masters to be irrelevant in a post-bourgeois society. (Half a century later, publicists debated who had 'inherited' the author of *1984*. Had Orwell still been alive, Michael Foot was sure he would have been an old-style socialist. Across the Atlantic, Norman Podhoretz was certain he would have joined the neo-conservatives.)

Becher tried to persuade the sceptical among the refugees that the communists had not abandoned Germany's literary giants to the Nazis. Nor did they favour only topical political poems about tractors. They genuinely cared for literature in the broader sense. At the same time Becher urged his Moscow headquarters to accept that some contemporary poets and novelists wanted to deal with bourgeois 'problems' such as love, life and death rather than with the achievements of socialism. Party leaders should recognise that a work could be true German literature as long as it was not pro-fascist. They should understand that 'we' loved the real 'Germany' more than 'they' did (the fascists).

On a lecture trip in Prague, Heinrich Mann was happy to learn from Becher that the communists no longer rejected bourgeois literature as part of their cultural heritage. That helped Mann overcome his doubts. He expressed his enthusiasm for the proselytising Becher's initiatives and agreed to serve on the committee of international writers that was Becher's goal. Becher reciprocated by passing on to Moscow Mann's request that the Soviets pay his royalties in hard currency.

In preparing the international writers' congress, a major assignment for Becher was to overcome the rivalry among émigré publishers, and the suspicious way communist and other refugee writers regarded one another. He scored a point when he won over the writer Henri Barbusse to the idea of a broad anti-fascist association in Paris that would prove more welcoming to non-communist writers than the revolutionary, dogmatic *Morp*. Barbusse had become enormously influential after the publication of *Under Fire*, his novel about the horrors of war in the trenches.

By the end of 1934, Becher's plan for an international congress was well advanced. A crucial step in that direction was taken at a public meeting of the German writers' guild in December 1934, when Klaus Mann, André Malraux and Ilya Ehrenburg, *Izvestia*'s Paris correspondent – Victor Serge called him a 'hack agitator novelist' – reported positively on the Moscow writers' congress. Anna Seghers, a communist writer and member of the association of proletarian writers, proposed that the guild ask individuals and organisations to help assemble Western Europe's 'progressive' literary forces at such a congress, tentatively fixed for the summer of 1935.

Guild members unanimously approved what many thought to be Anna Seghers's 'spontaneous' suggestion. In fact, Becher, adept functionary that he was, had made sure beforehand of the Communist Party's blessing. Becher had also persuaded Moscow's cultural supervisors to let the French take the initiative. The German writers' guild agreed that it would be tactful to let the French host the congress and assume the main responsibility for its organisation.

Paris appeared the obvious conference venue, not only because many internationally recognised writers were living there, but also because the Soviet Union was about to conclude a mutual assistance pact with the French government. Barbusse and Malraux, assisted by Ehrenburg, supervised the drafting of a manifesto calling for a writers' congress. It was presented to a gathering of writers in the Café Voltaire, and published by *Le Monde* in April. By the end of May 1935, Maria Osten, Koltsov's companion, could report from Paris to Klaus Mann that the French were blazing with enthusiasm: they were asserting that the congress would be a 'world event'.

Feuchtwanger and Heinrich Mann agreed to sign the manifesto, perhaps the result in part of Eva Herrmann's entreaties on Becher's behalf. In the following months national delegations met in Paris cafés to choose themes, speakers and guests. The pro-Soviet Malraux and Aragon headed the French group, while Ehrenburg and Mikhail Koltsov were in charge of the Soviet one. Alfred Kantorowicz, the communist writer who had been instrumental in setting up the German 'Freedom Library', and Gustav Regler, another communist writer who later served as a political commissar with the international brigades in the Spanish Civil War, helped Becher run the German branch.

Despite the inevitable last-minute financial problems and disputes over the division of responsibilities, Gide opened the congress on schedule. In the uninspiring words of the invitation, writers had come here to clarify the conditions of literary creation, and relations between writers and their public. Their purpose was to defend the culture that was under threat in some countries, which remained nameless.

Aragon, Barbusse and Malraux sat on the dais with Gide, emphasising the French character of the event. Klaus Mann's review *Die Sammlung* published a drawing by Eva Herrmann of Barbusse and Malraux on the dais. Maxim Gorky was originally down to represent the Soviet Union but withdrew, allegedly because of ill health. At the last minute, the Soviets sent Isaac Babel and Boris Pasternak as substitutes.

E. M. Forster, who headed the British delegation, failed to persuade Rebecca West, J. B. Priestley or Virginia and Leonard Woolf to join him. Like Huxley, Forster went along unenthusiastically: 'I don't suppose the conference is of any use – things have gone too far,' he told Virginia Woolf. At the same time he was sure that people like themselves, representing 'the last utterances of the civilised', had a duty to be present.

As speakers expounded during afternoon and evening sessions on a range of abstract topics – humanism, culture and the nation, the writer's role in society – a festive ambience surrounded the gathering.

'We Have Just Saved Culture'

Authors autographed their books, which were on sale in the foyer. Children presented flowers to writers. The beer flowed freely.

Gide created a sensation by publicly supporting communism, but it proved to be a short-lived conversion. Huxley and John Strachey dealt with the writer's role in society. Gaetano Salvemini reported on the persecution of intellectuals in Italy. Heinrich Mann described 'Les problèmes de la création et la dignité de la pensée.' Feuchtwanger recalled that historical novels were more than entertainment – they could also serve as a weapon in the ideological struggle. André Malraux recited a French translation of a poem by Pasternak. In a brief address, the Russian poet himself concentrated on his ailments.

Brecht's speech contradicted the congress goal of bringing communists and liberals closer together. His Marxist analysis turned into an attack on German liberals for refusing to link Nazi terror to capitalist conditions of property ownership. Not surprisingly, his words found little echo, even in the 'red' press. The Soviets' banishment of the Belgian-born revolutionary Victor Serge led to fierce wrangles, while moves to prevent the surrealist André Breton from speaking caused disturbances.

A contemporary photograph shows Forster, in a dark suit and waistcoat, standing behind a table and microphone as he addressed the first session. Sitting at the table is André Malraux, who had suggested guidelines for the English novelist's address. Forster rejected his interference, stating that he would make the same speech, whatever the title chosen. The title turned out to be 'Liberty in England', but his remarks do not seem to have impressed his audience. For one thing, Forster's own words were mostly inaudible as he did not use the microphone. What the audience heard from his interpreter, moreover, was probably not what they had expected. Forster's message was less about the threat the Continental dictators posed to England's liberty than about the censorship, secrecy and petty tyranny of the kingdom's own 'Fabio-Fascism'.

Inevitably, a certain tedium set in. The celebrated writers were not necessarily talented orators. Many speeches lost in translation whatever sparkle they may have had in the original. Some contributions were inordinately long. Malraux spoke for nearly an hour. Barbusse's oration and its consecutive translation lasted three-quarters of an hour and sent many into the foyer in search of refreshments. Émigré writers found much of the proceedings deadly boring, even though the congress was supposed to help them. They thought speakers stated the obvious – at great length – and argued about the wording of a resolution as if it were a complicated sales contract.

Klaus Mann had several criticisms. There was no contact between speakers and the public. He found Robert Musil's remarks very weak. He thought Kisch's address had barely reached the level of a speech that one expected to hear at a trade union assembly, and it was discourteous of the Czech journalist to speak for 45 minutes in German.

Huxley, who had expected 'serious, technical discussions', complained to Gide that there were too many communist paeans. Reviewing the congress in the *New Statesman*, Forster objected that some speakers had been journalists rather than creative artists, while others 'were congress-addicts who would travel any distance for their drug'.

One event that electrified the dozing audience was the sensational appearance of a masked speaker. Presented under the pseudonym 'Jan Petersen', he was a communist novelist and essayist who had slipped out of Berlin to assure his audience that in a land of hangmen there were still writers who were fighting for a better Germany. 'Petersen', who had been smuggling reports of Nazi terror to an exile periodical in Prague, did not return to Germany. He learned that an informer had betrayed his group in Berlin. Instead, he fled to Britain and penned early accounts of the resistance in Germany; Gollancz published his *Gestapo Trial* and Hutchinson his *Germany Beneath the Surface: Stories of the Underground Movement*.

One of Becher's anxieties during the congress was that a hostile participant might denounce the proceedings as communist-inspired. His close colleague Regler unintentionally did so, and threw Becher into a panic. As Regler was about to address a session presided over by Gide and Barbusse, the sight of so many faces – the *Internationale* of writers – looking attentively at him raised his spirits. He put aside his prepared text, pulled two pamphlets from his pocket, brandished them and challenged the Gestapo informers he presumed were in the hall to mount the tribune and examine them.

Handing the brochures to Gide and Barbusse, Regler said that Nazi agents had not prevented the resistance from smuggling copies of the pamphlets into Germany. The enemy would never throttle the writers' voices, their affection for the workers or their passion for the truth, he declaimed. His emotional words roused the audience into standing up and singing the *Internationale*. Regler then noticed Becher, offstage, gesticulating desperately at him. Wondering why, Regler advanced towards him.

'You have gone completely mad,' a livid Becher shrieked, according to the memoirs Regler wrote after he had broken with the communists.

'Can't you hear what they are singing?' an elated Regler responded.

'The *Internationale*, you idiot, of course I can. Now we have been unmasked, this is no longer a neutral congress, you are going to be thrown out of the party,' Becher cried, striking his forehead with his two fists.

As the singing continued, with Gide and the other presiding members all on their feet, Regler tried to reassure Becher that news of such a spontaneous event would cross the Rhine. Unmoved, Becher denounced Regler as a saboteur. Later the Communist Party reprimanded him: it was not a comrade's prerogative to decide when to sing the *Internationale*; with the Popular Front governing France, prudence was necessary. After Regler pleaded that the anthem had gushed from people's hearts, Anna Seghers told him to 'quit that sentimental drivel; this is a question of tactics'.

How significant was the Paris congress? Its ringing calls for writers to defend humanism against barbarism attracted wide attention. To continue its work, it set up a committee in Paris. Despite their misgivings, Forster and Huxley agreed to join; so did Gide, Barbusse, Heinrich Mann, Bernard Shaw and Sinclair Lewis. A second congress followed in Spain in 1937.

Even at the time, though, it was easy to ridicule the whole enterprise. What especially disappointed some participants was the way 'red gold' had financed, staged and dominated the congress. Huxley thought the gathering had missed an opportunity to achieve something more. He returned to Sanary, upset at the way French communist writers had exploited the congress to thrust themselves into the limelight, and the Russians to disseminate Soviet propaganda. The communist organisers' cynical indifference to the 'wretched little delegates from the Balkans' had appalled him. Writers had hoped for more understanding of their problems; instead, they 'found only endless communist demagogy in front of an audience of 2,000 people'.

For Huxley, the congress brought out the worst aspects of religion in the guise of communism: the refusal of people to use their intelligence because they needed the consolation of faith; and the cynical ambition of those who did not believe in anything, but were anxious to rise in the hierarchy. Ironically, a committee of the United States Congress would in 1951 classify Huxley as 'a communist fellow-traveler'.

For the apostate Victor Serge, who was not present, the 'communist back rooms' that specialised in organising congresses of that kind wanted 'to arouse a pro-Stalinist movement among the French intelligentsia and buy over a number of famous consciences'. Sylvia Beach, proprietor of the celebrated Left Bank bookshop, Shakespeare and Company, also condemned the 'strongly communistic' nature of the meeting. Forster said he agreed to sit on its executive board, less to strengthen the intellectual resistance to Hitler, than to prevent the communists from dominating it. He appealed to other British writers to do likewise.

A sarcastic Brecht made his 'important announcement' that 'we have just saved culture. It required four days, and we decided to sacrifice everything rather than let culture perish. We are willing to sacrifice ten to 20 million people, if necessary. Thank God, there were enough people willing to assume the responsibility for that.' Brecht told Becher the congress had been a success, especially bearing in mind that its committees had organised it in a hurry and with little money. Partly to ensure there would be an accurate record of his speech, he asked Becher to issue the speeches in book form and send copies to major newspapers. Brecht explained that a Swiss journal had upset him by publishing a garbled version of his address: 'I did not say what it reported, and it did not report what I said.'

With the benefit of hindsight, non-communist historians have had harsh words for 'one of the most thoroughly rigged and steam-rollered assemblages ever perpetrated on the face of Western literature in the name of culture and freedom'. The 'turgid deliberations' produced 'pedestrian' consequences. It was 'a carefully staged piece of intellectual theatre, designed to prepare the intellectual elite for the Popular Front'. Chroniclers judged that 'Stalin's congress' did not influence history, but benefited 'a militant party subservient to a terroristic foreign state.' Gustav Regler's account of the *Internationale* incident substantiated views that Gide and Malraux were Comintern puppets. (After the war, the US Central Intelligence Agency covertly funded the congress for 'cultural freedom' that took place in West Berlin in 1950.)

At the time, however, the Paris congress fulfilled the expectations of many German writers. Becher drafted enthusiastic reports for Moscow. He thought the evening on which Gide and Malraux spoke was of historical importance, while Aragon's polemic against the Surrealists had been extraordinarily effective. Becher praised the British delegation and the especially 'profitable' speeches by Forster and Huxley. He believed the congress had convinced Huxley, who was sceptical beforehand, of the need to work 'with us'. A few months later, Becher tried to get 'an original contribution' from

Huxley for *International Literature,* a Moscow-based review. 'We definitely need work from English friends,' he told Anna Seghers.

Klaus Mann thought the congress had splendidly achieved its goal of parading the great anti-fascist names. Joseph Roth admired the way speeches had unmasked the enemy and defended the émigrés' work. More generally, the émigré writers believed their participation had heightened concern about the merciless way the Nazis were dealing with German culture. Their public protests received wide and generally favourable press coverage. The congress brought them into the fold of internationally acknowledged authors, and reassured them that many influential writers stood at their side. They were satisfied that its work would continue. Émigré organisations in Paris welcomed the way the congress drew the world's attention to the fate of German anti-fascists in exile and political prisoners in Germany.

If the results achieved at the Mutualité were mundane, they were probably no more disappointing than those of other international protest meetings of intellectuals. If the communists did steamroller the congress, that was partly because no other group was sufficiently motivated and organised. As the writer Manes Sperber put it, even if you were a non-communist or a disillusioned communist émigré writer, you saw no alternative.

The overwhelming support for Hitler in the Saar plebiscite convinced the émigrés that a proletarian revolt was not going to happen in Germany. And it was obvious that the western democracies were too spineless to call Hitler's bluff. Believing that dissidence within the anti-Nazi opposition would weaken Moscow's struggle against Hitler, they were prepared, reluctantly, to make allowances for Stalin's purges, which were still to reach their zenith.

The Mutualité meeting was a well-planned and well-executed step in Moscow's new strategy of creating a broad political front against Hitler – a goal officially endorsed by the seventh world congress of the Communist International, held in Moscow the following month. The flow of speeches and discussions in Paris had helped to win over the socialist and radical press, and thereby large swathes of public opinion, to the idea of common action. More than that: the Mutualité audience had witnessed the advent of an émigrés' leader – Heinrich Mann.

When Mann mounted the podium, the many hundreds who had assembled in the huge hall at first remained silent as a mark of respect for the writer. Then the crowd rose and broke out into prolonged applause. The standing ovation left Mann visibly moved. The émigrés, both liberals and those to the left, acknowledged his position as 'a kind of Hindenburg of the exiled', as 'our secret Kaiser'. For Heinrich Mann's nephew Klaus, it was the culmination of the whole proceedings; a rare occasion when the audience stood up in homage to a participant (another was when they stood up to pay their respects to René Crevel, a friend of Klaus Mann's and one of the French organisers, who committed suicide during the congress).

Heinrich Mann had come to personify the 'other' – the struggling, suffering and exiled – Germany. With the Popular Front movement gathering strength in Spain and France, the émigré writers wanted to believe that the anti-fascist resistance was turning from the defensive to the offensive. They looked to Mann to harness and lead them in the coming anti-fascist crusade.

1 Sanary shortly after the war. After 1933 the small port near Toulon became a haven for persecuted German-language writers.
Roger-Viollet/Topfoto

2 A gathering at the Huxleys' home in Sanary: Marta Feuchtwanger, the novelist Arnold Zweig, who emigrated to Palestine, the 'lost generation' American writer William Seabrook (centre), and Lion Feuchtwanger (far right).
Courtesy of University of Southern California, on behalf of the USC Specialized Libraries and Archival Collections

3 Should he return to Germany? That was the question that tormented Thomas Mann as he sat on the terrace of the villa he rented in Sanary during the summer of 1933.
Bildarchiv Preussischer Kulturbesitz

4 *Die Brennessel* (nettle), the Nazi satirical magazine published from 1931 to 1938, caricatures Heinrich Mann as Marlene Dietrich in *Der Blaue Engel*. The acclaimed film was based on his 1904 novel, *Professor Unrat*.
Bildarchiv Preussischer Kulturbesitz/Kunstbibliothek, SMB/Dietmar Katz

5 A portrait of Lion Feuchtwanger's gymnastic wife Marta by Walter Bondy. The Prague-born writer, artist and photographer was part of Sanary's émigré community.
Photo © Walter Bondy. Collection of the Bibliothèque Municipale de Toulon

6 Lion Feuchtwanger, whose historical novels were popular in many languages in the 1930s, stayed in Sanary until the advent of the Second World War.
Bildarchiv Preussischer Kulturbesitz

7 Eva Herrmann, a gifted American-Jewish caricaturist who was a friend of Sybille Bedford. As Lion Feuchtwanger's lover, Herrmann accompanied him during his visit to the Soviet Union. Photograph by Walter Bondy.
Photo © Walter Bondy. Collection of the Bibliothèque Municipale de Toulon

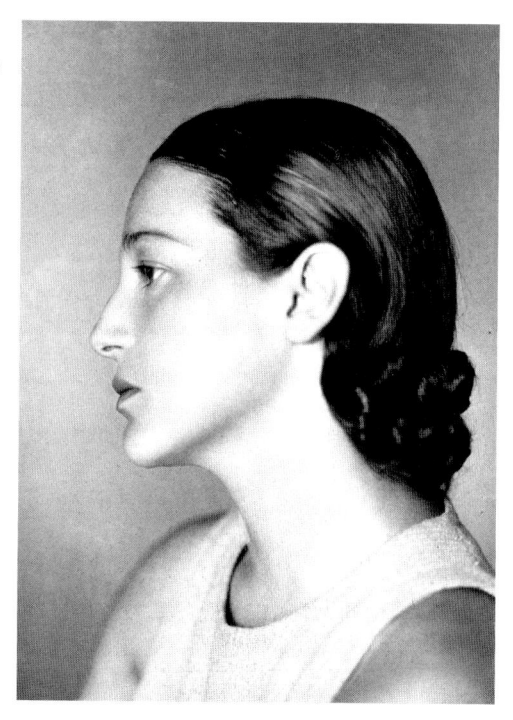

8 Thomas Mann's eldest son, Klaus, who founded a literary review for the refugee writers. The portrait is by Fred Stein, a German lawyer who became a renowned photographer after he fled to France and then to the United States.
Bildarchiv Preussischer Kulturbesitz/Fred Stein

9 Gottfried Benn, a leading expressionist poet who surprised the émigrés by siding with Hitler. The Nazis banned his writings after he changed his views.
© SV-Bilderdienst/Scherl

10 German students cheer while Goebbels harangues the crowd. The anti-Nazi cartoon depicts the notorious book-burning that students organised across the country in May 1933.
Bildarchiv Preussischer Kulturbesitz

11 H. G. Wells was president of the writers' 'international parliament', PEN. Its congress, held just after the book-burning, had to decide how to deal with PEN's German branch, which the Nazis had taken over.
TopFoto

12 Imprisoned after trying to set up a soviet republic in Bavaria after the First World War, the pacifist writer Ernst Toller fled from Germany in 1933. The brilliant orator's appearance at the 1933 PEN congress threw it into turmoil.
© Bettmann/Corbis

13 Thomas Mann's publisher Gottfried Bermann-Fischer, who took over the famous Fischer Verlag from his father-in-law. Reluctant to lose his lucrative German market, he at first tried to keep the Jewish firm in Berlin, but was finally forced to leave the country.
ullstein bild Berlin

14 Thomas Mann's eldest daughter Erika, who was instrumental in persuading him, after years of hesitation, to break with Nazi Germany. The portrait is by Lotte Jacobi, a distinguished photographer who emigrated from Germany to the United States in 1935.
Bildarchiv Preussischer Kulturbesitz/Lotte Jacobi

15 What one authority has called 'Far and away the best of all German émigré publications': Leopold Schwarzschild took the weekly he edited with him into exile, renaming it *Das Neue Tage-Buch*.
Bildarchiv Preussischer Kulturbesitz/SBB

16 Leopold Schwarzschild infuriated the Moscow-friendly émigrés in Paris because he condemned Stalin's totalitarian methods. Photograph by Fred Stein.
© FredStein.com (photo: Deutsche Nationalbibliothek, Deutsches Exilarchiv 1933–1945, Frankfurt)

17 Eva Herrmann caricatures two of the leading French participants at the Paris writers' congress in 1935: Henri Barbusse, who died that year and who achieved fame through his literary depiction of the horrors of *La Grande Guerre*; and André Malraux, one of France's leading anti-fascist intellectuals. Married at the time to a German-Jewish heiress, Malraux in 1935 published a novel about a communist imprisoned by the Nazis.
© DACS 2006

18 Lion Feuchtwanger and Bertolt Brecht at the 1935 writers' congress. In that year Brecht, whose exile was nomadic, completed his *Fear and Misery in the Third Reich*, based on eyewitness and newspaper accounts of life in Hitler's Germany.
Bildarchiv Preussischer Kulturbesitz/Fred Stein

19 André Gide looks up at E. M. Forster as he addresses the writers' congress in Paris. Forster was active in PEN and had recently become the first president of Britain's National Council for Civil Liberties. Gide, after strongly backing communism, became an apostate at the time of the Moscow purges, exasperating those on the far left.
Roger-Viollet/Topfoto

20 A portrait by Walter Bondy of Aldous Huxley, who wrote *Brave New World* while living in Sanary. Huxley was active in what he called the 'peace business'.
Photo © Walter Bondy. Collection of the Bibliothèque Municipale de Toulon

21 Georg Bernhard, who had edited one of Germany's most illustrious newspapers. Forced to flee Berlin in 1933, he that same year started a German-language daily in Paris for the refugees.
ullstein bild Berlin

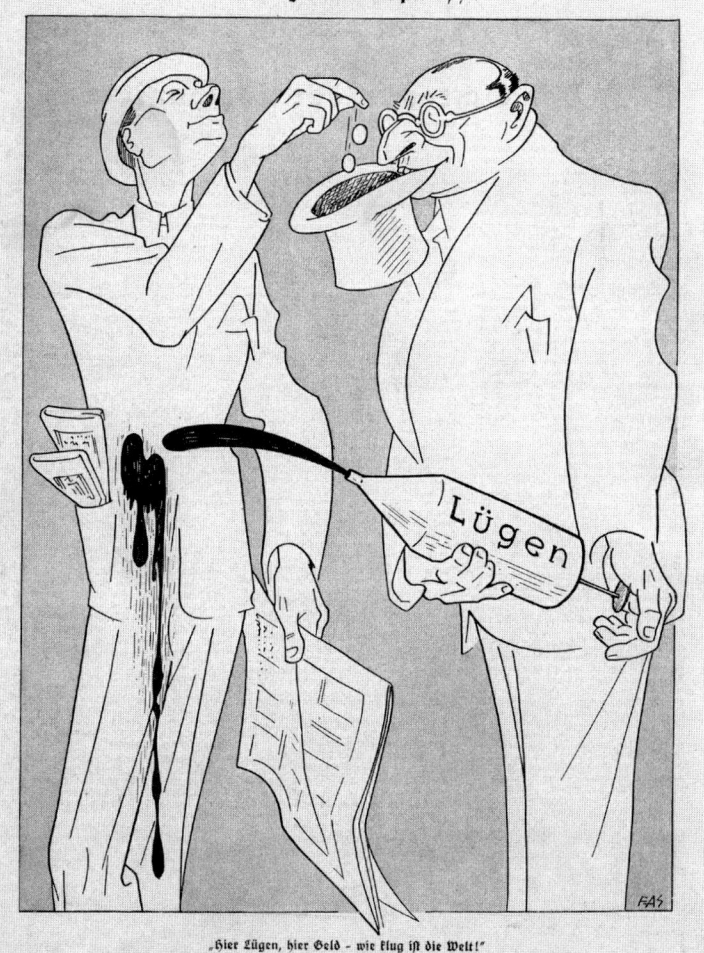

22 The political cartoon was a common Nazi propaganda weapon and the many brilliant German journalists in Parisian exile were a favourite target. 'You pay, we lie' is the caption to this one.
Photo courtesy Randall Bytwerk, German Propaganda Archive

23 'The émigré press … and its lies factory at work': this 1934 cartoon shows that the Nazis took the émigré press seriously.
Bildarchiv Preussischer Kulturbesitz

24 Heinrich Mann and André Gide, both of whom had their best work behind them by the late 1930s. While Gide would spend most of the war years in North Africa and receive the Nobel Prize in 1947, Mann escaped over the Pyrenees to Hollywood, where he vegetated until his death.
Roger-Viollet/Topfoto

25 'The pen is mightier …': the bodies of the Nazi and fascist dictators hanging from the pen of Walter Trier, yet another refugee from Hitler. He is remembered for his book illustrations, such as those for Erich Kästner's *Emil and the Detectives*, and his many covers for the *New Yorker* and for *Lilliput*, the pocket magazine that entertained British readers during the war.
© Walter Trier Estate, Canada (photo: Stiftung Archiv der Akademie der Künste, Berlin/Roman März)

26 Thomas Mann in Frankfurt, on his first post-war visit to Germany, in 1949. He ran into criticism for ignoring the Cold War division of Europe and going on the same trip to Weimar in East Germany. Both German states had wanted him to take part in their celebrations to mark the 200th anniversary of Goethe's birth.
Time Life Pictures/Getty Images

15 'I Came, I Saw, I Shall Write'

Feuchtwanger's Misguided Mission to Moscow

Like her husband, Marta Feuchtwanger enjoyed living on the Sanary peninsula, surrounded by water and cliffs. She nonetheless considered the Villa Lazare too small, primitive and especially unsuitable during cold spells. As the house-owner refused to improve the heating, the Feuchtwangers resolved to move. While her husband escaped to Paris for a few weeks, Marta began house-hunting again. She was not entirely mobile, having suffered a severe leg injury in a car accident. Maria Huxley had swiftly called a doctor and an ambulance, and alerted the hospital in Toulon.

By March 1934, the Feuchtwangers had found a house, comfortably but ordinarily furnished, some 20 minutes' walk from the Café de Lyon, on the way to Bandol. As Feuchtwanger could not stand noise, he rented the whole house, though the owner had converted it into three units. It was on three floors, had three kitchens, three bathrooms, three garages and some 18 rooms. The Villa Valmer, renamed Villa La Calanco, still exists on a south-facing slope on the Avenue Beausoleil, among other large freestanding villas in generous gardens.

Huxley, perhaps exaggerating, reported the 'exciting news' that the former Feuchtwanger residence, Villa Lazare, would be rechristened 'La Case à Papa' and turned into 'a bordel'. Huxley told friends that, when they next came down, they would know where to spend 'the tedious hours when inspiration flags and books seem to have lost their appeal'. According to Feuchtwanger's version, the villa was to serve as a night-club.

The move revived Marta's joie de vivre. Her only child had died as a baby, and she was inclined to pessimism. Her sharp tongue sometimes embarrassed her husband. Angered by what she regarded as foolish luxuries, she was of a thrifty and ascetic disposition; her slim figure reflected her fondness for sport, gymnastics in particular. Now, however, she enjoyed the house's fine view of the sea and islands, as well as its olives, figs, almonds and other fruits and nuts. She enthusiastically devoted time to the garden, with its daffodils, hyacinths, mimosa, geraniums, a rose garden, and the bougainvillaea that sheltered the terrace. She cultivated peas, artichokes, radishes and beans. She put up a chicken coop so that her husband could have fresh eggs in winter. Even in January, it was warm enough for her to watch Lion play with the cat in the garden (he hated dogs).

Marta busied herself with refurbishing the new home. She altered the garish wallpaper and, to ensure that her husband enjoyed the necessary tranquillity for his writing, wasted no time in turning one of the bathrooms into a library. Marta believed her alterations to the villa were of a provisional nature. Even though there seemed little that was ephemeral about her arrangements, in those first years of exile neither of them really believed, or wanted to believe, that the Germans would tolerate Hitler for much longer. As the crisis in Europe deepened, however, they, like so many other émigrés, slowly began to realise that they had bade a definitive good-bye to Berlin.

Lion, meanwhile, laboured on his historical trilogy *Josephus*, ordering books to replace the thousands he had lost in Berlin, or borrowing works from the London Library. Sometimes, Marta would listen to him reading from his work. Besides his books, Feuchtwanger had lost much of his fortune and other possessions when he fled Germany. His name was on the first list, published in August 1933 by the *Reichsanzeiger*, the official government gazette, of persons stripped of their German citizenship because of 'disloyalty to the German Reich and the German people'. Munich University rescinded the doctorate it had conferred upon him (restoring it after the war).

Feuchtwanger, nonetheless, felt at home and managed to live well in his fine villa. He sometimes did not leave the house for days. Though not a sporty type like his wife, Feuchtwanger joined her in a morning round of gymnastics. He considered himself a good swimmer, but an indifferent dancer. Huxley observed him through binoculars as he walked around his house 30 times in bathing trunks. Feuchtwanger would then climb down the steep cliff and enjoy a swim in the sea. Marta supervised her husband's physical exertions and spurred him on.

Supposedly on a diet, Feuchtwanger was something of a gourmet. He cleared the plates of snacks after Marta had gone shopping. He enjoyed contemplating which restaurants he would sample on his next visit to Paris, and which type of oyster and wine he would order. In a corner of the garden, the couple would grill fish, pigeons and rabbits on charcoal and rosemary. If Marta had to go into the kitchen, Lion would keep guard so that cats snatched nothing away.

The couple had an efficient maid, whose only fault was that she drank.

Even the precarious existence of a refugee did not upset Lion's methodical work habits. While he never attained the literary heights of Thomas Mann or Stefan Zweig, Feuchtwanger was virtually as successful in exile as he had been in Germany, for the simple reason that his works were also extremely popular in translation. Businesslike in his dealings with publishers and filmmakers, he saw himself as an industrious master of his craft, rather than as a genius.

After Thomas Mann moved to Switzerland, towards the end of 1933, Feuchtwanger became Sanary's best-known German writer in residence. To mark his 50th birthday, in 1934, Klaus Mann published in his review congratulatory messages from more than a dozen famous writers – among them Brecht, André Maurois and Joseph Roth. Huxley's was the shortest: 'Congratulations and best wishes.' Huxley had explained to Klaus beforehand that 'je suis dans une situation un peu difficile, car je n'ai jamais lu un de ses livres.'

Feuchtwanger acquired a stately eight-cylinder Talbot convertible, the fruit of his re-established success. Marta used it to bring friends and acquaintances to the villa from as far away as Nice. Chauffeured by his wife, the writer would pass other émigrés and occasionally, if they were lucky, alight from the vehicle to grant them a two-minute audience. They disdainfully referred to him as 'Lion the Great'.

Lion and Marta lived in the Villa Valmer until 1940. They invited Brecht, Arnold Zweig and other friends who shared their fate to visit them, particularly in the summer months. In the evenings, guests might often wander down to one of the cafés around the harbour. In September 1936, one of their guests recorded with a touch of hyperbole that 'half the emigration' had assembled in Sanary for a large tea party at the Feuchtwangers.

Like a child showing off his toy soldiers, Feuchtwanger would lead first-time visitors to his library on the first floor of the villa. Perhaps the bibliophile would show them some of the valuable collector's items on his shelves. While browsing in Paris bookshops he had gradually replaced some of the many books he had lost in Berlin. But he was more likely to invite them to admire translations of his own works into unusual languages such as Coptic and Albanian. Feuchtwanger invariably tried to impress friends and critics alike with statistics about the many readers around the globe reading one of his works at any given moment. His continuing worldwide success, even in exile, confirmed his own high opinion of himself as a writer. At the same time, the apparently effortless way in which he had resumed his comfortable way of life aroused the jealousy of his peers. As his secretary saw it, Feuchtwanger might generously help nine refugees less fortunate than himself, but if he refused the tenth, he would be called a miser.

Feuchtwanger's serenity, even in those most agitated times, impressed his neighbours. While the wild rumours that followed the assassination in Marseilles in 1934 of the French foreign minister Louis Barthou and King Alexander of Yugoslavia were leading other refugees to panic that the police might arrest them, Feuchtwanger lay in bed reading Plutarch. Klaus Mann always found Lion good-humoured and optimistic. Other friends and visitors regarded him as an amiable but superficial and monotonous personality. Aldous Huxley was among those who mocked his seemingly self-centred ways.

Feuchtwanger knew that erotic passages enhanced a novel's chance of success. He thought sex played a much smaller role in English novels of the era than it did in French and German fiction. He himself could give the impression of an ardent lover, even if he rarely opened up his heart in his letters and diaries. Although nervous and unattractive, his fame helped him win partners who satisfied not only his sexual desire, but also his need for praise. While many of his letters were sober, conventional and primarily concerned with publishing matters, his diaries, written in a form of shorthand, were notable above all for the meticulous way the stubby and apparently shy writer recorded his many sexual encounters. He was not averse to putting down cryptic but passionate references to stroking the breasts and other parts of a lover's body. At the same time, Feuchtwanger failed to appreciate his wife's jealousy. He complained about the 'egg dance' he had to perform between his wife, his secretary Lola Sernau, and the American artist Eva Herrmann, referring caustically to his wife's 'petty' or 'frightful Strindbergian' behaviour.

Congregating in Sanary's cafés, other émigrés would indulge in malicious gossip about Feuchtwanger, and especially about the many affairs that he supposedly enjoyed. His liaison with Eva Herrmann, a friend of the Mann family who shared a house with Sybille Bedford in the hills behind Sanary, was open and long-standing. Of German-Jewish origin, Herrmann was 17 years his junior, attractive and discreet. She was the great love of his life in the years of French exile, as the many letters he wrote to her testify. She had studied art in Germany and left a large collection of caricatures of famous writers of the period, from Maugham and Gide to Hemingway and, of course, Feuchtwanger himself. She designed covers for a number of

'I Came, I Saw, I Shall Write'

Feuchtwanger's books. It was Eva who accompanied him when he visited the Soviet Union, while Marta stayed behind. Eva Herrmann would later welcome Lion and Marta when they resettled near her in Los Angeles after fleeing from Europe.

It was in the summer of 1936 that the Soviet writers' union invited Lion Feuchtwanger to visit Russia. Mikhail Koltsov, *Pravda*'s correspondent in Paris, and his young German companion Maria Osten came down to Sanary to deliver the proposal to him personally. Koltsov was the member of the Soviet writers' union responsible for maintaining links with writers in France. Victor Serge, the Belgian-born Russian revolutionary writer banished to the Russian hinterland, thought Koltsov was 'a man as remarkable for his talent as for his pliant docility'. Maria Osten was a Communist journalist and cultural functionary in Moscow. The couple were on their way to Spain, where Franco had just launched his insurrection against the Republicans. Koltsov's task was to support the anti-Franco international brigades by publicising their role in the civil war.

Feuchtwanger had been hoping to visit Maxim Gorky, a Russian writer he admired who had been suffering from tuberculosis. Koltsov and Osten, who had met Feuchtwanger during his visits to Paris, appalled him when they recounted the shocking story that a 'Trotskyist' doctor had 'murdered' Gorky in June 1936. The doctor had supposedly frightened the ailing writer to death by telling him that he did not have long to live. The Soviets put the doctor on trial and executed him. Years later, stories went the rounds that Stalin had ordered the death of Gorky.

In an era when Stalin was equally abhorred and worshipped abroad, many left-leaning intellectuals and politicians wanted to see for themselves whether communism offered a third way of running a country, one that was superior to both brutal Nazi totalitarianism and to the unbridled bourgeois capitalism that had left the world in such an economic mess. The communists' propaganda activities, like those of governments and international organisations since, included a programme whereby the Kremlin encouraged distinguished personalities whose views were deemed to influence public opinion – 'multipliers' in the technical parlance of a later era – to make their own fact-finding tour.

Through its total control of the Soviet media, Moscow ensured that the guests' presence received wide publicity while they were admiring Soviet achievements, an attention that usually flattered them. Moscow would lay out the red carpet in particular for prominent figures from the West, such as Feuchtwanger and André

Gide, who were not party members, aware that sceptics would give more credence to their utterances than to those of the faithful.

Typical of such visitors was André Malraux, who travelled to Russia in 1934 accompanied by Ilya Ehrenburg, a well-known Russian Jewish foreign correspondent of the period. A sample of the conclusions brilliant but naive political scientists might draw were those of Britain's Harold Laski. He believed Stalin's chief prosecutor in the show trials, Andrei Vyshinsky, was a man whose passion was law reform and who was doing what any ideal minister of justice would do, 'if we had such a person in Great Britain'.

There was another reason why writers undertook the journey to Moscow. The Soviet Union didn't belong to the international copyright convention (it joined in 1970), and was prone to publish foreign writers' work without permission or payment of royalties. The Soviets would, however, allow favoured writers to open a ruble account, which they could use to travel in style during their visit. The Soviets might also invite such writers to negotiate film and other rights, making them eligible for further royalties.

Such was the case with Feuchtwanger. The Russians had hitherto simply published his works without paying. In September 1935, they pleasantly surprised him by doing so for the first time. Explaining that it had become possible for them to pay royalties, they sent him 4,000 francs, though he had not claimed anything.

Feuchtwanger was not a communist, but his sympathies certainly lay in that direction. He and his family were victims of Hitler. Feuchtwanger was convinced that Stalin was a more determined opponent of fascism than were the Western leaders. Like many others at the time, he cursed them for failing to oppose both Hitler when he marched into the Rhineland, and Mussolini when he invaded Abyssinia.

The Comintern was now preaching co-operation between communists and other anti-fascist forces. That had been the goal that the international congress of writers, attended by Feuchtwanger, had set itself in Paris in 1935. That too was the policy of Léon Blum's French Popular Front government, formed in May 1936, an event that profoundly influenced the Germans in French exile.

Unfortunately for Feuchtwanger and other Moscow sympathisers trying to unite the fragmented émigré resistance, Stalin was making it increasingly difficult for them to extol the workers' paradise. Following the assassination at the end of 1934 of Sergei Kirov, the Communist Party leader in Leningrad, Stalin had inaugurated a reign of terror involving political trials, deportations and executions of former Bolshevik allies. While Feuchtwanger was in Moscow, Stalin had opened another show trial in the capital. Stalin wished to eliminate further personalities, after forcing them to confess that they had conspired with foreign powers and the exiled Leon Trotsky, Lenin's former comrade-in-arms, to overthrow the state.

Feuchtwanger had long toyed with the idea of visiting Russia. He had hesitated, not because of Stalin's atrocities or other political reasons, but rather because of his self-imposed pressure of work. On consulting his records, he told Brecht jestingly, he had been horrified to note that besides the historical novel he was completing he still had to write 1,233 novels, 413 plays and 123,478 essays in the 24 years that still lay before him. He nevertheless accepted the invitation to the Soviet Union. He could look forward to negotiations about a Soviet film version of his novel *The Oppermanns*, and to discussions about his joining Brecht on the editorial board of a Moscow-based German-language literary magazine. Above all, the journey held out the prospect of a meeting with Stalin himself.

Feuchtwanger departed Sanary for Moscow towards the end of November 1936, travelling by train via Zurich, Vienna and Prague. Besides Eva Herrmann, with whom Feuchtwanger shared a coupé, his party comprised Maria Osten, his Sanary neighbours Ludwig and Sasha Marcuse, and a young German woman who was going along to help with the talks about filming *The Oppermanns*. The Soviets had invited the writer Ludwig Marcuse to discuss his working for the Moscow review, although he was less sympathetic towards communism than Feuchtwanger, but nothing was to materialise.

On reaching the Polish-Russian border, the group had a foretaste of the privileged treatment they would be receiving: a delegation from the Soviet writers' union met them and accompanied them in a saloon carriage to the capital. The Soviet hosts regaled them with caviar and vodka, but could not provide Eva Herrmann with a lemon. The local papers gave full and prominent coverage to Feuchtwanger's arrival. *Izvestia*, the government's official organ, reported that the democrat and world citizen Feuchtwanger saw in the country's great achievements guarantees for the humanist hopes that permeated his wonderful creations.

The Moscow *Daily News* published at the top of its front page a group photograph showing Feuchtwanger wearing a heavy overcoat and woollen cap. With him were 'Honoured Scientist S. K. Orlov; A. Guchigov, brigade leader of the Lenin's Path Collective Farm in Chechen-Ingushia' and 'K. A. Borin, famous combine operator of the Shteingartovsk Machine and Tractor Station in the Azov-Black Sea territory'. The paper informed readers that the 'noted anti-fascist writer' had watched nearly a million Muscovites parading across Red Square in a demonstration to mark the new Soviet constitution.

Feuchtwanger's hosts invited him to a Rembrandt exhibition, concerts, the theatre and the Bolshoi Ballet. He left an opera performance before it ended so that he could see Eva Herrmann, thereby arriving too late for a party held in his honour. His programme was full of appointments to visit factories, read from his works, give lectures or make broadcasts. In Sanary, his wife Marta picked up one of the broadcasts he made for listeners in Western Europe. His talks to workers about his books left him astonished at the way the proletariat thronged to the fountains of knowledge only 20 years after emerging from the darkness of pre-revolutionary Russia. Feuchtwanger met publishers and editors, and directors interested in staging or filming his works. Among the 40 contracts he signed was one for a Soviet film version of *The Oppermanns*.

During sightseeing excursions, his hosts encouraged him to admire the country's achievements since the October Revolution. He found that the ordinary Russians he met complained about some aspects of everyday life, but seemed generally content. He thought it unlikely that his hosts had 'arranged' all these chance meetings. The years of hunger were over, he concluded. Shops stocked a good choice of products at reasonable prices. Statistics proved to him that the Russians ate more and better food per head than did the Germans or the Italians.

Feuchtwanger attended the second of the notorious Moscow show trials. A group of 17 prominent Bolsheviks had to defend themselves against the charge that they were now 'anti-Soviet Trotskyists'. In January 1937, the court sentenced 13 to death for treason, and four (including the ex-*Izvestia* editor Karl Radek) to lifelong imprisonment. To some exiles in Moscow, the verdict appeared milder than the weather – minus 27 degrees at night. Feuchtwanger found the proceedings bland.

It took Feuchtwanger some time to get used to his hotel. He thought the Metropol luxurious but noisy, and not altogether comfortable. He was very happy nevertheless that he had come to Russia: 'I am convinced that the future lies here, especially for writers,' he wrote to Arnold Zweig. On the morning of 8 January, Feuchtwanger answered a telephone call in his hotel room. He learned that Stalin would receive him in the Kremlin at midday.

The writer went along unenthusiastically: he had slept badly, he had a cold and he had taken a laxative. The encounter lasted three hours, according to Feuchtwanger, and was the climax of his stay in Moscow. Yet his notes of the occasion are curiously little more than a dry enumeration of the topics discussed – artistic freedom, the cult of Stalin's personality, democracy and the political trials – and an observation about how unsatisfactory it is to converse through an interpreter.

It is from the book Feuchtwanger wrote later that we learn how a suave Stalin skilfully mollified the visitor. Stalin agreed not to smoke (Feuchtwanger could not tolerate tobacco), though he did later light up his pipe, and he purported to share Feuchtwanger's concern about the cult of personality. That phenomenon, Stalin explained, was a temporary weakness associated with the early days of socialism. An exhausted Feuchtwanger returned to his hotel and took Eva Herrmann out to dinner. The brilliant historical novelist was soon drawing flattering parallels between Moscow and Rome: 'If Lenin was the Soviet Union's Caesar, Stalin would become its Augustus.'

Feuchtwanger found that his stay – extended from a planned six weeks to nearly three months, so that he could recover in the Ukraine from illness – turned out to be more strenuous than his time in the army or his trip to America had been. Acclaimed and showered with honours, the subject of interviews and reports in the metropolitan as well as the regional Soviet press, Feuchtwanger soon proclaimed – not the first visitor from the capitalist world to do so – that western civilisation was ailing: 'The air one breathes in the west is stale.' The Soviet Union had welcomed him in such a triumphal fashion, he could tell Brecht, that it was difficult for him to avoid assuming megalomaniac tendencies.

On his return to France in February 1937, Feuchtwanger announced 'I came, I saw, I shall write.' The visit had profoundly moved him. But there was more: he found that his 'positive attitude towards the Moscow political trial' he attended had caused a fierce controversy in the West. He had accepted the guilt of the accused, and this in the view of many neutralised any critical comments he made about the trial.

As Feuchtwanger later explained in an interview, while in the Soviet Union he had judged what was good and bad in the country. He acknowledged that Stalin had greatly impressed him during their meeting. On the other hand, he had expressed his reservations about the cult of the personality, which amounted to a 'tasteless idolatry'. He had frowned on the 'standardised optimism' of Soviet arts policy, and the state's patronising ways.

There was a second reason why Feuchtwanger thought critics had subjected him to much abuse. In an article that appeared in February 1937, he had slated André Gide's heretical book about his travels to the Soviet Union. *Back From the USSR* had appeared the previous autumn. Even before Maria Osten had left Paris to accompany Feuchtwanger, she had uttered her shock over the French novelist's apostasy. During the visit of Feuchtwanger's party, the Kremlin was engaged in a furious campaign of vituperation against the French author's book, having failed to halt its publication.

It was not the first time Gide's travel reports had caused a stir. In the 1920s, the future Nobel Prize-winner had visited French Equatorial Africa at the invitation of the French colonial ministry. Appalled at the way the trading companies exploited the Africans, he mobilised public opinion until the government withdrew the companies' concessions. As a writer with a strong social conscience, Gide had initially praised communism with few caveats. At the beginning of the 1930s, he had applauded 'this gigantic and still so human enterprise'. Later he declared, 'If my life were necessary to ensure the success of the USSR, I should sacrifice it at once.'

His enthusiasm had not waned by the time he came to address the international writers' congress in Paris in 1935. In the summer of 1936, the Soviets were conducting Gide around the country, as they would Feuchtwanger after him. The two foreign writers, who in 1934 had worked together to set up the German Freedom Library in Paris, saw much the same sights. They received the same obsequious attention from their hosts. Both praised and criticised what they had seen. Yet Gide and Feuchtwanger reached different conclusions.

Where Feuchtwanger larded his overall praise with minor criticisms, Gide's disillusionment outweighed his praise for 'undoubted achievements' such as the parks of culture. He found Moscow hideous, the long queues outside stores unforgivable, the merchandise inside repulsive. When he spotted 'une prodigieuse quantité de melons', he recalled an 'impertinent' Persian proverb that he had heard only in English: 'Women for duty, boys for pleasure, melons for delight.' But even those Soviet melons were 'sans saveur'.

For Gide, the Soviet Union was backtracking on its initial tolerance of abortion and homosexuality. It had set up a dictatorship, not of a united proletariat, but of one man. A stifling conformity had replaced the liberating élan of the early years after the revolution. Severe punishment served to extinguish even minor protests. To the astonishment of the German émigrés in Paris, Gide wondered whether in any other country, even in Hitler's Germany, the spirit was less free and more terrorised than in Russia.

'I Came, I Saw, I Shall Write'

In a piece of doggerel circulating in Moscow at the time, the Communist Party apparatchiks hoped that the 'Yid' (Feuchtwanger) would not turn out to be another 'Gide' (in Russian, both sound roughly like 'zhid'.) They had little cause to worry. Feuchtwanger didn't think Gide's earlier conversion to the materialist credo was serious. It had been a question of mood; Gide could just as easily have turned to Jesus and Mary as to Marx and Lenin, he asserted.

Feuchtwanger saw Gide as a nitpicking Parisian egocentric who had failed to distinguish Stalin's democracy from the formal West European version. Gide had missed the overall picture, so obsessed had he been with the ugliness and many small inconveniences of everyday life. Yes, the Russians did use newspaper instead of toilet paper; yes, there was intolerance and uniformity. But fascism threatened the Soviet Union, the Spanish republic and socialism in France, and this oversaturated aesthete had helped the enemy. Feuchtwanger was not alone in castigating Gide. Romain Rolland, for one, found his *Back From the USSR* 'superficial', 'childish' and 'evil', but his comments did not elicit the same opprobrium as did those of Feuchtwanger.

Widespread criticism of Feuchtwanger's views on the political trials and on Gide spurred him to react. He told Eva Herrmann he had written a little book about Moscow – to take his mind off his deep longing for a certain lady. He anticipated that the work would provoke a storm of attacks against him. By April 1937, he had finished a draft of his book. Visiting him in Sanary the following month, Koltsov persuaded him to revise 'dangerous' passages dealing with Trotsky. Even so, Feuchtwanger was apprehensive about 'the few critical comments' he had made about the Soviet Union: that medicines and cosmetics were not always easy to obtain, or how the constant need to show one's identity papers or special certificates irritated the Muscovites.

Overall, however, Feuchtwanger concluded that living conditions under the planned economy were better than before. If he had drawn attention to some minor deficiencies in an otherwise positive balance, it was because he recognised that without them his work might have no influence in the West. His fears that the inclusion of some derogatory comments might provoke a hostile response to his book in Moscow were unfounded. The Russians quickly prepared a translation, and the edition of some 200,000 copies promptly sold out in the Soviet Union. But they did not reprint the work, and it did not remain long on the shelves of the Soviet Union's public libraries; perhaps the Kremlin had noticed its critical passages.

In Western Europe, on the other hand, Feuchtwanger encountered what he called 'reservations about publishing a pro-Bolshevist book'. Querido in Amsterdam read his manuscript and tried to get Feuchtwanger to drop the work. The author saw no grounds to do so. He was not a politician; he had merely drafted a subjective account of his trip. While acccepting that the work was generally sympathetic to the communists, Feuchtwanger insisted he had not shrunk from criticisms he thought necessary.

Querido published the German version of *Moscow 1937* in the summer of 1937, Victor Gollancz issuing the English version the same year. Emanuel Querido himself soon realised his misgivings were justified. In his misleadingly sub-titled *A Travel Report for My Friends*, Feuchtwanger recognised that not all was perfect in the Soviet Union. He criticised the cult of Stalin's personality and the way the state kept its artists in tutelage, giving preferential treatment to those who always introduced a heroic optimism into their works. He cited the example of a story about a record-breaking pilot whose aircraft crashed. The Soviet authorities had excised the tale from a collection of short stories because it was too pessimistic. The author was Feuchtwanger.

Readers of *Moscow 1937* gained the impression that the new system's lack of intellectual pluralism, the inadequate housing and the poor taste of Soviet architecture were minor details. Moscow was in a hurry to carry out its grand vision – bringing peaceful co-existence to the Soviet Union's many component nations, improving the country's transport network, and providing a generous range of welfare facilities for children, the sick and the aged.

But it was mainly Feuchtwanger's remarks on the political trials that unleashed controversy within the emigrant community. In France, Feuchtwanger had read press accounts of the previous trials. He had concluded that the 'hysterical confessions' extracted by the prosecution were not genuine. A witness at the second series, he now gave the prosecution the benefit of the doubt: there had to be some truth in the accusations. In his view, such a modest man as Stalin would not have enacted so coarse a comedy merely to humiliate his opponents. He was categoric: if the confessions of Radek and the others were 'lies or trumped-up, then I don't know what truth is.'

Liberal and social democrat émigrés failed to understand how Feuchtwanger justified such monstrous miscarriages of justice in his *Moscow 1937*. Card-carrying communists and fellow-travellers naturally welcomed his admiration for Stalin. Brecht as well as Heinrich Mann had kind words for him. For Brecht, *Moscow 1937* was the best book on the topic in European literature. Heinrich Mann praised Feuchtwanger's sympathetic approach. With Henri Barbusse, Louis Aragon and Romain Rolland, both were among those German and French left-wing intellectuals who had attacked the renegade Gide.

Thomas Mann found the work 'curious', his son Klaus thought it 'annoying'. Feuchtwanger's friend Arnold Zweig shook his head disapprovingly as he leafed through the book. Malicious tongues among the refugees whispered (unfairly) that the Soviets had bribed Feuchtwanger to paint such a flattering picture of Stalin and the USSR. They thought he had failed to recognise the gravity of Stalin's liquidation of the old Bolshevik guard. During a visit to Paris at the beginning of 1938, Feuchtwanger found himself 'vilely molested, especially by all the homosexuals'. He had distracted himself, he told Eva Herrmann, by frequenting a new and extremely elegant brothel – an experience he would later use in his novel about the refugees in Paris.

Leopold Schwarzschild's penetrating critique in his weekly *Neue Tage-Buch* of *Moscow 1937* had a wide impact. In a series of articles, Feuchtwanger's friend raised awkward questions for the hundreds of persecuted German writers who were wondering how best they could counter-attack the Nazis. Schwarzschild claimed Feuchtwanger had turned what was ostensibly an account of his travels into a political pamphlet. In it he had not only given a biased account of events, but had also wilfully misused a text by Lenin, so that Lenin emerged as favouring Stalin over Trotsky.

Feuchtwanger, he argued, had justified Stalin's assault on liberties and dictatorial ways because they had enabled him to improve the people's material conditions: the Soviet population now had more bread, butter and meat. Schwarzschild, who equated the Soviet and Nazi totalitarian systems, wanted to know how Feuchtwanger could praise Stalin's abominations while criticising Hitler's monstrosities. How could one cry 'bravo' here but 'brutality' there? Did pro-Soviet writers want to replace the Gestapo with the Soviet secret police, he wondered.

Feuchtwanger did not see himself as a writer used and abused by Moscow's propaganda experts. He didn't think the pomp and flattery surrounding his visit had intoxicated him. He was a non-communist who advocated a common anti-Nazi effort by all political groups in exile. It was his duty to set the record straight, even if that meant highlighting the sunny side of the Soviet scene. He had no regrets that, as he put it, he had returned to the West to land in the nettles. For him, it was Gide who had undermined the common cause.

Looking back, one can see why Feuchtwanger registered what he experienced in Russia through rose-tinted spectacles. He and his family had suffered directly at the hands of the Nazis. Like many other refugees, he believed the Soviet Union was the country most likely to resist Hitler decisively. He had hoped his book would help shore up the crumbling German anti-Nazi front in Paris, which the émigré intellectuals saw as their best hope of contributing to the political resistance. Instead, his complimentary comments about the Soviet Union ignited another controversy that sapped the energies of the German writers in exile. At the end of the day, *Moscow 1937* damaged Feuchtwanger's reputation.

After Stalin signed his non-aggression pact with Hitler in 1939, the Soviet Union temporarily repudiated the fellow-travelling Feuchtwanger. The Soviets withdrew their film version of *The Oppermanns* from the country's cinemas. A Soviet literary journal broke off its serialisation of his novel about the émigrés in Paris exile.

Feuchtwanger remained in Sanary until after the outbreak of war. The French twice interned the stateless writer, before he managed in 1940 to escape from Marseilles over the Pyrenees and ultimately to New York and California. For the second time he would lose his home and belongings, including the library he had again built up.

Feuchtwanger didn't return to the topic of communism in his later work, neither to justify what he had written, nor to admit that he had erred. His past nevertheless dogged him from the moment he arrived in America. The *Los Angeles Times* asked him in 1941 if he was, or had ever been, a communist sympathiser. He replied that he was the friend of anyone who was against Hitler. The Federal Bureau of Investigation and other intelligence agencies shadowed Feuchtwanger closely while he was living in Los Angeles: the Feuchtwanger file runs to nearly 1,000 pages.

After the war, he would have liked to return to Germany and spend summers there. In 1957, he told Eva Herrmann her depiction of the Black Forest had made him yearn for the land of his birth. He wondered if he could manage it 'without endangering everything here'. He feared that if he went abroad, Washington wouldn't allow him to re-enter the USA. The anti-Nazi who had lost his German nationality tried in vain, from 1948 until his death ten years later, to become an American citizen. Feuchtwanger lived in the United States for 18 years but never again visited Europe. He died stateless. For years after 1945, his works, though widely available in East German editions, would be out of favour with many West Germans of the Cold War generation.

'I Came, I Saw, I Shall Write'

A tragic end lay in store for Mikhail Koltsov and his companion Maria Osten, the couple who had arranged Feuchtwanger's mission from Sanary to Moscow. Koltsov went on to write a successful book about his experiences as a journalist covering the Spanish Civil War. He was elected a deputy to the Supreme Soviet in the summer of 1938. Then his star began to wane. That winter, he was not among the guests whom Stalin invited to a reception in the Kremlin for a Spanish republican general with whom Koltsov was friendly.

Later the Soviets arrested Stalin's former confidant in *Pravda*'s editorial office and tortured him. A tribunal that dealt with 'enemies of the people' found him guilty at the end of a 20-minute secret hearing. Koltsov was 'liquidated' early in 1940. His partner Maria Osten travelled to Moscow from Paris to try to rescue him. The Soviets also arrested her, tortured her and executed her as a spy in 1942.

Moscow rehabilitated both posthumously. Both occupy a minor but permanent place in the literary annals of the pre-war era. Ernest Hemingway portrayed them sympathetically, as Karkov and his lover, in his novel about the Spanish Civil War, *For Whom the Bell Tolls*. Hemingway has Koltsov, alias Karkov, voice a typically communist attitude to eliminating political opponents: 'the murderous hyenas of Bukharinite wreckers and such dregs of humanity as Zinoviev, Kamenev, Rykov and their henchmen ... the treacherous dogs of generals and the revolting spectacle of admirals unfaithful to their trust ... are destroyed. They are not assassinated.'

16 'Canaan-sur-Seine'
The Strange End of the *Pariser Tageblatt*

Although friends had advised Feuchtwanger to leave Sanary and emigrate – one recommended destination was Palestine – he preferred to remain there, despite its relative isolation in the south of France. After all, he could easily be in London or Paris overnight and he did travel frequently.

In London, he would stay in Mayfair hotels and meet publishers or film magnates. Michael Joseph asked him to propose books for his new firm. One of the film-producing Warner brothers, 'an old orthodox Jew', was 'very interested in me, but I am more interested in his pretty daughter'. In Paris, he negotiated contracts with publishers, took part in political and literary activities organised by groups of exiles, dined in fine restaurants, ordered shirts from the Paris branch of Hilditch and Key – and occasionally ventured into Parisian brothels.

For some time, he had been contemplating a major political novel about German refugees in Paris. He resolved to start writing it on his return to Sanary from the Soviet Union. Feuchtwanger had closely observed émigré life in the French capital. He claimed to run into more acquaintances on the Champs-Elysées than he would encounter, before 1933, in a similar area of central Berlin. After 1933, the elegant thoroughfare became known as the 'Boulevard de l'Assimilation' and the capital itself, disparagingly, as 'Canaan-sur-Seine' (to this day, Berlin has a district called Moabit, a promised land to which French Huguenots fled).

German delicatessen stores and bookshops sprang up in Paris. Refugee bankers, doctors and lawyers tried to resume their professional life there. So did many journalists. They started a German daily newspaper, the *Pariser Tageblatt*. Even if it was only a pale and struggling imitation, it recalled the great liberal dailies that had perished in Berlin.

The influx of Jews from Central Europe was all too obvious – and, for some, unwelcome. In *France-la-Doulce*, Paul Morand, a fashionable right-wing writer who had had a Jewish lover, describes a German film-producer arriving in Paris on the express train from Berlin in the early 1930s. The refugees have been pouring in every evening for the past three months – first one, then ten, then 100, then 50,000. Some, looking just like Boches, descend from first-class coaches; smiling and placid, they hand out large tips. Others are thin, dark, bearded and deformed. They resemble dirty 'wogs' (*bicots*), they carry no passports and they tip only a few sous.

For Morand, Paris was like a new quarantine station or an animal pound: from the Rue des Rosiers in the Jewish quarter to the Champs-Elysées, the city was absorbing the stray foreigners. Morand pleaded that the French ask Germany 'not to send us its men dressed as women, its musicians with their erotic and depressing talent or its doctors qualified in sexual research'. At the end of the book, the Berlin film-producer toasts France as 'the Good Lord's concentration camp'. And such was the book's title when a German translation appeared soon after.

Across the Seine, on the go-as-you-please Left Bank, there were also signs of social change. They upset, among others, Richard Aldington, the English writer and biographer of D. H. Lawrence, and later a literary expatriate in Hollywood, like Huxley and the Manns. He regretted the disappearance of those modest cafés where poor artists and writers, starving for an ideal, had congregated a few years earlier to find warmth. Aldington observed that they had given way to big flashy places 'occupied by a heterogeneous and unpleasing multitude of freaks and prostitutes – men-women and women-men, charlatans, pimps, amateur prostitutes, negroes, numerous wops and Middle-European Jews with American passports'.

Feuchtwanger, who claimed he received 714 anonymous 'dirty Jew' calls in 1935, portrayed the changing city with a more sympathetic eye in *Exil*, his lengthy novel about German emigrants in Paris. Weaving into the work many of the events he witnessed and the characters he met, he offered a penetrating insight into the highly-strung life of the average impoverished refugee in 1930s Paris. There are vivid aperçus of the dissension, the distress and the disillusionment that seem inseparable from political exile. He captures the refugees' nostalgia for the country that no longer wanted them. (Watching the traditional Bastille Day parade down the Champs-Elysées, one apocryphal old Berliner claims 'Our storm-troopers march more smartly'.) Feuchtwanger noted how émigrés from Munich might prefer sausages and beer to oysters and Chablis. There is a fascinating vignette of a dinner where the ex-Berliners try to recreate their German way of life. The conversation continually harps on the way most things were better 'bei uns' – 'chez nous' – in the old country that they had loved, and fled.

On his visits to the French capital, Feuchtwanger would sometimes stay for several weeks. Friends and acquaintances from Paris, in turn, visited him in Sanary. He read the exile press and corresponded with many émigrés. He was familiar with their everyday life in Paris. He knew of the red-tape they ran into as they rushed around town trying to obtain the vital identity documents. He was familiar with their efforts to learn the language and their struggle to make a living. He'd seen how middle-class professional families had tried to adjust to living in modest, often shabby hotels; and how cafés served as their living rooms. He was no stranger to their factions and interminable feuds.

Feuchtwanger had an acute sense of the way German diplomats, bankers and journalists in Paris intrigued against the refugees and prepared the road to Vichy collaboration. Two of his characters are thinly disguised versions of notorious Nazi 'termites': Otto Abetz, Ribbentrop's Paris agent in the 1930s and German ambassador in Paris during the war, and Friedrich Sieburg, the turncoat Paris correspondent of the leading German daily, *Frankfurter Zeitung*.

In *Exil*, Feuchtwanger reflects resentfully on the millions in Germany who read the *Frankfurter* and the few thousand who see the exile periodicals. In Berlin, émigré journalists had at least enjoyed the illusion that their work served some purpose and produced results. They provoked lawmakers to debate the issues they raised. London, Paris and New York quoted from their articles. Now they worked in a vacuum in which even glowing verses by Shakespeare or scathing essays by Swift would fail to curb Nazi barbarities.

After Hitler annexed Austria in 1938, Feuchtwanger feared he might be unable to complete the novel in Sanary. He ensured his travel documents were in order and prepared to apply for an American visa. He was thinking of leaving in the autumn, but then stayed on to finish his manuscript in Sanary in August 1939. Querido published the work in 1940, just before the Germans overran the Low Countries. While *Exil* is not great literature, it offers a broad panorama of characters and incidents, and a wealth of absorbing detail about the refugee community in 'Canaan-sur-Seine'. The historian Richard Grunberger, at the time a young Austrian refugee in Britain, later said he relied on the book to catch the flavour of refugee life across the Channel.

With *Erfolg* (*Success*) and *Geschwister Oppermann* (*The Oppermanns*), *Exil* made up Feuchtwanger's 'waiting-room' trilogy about Nazi Germany and the great German Jewish exodus. He never wrote a planned fourth novel that was going to deal with the return from exile. When Ben Huebsch's Viking Press brought out *Paris Gazette* in April 1940, Huebsch presented the American translation of *Exil* as 'Feuchtwanger's greatest novel'. His publicity office claimed that 'never before has he had a theme with such meaning and emotional impact for every one of us today'. Reviewing the novel the same month, the *New Yorker* was less enthusiastic. It found the book too long (a postwar paperback edition runs to almost 800 pages), too crowded and overburdened with plot: 'Feuchtwanger, a German, believes in the method of exhaustiveness', the weekly told its readers.

Set in Paris in 1935, *Exil* relates how the main character Sepp Trautwein, an exiled musician living in Paris, gets involved against his will in politics. He takes on a newspaper job in an attempt to campaign for the liberation of a journalist kidnapped by the Nazis. The Nazis free the abducted journalist but the misery of exile drives Trautwein's wife to suicide. Trautwein goes back to his music. Marta Feuchtwanger said her husband based Trautwein on an émigré in France who had been a professor at Heidelberg University and who established a reputation during the Weimar Republic as a pacifist and human-rights activist, but the musician is also, in part, a self-portrait.

Feuchtwanger acknowledged in an afterword to some editions that he based the book on two real events: how Nazi agents abducted the émigré journalist Berthold Jacob, and how they muzzled the hostile Saar newspaper *Westland* before a huge majority of the territory's electorate voted for its re-incorporation into Germany. Feuchtwanger denied any intentional resemblance between the characters in his novel and persons linked to any real German-language periodical in France. He emphasised that the real-life Vladimir Poliakov, the Russian émigré publisher of the real-life *Pariser Tageblatt*, had not inspired his dislikeable fictional publisher, Louis Gingold. His disclaimer is unconvincing but hardly matters: no fictional account could surpass the true story of the *Pariser Tageblatt*.

***

Vladimir Poliakov's son Leon was about to leave the family's Paris apartment on Thursday, 11 June 1936, to go to the local *mairie* where he and his fiancée Nathalie were to be married. After their honeymoon, they planned to move into a cosy apartment near the Bois de Boulogne, which the couple had furnished by taking advantage of the hire-purchase facilities that were becoming more popular. Vladimir Poliakov had already left for the office when the concierge slipped a newspaper under the apartment's front door. It was the *Pariser Tageblatt*, a daily journal edited by German journalists in exile for the German-speaking community and particularly for the swelling flood of refugees. Vladimir Poliakov was the paper's founder and proprietor.

A prominently displayed article on the *Tageblatt*'s front page left Leon dumbfounded. In it, the editorial staff alleged that his father had some ten days earlier visited the German consulate in the Rue Huysmans, near the Luxembourg Gardens. There, it claimed, Vladimir had conducted negotiations with Dr Artur Schmolz. Schmolz headed the German embassy's press and propaganda section and, as such, followed and reported to Berlin on the activities of the German writers in French exile. A *Sûreté* report had claimed in 1935 that Schmolz was responsible for subsidising French newspapers that treated Germany kindly.

Acccording to the *Tageblatt*'s article, Poliakov came back from the meeting with Schmolz and informed the paper's business manager that he would be replacing both him and the editor. The editor was Georg Bernhard, a prominent German refugee who was visiting New York at the time, partly to raise funds for the struggling paper. A reception in his honour the previous Monday had brought together the cream of East Coast Jewry, as well as non-Jewish establishment figures such as Helen Keller, Elmer Rice, John Dewey and Simon Schuster.

According to the article, Poliakov told the *Tageblatt* manager that Bernhard's successor would change the paper's political course and adopt a more neutral attitude to Hitler and his goals. The article explained that the editorial staff, warned in time, had been able to denounce their publisher's perfidious behaviour and forestall a propaganda coup for Hitler. They had resolved to leave the *Tageblatt*. The defectors planned to bring out a new daily, the *Pariser Tageszeitung*, under a new publisher, Fritz Wolff.

For Leon Poliakov as for most *Tageblatt* readers, the émigré journalists were insinuating that his father was allowing the long arm of Joseph Goebbels to turn the anti-Nazi *Tageblatt* into a crypto-Nazi paper, and that the émigrés' new *Pariser Tageszeitung* would replace it as the true organ of a free Germany.

When the first issue of the mutineers' *Tageszeitung* appeared in the newspaper kiosks of Paris the next day, it repeated their allegations across three columns, under a front-page headline, 'We Accuse!' Those words harked back to Emile Zola's sensational article defending Dreyfus as the innocent victim of an anti-Jewish conspiracy. Was that what the rebellious journalists were now suggesting? They were. They accused Poliakov of secretly accepting financial backing from the German embassy – in exchange for toning down the paper's attacks and bringing in tamer editorial staff. They would become the victims of his conspiracy.

Meanwhile, Leon's father had arrived at the *Tageblatt* office to find that his editorial staff had indeed carried out an insurrection. Not only had they deserted him; someone had wrought havoc in the office, disconnecting the telephone lines and removing files with details of the paper's subscribers. The Poliakovs, father and son, quickly approached two other émigrés who had shown an interest in working for the paper: Konstantin Leites, like Poliakov a businessman of Russian origin, and Richard Lewinsohn, another German refugee journalist.

With their help, the Poliakovs managed to prepare the next issue. In it, Vladimir Poliakov appealed to the German exiles to judge for themselves the truth of the slanderous allegations about him. Lewinsohn took the material to the usual printers, only to find that they were now also printing the breakaway *Tageszeitung*. What then happened isn't too clear. At some point, probably as Lewinsohn left the printers that night of 11 June, someone injured him with a knife. After editing that one issue of Poliakov's *Tageblatt*, Lewinsohn withdrew from the conflict.

The printer stopped printing Poliakov's paper. Perhaps the *Tageszeitung* team bribed the printer to do so. Poliakov's budget was shaky, and he hadn't paid the printer's bills on time. According to Leon Poliakov, the printer 'sold' or gave the rebels a 'formidable weapon' – a post-dated cheque from his father that had bounced.

Undeterred, the two Poliakovs put together as best they could, in an unfamiliar language, a one-sheet edition of the *Tageblatt*. Protected by friends acting as bodyguards, they took it to a small print-works. But the opposition was on their tracks. Georg Bernhard's deputy Kurt Caro was determined to crush the competition. He found out the address of Poliakov's new printer. A group of about 20 tried to storm the premises but found themselves locked out. Not to be outwitted, they telephoned Hachette, the newspaper distributors, and learned that they would be picking up the edition at one o'clock that morning. Pretending to be from Hachette, the gang turned up at the printer's and were let in. They seized some 3,500 copies, the bulk of the edition, and threw them into the Seine. It was the last issue of the *Pariser Tageblatt*. (Half a century later, French trade unionists in Paris hijacked a truck in an attempt to halt the distribution of a free newspaper, *Metro*.)

Armed with Poliakov's uncovered cheque, the *Tageszeitung* despatched an emissary to him to see if the two papers could settle their differences amicably. Under the émigrés' proposals, they would compensate Poliakov and regard the cheque as an 'oversight'. They said Vladimir's son Leon would also have to sign any accord. When he, for the first time in his life, saw his father about to 'capitulate', the intransigent youth persuaded him to reject the proposal, probably by warning his father that the journalists weren't willing to withdraw their slanderous allegations publicly.

A battle opened that dragged on for years. At stake was no longer Poliakov's paper, but his honour. The émigrés tried to hush up the affair but ultimately it turned into a public scandal, as many sordid details seeped out. In Sanary, Ludwig Marcuse wrote an enthusiastic letter to the German journalists in Paris, but regretted his action 15 minutes after posting it. He realised that 'this thing stinks to heaven'. The dispute drove the publicists into prolonged disarray and deflected their talents from the common cause – using their pens to help combat the Nazi swords. The intrigues and even violence surrounding the journalists' uprising did little to enhance the émigrés' credibility among those democratic governments they had been hoping to influence.

That German diplomats in Paris wanted to muffle the highly articulate voices around the *Tageblatt* was only natural: it is one of the main themes in Feuchtwanger's *Exil*. Yet was it plausible that Poliakov had been conspiring with the Nazis against his mainly German-Jewish staff? He was a Russian Jewish émigré, after all, even if he was a businessman in financial difficulties rather than a journalist. His alleged 'pact with the devil' took place as late as the summer of 1936, when the heinous nature of the Nazi regime was clear for all to see. What could have caused the *Tageblatt* journalists to make such grave accusations?

The Poliakov family burned all documents dealing with the charges and their aftermath during the war, to prevent them falling into the hands of the Nazis. Even long after the end of the war, surviving participants still refused to shed light on this 'can of worms'. Though researchers have failed to unravel all aspects of the debacle, its essential components were probably mutual mistrust, incompatible temperaments and conflicting views on how best to resist the Nazi menace.

At first, German refugees and prominent French intellectuals accepted the journalists' version of events. Russian and Polish exiles, on the other hand, sided with what they regarded as a cruelly and unjustly maligned Poliakov family. Leon Poliakov and his new wife, after only a week's honeymoon in the country, returned to their respective parental homes. For Leon, the urgent need to defend his father's reputation was reason enough for this inconsiderate attitude to his new partner. The young Madame Poliakov went on to suggest separation; not long after, she left Paris to work in London. Before the year was out, divorce proceedings were under way.

It was Leon who had originally encouraged his father to launch a daily paper for the middle-class professional Germans, mostly assimilated Jews, who were streaming into France. Happy memories of his schooldays in Berlin, where his family lived briefly but comfortably in the Weimar years, had left Leon a devoted Germanophile. His father's media expertise went back to Odessa, where he was born and where he had owned newspapers and advertising agencies. Vladimir Poliakov moved to St Petersburg in 1906, where he took over four dailies and where his son Leon was born in 1910. The family returned to Odessa to escape the famine that followed Russia's defeat in World War I and the turmoil and violence that accompanied the Bolshevik victory in the civil war.

As the Red Army approached the Black Sea, the Poliakovs fled to Paris, via Italy. They saw their flight as a precautionary and provisional measure: Poliakov shared the common opinion among White Russian émigrés that the fanatically oppressive Bolshevik regime couldn't last long. In fact, the family never returned to Russia and remained firmly opposed to communism, even when it later appeared to others as the best hope for slaying the Nazi monster. Instead, they moved temporarily in 1921 from Paris to Berlin, where Vladimir's sterling deposits in London had greater purchasing power.

By the middle of the decade, the Poliakovs were back in Paris, among the 250,000 Russians who found refuge in France from the Bolsheviks. Vladimir revived a family advertising agency, 'Publicité Metzl', that had flourished in Russia and now began to specialise in serving the foreign-language papers that had sprung up after war-displaced communities settled in the French capital. He shared premises with the *Dernières Nouvelles*, the main paper for Russian émigrés. His associate was Isaac Grodzenski, who had ties to the Yiddish paper *Pariser Haint*.

The way the latest diaspora was changing the face of Paris struck the young Leon when he returned from a vacation in Italy in the summer of 1933. While many German opposition politicians at first sought refuge in Prague or Moscow, German doctors, lawyers and businessmen preferred the French capital. With many French out of work at the time, the government made it difficult for refugees to take up employment, but there were fewer restraints on establishing business firms or professional practices.

By the end of 1933, more than 20,000 highly literate refugees had fled Germany for France, most of them settling in or near the capital. Two years later, that figure was probably nearer 40,000. In their large numbers and in their educated middle-class backgrounds, Leon saw fresh hope for restoring his father's languishing fortunes. He encouraged him to found a German-language daily. Vladimir Poliakov had publishing, printing and advertising expertise; he had access to the necessary financial resources. All that remained was to find a suitable editor.

Vladimir Poliakov must have thought himself exceptionally lucky. The cream of Weimar Republic journalism, itself regarded as a model of professionalism, surrounded him. The numerous journalists who had recently arrived in the French capital were itching to exercise their skills and earn a living again. Among them was Georg Bernhard, the former editor-in-chief of what the world at large had considered a most venerable German daily, the *Vossische Zeitung*. With a small team of other ex-Berliners, Bernhard was already producing an émigré weekly in Paris.

Born in 1875, Bernhard started his professional life in the last years of the Wilhelmian empire. He moved from the world of banking and finance into business journalism. In his thirties, he joined the influential Ullstein publishing concern. With its four Berlin dailies and more than a dozen weeklies and monthlies, it was at the time one of the biggest firms of its kind in Europe. There Bernhard rose to become editor of its flagship, the enlightened *Vossische Zeitung*. Founded in 1704, it was regarded, in the words of another staff-member, Arthur Koestler, as 'the bible of German liberalism'. Bernhard became manager of Ullstein's news services. In addition, he lectured on banking and currency questions and in the late 1920s briefly represented the newly created liberal German Democratic Party in the Reichstag.

Ullstein was one of the country's major publishing empires – conglomerates that published books, newspapers and magazines, had their own printing presses and in some cases ran photograph and travel agencies. Another Jewish family in Berlin ran the Mosse media concern; its upmarket paper was the liberal *Berliner Tageblatt*. Frankfurt housed another distinguished daily, the *Frankfurter Zeitung*, founded by Leopold Sonnemann. His son-in-law Heinrich Simon later controlled it, until he fled to Palestine in 1934. The daily paper that the émigrés would produce in Paris sought to emulate features of these prestigious journals, while combining them with the more sensational approach of what were known as Berlin's 'boulevard sheets'.

Most German-Jewish publishers and editors would have described themselves as Germans, first and foremost. They came from assimilated middle-class families. Many barely practised their religion and tended to regard Zionism as an ideal for the less emancipated Jews of Eastern Europe. Such distinctions were irrelevant for the Nazi movement. In its eyes, the Jewish liberal press represented precisely the values that Hitler's propaganda disparagingly portrayed as morally corrupt. For Nazi ideologues, the liberal press was internationalist, not nationalist. Its constituency was the cosmopolitan big city, with its supposedly immoral tendencies, rather than the small towns and countryside, with what Nazis regarded as their morally superior traditional values.

For the National Socialist movement, Ullstein and Mosse were too close to big business and mass-production. They were too prone to welcome 'decadent' contemporary arts. Their 'plutocratic' publications ignored the interests of small firms and artisans, the less adventurous tastes of the province, and the more conservative outlook of farmers. Inevitably, Ullstein and Mosse (Goebbels tried to get a job with them) became targets for the Nazi propaganda machine. It persuaded a growing number of Germans that the Jewish press barons and their staff commanded the printed word, just as they convinced their followers that the Jews controlled business, many professions and the arts. It was easy to make the public believe that such domination in all these fields was totally unhealthy.

Occupying one of the most prominent editorial positions in this Berlin publishing galaxy, Bernhard became a prime target of Nazi attacks on the liberal media. His advocacy in the 1920s of Franco-German reconciliation had provoked his critics to dub the *Vossische* the 'Foch gazette'. While revered within his own Berlin bourgeoisie world, Bernhard's headstrong temperament, his suspicious nature and his erratic views made for difficult relations with the management. He became embroiled in a bitter Ullstein family row that curiously foreshadowed in some ways the Paris newspaper scandal and Bernhard's final downfall a few years later.

By the end of the 1920s, the rise in Germany's jobless and the tidal advance of the National Socialist movement were causing the hitherto liberal Jewish publishers to trim their sails and edge closer to the conservatives. Jewish journalists in Berlin grew more inhibited.

They stopped talking about the 'lift-goys' who took them to and from their offices. Anxious to protect their companies' economic interests, managers reined in a largely Jewish editorial staff that wanted to step up their attacks on the extreme right.

Bernhard had already survived political differences with the Ullstein family, partly because he could shelter behind Franz Ullstein, one of the five brothers who had inherited the 'house' from its founder, Leopold Ullstein. Matters changed after Franz married a journalist, Rosie Gräfenberg, in 1929. Because she moved more comfortably in right-wing circles than in the liberal environment associated with his paper, Bernhard believed she threatened his political influence over her husband and even his own position as editor-in-chief. He suspected that she wanted the Ullsteins to replace him with the less combative Friedrich Sieburg, a future Nazi fellow-traveller and at the time the *Frankfurter Zeitung*'s correspondent in Paris, where Rosie Gräfenberg had worked as a freelance.

When rumours began to circulate that during her Paris days Gräfenberg had acted as an informer for the Germans, and perhaps for the French government as well, Bernhard mentioned the gossip in his paper and the Ullstein family removed Franz from its board of directors. While Arthur Koestler joined those staff-members who declared themselves 'Franciscans', others came out as 'Bernardines'. Georg Bernhard deserted Franz Ullstein and sided with the rest of the family. He went to Paris to investigate one source of the hearsay about Gräfenberg: documents held by Joseph Matthes, a shady journalist who would later play a role in Bernhard's row with Poliakov.

Franz Ullstein counter-attacked to protect himself and his wife against Bernhard's hints in his paper. He enlisted the help of Leopold Schwarzschild, editor of the influential *Tage-Buch*, who in exile would enter the scene in later stages of the Bernhard drama. A family quarrel turned into an open scandal as journals reverberated with charges and counter-charges. By relying on the politically dubious Matthes, Bernhard, now in his mid-fifties, drew widespread public criticism upon himself and turned into a major liability for the Ullsteins. In August 1930, they finally secured his resignation on alleged grounds of political differences, compensating him handsomely for doing so. The following year a court found Rosie innocent of the charges, and the *Voss* carried an apology from the Ullstein family.

Bernhard returned to his lecturing. He was organising a congress to promote free speech when he had to flee Berlin in 1933, shortly after the Reichstag fire. By April 1933, he and his family, who fled after him to Switzerland, were together again in a large Paris apartment. The following month Nazi students publicly burnt examples of Bernhard's 'alien journalism of democratic, Jewish coinage'. The *Voss*, to its credit, closed down before it was compelled to do so.

Bernhard swore he would never return to Germany. Soon the middle-aged but still dynamic editor showed that if he was down, he was in no way out. By the end of 1933, the deposed 'king of Kochstrasse', the street where the Ullstein empire had its headquarters in pre-war Berlin, was back in an editor's chair, this time in the Rue de Turbigo, near Les Halles. Vladimir Poliakov had chosen Georg Bernhard to edit the *Pariser Tageblatt*, after protracted negotiations with other eligible candidates. Ignoring the recommendations of his Russian circle, he bowed to the wishes of Isaac Grodzenski, editor and owner of the Yiddish *Pariser Haint*, and other Polish Jews who were willing to bear the editorial expenses. Poliakov himself was to assume the printing costs.

Assured that he would enjoy editorial freedom, Bernhard recruited a small team drawn from highbrow as well as popular Berlin papers. A couple of weeks later, on 12 December 1933, the first number of the *Pariser Tageblatt* appeared. After working for some of the world's wealthiest and most modern newspaper enterprises, the staff and especially the editor had to adjust to primitive working conditions. Their austere office comprised three tables and a couple of typewriters in two rooms. Bernhard understandably chose to work from his home much of the time. In *Paris Gazette*, Lion Feuchtwanger based a leading character on Bernhard. As editor of Berlin's most respected paper, the cigar-smoking Franz Heilbrunn is a man of great influence. His words and gestures are those of a grand seigneur. When in exile, Heilbrunn invites ridicule by trying to recreate his elegant Berlin lifestyle.

At the *Tageblatt*, journalists wrote much of the copy by hand. The typesetter was no linguist, and the printer in Montmartre used the same two veteran machines for the *Tageblatt* as he did for the Russian and Yiddish papers produced by Poliakov's associates. This production process tested the German journalists' proofreading skills to the limit. Yet by 1936 the paper was a financial success. Its circulation was in the region of 14,000, of which about 1,000 were subscription copies. Its readers were mainly in the Paris region, but the daily was also on sale abroad, from Norway to Palestine.

Like most expatriate publications, the *Tageblatt* had to cater to both high- and low-brow tastes. If the title recalled the intellectually demanding *Berliner Tageblatt*, much of the contents showed the influence of the deputy editor, Kurt Caro, who had come from the mass-circulation *Berliner Volkszeitung*. Comprising four pages during the week, the paper opened with political news, moving on to business and sport. A section on life in Paris ranged from a local entertainment 'what's on' to the latest French murder trial. The *Tageblatt* closed with the arts, humorous features and an instalment of some new novel, often by an exile on an émigré theme. Leisure topics – the arts and reviews, scientific news, Paris fashion – filled a weekend supplement.

If the *Tageblatt* was wont to sensationalise and trivialise the news from Germany – devoting considerable space to listing Göring's wedding presents – it also dealt with everyday problems of the refugees, from asylum policies of different countries to advice on emigration, especially to Palestine. It tried to be a 'normal' Parisian paper for German-speakers abroad who wanted to think things out for themselves, without 'guidance' from an authoritarian political party.

Displaying clear loyalty to France and the host country's democratic principles, the *Tageblatt* canvassed apolitical readers' support for the struggle against Hitler. It opened its columns to a wide spectrum of political points of view, running for example an interview granted by the famous Czech reporter Egon Erwin Kisch to a communist news agency.

Denouncing the course of German politics was inevitably one of Bernhard's prime concerns. He not only attacked the obvious targets, the Nazi politicians; he also denounced leading cultural figures who had stayed in Germany, such as the musicians Wilhelm Furtwängler and Richard Strauss, because in doing so they supported Nazi propaganda. For him, they were 'intellectual fellow-travellers', 'traitors' who lacked civil courage, 'soldiers of Goebbels' who were 'helping to prostitute Beethoven, Mozart and Haydn' – and as such an 'enemy' who should be subject to martial law.

In the continental tradition, the *Tageblatt* normally handled events in an interpretative fashion. As Arthur Koestler graphically put it, journalists couldn't expect the reader to consume raw facts as issued by news agencies; they had to cook and chew the facts and then serve them in their saliva. Thus the way the *Tageblatt* dealt with news out of Germany reflected the staff's anger and wishful thinking. Behind the 'night of the long knives' in 1934, when the Nazis massacred Ernst Röhm and other alleged conspirators, the *Tageblatt* perceived widespread opposition to the regime. At the same time, Bernhard was reluctant to give the 'Jewish question' pride of place in his columns, considering the refugees as Germans rather than Jews. For him, the Nazis threatened other religious groups, such as the Catholics, just as they did the Jews.

A dominant and no doubt highly popular aspect of the *Tageblatt* was the way it helped refugees adapt to living in exile. It published features on ways to overcome the bureaucratic hurdles they faced in obtaining permission to reside or seek work in France. It told readers where to find affordable French-language courses or day-care centres for their children.

The *Tageblatt* recorded extensively the manifold activities organised by and for the émigrés, from political meetings to cultural events. It regularly devoted a page to new films and its archives chronicled the achievements outside Germany of German filmmakers such as Max Ophüls, Wilhelm Dieterle, Robert Siodmak and Fritz Lang. It proudly announced that Marlene Dietrich was earning more in Hollywood than Mae West.

Loyal *Tageblatt* readers joined the staff's protests after the French film director René Clair criticised the creative and professional qualities of his German counterparts, excepting Fritz Lang, and complained about the undesirable competition they presented. One of the last stories the *Tageszeitung* published, as the Germans were advancing on Paris, announced Veit Harlan's forthcoming production in Germany of the notorious anti-Semitic film, *Jud Süss*.

Bernhard had hoped that editing the *Tageblatt* would be similar to editing the *Vossische*. But it proved much harder to bring out a foreign-language daily paper in Paris. He faced unprecedented editorial and financial constraints. It steadily became more difficult to get reliable information about the Third Reich. As Goebbels brought German news sources to heel, Bernhard had to rely on clandestine correspondents, who didn't necessarily have first-hand information. Increasingly, the *Tageblatt* – a daily, after all – would have to rewrite what appeared in the French press and run it the following day.

In his coverage of the French political scene, Bernhard employed techniques to minimise the risk of his being accused of meddling in the host country's affairs. He would quote reports and editorials from the French press as a way of appearing to be objective. To convey opinion, he would commission analyses from sympathetic French politicians, or rely on syndicated articles by eminent figures such as Winston Churchill.

The *Tageblatt*'s staff worked in a sombre environment. Enemies surrounded Bernhard and his staff. Paris was full of German spies and informers who recorded and reported on the movements of influential emigrants. Diplomats tried to hinder hostile emigrant politicians and journalists from resuming their activities in France. Analysing the types of refugee it had observed, the German embassy distinguished between loyal non-Jews who had fled in 'hysteria and panic' and 'the truly dangerous and influential ... group around [the former leader of the social democrats in the Reichstag, Rudolf] Breitscheid and Bernhard'.

Scholars have since suggested that Berlin may have overestimated the importance of the émigré press. At the time, however, the Nazis thought it vital to neutralise the politically vociferous refugee journalists who attacked them on every occasion. The Reich's propaganda experts feared the activities of bourgeois journalists such as Bernhard more than they did those of the communists. They considered German liberals more likely to influence middle-of-the road French governments and the officials and journalists around them. Having failed to prevent Bernhard from taking the reins of the prime émigré publication, the German embassy's mission was to sabotage him, rather than eliminate the publication itself.

Berlin could easily intimidate Germany's smaller neighbours. Both Danzig and Austria banned Bernhard's paper in 1934. The unscrupulous methods the German government employed to silence hostile voices were widely known. Kingsley Martin noted, in his *New Statesman* diary in January 1934, what a journalist in Paris 'told me about the foreign activities of the Nazis, how they had bought French newspapers, how they threatened to raid the houses of those suspected of having anti-Nazi correspondents in Germany ...'. The German embassy encouraged the French press, especially some mass-circulation papers, to fuel the French public's antipathy to the refugees. It may have played a role in building up pressure on the French government to make their life more difficult. So it was all too understandable that Bernhard and his staff should fear that the embassy would exploit any opportunity to undermine the *Tageblatt*.

Even if some French legislators, officials and journalists were on good terms with the *Tageblatt* staff, others favoured rapprochement with Nazi Germany. There were strong right-wing tendencies in French society. The authorities and the police in particular were already concerned at the way French fascist movements had created public disorder around the Left Bank cafés frequented by the refugees. They saw the émigré press as helping to provoke the agitators. The French government moreover had to exercise its responsibility to ensure that political exiles didn't use French soil to publish insulting remarks about other governments and their leaders.

Bernhard had to be wary of the growing apprehension even among established French Jews. They feared that the new flood of refugees now following previous waves from Russia and Eastern Europe, and the scandal in 1934 around Serge Stavisky's fraudulent financial manipulations, could only swell anti-Semitic currents. Bernhard became involved in a controversy with Baron Robert de Rothschild, a leader of the French Jewish community who had been instrumental in organising help for the refugees, after the baron complained about the German Jews' ingratitude and the way wealthy German refugees weren't adequately supporting their poorer brethren.

Superficially, dealings at the *Tageblatt* between proprietor and editor appeared to be amicable. Bernhard wrote a flattering article to mark Poliakov's 70th birthday in May 1934. When they celebrated the occasion at the Hôtel Lutétia, the anti-Hitler Bernard sat on Poliakov's left, while Paul Miliukov, the fervently anti-Stalinist owner of the Russian-language paper *Dernières Nouvelles*, sat on his right. Yet animosity between Poliakov and the paper's staff was smouldering, although Poliakov didn't interfere with Bernhard's editorial control. Friction was developing within the enterprise itself; it was creating mutual distrust and would lead to editorial upheaval. Besides the stresses of refugee life, there were the owner's straitened financial circumstances, the journalists' awareness that they could at any moment fall into a Nazi trap, and conflicting conceptions of the paper.

There were also cultural differences between the owners and the editorial staff. Victims of persecution and pogroms over the centuries, Jewish groups nevertheless liked to establish a pecking order amongst themselves. As Joseph Roth saw it, Frankfurt's Jews looked down on Berlin's Jews, who looked down on Vienna's Jews, who looked down on Warsaw's Jews, who looked down on Galician Jews – of whom Roth was one. It was a grading that corresponded roughly to the chronology of Jewish emancipation.

Even within the German emigration to France, those who arrived earliest after 1933 came to see themselves as their group's 'pilgrim fathers'. At the *Tageblatt*, however, it was a case of the 'cravats' versus the 'caftans', the way 'our crowd' – a prosperous and largely assimilated German-Jewish middle class – looked down on 'Ostjuden', whom they tended to regard as their uncouth, overzealous kin from the east.

In *Paris Gazette*, Feuchtwanger's fictional publisher, Gingold, is a pious, bead-counting Romanian Jew who lives in a large apartment near the Arc de Triomphe. He has a hard, fleshless face, small eyes, irregular teeth and a false smile. He has made money in property, and plays the currency markets. He resents freelancers using office staff to type their copy. Much of the novel deals with the way the editor and his staff oppose Gingold's efforts to tone down their attacks on Hitler and the Nazis. Gingold argues in effect that émigré hysteria encourages Berlin to treat even more harshly those Jews still in Germany. Among them are his own daughter and son-in-law.

The real editor, Bernhard, carped that he had to deal with thick-skulled 'Russian Jews of a most unpleasant type'. Poliakov's associate, Isaac Grodzenski, complained of the overbearing and arrogant disdain exhibited by the assimilated 'first-class German Jews' on the *Tageblatt*. The Poliakov family had sadly recognised that such was broadly the German Jews' attitude to Vladimir, even though theirs was a wealthy and refined family who had lived in Germany as well as in France. They didn't consider themselves orthodox, barely observing Jewish religious rites. Objecting to the contemptuous way Bernhard had crushed him and his Polish partner 'under your heel', the White Russian Poliakov pointed out how they as 'accommodating Slavs' had adjusted to his German mentality.

Poliakov's grievances weren't all social. He complained that the editor appeared only rarely in the office, and showed too little regard for readers' criticism about the low intellectual level of the paper. The proprietor developed an antipathy to the way his impetuous editor had moulded the paper to reflect his embattled situation.

Poliakov and other Polish and Russian émigrés with whom he associated believed the *Tageblatt* concentrated too much on the supposed interests of the refugees, rather than on the German-speaking community as a whole. He showed especial disquiet at the way Bernhard began to clamour repetitively and stridently for co-operation with the German communists in setting up an anti-fascist Popular Front. Bernhard had reasonably enough made the paper friendlier to the Soviets, after Moscow in August 1935 abandoned its hitherto hostile attitude to Europe's social democrats.

Poliakov, on the other hand, had experienced at first hand the Russian communists' brutal pursuit of exclusive power. While there is no evidence that he envisaged a gentler editorial stance towards Hitler's aggressive ambitions, he wasn't convinced that hard-hitting onslaughts on practically everything that was happening in Germany constituted good journalism.

It was probably Poliakov's accounting methods and his failure to build a solid financial foundation for his publishing enterprise that led to the showdown. When the *Tageblatt* showed a profit after a year or so, the staff resented the way Poliakov declined to reinvest the surplus in the under-capitalised paper. Instead, he siphoned it off to help balance the finances of his less successful ventures. Poliakov had bought out Grodzenski's share in the Yiddish paper *Haint* after it transpired in 1934 that Poliakov's partner had been helping himself to some of the paper's receipts. In so doing, however, Poliakov overreached himself.

He suffered a further financial blow when his advertising agency lost a major client, the Russian émigrés' paper. Because Poliakov was constantly short of cash, he paid or reimbursed staff and outside contributors irregularly, sometimes months in arrears. As Bernhard himself later remonstrated with Poliakov, financial stringency had forced the paper to dispense with news services and with contributors as prestigious as Heinrich Mann.

All could see that only an outside investor could restore the venture's declining fortunes. By the early summer of 1936, three courses were theoretically open to the *Tageblatt*. Poliakov or Bernhard could somehow secure the urgent financial infusion and remain in harness. A second possibility was that an increasingly desperate Poliakov would find new backers, but drop his editor. The third option was for the dissatisfied journalists to find a Maecenas who would put up enough money for them to buy out Poliakov.

While Bernhard and his colleagues were determined to preserve the integrity of the paper they had built up over the past two years, they suspected that Poliakov didn't share that concern. Judging Poliakov to be essentially a businessman who wouldn't hesitate to put profits before politics, they feared he might cede political control in exchange for a healthier balance sheet. By the spring of 1936, the situation looked critical and it seemed as if Poliakov was prepared to sound out anyone.

The staff had misgivings about his negotiations with Joseph Matthes, the disreputable figure on the fringes of journalism who had brought discredit on Bernhard over the Ullstein family dispute. Although they turned out to be unfruitful, Poliakov's contacts with Matthes nonetheless appeared to confirm the staff's suspicions. Poliakov engaged in talks with another Russian emigrant, Konstantin Leites, who ominously insisted that, as part of a rescue package, Poliakov should modify the paper's editorial content to widen its appeal. He also proposed a change of editor: he wanted to recruit Richard Lewinsohn, who ironically had edited the business pages of Bernhard's old *Vossische* in Berlin and was now working on Leopold Schwarzschild's weekly *Neue Tage-Buch*. A third interested party was Fritz Wolff, a political refugee who had contributed articles to the *Tageblatt*.

It's easy to picture the doom-laden scenarios churning by now in the minds of Bernhard and his editorial team. They would have vivid memories of the way the great liberal establishments of Ullstein and Mosse in Berlin had opportunistically 'Aryanised' their staff, in the hope of propitiating the menacing Nazi masters. Now, in Paris, it needed little effort to imagine that, behind the scenes, machinations by the German embassy were under way. Bernhard would have assumed that vigilant German diplomats, aware of the tensions at the *Tageblatt*, were ready to pounce at the appropriate moment. In the autumn of 1933, rumours had circulated about Nazi efforts to rescue the *Neue Pariser Zeitung*, an ailing German-language daily established in Paris in the 1920s. That paper had since gone under, but in the summer of 1934, the German embassy, informed of Poliakov's problems, was advocating the *NPZ*'s resuscitation as the best way of torpedoing the *Tageblatt*.

Other recent incidents nourished the anxieties of Bernhard and his staff. They showed how effectively Nazi agents could subvert the opposition abroad and muzzle its journalists. *Westland* was a weekly published in the Saar, at the time an autonomous entity under League of Nations administration. In a plebiscite scheduled for January 1935, the local population was to choose between the status quo, attachment to France or re-incorporation into Germany. *Westland*'s editorial policy was to support the status quo.

In the autumn of 1934, the paper's publisher found the business strapped for cash and negotiated an advance of 200,000 francs from one Joseph Weissenberg. Despite Weissenberg's assurances that he wouldn't interfere editorially, it transpired that he had been acting as a front for the German propaganda ministry. The editors swiftly abandoned *Westland* and started another paper, *Grenzland*. A *Tageblatt* headline at the end of November 1934 read, 'Goebbels Buys *Westland*'.

Then there was the abduction of Berthold Jacob, a German journalist who had emigrated to Strasbourg in 1932 and who was an expert on Germany's rearmament drive. Dr Jacob was friendly with another journalist, Hans Wesemann, a former socialist who had secretly gone over to the Nazis. Holding out the prospect of valuable information for Berthold Jacob's press service, Wesemann in March 1935 lured Jacob to a restaurant outside Basle, close to the Swiss border with Germany. Wesemann proved to be a generous host and the liquor flowed freely.

'Canaan-sur-Seine'

Jacob didn't know that Wesemann and the 'chauffeur' who came by in a taxi to collect the two journalists were Gestapo agents. As the vehicle approached the German frontier, the driver flashed his lights three times and accelerated. An astonished Swiss border official managed to jump out of the way in time. On the German side, the border was wide open. The Nazis had kidnapped Jacob. Although they released him nearly six months later, the abduction was further evidence that the Reich would stoop to any stratagem to silence awkward opponents. That April, rumours linked the Jacob scandal to the mysterious death in London of two left-wing exiles, Dora Fabian and Mathilde Wurm. The coroner concluded that the women had committed suicide by taking poison. As a Swiss investigator had come to London to question Dora Fabian about the kidnapping, that verdict failed to quell talk of foul play by Nazi agents.

Like Feuchtwanger, Aldous Huxley used the Jacob incident. In *Eyeless in Gaza*, Giesebrecht is a refugee from Germany 'not because of his nose – because of his politics'. An 'Aryan but communist', he is enticed to Basel, supposedly to meet a 'familiar and fabulous' character, reminiscent of Willi Münzenberg – 'this most resourceful and courageous of all the German comrades engaged in the dissemination of communist propaganda and censored news'. The Nazis kidnap Giesebrecht, take him over the border into Germany and kill him.

In 1936, a third incident heightened the atmosphere of angst in the *Tageblatt*'s editorial offices. Czech police uncovered the intelligence activities of a German emigrant, Peter Ochmann, who was ostensibly working for a refugee organisation in Prague. It turned out that he had been supplying Nazi agents with compromising information: the names and addresses of émigrés and of their families in Germany. The Nazis, like the East Germans after the war, would threaten reprisals against the families of politically active émigrés. The *Tageblatt* reported the news in May, just a month before the staff's coup against Poliakov.

As the mid-summer of 1936 approached, Poliakov faced a difficult editorial deadline. Bernhard's contract ran until the end of that year. If the embattled proprietor wanted to terminate it, he would have to notify Bernhard six months in advance, by the end of June. Bernhard sailed for New York on 28 May. Rabbi Stephen Wise, a prominent figure in America's liberal Jewish community, had invited Bernhard to the United States to alert apathetic Jews to the dangerous clouds that were darkening Europe. By that time, Poliakov had failed to close a deal with either Konstantin Leites or Fritz Wolff.

Bernhard had already left Paris when Poliakov on 2 June wrote to warn him that there could be changes in their partnership, if he failed to raise money for their paper during his stay in the United States. About the same time, Poliakov alerted the paper's business manager, Artur Grave, to the prospect of new owners taking over. Poliakov explained that they would require both Grave and Bernhard to resign. They would also expect the *Tageblatt* to treat Germany less harshly, believing that not everything there was bad.

Over the next few days, Kurt Caro, Fritz Wolff and Bernhard's wife Fritze met in the Bernhards' apartment, from where they drafted cables to the editor about his supposed dismissal, and other news. They claimed Poliakov was taking advantage of Bernhard's absence to 'sell to the embassy'. Urging maximum discretion, they said the staff could counter the Nazi manoeuvre by starting a new publication, and that they had raised 200,000 francs for that purpose.

In the meantime, Bernhard had written to his wife to find out if Caro had taken the *Tageblatt*'s files with him. By 9 June, the mutineers were ready to abandon the *Tageblatt*. Through Salomon Grumbach, a French socialist deputy from Alsace who wrote for the paper, they had even taken steps to secure the goodwill of the French government.

When Caro published the sensational charges against Poliakov on the front page of Poliakov's own paper, many German refugees thought them plausible and expressed sympathy and support for the heroic breakaway by the editorial staff. They weren't alone. The way French evening newspapers and the news agencies immediately carried their statement showed that the journalists' influence stretched beyond exile circles.

A caustic Leon Poliakov remarked how the Franco-German 'Gotha de la gauche', from André Gide to Heinrich Mann, had acclaimed the mutiny. In New York, Georg Bernhard denounced the 'perfidious Russian' and exploited the incident to collect money for the new paper. The *New York Times* published the story as early as 12 June, a sub-headline categorically stating 'Reich Embassy Gets Control of *Tageblatt*'. It based its one-sided account of 'how the *Pariser Tageblatt* was converted to a pro-Nazi paper' on an interview with Bernhard the previous evening. In a short editorial headed 'Goebbels in Paris', the *New York Times* referred without qualification to the 'purchase' of 'the only daily anti-Nazi newspaper in Europe' by 'the chief of the propaganda and press section' of the German embassy. On his return from the United States, Bernhard claimed he could prove in a court of law exactly when Poliakov had visited the German embassy.

'What about Poliakov and Schmolz [head of the German embassy's press section]?' asked the refugee writer, Maximilian Scheer, when he called on the rebels' *Tageszeitung* at their new offices immediately after the putsch. 'We put that in to make the story clearer,' Scheer later reported the professional journalists as having told him. In fact, according to later research into the confidential reports that the German embassy sent to Berlin at the time, the coup took Berlin's diplomats by surprise.

Then as now, it would be improper for a diplomatic mission to carry out a direct commercial transaction of that type. On the other hand, an occult operation via a front organisation was conceivable, especially after the *Westland* and Berthold Jacob incidents. They had helped to foment the prevailing 'mole' hysteria, so that a covert Nazi intrigue against Bernhard and his staff that summer was as credible for émigrés in Paris as for journalists on Manhattan.

Where then did the truth lie? In the penultimate issue of his *Tageblatt*, Poliakov appealed to the German émigrés to judge for themselves the veracity of the journalists' allegations. He already had the Russian émigrés and their newspaper on his side. A Jewish jury of honour examined the charges made, in the words of Poliakov's son Leon, by the 'German gangsters', but the journalists declined to co-operate. They considered it to be below their dignity as German emigrants to submit to the probing of such a blatantly unrepresentative panel. The only German member of the tribunal, they pointed out, was a Jew who had converted. All the others were Russians, including close associates of Poliakov and someone the *Tageszeitung* referred to as an 'infamous Zionist fascist'. The 'court' dismissed the accusations against Poliakov, but the journalists refused to acknowledge its findings.

Most émigrés might have remained on the side of what they saw as the valiant rebels. After all, Richard Lewinsohn's one and only edition of the *Tageblatt* had indeed been less aggressively anti-Nazi. That was even the judgment of pro-Berlin observers in Paris, as Nazi records unearthed later show. Yet some leading exile figures had second thoughts. It was one thing to assert that Poliakov had supped with the devil, but it was straining their credulity to suggest that Lewinsohn, a German refugee, would let himself become involved in any remotely pro-Hitler coup.

The rebels retorted that Lewinsohn might unwittingly have allowed the paper's opinions to stray from the path of unqualified opposition to Berlin. Bernhard recalled the allegations he had made in his Ullstein days against the 'Mannheim Jewess', Rosie Gräfenberg. Ultimately, he was vindicated: she had in fact published articles in the Jewish press that praised the Nazis.

Some members of the refugee community worried about the way Kurt Caro and company had resorted to storm-trooper methods to sabotage Poliakov's efforts to bring out his paper. They took for granted that the mutinous journalists were behind the attack on Lewinsohn and the 'hijacking' of the final issue. What of their removal of the *Tageblatt*'s list of subscribers? With the Ochmann revelations in Prague still fresh in their minds, German refugees in Paris could regard that as a justified precaution to prevent the names from falling into Gestapo hands. Or was it plain theft? A French court would later decide that Caro had stolen the files. It imposed a fine on him – a small one, as the paper had relatively few subscribers.

The French association of foreign journalists carried out a second attempt at arbitration. In December 1936, it condemned Bernhard and his group for illegally expropriating Poliakov's paper. The German journalists disagreed with the findings, partly because the supposedly impartial chairman had sided with Poliakov. Faced with the prospect of censure and expulsion from the association, they nonetheless forestalled such a move by resigning from the body.

During the inquiry, Bernhard raised a thought-provoking challenge to the normally accepted right of publishers to handle their newspapers as purely commercial objects. He argued that a newspaper was also an item of intellectual property, to which the editorial staff had a claim. For him, there was a particularly strong case for 'co-ownership', if the publication was a weapon in a struggle against despotism. He didn't convince the 'jury'.

Although the murky circumstances surrounding the *Tageblatt*'s demise caused disquiet in Latin Quarter cafés, the German emigrants hesitated to join the unsavoury spectacle of the two sides hanging out their dirty laundry in public. Their silence was their way of showing solidarity with the journalists. But once again, the 'lone wolf' Leopold Schwarzschild refused to close ranks. By expressing his doubts about the journalists' version of events and espousing Poliakov's cause in his *Neue Tage-Buch* at the beginning of July 1936, he forced the exiled writers to open the 'can of worms'.

Such 'shabby tricks' by an émigré shocked Bernhard. Caro held that Schwarzschild was unqualified to set himself up as the moral censor of the emigration. The association of German writers in exile appointed a five-member investigative commission to judge whether

Schwarzschild had libelled Bernhard and Caro, but the acrimonious proceedings turned into a post-mortem on the *Tageblatt*. The commission tried to shed conclusive light on whether the journalists had plotted against Poliakov, or whether Poliakov had conspired with the German embassy.

Caro rested his case partly on the staff's knowledge that Poliakov wished to modify the paper's political line and was contemplating staff changes. The plotters' *pièce de résistance*, as Leon Poliakov put it, was the much-bruited report, said to come from a police file on his father, about Vladimir Poliakov's alleged links to the German embassy. The French police, the story went, had tipped off the paper's staff about Poliakov's meeting with the embassy's press attaché, Schmolz. The French minister of the interior had supposedly assured Bernhard's French associate, Salomon Grumbach, of the veracity of the police account.

Police files on foreigners were to be expected. But was the report of Poliakov's meeting with Schmolz genuine? The Poliakovs suspected that one of the conspirators had slipped the document into the police dossier and that Grumbach, who received a monthly retainer from Bernhard for articles and information, had covered up for the group.

Bernhard had another version of events. According to him, Poliakov went to see Schmolz because the German government was about to sue Poliakov and the associated Metzl advertising agency. They hadn't paid a large debt they owed to a Saar newspaper that the German government had expropriated after the plebiscite. In this version, the French authorities had registered Poliakov's visit to the German embassy but had refused to produce their evidence, as that would have amounted to an official admission of surveillance activities.

Three commission members found that the journalists hadn't plotted against the *Tageblatt*'s owner, but nor had they proved Poliakov's alleged visit to the German diplomat. The other two members also vindicated Poliakov, maintaining that there was no way of establishing conclusively who wrote the crucial report in the police dossier about his talks at the embassy.

Meanwhile, Poliakov had taken his former editor to court. He claimed that Bernhard had defamed him in three editorials in June and July, after he returned from the United States. In these, Bernhard repeated the gist of the earlier accusations, adding that no one else could have competed with Poliakov's rescuer – Goebbels. Bernhard said he could prove in a French court exactly when Poliakov, despite his denials, had called on Schmolz. Finally, he called Poliakov a proprietor without a conscience, a man willing to sell a political publication as if it were a cheese shop. A lower court found Bernhard guilty of libel, but the case stretched on into 1938, when Bernhard finally lost his appeal.

No one proved that Vladimir Poliakov knowingly aided official Nazi services in their campaign to undermine the émigré paper. Morally, the inquiries and legal procedures left Poliakov the victor, but materially he was a ruined man. His paper had sunk and the family had to sell its assets. Poliakov's health declined and he died in 1939. His son Leon, who had encouraged him to challenge his editor, went on to become a distinguished historian whose learned works dealing with anti-Semitism appeared in many languages. He died in 1997.

Vladimir Poliakov had objected that Bernhard's *Tageblatt* was too concerned with émigré issues. Ironically, Bernhard turned the paper's successor into a truly partisan organ of émigré politics. Bernhard, the classic bourgeois liberal, overcame his misgivings about Moscow and used his editorial seat at the *Tageszeitung* to call on Catholics, liberals and social democrats to work with the hard-line communists whom they had hitherto shunned. Many non-communists, however, still suspected that Moscow's overtures were a tactical manoeuvre and that a 'dictatorship of the proletariat' remained its goal. Continued political purges confirmed their fears.

One interpretation of the *Tageblatt* scandal portrays it as a battle between two camps within the German émigré community. The communists wanted to stop the anti-communist White Russian Poliakov from replacing an editor who was becoming pro-Soviet. On the other side, anti-communists such as Leopold Schwarzschild opposed Bernhard's efforts to promote the German Popular Front. At the beginning of the campaign to unite the exile community's factions, Schwarzschild and Bernhard had worked together on drawing up constitutional drafts for a post-Hitler 'Fourth Reich'. As Schwarzschild became disillusioned with Moscow, he began to obstruct the communist-dominated organisations, such as the German writers' guild.

Bernhard's value for the German resistance decreased as the prolonged *Tageblatt* affair exposed his role in the plot against Poliakov. A tug of war for control of its successor, the *Tageszeitung*, developed after the German communists' chief propagandist Willi Münzenberg fell out with Moscow in 1936. Bernhard supported Münzenberg and demanded complete editorial authority, but the management feared that the pair wanted to take over the paper and would promote the views of only the Moscow-friendly faction.

Asked to resign in June 1938, Bernhard broke with the paper in the preceding January. It was the third occasion on which he failed to reconcile his differences with newspaper proprietors. He went on to work for émigré causes, attending the international conference in Evian on the growing refugee problem. He kept on calling for a Popular Front, until Stalin's pact with Hitler in August 1939 thoroughly chastened him. Interned by the French near Bordeaux after the outbreak of war, Bernhard managed to flee to the United States in 1941. He died in New York in 1944.

Meanwhile, debts continued to plague the *Tageszeitung*. An appeal to Winston Churchill brought no response. The scandal had made the paper less attractive for American donors. Just as the disagreeable affair was fading from public memory, Leon Poliakov published a pamphlet in 1938 that served to revive it.

After the outbreak of war, the paper fell on even harder times. The French severely restricted what it could publish, other than positive articles based on official French and British reports about military preparations. Its readership shrank drastically. The French were interning male refugees including *Tageszeitung* journalists; émigrés were fleeing from the Continent. Distribution became more difficult. The Germans banned the paper's sale in newly conquered Austria and Czechoslovakia, and put pressure on Switzerland and Hungary to do the same. The *Tageszeitung* remained desperately short of funds and finally the printer called a halt. The last issue appeared on 18 February 1940.

On entering Paris in June 1940, the Nazis assigned a special squad to appropriate documents and works of art. Some of its members entered Bernhard's apartment and carried off furniture, art objects and private papers. At the *Tageszeitung*'s office, an axe was used to open the door so that it could remove files and equipment. A Nazi journalist admitted using a typewriter that 'accidentally fell into our hands' in the office of the 'infamous' paper and 'whose keys were last touched by agile dirty Jewish fingers'. He found the office 'as dirty and wretched' as the publication itself. Though the journalists were 'insignificant creatures', he stated, they had managed to mislead the French about the 'real' Germany.

Scholars on the other hand believe both the *Blatt* and the *Zeitung* had little political influence. Their journalists were too polemical and too prone to exaggerate. Their sensational stories were often unreliable. Governments and opinion-formers became sceptical about their reports. The papers' achievements probably lie elsewhere: through the many practical services they provided, the two papers helped the refugees adjust to the harsh blow fate had dealt them.

17 'Secret Kaiser' and 'Red Czar'

Heinrich Mann, Willi Münzenberg and the *Volksfront*

Thomas Mann briefly visited Sanary and Le Lavandou in September 1936. With his wife, he drove down from Switzerland to meet friends and acquaintances from his earlier sojourn there. He savoured a 'Lucullus-like' dinner at the Feuchtwangers and enjoyed walks across a 'wonderfully illuminated' landscape. Heinrich came over from Nice and the two brothers discussed politics. Thomas noted in his diary that Heinrich was in a sanguine frame of mind and even thought a revolution might break out in Germany. They spent a few days together before Thomas returned to Switzerland, while Heinrich went to Brussels to attend a world peace congress.

Was Heinrich Mann's political optimism justified as the year 1936 approached its end? Exiled politicians and intellectuals had heard from their underground contacts that people in all parts of Germany were deeply dissatisfied, even if they acknowledged that Hitler had created new jobs and enabled the country to regain its self-respect. Reports filtered out about Germans who didn't expect the regime to last long, however solidly entrenched it might appear. Some complained they had become less well off, yet seemed resigned to remaining helpless bystanders. Others, one heard, resented the police state's excessive intrusion into their lives and the way it was disrupting the country's traditions. Against that background, and encouraged by the rise of anti-fascist coalitions in Spain and France, German émigrés believed the moment had arrived for them to bring their diverse groups under one roof – and launch their counter-offensive.

A more realistic assessment would surely have led to a different conclusion: after all, the Nazis had by then crushed the opposition and consolidated their regime in most important respects. They sat more firmly than ever in the saddle. Foreign protests hadn't deflected them from hounding the country's Jews or from preparing for war and conquest. With the proclamation of their Nuremberg laws a year earlier, they had put their anti-Semitic obsession on a broad legal basis that would enable them to persecute the country's Jews more effectively than any pogrom in history.

In March 1936, Hitler had reacted to the ratification of the Franco-Soviet mutual assistance pact with an audacious coup. His armed forces re-occupied the demilitarised Rhineland. Britain and France offered no resistance. For the Nazi press, Hitler had sundered the shackles of the Versailles treaty. The spectacular pomp and ceremony surrounding the Berlin Olympic Games in the summer of 1936 had left the world with vivid impressions of a disciplined and mighty *Volk* standing solidly behind its new masters.

The democracies had stood passively by in October 1935, as Mussolini embarked on a cruel war of conquest in Abyssinia. Whether Paris and London would intervene to counter the fierce insurrection General Franco had launched against the Spanish Republicans in July 1936 was still uncertain. Contrary to what many refugees had at first hoped, the German people hadn't come to their senses, nor had Britain and France shown any determination to help them do so.

From his own narrower perspective, on the other hand, Heinrich Mann was justified in expressing some self-satisfaction. He was pouring out a torrent of journalism attacking Berlin. He had published what critics considered an important literary work with political undertones, a long historical novel about France's enlightened King Henri IV.

Heinrich Mann appeared to be achieving his goal: leading the refugees in France to political unity. Tirelessly campaigning for the goals of the Popular Front and for what he himself termed the 'people's state' he wanted to see in a postwar Germany, Mann gave numerous speeches, in addition to writing many topical articles and essays. Brian Howard told Klaus Mann he was going to the Albert Hall in Kensington to hear Klaus's 'Uncle Heinrich speak on Spain at a great meeting, and I am reviewing his *Henri IV* in the [*New*] *Statesman*'.

At first, Heinrich Mann had ridiculed Hitler, heaped disdain on the Nazi regime and expressed disgust at its brutality. As the Third Reich took root, he regarded the Nazis more seriously, moving from psychological to economic analyses and emphasising the need for Hitler's German opponents to work with what he presented as a more moderate Kremlin. His enemy's enemy was his friend – that was Heinrich Mann's simple philosophy on this issue. And that was why he joined the Popular Front crowd in supporting the Soviet Union, even though he wasn't blind to its defects.

Heinrich Mann went back to journalism after he reached the south of France in the spring of 1933. Editors in Prague, Paris and elsewhere began to ask for articles and soon Mann was contributing to most émigré periodicals. Some of his German texts were among those that active anti-Nazis printed on thin paper and smuggled into Germany. Over the rest of the decade, he was to write regularly in French for the highly respected *Dépêche de Toulouse*, a provincial daily with a print order in the 1930s of some 350,000 copies.

Mann would go to the Café Monnot in Nice and read a courtesy copy of the *Dépêche de Toulouse* that the paper's management delivered to him. It was one of the few papers he read regularly. His *Dépêche* articles on current affairs incurred the wrath of the German authorities and in February 1934 provoked a protest by the German embassy to the French government. It proved ineffective, probably because the newspaper's proprietor was the brother of a Radical Party politician who served in some 20 ministries. As Mann used up the money he had transferred out of Germany, he relied increasingly on the modest income from his combative articles and essays, as well as his royalties and a retainer from Querido, his new publisher in Amsterdam.

Mann's articles – he later also gave political broadcasts on Moscow's German-language 'freedom radio' – chronicle the inexorable drift to war. He accused the Nazis of instigating the Reichstag fire and fiercely denounced Germany's fraudulent elections, as well as the arbitrary persecutions under way there. As early as March 1933, Mann foresaw the likelihood of Germany annexing Austria.

In July of that year, the Toulouse paper published his essay on 'l'éducation morale', one of his favourite topics. The German version was the piece that opened the first issue of Klaus Mann's review, and caused Thomas Mann's publisher in Berlin such anxiety. For a long time, Heinrich Mann's articles reflected his belief that it would be enough to appeal to the German people's reason. Then he grasped that Hitler's ideas had struck a chord with much of the population. He discarded his few illusions about the true nature of the regime or the chances of effective counter-measures from other European powers. Clearly, they weren't ready to halt Hitler's re-armament drive.

Mann was, nevertheless, determined to expose what he held to be the truth about the scoundrels in Berlin. To that end he wanted to re-issue his *Dépêche* articles in book form, though he didn't expect sales to exceed 8,000 to 10,000 copies. Mann translated them into his mother tongue for the German book version that Querido had agreed to issue as *Der Hass* (Hate). It appeared in the summer of 1934 and strong demand led to a second printing within a fortnight. The Nazis tried to stop the distribution of *Der Hass* after a German review unwittingly reproduced, uncut, Mann's unflattering essay contrasting Hitler with Hindenburg.

A French version, *La Haine*, ran into nine reprints. The Soviet publishing organisation brought out 50,000 copies, and the book also appeared in Polish and Rumanian. Although Lion Feuchtwanger took a copy to London on Heinrich Mann's behalf, he failed to find a publisher who showed a definite interest in an English-language edition. Mann's political texts are full of grandiose abstractions that make his writings probably even less digestible in translation than in the original. Yet it was precisely in the Anglo-Saxon world, Heinrich Mann argued, that people didn't fully appreciate what was happening in Germany. Apart from their quibbling over details, London publishers were reluctant to displease the Germans, Mann surmised.

For presumably the same reasons, the Swiss authorities banned the book. In Austria, the Viennese publisher of Mann's pre-exile books now told him it would bring out no further works by him. The firm added to the blow by refusing to release the rights to the Mann titles it had already acquired. There were no French or English translations of a second collection of Mann's anti-fascist articles published in 1935. By the time his third collection appeared, Hitler was about to invade Poland and Mann realised that publication of the essays was politically 'pointless' and of only literary significance.

To gain more time to gather enough journalistic material for *Der Hass*, Mann had set aside his draft novel about King Henry of Navarre, begun before he fled Germany. He was one of several writers in French exile who took to working on historical novels or biographies. In recalling past events and figures, many of them saw a way of conveying a lesson about the present. Such works also helped writers overcome a professional hurdle they faced in exile: they were increasingly isolated from Germany, but still unfamiliar with modern France.

Where Thomas Mann had found his inspiration in the Old Testament, Heinrich looked to the French renaissance. He chose Henri of Navarre who, as Henri IV, proclaimed the edict of Nantes that brought religious freedom to France's Protestants. Mann's idea dated back to a voyage to south-west France in the 1920s, during which he visited Pau, the king's birthplace. Mann researched deeply, and curiously had misgivings about incorporating so many 'inalterable facts'. He began to see himself as a plagiarist.

Behind the facts lay a purpose. In Mann's judgment, the 'social' novel hadn't developed in Germany to the same extent as in France and Russia. For him, literature was more than a means to educate the elite; it was also an instrument to bring what he regarded as a socialist humanism to the *Volk*. His *Henri IV* is partly a vehicle to express these political ideas. He threaded didactic strands into it much as Feuchtwanger and others were doing in their historical fiction.

Between the lines of the book, but without overburdening the narrative, Mann wove a political message for his contemporaries. To alert readers, the supporters of the wicked Catholic league might suggest Nazi storm-troopers. Followers of its leader, Henri de Guise, greet him with 'Heil' and outstretched right hands. Did Goebbels inspire Mann's Jean Boucher, the fanatical and deformed priest who barks out his harangues? Did Mann have in mind a more effective League of Nations when writing about the 'grand design' for Europe devised by Sully, Henri's minister? Above all, was the novel a call to the forces opposing Hitler to close ranks?

Completing the work in French exile, Mann had been drafting his section on the St Bartholomew's Day massacre of the Protestants when in 1934 Hitler ordered the slaying of Ernst Röhm and other alleged conspirators. By emphasising the French monarch's enlightened leadership during an epoch of savage religious strife in 16th-century Europe, Mann hoped the novel would help repulse the waves of bigotry sweeping over contemporary Europe. He might even have seen himself as a latter-day Henri IV, destined to bring about some form of rapprochement among the banished groups and lead them into intellectual battle against the Nazi tyrant. Mann's portrayal of Henri's mistress Gabrielle d'Estrées showed a resemblance to his own companion and later wife, Nelly Kroeger.

Querido published the work in two volumes, the first towards the end of 1935 and the second in 1938. Feuchtwanger saw the panoramic renaissance epic as a powerful Gobelin tapestry in which Mann had woven the life and deeds of a true leader, in contrast to the comic Führers 'that surround us'. Some critics hailed it at the time, and later, as a work that ranked among the finest historical novels of 20th-century Europe. Even before Mann completed the first volume, foreign publishers had acquired translation rights to what Secker in London would issue in three volumes.

By December 1937, the United States edition of *Young Henry of Navarre* had sold nearly 18,000 copies, and Metro-Goldwyn-Mayer was interested in producing a film version. The novel didn't entice French publishers, on the other hand; perhaps they assumed that

French readers knew enough about the life and loves of their great monarch. Or perhaps, like Brecht, they had unkindly concluded that few would be able to make head or tail of such a jumble of lifeless characters. One of Mann's British biographers judged the prose style to be 'virtually untranslatable'.

Mann had finished the first volume, on Henri's youth, a few days before he travelled to Paris for the international writers' congress in June 1935. It was a time of ferment among the German émigrés. For more than two years, they had been adjusting to life in exile, debating their next moves and carrying out their inevitable post-mortem on the end of the Weimar republic.

One explanation of how and why Hitler had come to power highlighted the divisions among parties on the left. Who was to blame for the mutual mistrust? For social democrats, the fault lay with the communists, who wanted to impose on Germany a Soviet-style dictatorship of the proletariat that would be incompatible with the accepted values of western democracies. For communists, the unreliable social democrats were to blame. They had, after all, joined bourgeois parties in forcibly suppressing communist demonstrations. They were 'social fascists' who weren't genuinely prepared to discard the worn-out capitalist system in favour of their proclaimed socialist goals.

If division had helped to let Hitler in, perhaps union could force him out. In Spain and France the parties of the centre and of the left had formed political alliances to halt the spreading fascist threat. They exhorted others to do likewise. In June 1935, some 60,000 people demonstrated in a Paris suburb for international solidarity of the left. Heinrich Mann welcomed this French 'interference' in the affairs of other countries. Émigré publications in Paris took up the call, Georg Bernhard exhorting readers of his Paris émigré daily newspaper to 'wake up'.

The mass meeting in Paris was one of a chain of protests, from London's Trafalgar Square to Australia and New Zealand, orchestrated by the Communist International's web of agents. Like the Paris writers' congress that summer, the demonstrations were signals from Moscow that it had reversed its earlier policy and was now willing to reach out to other anti-Hitler forces.

At its historic seventh congress in Moscow, a month after the Paris rally, the Communist International itself, which regulated the policies of national communist parties around the world, confirmed the Kremlin's new doctrine of co-operation. The German communists had to toe the latest Comintern line. The old guard, associated with the party's failure to halt Hitler, was to make way for a fresh command under Wilhelm Pieck and Walter Ulbricht, both of whom would later preside over East Germany's fortunes.

Despite Ulbricht's opposition, the Comintern's chief agent in Western Europe, Willi Münzenberg, joined the German CP's central committee. The Comintern instructed Münzenberg to encourage German émigré groups in Paris to gather around one table. Münzenberg found some writers and politicians were already meeting at the Hôtel des Sociétés Savantes in the rue Serpente, near the Odéon. They had set up a provisional committee under Heinrich Mann, their 'secret Kaiser', to work for freedom in Germany. Far from trying to compete with them, Münzenberg chose to work with and through Mann and the rest of the intelligentsia. A remarkable propagandist had joined forces with an outstanding publicist to lead the struggle to reverse the fascist onslaught.

If that appeared to be a daunting assignment, then Mann and Münzenberg looked like a formidable combination. No personality was more likely to forge a solid opposition than Heinrich Mann. The émigrés hadn't hesitated to choose Mann as their helmsman and spokesman. It was as if fate had moulded him expressly for the position of what some would term the 'uncrowned president of the Fourth Reich'.

Here was a public figure who stood above political groups, not bound to any of the factions that had carried their doctrinal disputes with them into exile. There lay much of his influence, and Mann welcomed the fact that the political camps appreciated rather than scorned his neutral position. Here was a carefully dressed patrician – with the bow tie and goatee of a French senator – whose reserved and unpretentious manner, as he himself acknowledged, radiated the authority needed to mediate in the many conflicts that arose. The gravitas of age – he was now in his mid-sixties – raised him indisputably above the rest.

Socially and culturally he was a highly respected figure, as he had been in the Weimar days. Exiles viewed his energetic crusade against the Nazi barbarians as a predestined continuation of his fight against the crass nationalism of the pre-World War I monarchy. His humanism, his tolerance, his belief in education and reason – he envisaged a republic governed by a 'dictatorship of reason' rather than a 'dictatorship of the proletariat' – all were attributes that appealed to his fellow emigrants.

Also to Mann's advantage was his deep familiarity with France, with the French mentality and with French intellectuals. He had close links to the French Popular Front movement. Even before 1933, in the harsh years of strife over German reparations, the Francophile Mann had been an honoured figure in France. Now, with rabid anti-Semitic and fascist sentiments rampant in the country, Mann had another trump: he was neither Jew nor communist.

Besides the time he devoted to his substantial journalistic and literary output, Mann attended committees and addressed conferences in Paris and elsewhere. He would travel from his home in Nice to support a multitude of political organisations engaged in intellectual opposition. He became a co-president of Romain Rolland's World Committee Against War and Fascism. Addressing the League of Nations in Geneva, he called for measures to make it easier for refugees to obtain identity papers. He became a leading light in the international association of writers, PEN. He served as president of the German émigrés' library in Paris. He was honorary president of the association of German writers in exile. Mann wanted to go on a lecture tour of the United States so that he could help awaken Americans to the looming crisis in Europe. He had to decline the invitation, as he could not assure the organisers that he was able to speak in English without a text.

Mann and Münzenberg complemented one another: one a patrician and the other a plebeian (though some claimed Münzenberg was an illegitimate nephew of Kaiser Wilhelm II). Mann, a dedicated liberal who in an era of demagogues still believed that reasoned arguments would suffice to sway the masses, joined forces with Münzenberg, a man of action who seemingly had few scruples about the methods he used to manipulate opinion.

For some, Münzenberg has gone down in history as a 'grand master' of the covertly controlled propaganda front, a sinister genius who secretly directed a crowd of gullible intellectual fellow-travellers, from Heinrich Mann to the American journalist Dorothy Thompson and Harold Laski, the London School of Economics' star political scientist.

Willi Münzenberg's proletarian background offered a striking contrast to that of the courtly Mann. Born in Erfurt in 1889, Münzenberg lost both parents as a child. He worked in a shoe factory, became a pacifist during the First World War and a member of the German Communist Party in 1919. He met Trotsky and Lenin in Switzerland during the war. In the early 1920s, Lenin asked the 'red czar' to set up in Berlin what turned into a powerful worldwide welfare and public relations organisation to help many thousands of starving Russians.

Fond of luxury cars and expensive clothes, Münzenberg organised mass-meetings and congresses, ran left-wing newspapers, magazines, book clubs and radio stations, and distributed propaganda films. He acquired an evening paper and rapidly increased its circulation from 3,000 to 100,000 copies. He acquired exclusive distribution rights to Soviet films, bringing Eisenstein's *Battleship Potemkin* to the west.

Exploiting imaginative publicity methods, Münzenberg seemingly managed to run his powerful German media empire without letting a stifling party apparatus fetter him. Adopting the techniques of the sensation-mongering capitalist press, he transformed the pedantic and pedestrian newspapers of the extreme left into popular revolutionary broadsheets.

A communist member of the Reichstag since 1924, Münzenberg had been campaigning in his constituency near Frankfurt-am-Main on the evening of the Reichstag fire. Hitler had dissolved the Reichstag four weeks earlier, setting the elections for 5 March 1933. During the interim, Münzenberg, like other deputies, temporarily lost his parliamentary immunity. After the fire, the police, who arrested more than 11,000 communists, social democrats and other opponents of Hitler, searched Münzenberg's Berlin apartment in the building where Magnus Hirschfeld had his sexology institute. They delivered their arrest warrant there.

Police and storm-troopers raided the office of Münzenberg's publishing, newspaper and welfare trust, ordered the undertaking to cease further publication and closed its accounts. Münzenberg's companion, Babette Gross, obtained a passport with a false name for him. A chauffeur from his Frankfurt office drove him over the border into the Saar, at the time administered by the League of Nations. From Saarbrücken he reached Paris, where Babette Gross joined him. He was already in exile when voters re-elected him to the Reichstag.

From his office near Les Halles, Münzenberg and his loyal émigré staff – communists and fellow-travellers – soon organised a congress against war and fascism. They helped to establish the German 'Freedom Library', took over the Éditions du Carrefour publishing house, launched a daily paper as well as a weekly publication, and set up the secretariat of a world committee to aid victims of German fascism. Münzenberg was a past master at working through Comintern-controlled front organisations and the world committee was a typical example. Camouflaged as a philanthropic body based in London, it had Henri Barbusse, the British scientist J. B. S. Haldane and other internationally renowned Marxist sympathisers as its patrons.

Münzenberg's organisational talent, his 'proletarian' charm and his intellectual temperament made him powerfully persuasive. Arthur Koestler and others who worked with him all admired his special ability for inveigling highly respected political and intellectual figures into attaching their names and moral authority to his initiatives, so endowing them with considerable weight and ensuring them international publicity.

As the Nazis prepared, in 1933, to put on trial in Leipzig the communists they accused of setting the Reichstag on fire, Münzenberg used his committee to launch a swift counter-offensive. He didn't dispute that the chief defendant, Marinus Van der Lubbe, had started the fire. Instead, he offered evidence in his *Brown Book of the Hitler Terror* that the Dutchman was a Nazi stooge. Only by passing through a tunnel linking the parliament to Göring's official residence, he noted, could Van der Lubbe have ignited the fire.

Münzenberg had no proof and relied on a mixture of facts, bluff and intelligent guesswork. At the same time, his *Brown Book* offered a wealth of documentation about the persecution of the Jews, the first concentration camps and the stifling of the arts. It became a handbook of the anti-fascist movement. The propaganda maestro used many articles clipped from the newspapers he voraciously read; he drew on reports from his secret agents in German cities and he questioned refugees newly arrived in Paris. Translations of the *Brown Book* were soon available in large quantities around the world.

Münzenberg smuggled into Germany anti-Nazi propaganda disguised as paperback classics by Schiller and Goethe. He and his chief lieutenant, Otto Katz, alias André Simon (whom the communists would hang in Prague in 1952 as a British spy and Zionist conspirator), organised a 'counter-trial' in London at which an international group of notable lawyers examined the origins of the Reichstag fire. Katz called it 'an unofficial tribunal whose mandate was conferred by the conscience of the world'. The lawyers announced their 'verdict' – the Nazis were naturally the guilty party – the day before the real trial opened in Leipzig. Münzenberg's astute campaign to mobilise international opinion had put the Nazis on the defensive; the supreme court found Van der Lubbe guilty, but acquitted his four alleged accomplices. By any standards, it was a remarkable victory for the Paris scribes.

Now, two years later, the question was whether the Münzenberg-Mann tandem could successfully run an even more challenging campaign. Having agreed to Heinrich Mann's proposal to merge the different émigré groups, Münzenberg orchestrated a first joint meeting in September 1935 at the Hôtel Lutétia, a large Belle Époque establishment on Boulevard Raspail, near the Bon Marché department store.

Appropriately situated between the artistic Montparnasse and the literary-political Boulevard Saint Germain, the Lutétia had, in the 1920s, hosted New Year balls to raise money for poor Russian émigré writers. Now, it came to represent the endeavours of a broad spectrum of German refugees to settle their political differences and build an effective coalition. It was one of the hotels that became landmarks of the exiled intellectuals' pariah years. The Hôtel Lux was where German communists congregated in Moscow. The Hôtel de la Tour recalls the relatively agreeable early years of many writers in Sanary. The Hôtel Splendide in Marseilles is associated with Varian Fry's desperate efforts, after the fall of France, to rescue the more prominent intellectuals who flocked to the last major French port not controlled by the Nazis.

As the émigré representatives gathered in the salons of the Hôtel Lutétia in that September of 1935, one of Germany's opposition political parties wasn't formally present – though it had attracted one fifth of the votes at the end of the Weimar Republic. The Socialist International had allowed individual national parties to decide for themselves whether they wished to work with the communists. Like other social democrat parties in northwestern Europe, the German social democrats had declined to do so. Their absence from the Lutétia meeting was an unfortunate omission. Banned in June 1933, the party had moved to Prague and ran probably the most effective underground resistance network in Germany. It was left to those prominent party members who had settled in Paris to attend as individuals. Among them was Rudolf Breitscheid, who had presided over the social democrat group in the Reichstag.

Participants unanimously accepted Münzenberg's proposal that Heinrich Mann head a committee to steer their work forward. The administrative task facing Mann and Münzenberg was to create a viable organisation, but to what end? The embryonic German Popular Front had no electorate to whom it could appeal, whereas its Spanish and French equivalents were alliances of parties that contested elections and formed governments. A German resistance movement, however united, was unlikely to start recruiting volunteers for a guerrilla war behind the enemy's lines.

Then there was, from the beginning, a simmering conflict over what the participants understood by 'democracy'. The atmosphere of confusion developed into an abrasive ambivalence between writers and politicians about what they were trying to do. Münzenberg and Mann, perhaps seeing themselves and an inner-Lutétia fraternity as latter-day American 'founding fathers', believed their job was to draft and publicise detailed declarations. They wanted to agree among themselves as to their goals, spell out the nature of the post-Nazi German polity and issue proclamations based on this. They hoped that their vision of a better world, once communicated illegally to the oppressed German masses, would provoke unrest, resistance and perhaps an uprising.

What form should a new Germany take? To recommend a straightforward restoration, a return to some form of the discredited Weimar Republic, was obviously out of the question. On the other hand, Münzenberg thought it illusory for communists to maintain that a 'dictatorship of the proletariat' could simply replace Hitler's dictatorship without a transition phase. He knew that Nazi propaganda was effectively exploiting the widespread fear that a Soviet regime would mean chaos.

Having agreed that the new Germany would be some form of social democracy, the Lutétians in September 1935 asked a small group, which included the two bourgeois journalists, Leopold Schwarzschild and Georg Bernhard, to put their ideas on paper. For a while, an atmosphere of confidence prevailed in the salons of the Hôtel Lutétia. In his weekly *Das Neue Tage-Buch*, Schwarzschild claimed in November 1935 that observers in and outside Germany believed the Nazi regime had passed its zenith. As the Lutétia participants saw it, their task was to penetrate the Reich and reassure disappointed Germans and those with a grudge that Hitler's demise wouldn't mean chaos, terror and hunger.

Did Münzenberg have Moscow's approval for letting non-communist members of the liberal intelligentsia outline the main features of a new German constitution? Probably not, for the German communist leaders in Paris warned the Lutétia group that abstract discussions on future government programmes threatened to turn the meetings into endless palavers. In any case, the communists didn't see how one could formally constitute a German anti-fascist alliance without the official participation of the 'Sopade', the Social Democrat Party in exile in Prague.

Ulbricht himself met with the social democrats in the Czech capital in November 1935, in an attempt to overcome the fratricidal combat between parties of the left. He learned that the Sopade continued to distrust the German communists' professions of their faith in democracy, despite the change in their discourse. By the middle of

1936, Pieck and other communist leaders were calling for a 'democratic republic' rather than a 'dictatorship of the proletariat'. On closer analysis, however, it appeared that the new terminology had concealed rather than replaced the old.

German communists held that a democratic republic alone wouldn't mean the end of capitalist exploitation and the beginning of socialism. They still saw a dictatorship of the proletariat as their goal, and assumed they could bring it about if backed by the bulk of the workers. The German Communist Party, therefore, set about winning workers' support. In campaigning for that goal, the party now expected to enjoy the same rights as all other components of a Popular Front coalition.

It was hardly surprising, therefore, that the social democrats remained sceptical. They interpreted the Communist Party's assent to an alliance as little more than a tactical propaganda move on its part: a German Popular Front would simply serve as a stepping-stone to the unchanged communist objective of a Soviet Germany. Hadn't the title of a book by Wilhelm Pieck been *We Are Fighting for a Soviet Germany* (in the English translation published in London in 1934)?

Despite mutterings that the Popular Front organisers relied too heavily on journalists, the politicians didn't interfere. The writers expected to announce their blueprint for what Georg Bernhard called the 'Fourth Reich' at a plenary meeting of the Lutétia circle early in 1936. As the German phrase has it, they were like hunters trying to sell the pelt before they had killed the bear.

They outlined a programme for the first four days after the overthrow of the Nazis. Besides the formation of a provisional government representing all political groups in exile, they wanted the Vatican's blessing for the new Germany, and ceremonies at which they would burn the contents of Nazi offices. There were some unexpectedly authoritarian traits: only adults over the age of 30 would have the right to vote, and the government would restrict freedom of the press.

Control of newspapers reflected the journalists' concern to avoid a fresh drift to right-wing extremism and to ensure democratic control over freedom of expression. They wanted to prevent proprietors of newspaper empires, such as the conservative Hugenberg complex in the Weimar era, from inciting readers against a democratically elected government. Leopold Schwarzschild recommended that a 'qualified publicist' sit on editorial boards of newspapers. It would be for editors rather than proprietors to decide who was a competent information specialist.

The group also envisaged the next Germany as being part of what they variously called a 'European community', a 'united states of Europe', or a 'supranational Europe'. The economic measures they advocated, such as the expropriation of large estates and the nationalisation of banking and heavy industry, would become common features of postwar Europe.

Heinrich Mann convoked the plenary session of the Lutétia circle for 2 February 1936. On the preceding day, the left-wing and liberal political groups held separate preparatory gatherings to consider the detailed papers that Bernhard and his colleagues had drawn up for them. The politicians rejected the writers' more specific proposals, saying they would accept from them nothing more than a general statement of principles. What had gone wrong?

Communists or radical socialists were unlikely to adopt the bourgeois journalists' plans for the 'Fourth Reich', premised as they were on a modified capitalist system. Ideological barriers between social democrats and communists, moreover, impeded consensus on such precise details of a far-distant new German state. In any case, the Communist Party's priority was the immediate joint combat to overthrow the Nazis. In its view, a Popular Front meant an alliance among political parties; it was the parties' role to work out any common platform.

Münzenberg had the unenviable task of telling the writers that their labours had been a waste of time. He had initially supported their approach, but had since grasped that the communist hierarchy disapproved of his close partnership with the liberals. He now had to persuade the writers to prepare a fuzzy declaration on liberties and human rights acceptable to all groups.

They did so and, at the plenary on 2 February, their declaration was the only item on the agenda, apart from an amnesty appeal. Nearly 120 leading figures from the 'other' Germany congregated in the hotel to hear Bernhard explain the document. Breitscheid and others criticised some of its passages and complained that the organisers hadn't circulated the text in advance.

Heinrich Mann accepted most objections to the document. While he could conjure up a vision of the future Germany as poetic as that of any writer, he sensed where the power lay. He later said his fellow scribes had been grateful for, rather than upset by, his willingness to compromise.

Mann undertook the thankless chore of asking a group of mediators to amend the declaration. All present accepted the new text and its call for a workers' democracy. But that wasn't the end of the story. Party officials were infuriated that some publications reproduced the writers' original version. Germany's anti-Hitler politicians never again allowed poets to become so directly involved in their business.

Outside observers, however, reckoned the conference and its vague call for German unity a noteworthy event. They expected the hitherto insignificant debating club might turn into a solid political movement. Nazi agents reported to Berlin that Heinrich Mann and his colleagues had the makings of a government in exile. Perhaps they really feared the émigrés could provoke an uprising against Hitler.

Armed with the Lutétia circle's declaration, Heinrich Mann and Münzenberg could now lead the anti-Nazi struggle. They expected to win public sympathy and strengthen the resolve of western governments to oppose the Führer. They hoped to help Hitler's many political prisoners more effectively. They wanted to embolden Germany's underground resistance, which they thought remained widespread. They planned to distribute anti-Nazi material, to commit acts of sabotage and to incite workers to strike.

The timing of the plenary session had been fortunate. In that same February 1936, Spain's Popular Front parties were victorious in national elections. The following May, France's Popular Front notched up a similar success. Broad masses backed the Spanish and French movements, but the Lutétia circle's direct support came from a few thousand exiles in Paris.

In the following months, the Lutétia circle formed an executive committee, produced a thrice-weekly publication and launched a series of political statements. Its activities culminated, in December 1936, in yet another supplication to the German people to unite against Hitler. With the notable exception of Leopold Schwarzschild, who had withdrawn from the 'experiment' in the summer of 1936, the familiar band of writers, from Lion Feuchtwanger to Klaus Mann, appended their names to the revised appeal. Couched in terms general enough to secure the signature of Wilhelm Pieck and Walter Ulbricht for the communists, and Willy Brandt on behalf of the splinter Socialist Workers Party, the document had the support of individual social democrats in Paris, but not of the party as such in Prague. Over all those months of attempts to ally Germany's two major left-wing parties in exile, the socialists and the communists undertook only one joint action – a protest against the Nazis' execution of a communist militant.

By the end of 1936, it wasn't, as some émigrés had imagined, the government in Berlin that had passed its peak – it was the German

Popular Front campaign in Paris. The momentum was evaporating. As the months advanced, events impelled Heinrich Mann to admit that his appeals for a united resistance to Hitler were becoming increasingly unrealistic. Following Schwarzschild, other liberals and Catholic representatives had withdrawn from the organisation.

The émigrés wanted to alarm the western powers and exhort them to halt the impending disasters. Reaction to the Spanish Civil War showed them the futility of their exertions. Within France itself, the German resistance found itself competing with the German government to win over the local population. As Lion Feuchtwanger narrated in *Paris Gazette*, his novel about refugees in Paris, suave German diplomats and journalists supported the extreme right, who hated Léon Blum and his Popular Front government. They also backed campaigns to encourage war veterans, pacifists and the young generation to rally for peace through reconciliation – 'rapprochement' – with Germany.

It was, however, Stalin rather than Hitler who ultimately torpedoed the German resistance. The first political trials took place in Moscow in the summer of 1936, when Soviet judges sentenced long-standing colleagues of Lenin to death for 'Trotskyist disloyalty' and supposedly plotting assassinations. Heinrich Mann expressed his regret but didn't protest, though asked several times to do so. If those sentenced to death had conspired against the revolution, he wrote, it was necessary to eliminate them rapidly. He abased himself less than Boris Pasternak, one of 16 Soviet writers who publicly bayed for the heads of the senior party figures accused of terrorism. Their tract was headed 'Wipe them from the face of the earth'.

As the trials extended into 1938, they increased the mistrust of émigrés who had hitherto looked sympathetically on the Soviet Union. André Gide's disillusioned observations about the Soviet Union, published in November 1936, became a bestseller and influenced many wavering Germans in exile. The judicial farces almost nullified the conciliatory gestures the communists had made to the other anti-fascist bodies.

The Moscow purges turned into a watershed for the struggling German *Volksfront*. The German Communist Party found it increasingly awkward to co-operate with émigré groups who were attacking Stalin for liquidating the political veterans around him. Within the Lutétia circle, the Comintern's attempts to stifle open discussion and dominate the group's activities – in effect to make the Hôtel Lutétia subservient to the Hôtel Lux – steadily undermined the circle's initial enthusiasm.

The disparate composition of the émigré coalition offered little room for doctrinal consensus. There was no way to reconcile dogmatic Communist Party functionaries and veteran liberal wordsmiths. Perhaps, as George Orwell argued, the Popular Front was an unholy alliance between robbers and robbed that had 'about as much right to exist as a pig with two heads'.

Since Heinrich Mann chose to remain above the organisational disputes and day-to-day intrigues, he failed to fully exert his unquestioned moral authority. He paid only brief visits to Paris, preferring to tarry in Nice. Much as Mann tried, in the self-appointed role of honest broker, to guide the movement to a loftier plane, he was ultimately drawn into a bitter conflict that involved his right-hand man, Willi Münzenberg.

Though Münzenberg had been content to direct operations from behind the scenes, there was an element of hubris about his methods. He was an outstanding propagandist but a poor bureaucrat. Münzenberg's unconventional approach, hitherto so successful, and his ill-disguised contempt for sycophancy, manoeuvering and hair-splitting, had earned him the hostility of the more orthodox Communist Party hacks. Münzenberg had originally justified the political trials, claiming that the accused had engaged in espionage and endangered the Soviet Union's security. Disturbing reports now reached Moscow of his growing unease over the liquidations.

Münzenberg believed he was still a true communist, but his party peers saw him as a maverick who had turned into a bourgeois deviant. For Wilhelm Pieck and Walter Ulbricht, he had become too headstrong. He was unwilling to bow to party discipline, just when unity was primordial. In preparing for a catastrophic collision with the Third Reich, the Soviet Union couldn't tolerate any internal opposition. Even émigrés who weren't full-blooded communists understood that, as they observed the ineffectual snarling and snapping of France and Britain. Münzenberg's downfall was only a matter of time.

In the summer of 1936, the Comintern offered Münzenberg a position in the propaganda section of its headquarters. By the time he went to Moscow in October 1936, ostensibly to prepare for his new responsibilities, he knew he had fallen out of favour with the Party. A Comintern disciplinary board questioned him about his and his colleagues' activities in Paris. He declined to sign a statement denying rumours of his refusal to carry out tasks assigned to him by the Comintern. Münzenberg's superiors nonetheless let him return to Paris, accepting his explanation that he needed to settle his affairs in the French capital. He knew that in Moscow he probably faced banishment or even liquidation – and he resolved not to go back there.

After a few months' respite, Ulbricht returned to the attack, but from a different angle. In the spring of 1937, Ulbricht informed Heinrich Mann that he, the party apparatchik, would be replacing Münzenberg on the *Volksfront* committee, because Münzenberg would be absent from Paris for a long time. A perturbed Mann insisted that it wasn't the Communist Party but the committee, as an autonomous body, that determined who its members should be. The social democrats, who were also unhappy with the communists' manoeuvres, joined Heinrich Mann in asking the Communist Party to replace Ulbricht.

Ulbricht told a powerless Mann that the Communist Party couldn't let the social democrats dictate who should represent it. The CP's official reply, in May 1938, confirmed Ulbricht's view. The German communists now made their position clear. The Lutétia committee could pass resolutions, but shouldn't have any other power of decision. In the party's view, the committee's job was to help the masses by acting as an information agency. Because of its mixed composition, it couldn't be an autonomous operational organ directing the struggle of the masses in Germany.

While the non-communists had found Münzenberg an amenable partner, Ulbricht's arrival on the scene soon led to quarrels within the Lutétia circle. Mann and others complained that the communists no longer respected committee decisions and were trying to sabotage its work. Despite Ulbricht's assurances that he would co-operate loyally to restore the previous mutual trust, there was little improvement. Mann told an acquaintance in 1937 that he wouldn't confer with Ulbricht again. He couldn't sit at a table with someone who suddenly claimed that the table was in fact a duck-pond and expected Mann to agree with him.

By September 1937, relations were so bad that, on behalf of the committee, Heinrich Mann protested to Moscow about Ulbricht's unscrupulous schemes to bring the movement under communist control. In the spring of 1938, Ulbricht lost his position as the German communist leader in Paris and moved to Moscow, where he served as the German Communist Party's representative in the Comintern. By that time, non-communists had ruefully acknowledged that they couldn't work with the communists on an equal footing. Discord paralysed the German Popular Front and it disintegrated in September 1938.

Münzenberg, meanwhile, though excluded from the Popular

Front's activities, refused to leave Paris for Moscow, where his superiors wished to 'clarify his position' with him, as they put it. When the German Communist Party failed to get the Comintern to set him a deadline, it took matters into its own hands. It accused him of holding unapproved talks with bourgeois conservatives. It ordered Münzenberg to appear before the party leadership to answer charges that he had intrigued against the party's Popular Front policy and infringed basic party principles. His refusal to comply led the party to strip Münzenberg of all his party functions and expel him from the Central Committee, on which he had sat since 1924. By 1938, it had driven him completely out of the party he had joined at its inception. He appealed unsuccessfully against his removal.

Münzenberg went on to start his last paper, *Die Zukunft* (The Future). Another disillusioned communist, Arthur Koestler, helped him. The French foreign office and possibly some rich friends of Anthony Eden's, who had by then resigned as Britain's foreign secretary, financed him. Münzenberg denounced Hitler's non-aggression pact with Stalin in August 1939. He called Stalin's occupation of part of Poland a stab in the back.

The French interned Münzenberg as an enemy alien in central France in the summer of 1940, at the end of the 'phoney war'. The camp commander freed the political refugees just before the fall of Paris, as German troops approached the camp. Witnesses last saw Münzenberg in the company of two young men, unknown in refugee circles but supposedly German social democrats. On 17 October 1940, local farmers found Münzenberg hanging from a tree near Grenoble.

The cause of his death has remained a mystery. Koestler suspected murder (the Soviets murdered Trotsky in Mexico the same year). It could have been suicide: Walter Benjamin and other émigré writers killed themselves at this time. No one has conclusively linked Münzenberg's death to the Soviet secret police, to the Gestapo or even to simple highway robbers.

After the collapse of the German *Volksfront*, an ever-hopeful Heinrich Mann became president of yet another action committee, with Bernhard and Feuchtwanger still at his side. He ignored suggestions that he sever his ties of friendship with Münzenberg, and contributed to early issues of Münzenberg's last paper. Münzenberg in turn, with Johannes Becher, tried to promote Mann as a candidate for the Nobel Prize for literature.

Heinrich Mann didn't break with Moscow and didn't openly criticise Stalin's pact with Hitler. He had never visited the Soviet

Union, though often invited to do so. After the war had begun, he turned down the offer of a visa to enter Russia that he learned was awaiting him at the embassy in Paris. Mann was reluctant to leave France. When the Vichy regime took control of southern France, the right-wing French press began castigating him, the ardent promoter of Franco-German reconciliation, as one of the émigrés chiefly responsible for France's plight. Mann realised his life was in danger.

Heinrich Mann, now nearly 70 years old, and his wife secretly made their way from Nice to Marseilles. There Varian Fry, the 'American pimpernel' sent to France by the Emergency Rescue Committee, helped them, as well as Mann's nephew Golo and Franz and Alma Werfel, to cross the Pyrenees on foot and slip into neutral Spain. They proceeded to Barcelona and Madrid and reached Lisbon on a Lufthansa flight. Thomas Mann arranged United States entry visas for his family, and paid their trans-Atlantic berths on a Greek ship.

The *New York Times* recorded the party's arrival in Hoboken. Legend has it that the newspaper was unaware of Heinrich Mann's status as a writer. As Christopher Hampton puts it in his play, *Tales from Hollywood*, the *Times* 'welcomed the arrival of the famous German author, Golo Mann. Then they said he was accompanied by his Uncle Heinrich.' In fact, the report didn't call Golo 'famous'. Its headlines mentioned only Heinrich Mann and Franz Werfel, and it published photos only of Werfel and of Heinrich Mann and his wife. What the paper did ignore was Heinrich Mann's political role as an émigré leader during his exile in France.

Mann's second flight heralded a steep decline in his literary career. In July 1939, the *Times Literary Supplement* had selected his concluding volume about Henri IV as its book of the month. It was his last work to be translated into English. Mann had a frustrating year as a scriptwriter in Hollywood, where he complained of loneliness and ingratitude. He became virtually destitute and relied on his brother's financial help. His wife Nelly took an overdose of sleeping pills in 1944.

Heinrich Mann found life in the USA difficult partly because he had never visited that country before. Thomas, on the other hand, had toured it widely and received several honorary degrees from American universities. He knew many influential Americans, such as the journalist Dorothy Thompson or Agnes Meyer, wife of the proprietor of the *Washington Post*.

A chance to escape from humiliating poverty, isolation and obscurity came in May 1949 when the reconstituted German academy of the arts invited Heinrich Mann to become its first president. Johannes Becher's offer of a villa in Berlin, a chauffeur and an office in the academy made it an especially tempting proposition. There was a further inducement. His East German publishers told him that his books enjoyed such large sales there that, if he returned, he would become a millionaire – in non-convertible East German marks.

In the United States, on the other hand, publishers had shunned Mann's work for a decade. The persecution of communists and 'progressive' émigrés was under way. Heinrich Mann didn't consider going back to West Germany. He believed the country was reverting to its prewar capitalist system and rebuffing him completely. He began to prepare his departure from California, aware that he would probably have to sit at a table with Ulbricht again and that, following the formal division of Germany that occurred in the autumn of 1949, he would preside over a rump academy. As it turned out, he had to cope with neither inconvenience. Mann booked to sail to the Polish port of Gydinia at the end of April 1950, but he died in March and lies buried in Santa Monica.

The German Popular Front, if not stillborn, never developed into a viable movement likely to pose a grave threat across the Rhine. The émigré leaders had misjudged their ability to penetrate Germany with their message and overestimated the strength of the opposition to Hitler in the Reich itself. By the time the intelligentsia's generals in France and Russia had prepared their offensive, the Nazis had in effect decimated their armies in Germany. It was a fantasy to believe that broad swathes of the German population were so discontented with their government that they were seriously ready to offer open resistance.

The German Popular Front turned out to be an intellectual initiative that inspired great hopes among the émigrés, but did little to prevent or help win the war. Yet it had its significance, however ephemeral. In uncovering the contradictory ideologies within the German exodus, Mann, Münzenberg, Ulbricht and company were rehearsing the roles their incompatible factions would play in Cold War Germany.

In January 1938, Ulbricht left France for Moscow. He and other German communist politicians and writers in Moscow – among them Wilhelm Pieck, Johannes Becher and Friedrich Wolf (a doctor turned playwright, briefly a refugee in Sanary, and the father of Markus Wolf, the East German 'master spy') – set up a national committee for a 'free Germany'. At the end of January 1939, the German Communist Party met south of Paris and outlined a future 'German

Democratic Republic', based on radical land reform and a merger of the Communist and Social Democrat Parties. The party had planted at least some of the seeds of Germany's postwar division.

Located near the German embassy, the Hôtel Lutétia had also served other Germans. In the 1930s, it had hosted meetings between Nazis and future French *collaborateurs*. During the war, the Nazis requisitioned the hotel after they occupied Paris. Admiral Wilhelm Canaris, head of the Abwehr military intelligence service, directed espionage activities from room 109.

18 Back from Oblivion
Postwar Germany's Mixed Feelings About Its Exile Writers

Like a Churchill or a De Gaulle waiting in the wings for the voters to encore them back into the limelight, German exile writers expected their long-lost public to hastily summon them home after the Allied victory. Though many had languished in limbo, they imagined that their anti-fascist record, and the humiliation and suffering they had endured, would spur Germans to welcome them warmly. They assumed the defeated nation would be eager to read their work – the books the Nazis had burned, and banned for more than a decade. The writers didn't regard themselves as survivors of a vanquished civilisation, but rather as architects of a new Germany. They hoped its prospective owners and occupiers would show them sympathy and gratitude.

It was as an advanced brigade of political construction workers that a small group of key German communists, led by Walter Ulbricht, followed the victorious Red Army westwards. They marched into Berlin from Moscow at the end of April 1945, a week before Germany capitulated unconditionally. Ulbricht's exile troupe was one of three the Soviets planted in their occupation zone to help the liberators rebuild the ruined country's administration.

In their briefcases Ulbricht's team had the blueprints of a new society, based partly on the plans for a 'socialist' Germany drawn up in Paris before 1940. During the war, German communists had set up their 'Free Germany' committee in Moscow to pave the way for them to take over vital bureaucratic positions in the Soviet zone of occupation. Supervised by the James-Bond-sounding SMAD – the Soviet Military Administration in Deutschland – they were going to demolish all relics of the disastrous Nazi militarist ideology and lay 'socialist' foundations for the new German state.

The political poet and stern functionary Johannes Becher was among the writers in Ulbricht's entourage; he took over culture. So was Friedrich Wolf, who administered cinema. As Becher set about reshaping the arts in the new mould, he favoured writers, musicians and artists with a proven anti-fascist record. For him, the only decent

Germans were those who had been active 'antifa[scist]s'. A new publishing house, appropriately called *Aufbau* (build-up), soon began to reissue the works of Heinrich Mann, Arnold Zweig, Feuchtwanger and other progressives.

Moscow supervised the German communists' efforts. It encouraged exiled 'antifa' intellectuals around the world to return, going so far as to divert a freighter 2,000 kilometres to pick up two writers who had found refuge in Mexico. The authorities in the Soviet zone honoured the former outcasts and granted them privileges, from housing to easier travel abroad. It would have been a major coup for them, if Heinrich Mann had returned to East Berlin from California.

For a couple of years, the Soviet occupiers showed unexpectedly liberal traits. They tolerated the foundation of social democrat, liberal and even Christian democrat parties. Did Moscow and the German communists, in that early phase, seriously intend to create the sort of social democracy outlined in the pre-war Popular Front statements that the émigrés had drafted in the Hôtel Lutétia? It is easy to understand, in retrospect, how some exiles could have believed so. Thomas Mann had no hesitation in contributing to an East German review, *Aufbau*. From his New York exile, Alfred Kantorowicz returned to the Soviet sector of Berlin to publish another review. A decade later, he would flee to West Germany as an embittered ex-Communist. As the confrontation between capitalism and communism became sharper, East Germany stepped up its persecution of intellectuals who overstepped the party line, and its control of what its citizens could read.

In Prague, the Czechs warmly embraced Egon Erwin Kisch when he came back from Mexico in 1946. He was soon disillusioned, nonetheless. The city was no longer a German-language metropolis. The Nazis, bizarrely, had rooted out German culture, closely entwined as it had been with the country's German-speaking Jewish population. Many of Kisch's family and friends were among those killed. Then Czechoslovakia's President Eduard Benes expelled the country's Sudeten Germans, many of whom had collaborated with the Nazis. The country's Slav speakers despised the German language. They might even molest people heard speaking it on the streets. Anti-German sentiment was so strong that the Czech PEN excluded German-language writers. Shortly before he died in 1948, Kisch couldn't find a German-language publisher for his last book, stories about ghetto life. It appeared first in an English translation.

Half a century after his death, Kisch was the subject of a major exhibition – in Vienna. Today, Austria is proud to claim distinguished 'Danubian' German-speaking Jews as a part of the legacy of its glorious imperial past. In the early postwar years, however, Austria tended to ignore them, happy to accept the role the allies had conferred on it – 'Hitler's first victim'.

While some of Austria's exile writers did manage to re-integrate, usually by associating with a political party, others found themselves 'strangers at home'. The cultural establishment preferred to honour writers who had remained in Austria, even though they might have denounced anti-Nazis, praised Hitler or shaken Goebbels's hand when he awarded them a prize. Official Austria overlooked writers such as Arthur Koestler or Elias Canetti, a future Nobel Prize winner, because they lived abroad. It defended its stance by arguing that both the Austrian public and struggling young writers would resent steps to lionise them.

It took many years for the country to come to terms with its active role in Hitler's war. By the time Austria marked the 50th anniversary of its attachment to the Third Reich, a new generation had critically reappraised those dark years. Their research, conferences and exhibitions paved the way for a general rehabilitation of Austria's *Exilliteratur*.

A similar development took place in what the Western allies shaped into West Germany. At first, there was no rush to reissue books by émigrés. Many teachers, journalists and officials who had served the Reich at middle level kept their jobs, despite the de-Nazification policy. They were unlikely to encourage the demand for works by exiles. They favoured books by those 'inner émigrés' who had stayed behind, or by mainstream conventional writers of the Weimar era.

German publishers were likely to be cautious. They faced paper rationing, damaged or destroyed printing works, and scarce foreign currency to acquire book rights. They wanted to let readers catch up with foreign and especially avant-garde authors whose work had been beyond their reach all those years. What interest a sullen populace did show for exile literature tended to be for authors whom critics would classify as 'trivial', such as Remarque, as non-political, such as Musil, or 'rabidly anti-communist', such as Koestler.

If a war-weary society displayed little enthusiasm for the exiles' books, it also ignored many exiled writers themselves. It scorned those who had sympathised with communism before the war, and then wholeheartedly supported the Red Army's onslaught on their own country. Feuchtwanger complained in the spring of 1948 that it was proving impossible to deliver copies of his *Exil* from East to West Berlin.

Germans resented those intellectuals who, as they saw it, had sided with Stalin, run away from the rigours of the war, and led a cushioned life abroad. They esteemed more highly those who stoically stayed and shut up. For many, the real heroes were those who risked and lost their lives in attempts to organise a resistance, or even to kill the Führer. Someone told Klaus Mann, 'You don't give up your career because you don't like Hitler's nose.' It wasn't a peculiarly German phenomenon: the French looked down on writers and painters who had abandoned the country, while praising Picasso because he stayed on and helped the *Résistance*.

But many well-known émigré writers and other intellectuals didn't want to 'come home'. They had become too accustomed to the charms of New England, California or Oxbridge. Their experiences during the Hitler years had altered their outlook and they now found they had little in common, even with staunch anti-fascists who had remained in the country.

Some returned as part of the occupying forces and had to work on their behalf. Klaus Mann, for one, was wearing an American army uniform and travelling in an army jeep when, a few days after Ulbricht and Becher had returned to Berlin, he visited his parents' severely damaged home in Munich. Mann was reporting on postwar Germany as a special correspondent for the US army's daily newspaper, *Stars and Stripes*. Like his father and many other émigrés who ended up in the United States, Klaus Mann had acquired an American passport. In the few years left to him before he committed suicide in France in 1949, he never again lived in Germany. Alfred Döblin returned as a French citizen, wanting to help revive literary life in West Germany. He founded a new journal but its liberal, humanist outlook failed to appeal, and a disillusioned Döblin returned to Paris.

Thomas Mann re-emerged as the leading representative of German letters after 1945, even though he remained in the United States. His works were popular in West Germany and an irritated Mann thought his publisher, Fischer, was too slow in reprinting his novels. He also resented Fischer's legalistic approach to licensing East German editions, because of difficulties about remitting royalties in hard currency.

Yet Thomas Mann again became a highly controversial figure. Much of the postwar dispute about the pre-war flight of the intellectuals centred on him. During the wartime debates on Germany's future, Mann had sided with those who opposed a 'soft' peace. He had angered the German people as a whole, by contending in his wartime broadcasts that they were collectively responsible for the horrors of the Nazi regime and the catastrophe that had befallen them. As the war ended, he told his former compatriots that they hadn't done enough to encourage resistance, and that the concentration and extermination camps disgraced the German people as a whole. Hostile readers resented his view that since the Germans had proved unable to free themselves, the occupiers might have to run the country for a long while yet.

Even so, some Germans urged him to come home and use his status and authority to help the prostrate country recover. Others still had serious misgivings. They queried whether Mann and other writers had been right to abandon the fatherland in its time of need, when racial or political persecution hadn't compelled them to do so. In an open letter to Thomas Mann, the writer Frank Thiess argued that Mann and other non-Jewish writers should have stayed in Germany as a matter of honour. They shouldn't have observed the German tragedy unfold from their comfortable *loge* and stall seats abroad, he maintained.

Thiess had supported the Nazis at first, only to have some of his own books blacklisted later. He now revived the 'inner migration' controversy that had locked Klaus Mann in his prewar combat with Gottfried Benn. Thiess took the side of those who had starved, seen their own houses in flames and endured the bombing of German cities (Gerhart Hauptmann, for example, had witnessed Allied bombers destroy Dresden). Thiess distanced himself from those who, as he put it, had from afar watched newsreels and read press accounts of German suffering. He defended writers who stayed behind and chose to silence their voices, rather than warn Germans about the Nazi peril. He thought writers in exile had unfairly condemned such an attitude as a dereliction of duty. Thiess presented the 'internal exiles' as the real literary heroes and martyrs. They hadn't collaborated with the Nazis but had, artistically, withdrawn into their shells and shared the people's sufferings.

Mann confided to his son Golo that he thought it a 'shameless falsification' of his position to classify him and other 'Aryan' émigré writers as cowards. It was ridiculous to suggest that such people were traitors and deserters who could have survived in Germany after 1933. Publicly, Mann tried to reassure the Germans that strong emotional ties still bound him to his native land, but he emphasised that he wasn't going to return. He recalled the physical and psychological hardships of exile and his subsequent alienation from Germany, and expressed his gratitude to the United States for adopting him as its own.

So intense was the animosity towards Mann that he bypassed Germany on his first postwar visit to Europe, in the spring of 1947. He feared his presence might provoke disturbances. Yet East and West Germany courted him – one of the few exile writers still living outside Germany who received such flattering attention. Declaring that he didn't recognise the Allied zones of occupation, he insisted on receiving awards from both sides when invited to take part in Goethe and Schiller anniversaries, in 1949 and 1955 respectively.

If Mann's balancing act displeased West Germans, it also rang alarm bells in Washington. Besides Mann's neutral attitude to Germany, there was his support for American civil-rights activists who protested against United States persecution of German left-wing exiles, such as Hanns Eisler. Mann publicly congratulated Johannes Becher on his 60th birthday, a gesture that led a US Congressman to call Mann a front-rank apologist for Stalin.

The House of Representatives' Un-American Activities Committee ordered Mann to appear before a sub-committee so that it could investigate his record more closely. For some, he was 'America's fellow-traveller No. 1'. Hostile publicity generated by McCarthyism drove Mann back to Europe in 1952, and into his final exile in Switzerland. At his memorial service in 1955, Bonn's ambassador in Bern and its consul-general in Zurich represented West Germany. East Berlin, however, sent a high-level delegation headed by its minister of culture, Johannes Becher. To the end of his life, Thomas Mann remained a contentious writer for Germans.

In the 1940s, the United States government had fretted that some politically active writers and other émigrés in America were, wittingly or otherwise, helping to set up a regime in postwar Germany that would be subservient to Moscow. Throughout the war, the Federal Bureau of Investigation and other US intelligence services closely tracked German anti-Nazis in the Americas, north and south. J. Edgar Hoover and his colleagues suspected what Hoover called 'communazis' of being mushy on communism – hadn't Feuchtwanger praised Stalin and his Soviet Union? – and kept them under constant surveillance.

Thousands of agents shadowed 'red' writers, bugged their homes and intercepted their mail. They reported on the émigrés' political unreliability as on their moral peccadilloes. They monitored the activities of the Mann family. They observed Klaus Mann as he picked up a soldier and took him back to his New York hotel room. They forced Feuchtwanger to deny that he had slept with Eva Herrmann.

During the war, German exiles found that the United States didn't encourage them to create a countervailing authority to the Nazis. In that respect, their situation differed from that of other European exiles. Washington feared that if it failed to agree with Moscow on the future of Germany, as seemed likely, the German exile writers might throw their weight on the Soviet side. American intelligence services heard about plans to get Thomas Mann to head a 'Free Germany' movement in the United States. Given his international prestige, the last thing the State Department wanted was to see Thomas Mann heading anything like an unreliable German government in exile. The government foiled the plan. As Mann was applying for United States citizenship and expecting to remain in the country permanently, it was easy to manipulate Mann to keep out of exile politics.

As the predominant occupying power in West Germany after 1945, Washington strongly influenced the defeated nation's wary attitude to many of its prominent émigrés. The State and War Departments discouraged some overly independent Germans from returning by subjecting them to bureaucratic procedures so rigorous that the exiles wondered if they were on trial. The US wouldn't let Brecht travel to East Berlin through its occupation zone. Hanns Eisler had to leave America illegally on a Polish freighter.

Through the vast re-education programme it carried out between 1945 and 1948, the United States controlled what Germans could read and learn. Visiting Frankfurt in 1947, Arthur Miller heard from Theodor Adorno that Washington was compelling the German educational authorities to use textbooks that left a void for the Hitler years. The US government distributed some 10,000,000 American books and pamphlets intended to cultivate a democratic outlook and eradicate any remnants of a militarist mentality, while stressing the American nation's achievements in the arts and sciences.

Across a chain of 'Amerika Haus' libraries, Germans could avidly flick through glossy magazines that revealed the cornucopia spreading over part of the other hemisphere. But there was little room for the work of eminent German writers who had settled in the United States, or indeed for 'progressive' American literature. American censors approved of Benjamin Franklin's autobiography, but regarded everything by Erskine Caldwell or William Faulkner as liable to taint German minds. They acknowledged such books had literary merit, but deplored the negative picture of American civilisation. Arthur Miller's *All My Sons* was unsuitable and so were unexpurgated versions of Hemingway's *Men Without Women*.

The lot of the exile writers barely improved after the occupation ended, and the three western zones became the Federal Republic. Under Konrad Adenauer's 'restoration' in the early 1950s, many former Nazis re-entered public life. Publishers favoured writers of the Weimar era who shared the chancellor's conservative outlook. Yet behind the scenes, a handful of devoted scholars had been working to rescue the émigré writers' works from oblivion. A few refugee writers had been trying to draw attention to 'exile literature' as a phenomenon, but there was little resonance. In 1947, one publisher rejected a proposed survey as a 'pamphlet against those who stayed behind'.

A first, enormous task was simply to find out what writers had published in the various countries where they had lived as refugees. Curiously, Germany's pre-war national library in Leipzig had remained a depository for their books, even during the Hitler years. West Germany, on the other hand, had to start from scratch. Its national library in Frankfurt had begun in the late 1940s to amass and catalogue what today amounts to some 16,000 documents – probably the most complete collection anywhere of books, periodicals, pamphlets and newspaper articles published in exile between 1933 and 1945. By 1965, the *Deutsche Bibliothek* was ready to display a selection of its archives in Frankfurt.

The exhibition of 'exile literature' was a seminal event. The worst years of the Cold War were over. Both Bonn and East Berlin had accepted the status quo and the need for peaceful co-existence. The influence of Adenauer's generation had waned; the old guard had given way to younger Germans curious to know more about all aspects of the Third Reich. West Germans were now more receptive to the literary output of the outcasts. They began to rehabilitate the exile writers and gradually recognised the value of their literary legacy. In communist Germany, ironically, some émigré writers now fell into disgrace and several chose to end their days in the West.

By the late 1960s, 'exile literature' had become a thriving field of research in universities, not just in Germany but also in centres of learning elsewhere, especially those that employed refugee academics. Scholars explored all facets of the topic in congresses and symposia, in radio and television documentaries, in learned journals and popular books. Publishers now vied for memoirs and biographies. The 50th anniversary of the book-burning stimulated a nationwide review of the fate of the émigré authors. An awakened interest emboldened publishers to reissue the works of near-forgotten authors.

Fascination trickled down to the local level. In 1993, the small town of Bad Säckingen, south of Freiburg, held an exhibition on the fate of 15 exiled writers who had lived in the French port with which it had been twinned for 20 years – Sanary. An enlarged version of the exhibition, covering 28 writers, toured Germany three years later. The exhibition and the publicity it created encouraged the port to exploit this literary heritage. Its tourism office prepared a leaflet in French and German. Sanary began to organise literary walking tours that included Huxley's home, though at first it wrongly identified the 'Villa Huxley'. Sanary's website featured a section about '*les écrivains allemands*'. There were reports that the German government, having helped transform Feuchtwanger's California home into a study centre, might do the same for his villa in Sanary.

Sanary is no longer the 'secret capital' of German literature. Instead, the small port and its outcasts have, late in the day, become part of a chapter in modern Germany's literary history.

Bibliography

Abels, Norbert, *Franz Werfel* (Reinbek: Rowohlt, 1990)
Ambler, Eric, *Epitaph for a Spy* (New York: Carroll & Graf, 1991)
Arnold, Heinz Ludwig (ed.), *Deutsche Literatur im Exil 1933–1945* (Frankfurt: Athenäum, 1974)
Assouline, Pierre, *Gaston Gallimard* (Paris: Seuil, 2001)

Badia, Gilbert, et al., *Les barbelés de l'exil* (Grenoble: Presses universitaires de Grenoble, 1979)
Badia, Gilbert, et al., *Les bannis de Hitler* (Presses universitaires de Vincennes, 1984)
Bance, Alan (ed.), *Weimar Germany: Writers and Politics* (Edinburgh: Scottish Academic Press, 1984)
Banuls, André, *Heinrich Mann* (Paris: Klincksieck, 1966)
Barron, Stephanie, et al., *Exiles & Émigrés* (Los Angeles County Museum of Art/New York: Abrams, 1997)
Bedford, Sybille, *A Legacy* (London: Weidenfeld & Nicolson, 1956)
Bedford, Sybille, *Aldous Huxley* (New York: Knopf, 1974)
Bedford, Sybille, *Jigsaw* (Harmondsworth: Penguin, 1990)
Bedford, Sybille, *A Favourite of the Gods* (London: Virago, 1993)
Behmer, Markus, *Von der Schwierigheit, gegen Illusionen zu kämpfen – Der Publizist Leopold Schwarzschild* (Münster: Lit, 1996)
Behmer, Markus (ed.), *Deutsche Publizistik im Exil 1933 bis 1945* (Münster: Lit, 2000)
Benn, Gottfried, *Doppelleben* (Wiesbaden: Limes, 1950)
Bentmann, Friederich (ed.), *René Schickele – Leben und Werk in Dokumenten* (Nuremberg: Carl, 1974)
Benz, Wolfgang, *Das Exil der kleinen Leute* (Munich: Beck, 1994)
Benz, Wolfgang, *Flucht aus Deutschland* (Munich: dtv, 2001)
Bermann Fischer, Gottfried, *Bedroht Bewahrt* (Frankfurt: Fischer, 1967)
Berthold, Werner, and Eckert, Brita, *Der deutsche PEN-Club im Exil* (Frankfurt: Deutsche Bibliothek, 1980)

Betz, Albrecht, *Exil und Engagement* (Munich: edition text + kritik, 1988)
Bock, Hans Manfred *et al.*, *Entre Locarno et Vichy* (Paris: CNRS, 1993)
Bollenbeck Georg, *Oskar Maria Graf* (Reinbek: Rowohlt, 1989)
Bracher, Karl Dietrich, *The German Dictatorship* (Harmondsworth: Penguin, 1970)
Brecht, Bertolt, *Werke* (Berlin: Aufbau, 1989)
Brod, Max, *Prager Tagblatt* (Frankfurt: Fischer, 1979)
Bronsen, David, *Joseph Roth* (Cologne: Kiepenheuer & Witsch, 1975)
Buckard, Christian, *Arthur Koestler* (Munich: Beck, 2004)
Burrin, Philippe, *La France à l'heure allemande* (Paris: Seuil, 1995)

Campbell, Roy, *Light on a Dark Horse* (Harmondsworth: Penguin, 1969)
Canetti, Elias, *Die Gerettete Zunge* (Frankfurt: Fischer, 1979)
Cate, Curtis, *André Malraux* (Paris: Flammarion, 1994)
Cesarani, David, *Arthur Koestler* (London: Heinemann, 1998)
Chapsal, Jacques, *La vie politique en France depuis 1940* (Paris: Presses universitaires de France, 1969)
Conseil Général des Bouches-du-Rhône, *Varian Fry – Mission américaine de sauvetage des intellectuels anti-nazis* (Arles: Actes Sud, 1999)
Conseil Général des Bouches-du-Rhône, *Varian Fry et les candidats à l'exil* (Arles: Actes Sud, 1999)
Craig, Gordon A., *Germany 1866–1945* (Oxford: Oxford University Press, 1978)

Daix, Pierre, *Aragon* (Paris: Flammarion, 1994)
Daviau, Donald and Fischer, Ludwig (ed.), *Das Exilerlebnis* (Columbia, SC: Camden House, 1982)
Dawidowicz, Lucy, *The War Against the Jews* (New York: Bantam, 1976)
De-la-Noy, Michael, *Eddy: The Life of Edward Sackville-West* (London: Bodley Head, 1988)
Deutsche Bibliothek, *Exil-Literatur 1933–1945* (Frankfurt: Deutsche Bibliothek, 1966)
Dirschauer, Wilfried (ed.), *Klaus Mann und das Exil* (Worms: Lendle, 1973)
Dittberner, Hugo, *Heinrich Mann* (Frankfurt: Athenäum, 1974)
Döblin, Alfred, *Schicksalsreise* (Munich: dtv, 1986)

Bibliography

Dove, Richard, *He was a German: A Biography of Ernst Toller* (London: Libris, 1990)
Dufay, François, *Le voyage d'automne* (Paris: Plon, 2000)
Durzak, Manfred (ed.), *Die deutsche Exilliteratur 1933–1945* (Ditzingen: Reclam, 1973)
Dwars, Jens-Fietje, *Abgrund des Widerspruchs – Das Leben des Johannes R. Becher* (Berlin: Aufbau, 1999)

Eckert, Brita (ed.), *Die jüdische Emigration aus Deutschland 1933–1941* (Frankfurt: Deutsche Bibliothek, 1986)
Ellmann, Richard, *James Joyce* (Oxford: Oxford University Press, 1965)
Emmerich, Wolfgang, *Kleine Literaturgeschichte der DDR* (Darmstadt: Luchterhand, 1981)

Faure, Ulrich, *Im Knotenpunkt des Weltverkehrs* (Berlin: Aufbau, 1992)
Feuchtwanger, Lion, *Erfolg* (Berlin: Kiepenheuer, 1930)
Feuchtwanger, Lion, *The Oppermanns* (London: Secker, 1934)
Feuchtwanger, Lion, *Centum Opuscula* (Rudolstadt: Greifen, 1956)
Feuchtwanger, Lion, *Exil* (Frankfurt: Fischer, 1979)
Feuchtwanger, Lion, and Zweig, Arnold, *Briefwechsel 1933–1958* (Berlin: Aufbau, 1984)
Feuchtwanger, Lion (trans.), *Le Diable en France* (Paris: Godefroy, 1985)
Feuchtwanger, Lion, *Briefwechsel mit Freunden 1933–1958* (Berlin: Aufbau, 1991)
Feuchtwanger, Lion, *Moskau 1937* (Berlin: Aufbau, 1993)
Feuchtwanger, Marta, *Nur eine Frau* (Berlin: Aufbau, 1983)
Fischer, Brigitte, *Sie schrieben mir* (Zurich: Classen, 1978)
Fisher, Clive, *Cyril Connolly* (London: Macmillan, 1995)
Flinker, Martin, *Thomas Manns Politische Betrachtungen* (The Hague: Mouton, 1959)
Flügge, Manfred (ed.), *Letzte Heimkehr nach Paris* (Berlin: Arsenal, 1989)
Flügge, Manfred, *Gesprungene Liebe* (Berlin: Aufbau, 1993)
Flügge, Manfred, *Wider Willen im Paradies* (Berlin: Aufbau, 1996)
Forster, Heinz und Riegel, Paul, *Deutsche Literaturgeschichte – Die Nachkriegszeit 1945–1968* (Munich: dtv, 1995)
François-Poncet, André (trans.), *Botschafter in Berlin 1931–1938* (Mainz: Kupferberg, 1962)
Frank, Bruno, *Der Reisepass* (Amsterdam: Querido, 1937)

Frank, Mario, *Walter Ulbricht* (Berlin: Siedler, 2001)
Freyermuth, Gundolf S., *Reise in die Verlorengegangenheit* (Hamburg: Rasch und Röhrig, 1990)
Friedländer, Saul, *Nazi Germany & the Jews* (London: Phoenix, 1998)
Fritsch, Christian, and Winckler, Lutz (eds.), *Faschismuskritik und Deutschlandbild im Exilroman* (Berlin: Argument, 1981)
Fry, Varian, *Surrender on Demand* (New York: Random House, 1945)
Fryer, Jonathan, *Isherwood* (London: New English Library, 1977)
Fuegi, John, *The Life and Lies of Bertolt Brecht* (London: Flamingo, 1995)
Furbank, P. N., *E. M. Forster: A Life* (Oxford: Oxford University Press, 1979)

Georgiadou, Areti, *Annemarie Schwarzenbach* (Munich: dtv, 1998)
Gide, André, *Retour de l'U.R.S.S.* (Paris: Gallimard, 1936)
Gilbert, Martin, *Atlas of Jewish History* (New York: Dorset Press, 1984)
Gilbert, Martin, and Gott, Richard, *The Appeasers* (London: Phoenix, 2000)
Gold, Mary Jayne, *Crossroads Marseilles 1940* (Garden City: Doubleday, 1980)
Grab, Walter, *Der deutsche Weg der Judenemanzipation* (Munich: Piper, 1991)
Grandjonc, Jacques and Grundtner, Theresia (eds), *Zone d'ombres 1933–1944* (Aix-en-Provence: Alinea, 1990)
Green, Martin, *Children of the Sun* (New York: Basic Books, 1976)
Gross, Babette, *Willi Münzenberg* (Leipzig: Forum, 1991)
Grosser, Alfred, *Germany in Our Time* (New York: Praeger, 1971)
Grunberger, Richard, *A Social History of the Third Reich* (Harmondsworth: Penguin, 1974)

Hamilton, Nigel, *The Brothers Mann* (New Haven, CT: Yale University Press, 1979)
Hampton, Christopher, *Tales From Hollywood* (London: Samuel French, 1983)
Hartung, Günter, *Klaus Manns Zeitschrift 'Die Sammlung'* (In: Weimarer Beiträge 19. Jg., H. 5, H. 6, Berlin: 1973)
Hasenclever, Walter, *Irrtum und Leidenschaft* (Berlin: Herbig, 1977)
Haumann, Heiko, *Die Geschichte der Ostjuden* (Munich: dtv, 1990)

Haupt, Jürgen, *Heinrich Mann* (Stuttgart: Metzler, 1980)
Hayman, Ronald, *Bertolt Brecht* (Munich: Heyne, 1983)
Heilbut, Anthony, *Exiled in Paradise* (New York: Viking, 1981)
Heilbut, Anthony, *Thomas Mann* (London: Papermac, 1997)
Heller, Erich, *Thomas Mann* (Frankfurt: Suhrkamp, 1959)
Heller, Gerhard, *Un allemand à Paris* (Paris: Seuil, 1981)
Hessel, Stéphane, *Danse avec le siècle* (Paris: Seuil, 1997)
Hilberg, Raul, *Täter, Opfer, Zuschauer* (Frankfurt: Fischer, 1996)
Hingley, Ronald, *Pasternak* (London: Unwin, 1985)
Hirschfeld, Gerhard (ed.), *Exile in Great Britain* (Leamington: Berg, 1984)
Hofer, Walther (ed.), *Der Nationalsozialismus* (Frankfurt: Fischer, 1957)
Holz, Keith, and Schopf, Wolfgang, *Im Auge des Exils* (Berlin: Aufbau, 2001)
Holzner, Johann, Scheichl, Sigurd, Paul, and Wiesmüller, Wolfgang (eds.), *Eine schwierige eimkehr: Oesterreichische Literatur im Exil 1938–1945* (Innsbruck: Innsbruck University, 1991)
Huxley, Aldous, *Eyeless in Gaza* (Harmondsworth: Penguin, 1962)
Huxley, Aldous, *Letters*, edited by Grover Smith (London: Chatto & Windus, 1969)
Huxley, Julian (ed.), *Aldous Huxley 1894–1963 – A Memorial Volume* (London: Chatto & Windus, 1965)

Ihme-Tuchel, Beate, *Die SED und die Schriftsteller 1946 bis 1956*. In *Aus Politik und Zeitgeschichte* B13/2000 (Bonn: Bundeszentrale für politische Bildung, 2000)
Isherwood, Christopher, *Christopher and His Kind* (New York: Farrar Straus Giroux, 1976)
Israel, Jonathan, *European Jewry in the Age of Mercantilism 1550–1750* (Oxford: Littman, 1998)

Jaretzky, Reinhold, *Lion Feuchtwanger* (Reinbek: Rowohlt, 1983)
Jasper, Willi, *Der Bruder Heinrich Mann* (Frankfurt: Fischer, 1994)
Jasper, Willi, *Hôtel Lutétia* (Paris: Michalon, 1995)
Jens, Inge and Walter, *Frau Thomas Mann* (Reinbek: Rowohlt, 2003)
Johannes-R.-Becher Archiv (ed.) *Erinnerungen an Johannes R. Becher* (Frankfurt: Röderberg, 1974)
Jungk, Peter Stephan, *A Life Torn By History – Franz Werfel 1890–1945* (London: Weidenfeld & Nicolson, 1990)

Kantorowicz, Alfred, *Deutsches Tagebuch* Band I (Berlin: Kindler, 1964)
Kantorowicz, Alfred, *Exil im Frankreich* (Bremen: Schünemann, 1971)
Kantorowicz, Alfred, *Politik und Literatur im Exil* (Munich: dtv, 1987)
Kaukoreit, Volker and Pfoser, Kristina (ed.), *Die oesterreichische Literatur seid 1945* (Ditzingen: Reclam, 2000)
Kessler, Harry Graf, *Tagebücher, 1918–1937* (Frankfurt: Insel, 1996)
Kesten, Hermann, *Meine Freunde die Poeten* (Frankfurt: Ullstein, 1980)
Kesten, Hermann, *Dichter im Café* (Frankfurt: Ullstein, 1983)
Keun, Irmgard, *Wenn wir alle gut wären* (Cologne: Kiwi, 1983)
Koch, Gerd (ed.), *Literarisches Leben, Exil und Nationalsozialismus* (Frankfurt: Brandes & Apsel, 1996)
Koch, Stephen, *Double Lives* (New York: Free Press, 1994)
Koestler, Arthur, *Darkness at Noon* (London: Macmillan, 1941)
Koestler, Arthur, *Scum of the Earth* (London: Cape, 1941)
Koestler, Arthur, *Arrival and Departure* (London: Cape, 1947)
Koestler, Arthur, *The Yogi and the Commissar* (London: Cape, 1947)
Koestler, Arthur, *Arrow in the Blue* (London: Collins, 1952)
Koestler, Arthur, *The Invisible Writing* (London: Hutchinson, 1969)
Krispyn, Egbert, *Anti-Nazi Writers in Exile* (Athens, GA: University Press, 1978)
Kröhnke, Karl, *Lion Feuchtwanger – Der Ästhet in der Sowjetunion* (Stuttgart: Metzler, 1991)
Kurth, Peter, *American Cassandra – The Life of Dorothy Thompson* (New York: Little, Brown, 1990)
Kurzke, Hermann (ed.), *Thomas Mann's Essays* (Frankfurt: Fischer, 1977)

Lacquer, Walter, *Weimar* (New York: Perigee, 1980)
Lambertz, Thomas, *Eva Herrmann und das literarische Exil* (Cologne: Galerie ON, 1997)
Lancaster, Marie-Jacqueline, *Brian Howard: Portrait of a Failure* (London: Blond, 1968)
Landshoff, Fritz H., *Erinnerungen eines Verlegers* (Berlin: Aufbau, 1991)
Langkau-Alex, Ursula, *Deutsche Emigrationspresse* (In: *International Review of Social History*, 2/1970, Amsterdam: 1970)

Bibliography

Langkau-Alex, Ursula, *Volksfront für Deutschland* (Bodenheim: Syndikat, 1977)
Leonhard, Wolfgang, *Die Revolution entlässt ihre Kinder* (Cologne: Kiepenheuer und Witsch, 1955)
Loewy, Ernst (ed.), *Exil. Literarische und politische Texte aus dem deutschen Exil 1933–1945* (Frankfurt: Fischer, 1981)
Loring, Marianne, *Flucht aus Frankreich 1940* (Frankfurt: Fischer, 1996)
Lottman, Herbert, *The Left Bank* (London: Heinemann, 1982)
Lühe, Irmela von der, *Erika Mann* (Frankfurt: Campus, 1994)

Maas, Lieselotte, *Kürfürstendamm auf den Champs-Elysées?* (in *Exilforschung*, Band No. 3; Berlin: edition text + kritik, 1985)
Maas, Lieselotte, *Handbuch der deutschen Exilpresse 1933–1945* (Munich: Hanser, 1976)
MacKenzie, Norman and Jeanne, *H. G. Wells* (New York: Simon & Schuster, 1973)
Mahler-Werfel, Alma, *Mein Leben* (Frankfurt: Fischer, 1986)
Mann, Erika, *Briefe und Antworten 1922–1950* (Munich: dtv, 1988)
Mann, Erika, *Mein Vater, der Zauberer* (Reinbek: Rowohlt, 1996)
Mann, Erika and Klaus, *Das Buch von der Riviera* (Reinbek: Rowohlt, 2002)
Mann, Erika and Klaus, *Escape to Life* (Boston: Houghton Mifflin, 1939)
Mann, Golo: *Erinnerungen und Gedanken – Eine Jugend in Deutschland* (Frankfurt: Fischer, 1991)
Mann, Golo: *Erinnerungen und Gedanken – Lehrjahre in Frankreich* (Frankfurt: Fischer, 1999)
Mann, Heinrich, *Die Jugend des Königs Henri Quatre* (Frankfurt: Büchergilde Gutenberg, 1966)
Mann, Heinrich, *Ein Zeitalter wird besichtigt* (Reinbek: Rowohlt, 1976)
Mann, Katia, *Meine ungeschriebenen Memoiren* (Frankfurt: Fischer, 2001)
Mann, Klaus, *Heute und Morgen* (Munich: Nymphenburger, 1969)
Mann, Klaus, *Mephisto* (Reinbek: Rowohlt, 1981)
Mann, Klaus, *Die Neuen Eltern* (Reinbek: Rowohlt, 1992)
Mann, Klaus, *Briefe und Antworten 1922–1949* (Reinbek: Rowohlt, 1991)
Mann, Klaus (ed.), *Die Sammlung* (Frankfurt: Zweitausendeins, 1986)

Mann, Klaus, *Tagebücher 1931–1949* (Reinbek: Rowohlt, 1991)
Mann, Klaus, *Der Wendepunkt* (Reinbek: Rowohlt, 1996)
Mann, Klaus, *Der Vulkan* (Reinbek: Rowohlt, 1995)
Mann, Thomas, *Briefe 1889–1936* (Frankfurt: Fischer, 1961)
Mann, Thomas, *Briefe 1937–1947* (Frankfurt: Fischer, 1963)
Mann, Thomas – Mann, Heinrich, *Briefwechsel 1900–1949* (Frankfurt: Fischer, 1995)
Mann, Thomas, *Briefwechsel mit Autoren* (Frankfurt: Fischer, 1988)
Mann, Thomas, *Briefwechsel mit seinem Verleger Gottfried Bermann Fischer* (Frankfurt: Fischer, 1973)
Mann, Thomas, *Essays*, Band 2, *Politik* (Frankfurt: Fischer, 1977)
Mann, Thomas, *Tagebücher 1933–1934* (Frankfurt: Fischer, 1977); *1935–1936* (Frankfurt: Fischer, 1978)
Marcuse, Ludwig, *Mein zwanzigstes Jahrhundert* (Zurich: Diogenes, 1975)
Marino, Andy, *American Pimpernel – The Story of Varian Fry* (London: Hutchinson, 1999)
Martin, Claude, *Gide* (Reinbek: Rowohlt, 1995)
Maugham, W. Somerset, *Strictly Personal* (New York: Arno, 1977)
Mayenburg, Ruth von, *Hotel Lux* (Frankfurt: Ullstein, 1981)
McMeekin, Sean, *The Red Millionaire: A Political Biography of Willi Münzenberg* (New Haven, CT: Yale University Press, 2004)
Mehring, Walter, *Die verlorene Bibliothek* (Munich: Heyne, 1972)
Mendelssohn, Peter de, *Unterwegs mit Reiseschatten* (Frankfurt: Fischer, 1977)
Mertens, Pierre, *Les éblouissements* (Paris: Seuil, 1987)
Michel, Henri, *Pétain et le régime de Vichy* (Paris: Presses Universitaires de France, 1978)
Miller, Arthur, *Timebends – A Life* (London: Methuen, 1987)
Mittenzwei, Werner, *Das Leben des Bertolt Brecht* (Berlin: Aufbau, 1988)
Morgenstern, Soma, *Joseph Roths Flucht und Ende* (Berlin: Aufbau, 1998)
Mosse, George L., *Germans and Jews* (New York: Grosset & Dunlap, 1970)
Müller-Salget, Klaus, *Alfred Döblin* (Bonn: Bouvier, 1972)
Murray, Nicholas, *Aldous Huxley: An English Intellectual* (London: Abacus, 2002)

Naumann, Uwe, *Klaus Mann* (Reinbek: Rowohlt, 1994)

Bibliography

Niémetz, Serge, *Stefan Zweig* (Belfond, 1996)
Noth, Ernst Erich, *Mémoires d'un allemand* (Paris: Juillard, 1970)

Orwell, George, *Collected Essays, Vol. 1* (Harmondsworth: Penguin, 1970)

Palmier, Jean-Michel, *Weimar en exil* (Paris: Payot, 1988)
Parmelin, Hélène, *Une passion pour Sanary* (Aix-en-Provence: Édisud, 1980)
Petersen, Walter F., *The Berlin Liberal Press in Exile* (Tübingen: Max Niemeyer, 1987)
Pike, David, *German Writers in Soviet Exile 1933–1945* (Chapel Hill, NC: North Carolina University Press, 1982)
Poliakov, Léon, *L'auberge des musiciens* (Paris: Mazarine, 1981)
Powell, Anthony, *What's Become of Waring* (London: Mandarin, 1992)
Prater, Donald, *European of Yesterday. A Biography of Stefan Zweig* (Oxford: Oxford University Press, 1972)
Prater, Donald, *Thomas Mann – A Life* (Oxford: Oxford University Press, 1995)
Pryce-Jones, David, *Cyril Connolly* (New York: Ticknor & Fields, 1984)
Pulzer, P. G. J., *The Rise of Political Anti-Semitism in Germany and Austria* (New York: Wiley, 1964)

Regler, Gustav, *Das Ohr des Malchus* (Frankfurt: Suhrkamp, 1975)
Reich-Ranicki, Marcel, *Thomas Mann and His Family* (London: Fontana, 1989)
Reich-Ranicki, Marcel, *Mein Leben* (Stuttgart: DVA, 1999)
Remarque, Erich Maria, *The Night in Lisbon* (New York: Harcourt, Brace & World, 1964)
Remarque, Erich Maria, *Arc de Triomphe* (Frankfurt: Ullstein, 1980)
Ritchie, J. M., *Gottfried Benn* (London: Wolff, 1972)
Ritchie, J. M., *German Literature under National Socialism* (London: Croom Helm, 1983)
Robinson, Armin L. (ed.), *Die zehn Gebote* (Frankfurt: Fischer, 1988)
Roché, Henri-Pierre, *Jules et Jim* (Paris: Folio, 1953)
Roth, Joseph, *Briefe 1911–1939* (Cologne: Kiepenheuer & Witsch, 1970)
Rubenstein, Joshua, *Tangled Loyalties – The Life and Times of Ilya Ehrenberg* (New York: Basic Books, 1996)

Ryder, A. J., *Twentieth-Century Germany* (London: Macmillan, 1973)

Sahl, Hans, *Das Exil im Exil* (Munich: dtv, 1994)
Sahl, Hans, *Die Wenigen und die Vielen* (Frankfurt: Fischer, 1959)
Salmon, André, *Souvenirs sans fin* (Paris: Gallimard, 1961)
Saint Sauveur-Henn, Anne (ed.), *Fluchtziel Paris* (Berlin: Metropol, 2002)
Scheer, Maximilian, *So war es in Paris* (Berlin: Verlag der Nation, 1972)
Schickele, René, *Werke* (Cologne: Kiepenheuer & Witsch, 1959)
Schöffling, Klaus (ed.), *Dort wo man Bücher verbrennt* (Frankfurt: Suhrkamp, 1983)
Schröter, Klaus, *Thomas Mann im Urteil seiner Zeit* (Hamburg: Wegner, 1969)
Schröter, Klaus, *Thomas Mann* (Reinbek: Rowohlt, 1967)
Schröter, Klaus, *Heinrich Mann* (Reinbek: Rowohlt, 1996)
Schröter, Klaus, *Döblin* (Reinbek: Rowohlt, 1993)
Schwarzschild, Leopold, *Die Lunte am Pulverfass* (Hamburg: Wegner, 1965)
Seabrook, William, *No Hiding Place* (Philadelphia: Lippincott, 1942)
Serge, Victor, *Memoirs of a Revolutionary* (Oxford: Oxford University Press, 1980)
Serke, Juergen, *Die verbrannten Dichter* (Weinheim: Beltz & Gelberg, 1977)
Seghers, Anna, *Transit* (Reinbek: Rowohlt, 1966)
Shattuck, Roger, *Writers for the Defense of Culture* (Boston, *Partisan Review* No. 3, 1984)
Shirer, William L., *The Collapse of the Third Republic* (New York: Simon & Schuster, 1969)
Shirer, William L., *The Rise and Fall of the Third Reich* (New York: Simon & Schuster, 1985)
Simon, André, *Men of Europe* (New York: Modern Age, 1941)
Skierka, Volker, *Lion Feuchtwanger* (Berlin: Quadriga, 1984)
Snowman, Daniel, *The Hitler Emigrés* (London: Pimlico, 2002)
Sontheimer, Kurt, *Antidemokratisches Denken in der Weimarer Republik* (Munich: dtv, 1983)
Spalek, John M., Feilchenfeldt, Konrad, and Hawrylchak, Sandra, *German-Language Exile Literature since 1933* (Munich: Saur, 1976)
Spender, Stephen, *World Within World* (London: Hamish Hamilton, 1953)

Bibliography

Spiel, Hilde, *Die hellen und die finsteren Zeiten* (Berlin: Paul List, 1989)
Stephan, Alexander, *Die deutsche Exilliteratur 1933–1945* (Munich: Beck, 1979)
Stephan, Alexander, *Im Visier des FBI* (Berlin: Aufbau, 1998)
Stern, Guy, *Literature and Culture in Exile* (Dresden: Dresden University Press, 1998)
Stern, Carola, *Ulbricht* (Frankfurt: Ullstein, 1966)
Sternburg, Wilhelm von, *Lion Feuchtwanger* (Berlin: Aufbau, 1994)
Sternburg, Wilhelm von, *Arnold Zweig* (Rudolstadt: Anton Hain, 1990)
Strelka, Joseph Peter (ed.), *Flucht und Exil* (Frankfurt: Insel, 1988)

Taylor, James, and Shaw, Warren, *A Dictionary of the Third Reich* (London: Grafton, 1988)
Taylor, John Russell, *Strangers in Paradise* (London: Faber, 1983)
Thalmann, Rita, *L'immigration allemande et l'opinion publique en France de 1933 à 1936,* in *La France & l'Allemagne 1932–1936* (Paris: CNRS, 1980)
Thalmann, Rita, *L'émigration allemande et l'opinion française de 1936 à 1939,* in *La France & l'Allemagne 1932–1936* (Munich: Artemis, 1981)
Toller, Ernst, *Eine Jugend in Deutschland* (Reinbek: Rowohlt, 1996)
Touchard, Jean, *La gauche en France depuis 1900* (Paris: Seuil, 1977)

Vegesack, Thomas von, *De intellectuellen* (Amsterdam: Meulenhoff, 1989)

Walter, Hans-Albert, *Der Streit um die 'Sammlung'* (In: *Frankfurter Hefte*, 21. Jg., H. 12, Frankfurt: Neue Verlagsgesellschaft, 1966)
Walter, Hans-Albert, *Deutsche Exilliteratur 1933–1950,* Vol. 7 *Exilpresse* (Darmstadt: Luchterhand, 1974)
Walter, Hans-Albert, *Fritz H. Landshoff und der Querido Verlag 1933–1950* (Marbach: Deutsche Schillergesellschaft, 1997)
Watts, Marjorie, *Mrs Sappho* (London: Duckworth, 1987)
Waugh, Evelyn, *Diaries,* edited by Michael Davie (London: Weidenfeld & Nicolson, 1976)
Waugh, Evelyn, *Letters,* edited by Mark Amory (New York: Ticknor & Fields, 1980)
Weber, Eugen, *The Hollow Years – France in the 1930s* (London:

Sinclair-Stevenson, 1995)

Wegner, Matthias (ed.), *Exil und Literatur* (Frankfurt: Athenäum, 1968)

Weil, Bernd, *Klaus Mann: Leben und Literarisches Werk im Exil* (Frankfurt: Rita Fischer, 1983)

Wells, G. P. (ed.), *H. G. Wells in Love* (London: Faber, 1984)

Wells, H. G., *Experiment in Autobiography* (London: Faber, 1984)

Werfel, Franz, *Jacobowsky und der Oberst* (Frankfurt: Fischer, 1962)

Wessel, Harald, *Münzenbergs Ende* (Berlin: Dietz, 1991)

Wilkinson, James D., *The Intellectual Resistance in Europe* (Cambridge, MA: Harvard University Press, 1981)

Wilson, Edmund, *The Shores of Light* (New York: Farrar Straus Giroux, 1952)

Witte, Bernd, *Walter Benjamin* (Reinbek: Rowohlt, 1985)

Winkler, Michael (ed.), *Deutsche Literatur im Exil 1933–1945* (Ditzingen: Reclam, 1977)

Wolff, Charlotte, *Hindsight* (London: Quartet, 1980)

Wolff, Rudolf (ed.), *Klaus Mann* (Bonn: Bouvier, 1981)

Worthington, Marjorie, *Come, My Coach* (New York: Knopf, 1935)

Worthington, Marjorie, *The Strange World of Willie Seabrook* (New York: Harcourt, Brace & World, 1966)

Wulf, Josef, *Kultur im Dritten Reich* (Frankfurt: Ullstein, 1989)

Wunderlich, Heinke, and Menke, Stefanie, *Sanary-sur-Mer* (Stuttgart: Metzler, 1996)

Wunderlich, Heinke, *Spaziergänge an der Côte d'Azur der Literaten* (Zurich: Arche, 1993)

Zehl Romero, Christiane, *Anna Seghers* (Reinbek: Rowohlt, 1994)

Zweig, Stefan, *Die Welt von Gestern* (Frankfurt: Fischer, 1992)

Index

Please note that references in **bold** relate to major mentions of topics

A la Recherche du Temps Perdu (M. Proust), 19
Abetz, Otto, 182
Abyssinia, Mussolini, invasion by (1935), 170, 207
academy of the arts, Prussian, 53–54, 74
Action Française (right-wing movement), 35
Adenauer, Konrad, 235
Adorno, Theodor, 234
Afternoon Men (A. Powell), 3
Aldington, Richard, 181
All My Sons (A. Miller), 235
Almansor (tragedy), 62
Altmann, Toni, 4, 16, 18
Amann, Max, 27
Ambler, Eric, 14
'Amerika Haus' libraries, 234
Amsterdam, international conference (1932), 149; Mann (Klaus) in, 95; Querido (publisher) *see* Querido, Emanuel (Amsterdam publisher)
Anschluss, 132
anti-Semitism, and Feuchtwanger, 49; in France, 14; 'Germanomania', 62; and Herzog, 3; by Hitler/Nazis, 43, 117, 206–7; *Je Suis Partout* (anti-Semitic publication), 84; and Mann (Thomas), 27; *see also* Jews; Nazis
Aragon, Louis, 177
Aron, Raymond, 32, 89
Asch, Shalom, 76, 79
Ashcroft, Peggy, 43
'asphalt literture', 63
Asquith, Margot, 70, 71, 72
Association des Ecrivains et Artistes Révolutionnaires, 154
Auden, W. H., 5, 51, 55, 56, 65, 153
Aufbau (publishing house), 229
Aurora (publishing firm), 68
Auschwitz, 143
Austria, *Exilliteratur*, 230; Fischer (Gottfried Bermann), move to, 131;

and Hitler, 1, 130, 182, 208; and Jews, 230
Autocracy of Mr Parma (H. G. Wells), 79

Babel, Isaac, 158
Bad Säckingen (town), 236
Bambi (F. Salten), 73
Bandol (Côte d'Azur), 32, 46; Grand Hôtel, 29, 31, 33
banning of books, 63, 64, 68, 95, 103; *see also* book-burning
Barbusse, Henri, *Association des Ecrivains et Artistes Révolutionnaires* set up by, 154; and Gide, 177; and Münzenberg, 214; and Paris Writers' Congress (1935), 148, 150, 157, 158, 159, 160
Barcelona, 17
Barth, Karl, 102
BASF (chemical company), 143
'Bastide Juliette' (house in Sanary), 4
Bastille Day, 181
Battleship Potemkin (Eisenstein), 214
Baum, Vicki, 44
Bayer (chemical company), 143
Beach, Sylvia, 162
Becher, Johannes, and Mann family, 126, 226; and Paris Writers' Congress (1935), 150–3, 154, 155, 162; and post-war period, 228–9, 233
Bedford, Sybille, escape from France, 19; and Feuchtwanger (Marta), 46; and Herrmann, 168; Huxley, biography of, xi; and Mann family, 86, 101; in Sanary, 16
Bedford, Walter, 4, 16
Bel Ami (G. de Maupassant), 37
Ben Huebsch (publisher), 50, 86, 183
Benjamin, Walter, 19, 111
Benn, Gottfried, autobiography, 60; and Becher, 150; and German leadership, 52, 54, 59–60; and Mann

249

(Klaus), 39, 53, 54, 57, 58, 59, 102, 232; new regime drawn up by, 113; as vice-president of Union of National Writers, 83; *also mentioned*, 51
Berlin, 'boulevard sheets', 189; and Fischer (Gottfried Bermann), 89–90; head office for students, 62; international conference in (1929), 149; Moabit district, 180; Olympic Games (1936), 207
Berliner Tageblatt, 188, 192
Berliner Volkszeitung, 192
Bernhard, Georg, and *Das Neue Tagebuch*, 139; and Freedom Library, 69; *Pariser Tageblatt*, editor of, 139, 185, 190–3, 197, 200–1, 204–5; *also mentioned*, 211
Bertaux, Félix, 38
Bertaux, Pierre, 132
Beyle, M. H. (Stendhal), 43
Beyond the Mexique Bay (A. Huxley), 111
'bibliocaust', 61
bills of exchange, 140–1, 142
blacklisted publications, 13, 63, 64, 68, 95
Bleichröder, Gerson, 37
Blue Angel, The (H. Mann), 8, 37, 40
Blum, Léon, 170, 221
book-burning, and blacklists, 63; *Buddenbrooks* (T. Mann), 24, 62; 50th anniversary, ix, 236; and PEN (writers' association), 75; by students, 61, 62, 63, 66, 67, 68; *see also* banning of books; students, 'cleansing' of literature by
booksellers, denouncement of, 63
Börger, Thomas, x
Borin, K. A., 171
Börsenblatt, 106, 107
Boulevard Beausoleil (Sanary), 2
Boulevard de la Plage (Côte d'Azur), 46
Boulevard St Germain, Nazi book exhibition in, 69
Bourget, Paul, 35
Brandt, Willy, 220
Brave New World (A. Huxley), 2
Brecht, Berthold, and Becher, 150, 151; and book-burning, 68; and Paris Writers' Congress (1935), 159; publications by, 111; Sanary, visit to, 12; *also mentioned*, 1, 10, 126, 149

Breitscheid, Rudolf, 216
Breton, André, 159
Brideshead Revisited (E. Waugh), 3
Brown Book, 152, 215
Brownshirts (Nazis), 35
Bruno Cassirer, 123
Budberg, Moura, 76
Buddenbrooks (T. Mann), 23, 24, 62, 89
Bundesverdienstkreuz (Federal order of merit), x
Busch, Fritz Otto, 75

Café de la Marine (Sanary), 4
Café du Dôme (Montparnasse), 4
Café Monnot (Nice), 208
Cahn, Werner, 47
Campbell, Roy, 101
'Canaan-sur-Seine', refugee community in, 182
Canaris, Admiral Wilhelm, 227
Canby, Henry Seidel, 76, 77, 78, 84
Canetti, Elias, 230
Cape, Jonathan, 99
Capek, Karel, 83
Caro, Kurt, 185, 192, 200, 202
Cavell, Edith, 52
Central Intelligence Agency (CIA), 162
chamber of culture (Reich), 52
Chamberlain, Neville, 130
Chamberlain, Sir Austen, 144
Channon, Sir Henry 'Chips', 54
Chemin de la Colline (Sanary), 2, 33
Churchill, Winston, 19, 144, 205
CIA (Central Intelligence Agency), 162
City of Benares (vessel), destruction by Germans, 84–5
Clair, René, 193
Clark, Kenneth, 3
Clerkenwell, Karl Marx memorial library in, 68
Cleugh, James, 48
co-operation doctrine, 211
Cocteau, Jean, 5, 6, 56, 102
Cold War, 85
Comintern, 212, 221, 222
Communist International, 155
Communist Party, 11, 150, 151, 218, 226–7
concentration camps, 14, 15, 25, 26
Connolly, Cyril, 3, 17, 18
conspiracy theories, 14
Cooke, Alistair, 43
Côte d'Azur, Boulevard de la Plage,

Index

46; and Mann family, 41, 56; Schwarzschild in, 138; *see also* Bandol (Côte d'Azur); France; Sanary-sur-Mer (Côte d'Azur)
Coudenhove-Kalergi, Count Richard, 38, 56
Coudenhove-Kalergi, Ida (neé Roland), 38
credit, Wechsel distinguished, 141
Crémieux, Benjamin, 76, 78, 84
Crevel, René, 164
'culture', terminology, 51–2
Curie, Eve, 131
Curie, Marie, 131

D. H. Lawrence, 2, 3, 8
Dachau concentration camp, 25, 26
Daily Mail, 144
Das Neue Tage-Buch (weekly), citing from, 143–4; controversial article in, 119; final appearance (1940), 147; and Fischer (Bermann), 120, 121; and Mefo mechanism, 142; and PEN (writers' association), 82; and Schacht, 140; Schwarzschild, edited by, 119, 136, 138, 139, 197, 217
Dawson Scott, Catharine Amy, 73
De Gaulle, Charles, 20
de Guise, Henri, 210
death camps, 143
Dell, Robert, 144
Dépêche de Toulouse, 208
Der fromme Tanz (K. Mann), 55
Der Hass (Hate), 208–9
Der jüdische Krieg (The Jewish War) (L. Feuchtwanger), 26
Der Stürmer (J. Streicher), 69, 120
Der Untertan (H. Mann), 37
Dernières Nouvelles, 195
d'Estrées, Gabrielle, 210
Deutsch, André, 129
Deutschlandfunk (German radio station), xi
Dichter (writers), 63
Die Brennessel (Stinging Nettle), 39–40
Die kleine Stadt (H. Mann), 37
Die Sammlung magazine, Austria, banning by, 110; and Döblin, 102, 106; and Howard, 111; and Huxley, 100; journals succeeding, 112; literary character, 104; and Mann (Klaus), 100, 101–8; and Mann (Thomas), 102, 107, 111, 113, 114; patrons of, 100; popularity of, 111; and Roth, 100, 102, 107–8, 109; and Schickele, 102, 106, 107, 109; and Zweig, 102, 104; also mentioned, 158
Die Söhne (L. Feuchtwanger), 46
Die Zukunft, 224
Dietrich, Marlene, 8, 37, 40, 193
Döblin, Alfred, as banned writer, 95; and *Die Sammlung* magazine, 102, 106; and PEN (writers' association), 75; Prussian academy, resignation from, 53; publications by, 111; and Querido (Dutch publisher), 115; and Roth, 110
Dollfuss, Engelbert, 116, 152
Doppelleben (G. Benn), 60
Dreyfus, Captain Alfred, 184
Driberg, Tom, 51
Dubrovnik (*previously* Ragusa) *see* Ragusa (*later* Dubrovnik)
Dumas, Alexandre, 43
Düsseldorf, hosting of exhibition at (1996), x

economic slump (1930s), 8
Edict of Nantes, 209
Edward II (C. Marlowe), 42
Ehrenburg, Ilya, 157, 158, 170
Einstein, Albert, 26, 32, 33, 149
Eisler, Hanns, 155, 233, 234
Elster, Hanns Martin, 75, 83
Emergency Rescue Committee, 147, 225
English Passengers (R. Olden), 84
Entjudung (Jews, removal from judiciary), 27
Entretiens de Pontigny (T. Mann), 38
Epitaph for a Spy (E. Ambler), 14
Erbfrage, 156
Erfolg (L. Feuchtwanger), 43–4
Escape to Life (Klaus and Erika Mann), 19, 57
Evans, Charles, 119
Exil (L. Feuchtwanger), 181, 182–3, 186
'exile literature', 235
Exilliteratur (Austria), 230
Eyeless in Gaza (A. Huxley), 2, 148, 199

Fabian, Dora, 199
Fadiman, Clifton, 43
Federal Bureau of Investigation (US), 233
Ferrero, Guglielmo, 87
Feuchtwanger, Lion, **42–50**; 'Anglo-Saxon' friends of, 63; attacks on, 44; banning of books, 95; and Becher,

251

150, 158; character, 168; death, 178; *Exil*, 181, 182–3, 186; in France, 1, 2, 8, 10, 15, 16, 46, 48, 165–6, 167, 178, 181, 182; and Freedom Library, 70, 153; and Gide, 174, 175; and Herrmann, 234; and Koestler, 13; Les Milles, detention in, 14; and Lutétia circle, 220; and Mann family, 39, 86, 177, 209; and Moscow mission, 169–79; and Nazi regime, 26, 47; *Oppermanns, The* (anti-Nazi novel), 47–50, 58, 118, 171, 178; and Paris Writers' Congress (1935), 148, 159; and PEN (writers' association), 75, 83; physical appearance, 46–7; and Popular Front, 221; in Sanary, 1, 2, 8, 10, 15, 48, 165–6, 167, 178, 182; and Schwarzschild, 146; on sexuality, 168; and sports, 166; on Stalin, 173, 177; students' actions against, 64, 66; success of, 167; *also mentioned*, 12

Feuchtwanger, Marta, 10, 15, 45, 46, 165–6, 172

Feuchtwanger, Martin, 50

Fielding, Henry, 43

Finnegan's Wake (J. Joyce), 112

First World War, 23, 38, 73, 79

Fischer, Brigitte, 67, 88

Fischer, Gottfried Bermann, Austria, move to, 131; and Berlin, remaining in, 89–90; and Fischer (Samuel), 88–9; and Fischer Verlag (Jewish publishing business), 26, 118; on flying, 90; and Hauptmann, 132; and Korrodi, 130; Landshoff Bermann Fischer publishing corporation, founding of, 135; and Mann (Klaus), 95, 101–2, 103, 105, 112; and Mann (Thomas), 21, 24–5, **92–4, 96–8**, 103, 106, 111, 115–16, 121, 122, 123, 127, 129, 133, 134; and Nazi regime, 90–2, 118, 119–20, 129; as 'protected' Jew (*Schutzjude*), 119; and Roth, 107; and Schwarzschild, 91, 124–5, 146; in Sweden, 134

Fischer, Hedwig, 118, 119

Fischer, Samuel, 21, 23, 32, 88, 119, 121; *see also* Fischer, Gottfried Bermann

Fischer Verlag (Jewish publishing business), and *Die Sammlung* magazine publication, 111; and Fischer, Gottfried Bermann, 21, 118; legal action, threat of, 115; limitation of activities, 90; and Mann family, 36, 92, 117; and Nazi regime/blacklisted works, 26, 63; shortcomings of, 88

Fischer-Heinemann, 123

fonctionnaires, 15

For Whom the Bell Tolls (E. Hemingway), 179

Foreign Legion, French, 15

Forster, E. M., and Paris writers' congress (1935), 149, 158, 159, 161, 162

Forsyte Saga (J. Galsworthy), 73

France, anti-Semitism, 14; Bedford's escape from, 19; Germany, invasion by (1940), 16; and Mann (Heinrich), 212–13; political asylum tradition, 9; Renaissance, 209; Toulon, 14, 20, 31; *see also* Côte d' Azur; Paris; Sanary-sur-Mer (Côte d'Azur)

France-la-Doulce, 180–1

Franco, General, 207

Franco-Soviet mutual assistance pact (1936), 207

François-Poncet, André (French ambassador), 32, 40

Frank, Bruno, 1, 10, 12

Frank, Leonhard, 126

Frank, Waldo, 149

Frederick the Great, 53

Freedom Library (burned and banned books), 68–9, 70, 72, 153, 174, 214

Freud, Sigmund, 8, 19, 28, 131

Fry, Varian, 216, 225

fugitives, political, 9

Fürtwängler, Wilhelm, 25

Galsworthy, John, 44, 73, 75, 78, 83, 101

Gaston Gallimard (French publisher), 69, 76

gendarmes, 15

George, Stefan, 12

German People's Party, dissolution, 92

Germany, bills of exchange, issue of, 140–1, 142; 'black' debt, concealed, 142; bombing of cities, 232; book-trade association, 64; Communist Party, 11, 150, 151, 218, 226–7; France, invasion of (1940), 16; 'job creation', 140; League of Nations, withdrawal from (1933), 83, 116; liquidity, increase of, 140–1; Munich, 21–2, 23, 27, 29, 31, 38; Popular Front, 145, 161, 164, 207,

Index

218, 224, 226; Second Reich, 36; and sexual relations, 63; Social Democrat Party, 24, 139; tanks of, 143; Third Reich, 50, 67, 103, 116, 207; travellers, ban on leaving, 26; unification (1871), 37; writers' guild, 153; *see also* Berlin; Hitler, Adolf; Nazis; Weimar Republic
Gestapo, 27, 92, 133
Gide, André, *Association des Ecrivains et Artistes Révolutionnaires* set up by, 154; and Feuchtwanger, 174, 175; and Freedom Library, 69, 72; and Hirschfeld, 65; and Huxley, 148; and Mann family, 38, 56, 100; and Paris Writers' Congress (1935), 149, 158, 159, 160, 161, 162; at Sanary, 5; on Soviet Union, 221
Gilliat, Sidney, 47
Giraudoux, Jean, 15, 29, 89
Gleichschaltung, concept of, 51
Goebbels, Joseph, and Bermann Fischer, 121; book exhibition, Boulevard St Germain, 69; and book-burning, 61, 63; on 'culture', 51–2; and D. H. Lawrence, 8; and Mann (Thomas), 93, 127; 'Ministry of Propaganda and Popular Enlightenment', headed by, 51, 62; and *Schutzverband Deutscher Schriftsteller* (German writers' guild), 153; and *Tageblatt*, 184
Goethe Institute, xi
Gold, Michael, 149
Gollancz, Victor, 176
Göring, Hermann, 90, 91
Gorky, Maxim, 76, 150, 158, 169
Graf, Oskar Maria, 67–8, 126
Gräfenberg, Rosie, 190, 202
Grand Hôtel, Bandol, 29, 31, 33
Grass, Günter, 72
Grave, Artur, 200
Green, Julien, 5, 56
Grenzland, 198
Grimme, Adolf, 39
Grodzenski, Isaac, 187, 196, 197
Gross, Babette, 214
Grosz, George, 91
Grunberger, Richard, 50, 182
Guderian, General Heinz, 143
Gushigov, A., 171

Haldane, J. B. S., 214
Hamsun, Knut, 122
Harlan, Veit, 43
Harper, Allanah, 16
Harrap, George, 6
Hastings, Warren, 42
Hauptmann, Gerhart, 81, 88, 114, 131–2, 232
Hauser, Heinrich, 90, 91
Heilbrunn, Franz, 191
Heimat literature, 68, 116
Heine, Heinrich, x, 61, 62
Heinemann (London publishing business), 119, 130, 133
Heins, Valentin, 27, 30
Hemingway, Ernest, 179, 235
Henri IV (of Navarre), 209, 210, 211
Hermann Abs (banker), 119
Herrmann, Eva, artistic ability, 168–9; and Becher, 158; and Bedford, 168; and Feuchtwanger, 175; and Mann family, 19, 234; at Sanary, 4, 5, 16; *also mentioned*, xi, 171
Herzog, Wilhelm, 3, 11, 35, 41, 87
Hesse, Hermann, 100, 120, 123, 126, 150
Hessel, Franz, 19
Heydrich, Reinhard, 97
Himmler, Heinrich, 116
Hindenburg, Paul von, 11, 22, 38, 117
Hirschfeld, Magnus, 64–5, 66, 214
Hitler, Adolf, anti-Semitic laws, decree of, 117; and Austria, 1, 130, 182, 208; cultural ideology, 54; economic programmes, 139; election successes, 22; as German chancellor (1933), 9, 22; military conscription, re-introduction of, 117; Nazi–Soviet non-aggression pact (1939), 14, 146, 178, 205, 224; Polish invasion, 209; public-works projects, 139; putsch (1923), 43; rabble-rousing activities, 45; reasons for power, 211; Rhineland, march into, 170; *see also* Germany; Gestapo; Nazis
Hitler Youth, 17, 66
Hoechst (chemical company), 143
Hoffmannsthal, Hugo von, 54
Holzner, Hans (chauffeur), 22, 27, 29–30
homosexuality, 64–5, 174
Hoover, J. Edgar, 233
Horizon (C. Connolly), 18
Horst Wessel (Nazis' marching tune), 25, 65
Hôtel de la Tour, 2, 17, 20, 33, 57, 61, 100
Hôtel des Sociétés Savantes, 212
Hôtel Lutétia, 216, 221, 227, 229; *see also* Lutétia circle

253

Hôtel Lux, 216, 221
Hôtel Splendide, 216
Howard, Brian: on anti-Nazis, 16–17; and *Die Sammlung* magazine, 111; and Mann family, 18–19, 99, 101, 207; and Maugham, 17–18; in Sanary, 3–4, 5
Huebsch, Ben, 86
Hugo, Victor, 38, 107
Huxley, Aldous: and Bedford (Sybille), xi, 19; and *Die Sammlung* magazine, 100; and Mann (Klaus), 100, 110; on Nazi movement, 8; and Paris Writers' Congress (1935), 159; publications by, 2, 111, 148, 199; and Sackville-West, 5
Huxley, Julian, 148
Huxley, Maria, 2, 7, 165
Huxley, Matthew, 7

Ibsen, Henrik, 90
IG Farben (chemical undertaking), 143
In the Land of Cockaigne (H. Mann), 37
Institute of Physical Education, 64
Isherwood, Christopher, and Altmann, 4; and Auden, 5; and Hirschfeld, 65; and Mann (Klaus), 99; and politics versus creativity, 153; on refugees, 9; United States, escape to, 51

Jacob, Berthold, 142, 143, 183, 199
Jameson, Storm, 84
Je Suis Partout (anti-Semitic publication), 84
Jew Suess (L. Feuchtwanger), 43
Jews, Austrian, 230; editorial offices, banned from, 52; French, 195; German, 70, 119, 195; international outlook, 126; *Literaten* (writers), 63; and Mann (Thomas), 25; national groups, 195; Nazi Germany, conditions in, 50; *see also* anti-Semitism
Johst, Hanns, 68, 74, 83, 105
Joseph in Egypt (T. Mann), 131
Joseph and His Brothers (T. Mann), 12, 26, 94, 96
Joseph, Michael, 180
Josephus, Flavius, 45, 46, 47
Joyce, James, 83, 112
Jud Süß (L. Feuchtwanger), 42–43
Jud Süess (L. Feuchtwanger), 8, 50
Jules et Jim (F. Truffaut), 20

Kafka, Franz, 111

Kampfbund (militant federation), 62, 74
Kantorowicz, Alfred, 19, 70, 71, 158, 229
Karl Marx memorial library, Clerkenwell, 68
Katz, Otto, 215
Kerr, Alfred, 27, 74, 75, 84, 102
Kerr, Judith, 84
Kesten, Hermann, 12, 41
Keun, Odette, 76
Kiepenheuer (publishing firm), 53
Kipps (H. G. Wells), 79
Kirov, Sergei, 170
Kisch, Egon Erwin, 2, 12, 69, 192, 229–30
Klee, Paul, 80
Kleist, Heinrich von, 41
Klossovski, Erich, 4
Kneale, Matthew, 84
Knopf, Alfred A., 94, 95
Koestler, Arthur, and Austria, 230; and Bernhard, 188; and Feuchtwanger, 13; on Münzenberg, 215, 224; and Schwarzschild, 147; suicide of, 1; and *Tageblatt*, 192; *also mentioned*, 190
Kolb, Annette, 120, 123, 126
Kollwitz, Käthe, 39
Koltsov, Mikhail, 148, 158, 169, 179
Koopman, Helmut, xi
Korrodi, Eduard, 125, 126, 130
Kremlin, 169, 174, 211
Kristallnacht, 123, 192
Kroeger, Nelly, 40, 210
Kutzner, Rupert, 43–44

Landshoff, Fritz, 135
Lasker-Schüler, Else, 52, 126
Laski, Harold, 170
Lawrence, D. H., 2, 3, 8
Le Figaro, 144
Le Lavandou, 29, 31, 57, 206
Le Nautique (Sanary), 2
Le Tourbillon (waltz), 20
League of Nations, 29, 83, 116, 155, 210
Legacy, A (S. Bedford), 19
Leites, Konstantin, 185, 197, 199
Lenin, Vladimir, 177
Les Milles, 14, 17
Les Milles – Le Train de la Liberté (film), 16
Lewinsohn, Richard, 185, 197, 201–2
Lewis, Sinclair, 44, 102, 161
liberal press, 188, 189

Index

Liberté, Egalité, Fraternité, 13
libraries, alleged harmful role of, 63–4
Liebermann, Max, 39
'literary brothels', 64
Literaten, Jewish, 63
literature 'cleansing' *see* book-burning
Lloyd George, David, 144
Loon, Hendrik Willem van, 134–5
Los Angeles Times, 178
Lowe-Porter, Helen, 94, 99
Löwenstein, Hubertus Prinz zu, 71–2
Lübeck (home of Thomas and Heinrich Mann), x
Ludwig, Emil, 63, 75
Luftwaffe, 142
Lutétia circle, 217, 219, 220; *see also* Hôtel Lutétia
Luther, Martin, 62, 100

MS *Krajl Aleksander* (steamer), 73
Maß und Wert (journal), 112
MacDonald, Ramsay, 44, 47
Maclean, Donald, 17
Magic Mountain, The (T. Mann), 23, 24, 30, 89
Magnus Hirschfeld Institute for Sexual Science, 64–5
Mahler-Werfel, Alma (wife of Franz Werfel), 1, 2, 15–16, 131, 137
Malraux, André, and Freedom Library, 69; and Moscow Writers' Congress (1934), 157; and Paris Writers' Congress (1935), 148, 149, 158, 159, 162; Russian visit (1934), 170
Man Without Qualities, The (R. Musil), 2, 131
Manchester Guardian, 43, 81, 144
Mann, Elisabeth ('Medi'), 21, 25, 29, 86
Mann, Erika, Auden, marriage to, 5; *Escape to Life*, 19; and family, 26, 31, 41, 86, 88, 94, 95–6, 125; on Fischer (Bermann), 95; and Nazi regime, 21; physical appearance, 22; publications by, 12; and Querido, Emanuel, 115; Riviera, guide to, 4; at Sanary, 1, 33; and Schwarzschild, 122; in Switzerland, 22; and United States, 99
Mann, Golo, and family, 27, 28, 86, 232; Fischer (Samuel), meeting with, 32; Göttingen, interruption of studies at, 26; as historian, 56; and Holzner (chauffeur), 29–30; and Jünger, 12; in Sanary, 1
Mann, Heinrich, 35–41; academy of arts, resignation from, 53, 74; at Amsterdam conference (1932), 149; and Becher, 150, 157, 158; and Benn, 53; early life/education, 36; as enemy of morality, 67; and family, 22, 36–7, 103, 114, 122, 126, 206; and Feuchtwanger, 44; and France, 212–13; and Freedom Library, 153; *Henri IV*, 209, 210, 211; and Hitler/Nazis, 27, 220, 221; and Huxley, 7, 8, 148; Jews, attitudes towards, 36; and journalism, 208; as leader, 225; literary contributions, 36; and Lutétia circle, 219, 220; and Münzenberg, 213, 216, 222; opposition/destruction of works of, 64, 95; and Paris Writers' Congress (1935), 159, 163–4; and PEN (writers' association), 75, 83; political attitudes, 37–8, 206; in Sanary, 1, 41; in United States, 225, 226; and Weimer Republic, 36, 38–9; *also mentioned*, 29, 100, 220
Mann, Katia (neé Pringsheim), on Germany, return to, 30–1; *Magic Mountain* letters, 30; marriage to Thomas, 23; as mother, 54; in Sanary, 33; in Switzerland, 21; *also mentioned*, 25, 26, 86, 114, 122–3
Mann, Klaus, 51–60, 99–112; in Amsterdam, 95; attack on, 100; and Becher, 150; and Benn, 39, 53, 54, 57, 58, 59, 102, 232; *Die Sammlung* magazine, 100, 101–8; early years, 54; *Escape to Life*, 19, 57; essays by, 12; and family, 31, 41, 86; and Fischer (Bermann), 95, 101–2, 103, 105, 112; in France, 1, 29, 33, 51, 61; and Howard, 16, 17, 207; and Korrodi, 125; literary review of, 148; on Moscow writers' congress, 157; and Nazi regime/Hitler, 10, 21, 53, 57, 110, 231; and Paris Writers' Congress (1935), 160, 163; and PEN (writers' association), 83; physical appearance, 22; post-war period, 234; publications of, 4; in Sanary, 1, 33, 51, 61; and Schwarzschild, 137, 146, 147; suicide of, 60; and Thomas Mann (father), 28, 88; travels of, 55; and 'Zhdanovism', 155; and Zweig (Stefan), 101, 105
Mann, Michael, 29, 86
Mann, Monika, 32, 59, 84, 85
Mann, Thomas, attacks on, 23–4, 27–9; and Becher, 150, 153;

255

Buddenbrooks, 23, 24, 62, 89; and *Die Sammlung* magazine, 102, 107, 111, 113, 114; essays, 115; fame of, 128; and family, 55; and Feuchtwanger, 167; and Fischer (Gottfried Bermann), 21, 24–25, **92–4, 96–8**, 103, 106, 111, 115–16, 121, 122, 123, 127, 129, 133, 134; and Fischer (Samuel), 21, 23, 121; in France, 1, 2, 20, 33, 86, 87; German nationality, 127; on Germany, 30–1; Harvard, honorary doctorate from, 116, 127; health, 88; and Heinrich Mann (brother), 22, 36–7, 114, 122, 126, 206; and Hitler, 127, 128; homosexual inclinations, 31; and Huxley, 7; *Joseph in Egypt*, 131; *Joseph and His Brothers*, 12, 26, 94, 96; *Magic Mountain, The*, 23, 24, 30, 89; marriage, 23; and Nazi regime, 22, 23, 25, 26, 31, 87, 108, 114–15, 127; Nobel Prize, winner of (1929), 7–8, 23, 37, 89, 108; and Old Testament, 209; and Paris Writers' Congress (1935), 149; and PEN (writers' association), 75; political views, 23, 24, 113, 114–15, 127; 'politicum' of, 115, 117, 125; post-war period, 231–3; in Sanary, 1, 2, 20, 33, 86, 87; and Schickele, 115; in Switzerland, 21, 24, 167; *Tales of Jacob*, 94, 103, 105, 109, 113–14; villa inhabited by, x, 34, 86, 87; on Wagner (Richard), 21–2, 27, 28, 29, 93; and Zweig (Stefan), 127; *also mentioned*, 64

Mansfield, Katherine, 3
Marchesani, Lisa, 4, 33, 78, 87
Marcuse, Ludwig, 4, 127, 171
Marcuse, Sasha, 171
Marlowe, Christopher, 42
Martin, Kingsley, 84, 194
Marx, Karl, German attitudes towards, 67
Marxist writers, 155
Masaryk, Thomas, 40
Matthes, Joseph, 190
Maugham, Somerset, 15, 17–18
Maupassant, Guy de, 37
Maurois, André, 83, 144
Mefos/'Mefo-Wechsel' system, 141, 142
Meier-Graefe, Julius, 3
Mein Kampf, 47, 68
Men of Good Will (J. Romains), 78
Men Without Women (E. Hemingway), 235

Mencken, H. L., 102
Mendès-France, Pierre, 144
'Metallurgische Forschungsanstalt mbH', 141
Meyer, Agnes, 225
Miliukov, Paul, 195
Miller, Arthur, 234, 235
Morand, Paul, 180–1
Moreau, Jeanne, 20
Morp (Russian writers' association), 150, 151, 154, 155
Mortimer, Raymond, 4, 17, 101
Moscow 1937, 176–7, 178
Moscow, Feuchtwanger, mission of, 169–79; 'Free Germany' committee in, 228; writers' congress, 157
Mosley, Sir Oswald (Tom), 7
Mosse, Rudolf, 189
Muggeridge, Malcolm, 72
Munich, 21–2, 23, 27, 29, 31, 38
Münzenberg, Willi, abilities, 215; background, 213; *Brown Book*, 152; and Comintern, 212; and Mann (Heinrich), 213, 216, 222; political activities, 214, 215–16, 217, 223–4; suicide, 224
Musil, Robert, and Fischer family, 131; and Mann (Heinrich), 38; and Paris Writers' Congress (1935), 149, 160; in Sanary, 2; *also mentioned*, 102
Mussolini, Benito, 20, 87, 130; Abyssinia conquest (1935), 170, 207
Mutualité, 149, 163

National People's Party, Germany, 23
National Socialist Party, 23, 29, 139; *see also* Nazis
Nazi–Soviet non-aggression pact (1939), 14, 146, 178, 205, 224
Nazis, blacklisted publications, 13, 63, 64, 68, 95; book-burning by *see* book-burning by Nazis; Brownshirts, 35; and Communist Party members, 11; election successes, 24, 56; and Fischer, Gottfried Bermann, 90–2, 118, 119–20, 129; Jews, hatred of, 126; and Mann (Klaus), 10, 21, 53, 57, 110; and Mann (Thomas), 22, 23, 25, 26, 31, 87, 108, 114–15; propaganda, 24, 43, 45, 69; storm-troopers, 45; terrorist activities by, 23; *see also* Germany; Gestapo; Hitler, Adolf; Jews, persecution of; National Socialist Party
Neue Rundschau (intellectual review), 28

Neue Tage-Buch (weekly) *see Das Neue Tage-Buch* (weekly)
Neue Zürcher Zeitung, 121, 122, 125, 130
Neueste Nachrichten, 28
New Statesman, 19, 99, 160
New York Times, 225
News Chronicle, 99
Nicholson, Harold, 54
'night of the long knives', 123, 192
Nizan, Paul, 149
NTB see Das Neue Tage-Buch (weekly)
Nuremberg, anti-Semitic laws, 117, 206

Observer, The, 82
Ochmann, Peter, 199
Odenwald (German boarding school), 54
Olden, Rudolf, 84–5
Oppenheimer, Josef Süß, 42–3
Oppermanns, The (L. Feuchtwanger), 47–50, 58, 118, 171, 178
Orlov, S. K., 171
Orwell, George, 3, 222
Ossietzky, Carl von, 45, 122
Osten, Maria, 158, 169, 171, 174, 179
Ould, Hermon, 74, 84
Outline of History (H. G. Wells), 79
Overwien, Anita, xi
Oxford, Lady, 70, 71

Paris, as centre of political opposition to Hitler, 9–10; Feuchtwanger on, 181; library of banned books in, 19; refugees from, 181; Writers' Congress (1935), 148–64; *see also* France
Paris Gazette, 183, 191
Pariser Haint, 191
Pariser Tageblatt (newspaper), 139, **180–205**
Pariser Tageszeitung, 145
Pasternak, Boris, 149, 158, 159, 221
PEN (world writers' association), 73–85; and book-burning, 75; branches, 75; Czech, 229; founding of, 73; German members, 74–5; and Mann (Heinrich), 213; Ragusa conference (1933), 73, 75–82; and Wells, 76, 80, 81–2; withdrawal from by Germans, 83
Peppermill, The (anti-Nazi cabaret), 22
'Petersen', Jan, masked speaker, 160
Pfitzner, Hans (composer), 27, 54, 93
'phoney war', 15

Pieck, Wilhelm, 212, 218, 220, 222, 226
Pirandello, Luigi, 78
Plage de la Gorguette (Sanary), 2
Podhoretz, Norman, 156
Point Counter Point (A. Huxley), 2
Poliakov, Germaine, xi
Poliakov, Leon, 183, 184, 187, 201, 203, 205
Poliakov, Vladimir, and *Tageblatt*, 183–5, 187, 188, 191, 196, 197, 200, 203, 204
Popular Front, German, 145, 161, 164, 207, 218, 224, 226; Orwell on, 222; Spain, 220
Powell, Anthony, 3
Power (L. Feuchtwanger), 43
Priestley, J. B., 83, 158
Prittwitz, Friedrich Wilhelm von, 42
Proust, Marcel, 19
Put Out More Flags (E. Waugh), 3, 18, 51

Quai Cronstadt (Toulon), 6
Quai d'Orsay, 30, 70
Quartier St Trinide (Sanary), 4
Querido, Emanuel (Amsterdam publisher), *Der Hass*, 208–9; and Feuchtwanger, 46, 47, 48, 49–50, 176; and Fischer (Bermann), 98; and Howard, 99; and Mann (Erica), 115; and Mann (Klaus), 95, 96; Poland, deportation to, 135
Quincey, Thomas de, 12

Radek, Karl, 151, 172
Ragusa (later Dubrovnik), French *déclaration* (PEN conference), 81; PEN conference (1933), 73, 75–82; as 'Salzburg-on-Sea', 77
Rats, The (G. Hauptmann), 131–2
Regler, Gustav, and Paris Writers' Congress (1935), 158, 160, 161, 162
Reichsanzeiger (government gazette), 166
Reichsbank, change in statutes, 139; money, printing of, 141
Reichstag, burning of (1933), 9, 11, 40; *Brown Book* on, 152
Remarque, Erich Maria, 44, 63, 64, 67, 230
Rhondda, Viscountess, 72
Roché, Henri-Pierre, 20
Röhm, Ernst, execution of, 10, 59, 116, 192, 210
Rolland, Romain, *Association des*

Ecrivains et Artistes Révolutionnaires set up by, 154; and Feuchtwanger, 69, 177; and Gide, 177; and Mann (Klaus), 107; and Paris Writers' Congress (1935), 148; World Committee Against War and Fascism, 213; and Zweig (Stefan), 106; *also mentioned*, 102
Romains, Jules, 15, 78, 79, 84
Roosevelt, Eleanor, 44–5
Roosevelt, Franklin Delano, 42, 44
Rosebery, Countess, 71–2
Rosenberg, Alfred, 52, 68, 105, 156
Rosenthal, Tom, 129
Rotarians, 25
Rotger, Barthélémy, x
Roth, Joseph: as banned writer, 95; and *Die Sammlung* magazine, 100, 102, 107–8, 109; and Döblin, 110; on Jewish groups, 195; and Paris Congress (1935), 163; and Querido, Emanuel (Dutch publisher), 115; *also mentioned*, 1, 153
Rothschild, Lionel de, 70
Rothschild, Robert de, 195
Rudolf (Austrian crown prince), 4
Russell, Bertrand, 65, 144
Russia *see* Soviet Union

Saar, territory of, 9
Sackville-West, Edward, 5
Saenger, Samuel, 32, 102–4
Salten, Felix, 73
Salvemini, Gaetano, 87, 159
Sammlung magazine affair *see Die Sammlung* magazine
Samuel Fischer Verlag (Jewish publishing business) *see* Fischer Verlag (Jewish publishing business)
'Sanary' (poem), 3
Sanary-sur-Mer (Côte d'Azur), x; Allies, bombing by, 20; 'Bastide Juliette' house, 4; Boulevard Beausoleil, 2; Café de la Marine, 4; Chemin de la Colline, 2, 33; contemporary state of, 33–4; Feuchtwangers at, 1, 2, 10, 15, 48, 165–6, 178, 182; German capture of, 20; historical works produced in, 12; Hitler's enemies in, 14; Hôtel de la Tour, 2, 17, 20, 33, 57, 61, 100; impact of approaching war on, 13; importance of, 236; internment of refugees, 16; La Gorguette peninsula, 49; Le Nautique, 2; liberation of port (1944), 20; as 'literary capital', 20; Mann (Thomas) at, 1, 2, 20, 33, 86, 87; Plage de la Gorguette, 2; Quartier St Trinide, 4; Villa Valmer, 2; as 'Weimar-on-Sea', 3; as writers' refuge, 1–20, 51; *see also* France
Schacht, Hjalmar, 139, 140, 141
Schickele, Anna (wife of René), 29
Schickele, René, and academy of arts (Prussian), 53; and *Die Sammlung* magazine, 102, 106, 107, 109; and Mann family, 29, 31–2, 103, 115; and Nazi regime, 10, 11, 122; in Sanary, 3, 4; and Seabrook, 8
Schirach, Baldur von, 156
Schmidt-Pauli, Edgar von, 75, 77, 79, 80, 82, 83
Schmolz, Artur, 184
Schmutz und Schund ('smut and trash' literature), 124
Schnitzler, Arthur, 111
Schönebeck, Sybille von: education, 4; on Nazi horror, 5
Schriftsteller (writers), 63
Schutzverband Deutscher Schriftsteller (German writers' guild), 52, 153
Schwarzes Korps (SS paper), 69
Schwarzschild, Leopold, **136–47**; anti-Communism of, 146, 147; *Das Neue Tage-Buch* edited by, 119, 136, 138, 139, 197, 217; death, 147; and Feuchtwanger, 146; and Fischer, Gottfried Bermann, 91, 124–5, 146; and Hitler/Nazi regime, 122, 138, 145; journalistic talent, 138; and Mann (Erika), 122; and Mann (Klaus), 137, 146, 147; and Mann (Thomas), 123; on *Moscow 1937*, 177; Paris, emigration to, 136; readers of, 143; and Toller, 144; *also mentioned*, 153, 202, 218, 220
Schwarzschild, Valerie, 136–8
Seabrook, William, 5–6; party for Germans hosted by, 7–8
Secker, Martin, 43, 48, 50
Second Reich, 36
'Secret of Mayerling, The' (B. Howard), 4
Seghers, Anna, 157, 161, 163
Seigfried Line, Franco-German border, 143
Serge, Victor, 159, 161, 169
Sergeant Grisha (A. Zweig), 2
Sernau, Lola, 40, 43, 47–8, 168
sexual relations, German attitudes to, 63, 64–5
Sforza, Count Carlo, 87

Shape of Things to Come, The (H. G. Wells), 144
Shaw, George Bernard, 44, 78, 90, 149, 161
Sieburg, Friedrich, 182, 190
Simon, André, 215
Simon, Heinrich, 188
Simpson (E. Sackville-West), 5
SMAD (Soviet Military Administration in Deutschland), 228
Small Town, The (H. Mann), 41
Social Democrat Party (Germany), 24, 139
Sonnemann, Leopold, 188
Soviet Union, on abortion, 174; Franco-Soviet mutual assistance pact (1936), 207; on homosexuality, 174; Kremlin, 169, 174; League of Nations, joining, 155; Moscow mission of Feuchtwanger, 169–79; Nazi–Soviet non-aggression pact (1939), 14, 146, 178, 205, 224; SMAD (Soviet Military Administration in Deutschland), 228
Spanish Civil War, 72, 221
Spender, Jane, xi
Sperber, Manes, 163
Staats-Zeitung, 28
Stalin, Joseph, and Becher, 155; Feuchtwanger on, 173, 177; and German resistance, 221; Nazi–Soviet non-aggression pact (1939), 14, 146, 178, 205, 224; personality, 176; *also mentioned*, 12–13, 145, 171, 173
Stavisky, Serge, 195
Steed, Wickham, 70, 72, 144
Stendhal (M. H. Beyle), 43
Sternheim, Carl, 5
Sternheim, Thea (Mopsa), 5
Story of Mankind (H. W. van Loon), 134–5
Strachey, John, 159
Strachey, Lytton, 90
Strauss, Marcel, 145
Strauss, Richard, 25, 27, 114
Streicher, Julius, 69, 120
students, 'cleansing' of literature by, 61–72; book types condemned, 62–3; booksellers, denouncing of, 63; burning activities, 61, 62, 63, 66, 67, 68; head office, Berlin, 62; libraries, alleged harmful role of, 63–4; in modern times, 72; raids, 66; 'twelve theses', condemning alien writings, 61–2; world attention, 68; *see also* book-burning

Sufferings and Greatness of the Masters (T. Mann), 115
Suhrkamp, Peter, 94, 118–19, 135
swastika, 48

Tage-Buch (weekly) *see Das Neue Tage-Buch* (weekly)
Tageblatt see Pariser Tageblatt (newspaper)
Tales of Jacob (T. Mann), 94, 103, 105, 109, 113–14
Thiess, Frank, 232
Third Reich, 50, 67, 103, 116, 207; *see also* Nazis
Thompson, Dorothy, 213, 225
Threepenny Opera (B. Brecht), 111
Toller, Ernst, detention for treason, 78; and Ould, 74; pacifist views, 78; and PEN (writers' association), 83; at Sanary, 78; and Schwarzschild, 144; speech of, 80–1; student opposition to works of, 64; war experiences, 77–8; and Wells, 79; *also mentioned*, 2, 70
Toulon, 14, 20, 31
Trenet, Charles, 10
Tristan and Isolde, 131
Trotsky, Leon, 171
Truffaut, François, 20
Tucholsky, Kurt, 50, 64
Turning Point, The (K. Mann's autobiography), 56

Ulbricht, Walter, 72, 212, 217, 220, 222, 223, 226, 228
Ullstein, Franz, 190
Ullstein, Leopold, 189, 190
Union of National Writers, 83
United States, 8, 162, 233

Valéry, Paul, 87
Van der Lubbe, Marinus, 215
van Loon, Hendrik Willem, 134–5
Veidt, Conrad, 43
Versailles Treaty (1919), 38, 62; Schacht, opposition by, 139
Vetsera, Maria, 4
Villa des Roseaux, 6
Villa Lazare, 46, 47, 49, 165
Villa Tranquille, x, 34, 86, 87, 113
Villa Valmer, 2, 165, 167
Volcano, The (K. Mann), 56
Volk, 58
Völkischer Beobachter (government sheet), 22, 23, 27, 40, 74
Volksfront, 224

von Epp, General Franz, 23, 28
von Hindenburg, Paul, 11, 22, 38, 117
von Hoffmannsthal, Hugo, 54
von Kleist, Heinrich, 41
von Ossietzky, Carl, 45, 122
von Prittwitz, Friedrich Wilhelm, 42
von Schirach, Baldur, 156
von Schmidt-Pauli, Edgar, 75, 77, 79, 80, 82, 83
Vossische Zeitung, 188, 189, 193, 197
Vyshinsky, Andrei, 170

Wagner, Richard, Mann on, 21–2, 27, 28, 29, 93
Walter, Bruno, 25, 54, 80, 81, 131
Wartburg festivities (1817), 62
Wassermann, Jacob, 35, 108, 111, 115
Waugh, Evelyn, 3, 18, 51
We Are Fighting for a Soviet Germany (W. Pieck), 218
We are Prisoners (O. M. Graf), 67
Weidenfeld, George, 14
Weill, Kurt, 1
Weimar Republic, and Feuchtwanger, 44; final years, 23; German students' opposition to, 62; liberalism of, 53; and Mann (Heinrich), 36, 38–9; and 'new Germany', 217; *Schutzverband Deutscher Schriftsteller* (German writers' guild), 153; *see also* Germany
'Weimar-on-Sea' *see* Sanary-sur-Mer (Côte d'Azur)
Weinberg, Rudolph, 49
Weiner, Joyce, 40, 46, 47
Weissenberg, Joseph, 198
Wells, H. G., 73–85; and Feuchtwanger, 44; and Freedom Library, 70; on Jews, 79; and Keun, Odette, 76; and Library of the Burned Books, 84; and Paris Writers' Congress (1935), 149; and PEN (writers' association), 76, 80, 81–2; publications by, 79, 144; on Schmidt-Pauli, 83
Werfel, Alma, 1, 2, 15–16, 131, 137
Werfel, Franz, and academy of arts (Prussian), 53; burning of publications of, 67; identity check of, 15; and PEN (writers' association), 83; *also mentioned*, 1, 2, 16, 126, 131

Werner, Oscar, 19–20
West, Mae, 193
West, Rebecca, 76, 158
Westland (Saar newspaper), 183, 198, 201
What's Become of Waring (A. Powell), 3
When Hitler Stole Pink Rabbit (J. Kerr), 84
Wilhelm II (Kaiser), 36, 38, 213
Wilson, Edmund, 3
Wise, Stephen, 199
Wolf, Friedrich, 226, 228
Wolff, Charlotte, 66
Wolff, Fritz, 198, 199, 200
Wolff, Kurt, 87
Woolf, Leonard, 158
Woolf, Virginia, 158
World Committee Against War and Fascism, 213
World in Trance (L. Schwarzschild), 147
World War I, 23, 38, 73, 79
Worthington, Marjorie, 6, 7
Wunderlich, Heinke, x–xi

xenophobia, 14

Yakuba, Père, 6
Young Joseph, The (T. Mann), 111–12

Zhdanov, Andrei, 155
Zionism, 189
Zola, Emile, 36, 184
Zuckmayer, Carl, 44
Zweig, Arnold, anti-militarist novels of, 8; and Feuchtwanger, 172, 177; on German Jewry, 12; and Huxley, 7; at Sanary, 1–2, 10
Zweig, Friederike, 74
Zweig, Stefan, and Becker, 153; and *Die Sammlung* magazine, 102, 104; and Feuchtwanger, 167; and Hesse, 100; and libraries, 64; and Mann (Klaus), 56, 101; and Mann (Thomas), 127; and Paris Writers' Congress (1935), 149; and PEN (writers' association), 73–74; and Roth, 108; at Sanary, 1; and Toller, 81
Zyklon-B gas poison, 143